Cassell's Movie Quotations

Cassell's Movie

Quotations

Nigel Rees

CASSELL&CO

First published in the UK 2000 by
Cassell & Co
Wellington House
125 Strand
London
WC2R OBB

This edition 2002

Distributed in the United States by
Sterling Publishing Co. Inc.
387 Park Avenue South
New York, NY 10016, USA

British Library Cataloguing-in-Publication Data
A catalogue entry for this book
is available from the British Library

ISBN 0-304-36224-7

Designed and typeset by Harry Green

Printed and bound in Great Britain
by Bookmarque Ltd, Croydon, Surrey

Contents

Introduction

This is the first major dictionary of movie quotations – that is to say, a book containing not only quotable lines of dialogue from films but also quotable remarks by and about film-makers and, indeed, filmgoers. Film titles and names of people are presented in alphabetical sequence. Lines from films – as well as critical comments and other relevant material – are presented under the title of the film. Quotations of what film people have said are presented under their names, as also comments about them (so Billy Wilder on Marilyn Monroe appears under Marilyn **MONROE** rather than Billy **WILDER**).

There are also special sections devoted to Anonymous quotations, Catchphrases, Clichés, Screen titles, Slogans and Titles of films (that are in themselves quotations or have become popular sayings in their own right). Particular attention has been paid to the actual use of quotations in film titles (for example, ***NOW VOYAGER*** 310:8) and when incorporated in screenplays (for example, ***The PIANO*** 327:2). Generally speaking, however, where a title quotation was established before it was used as the title of a film, then it has not been featured. Similarly, lines from plays and books that have been included in screenplays of those plays and books are only featured when a significant change has been made to them, or where it can be said that their quotability derives from the film use.

There have, of course, been books that have endeavoured to present film quotations in *some* of these categories in the past, but I doubt whether there has been a book that has attempted to cover *all* of them before. I have set particular store on trying to reproduce dialogue *as it is spoken in the films*, rather than as it may have been set down in the original scripts or in later published scripts. My experience of the several books of 'film quotes' already published is that they are based on very rough transcriptions of soundtrack material. One rather imagines the editors jotting things down in the dark or trying to recall them afterwards, so vaguely are they related to what is actually said in the movies. Where possible I have listened again to the original soundtrack to obtain my version. Where this has not been possible and I have erred, I look forward to having any inaccuracies pointed out to me.

Even with the ability to review films over and over again on video, it is often very difficult to decide what is actually said in them. The speed at which dialogue is delivered in a Woody Allen movie, say, is extraordinarily fast. It can also bear little relevance to published versions of his scripts. Allen's actors are encouraged to improvise around his lines just as much as he does. There is nothing sacrosanct about them. But, to my mind, a book of movie quotations needs to record what is actually heard on the soundtrack rather than what is in the screenwriter's script.

Another consideration when selecting entries for this book has been, 'What exactly *is* a movie *quotation*?' This is necessary because there has grown up a vast store of reported comments by and about film people – much of it taken from journalistic interviews, fan magazines and the like – which, to my mind, are not quotations at all. A quotation should *say something in a particular way* – perhaps wittily, pithily, vividly – but in such a way that it demands to be repeated by others. Casual comments and expressions of view do not necessarily reach this standard.

Accordingly, from the vast amount of film-makers' and filmgoers' remarks, entries have been selected on the basis that they are quotable observations on (1) cinema, (2) the art of film-making in all its aspects, (3) critical assessments of individual films and of actors, directors and other film-makers, (4) biographical descriptions of such people. Utterances by film people are restricted to film-related matters, though sometimes a saying that is simply characteristic of their personalities or that sheds some light on their lives and careers has been included. As with lines of dialogue, the basic selection criterion has been that the observation or remark *has already been quoted somewhere else* – and thus is not merely something that has caught the editor's fancy (although, inevitably, there are exceptions to this rule ...).

●

My chief impression on completing this book – a labour of love, if ever there was cause to use that phrase so favoured of Introductions – is amazement at the sheer number of films that have been made over the past hundred or so years. Call films an art form or just a means of entertainment, the growth and spread of cinema in this period has been nothing short of astonishing. But equally notable, as far as I am concerned, is the extraordinary amount that has been written about the medium – in newspapers and magazines and in countless books. The 'literature' of the cinema is enormous – not just the fan-fodder, but also the serious critical works on the art and the people involved. Inevitably, the quotations included in this dictionary represent the tiniest fraction of all the millions of words that have been expended on this mightiest of all means of popular entertainment.

I have always been a devoted filmgoer. Since my earliest youth I have haunted the picture palaces (I think *Bambi* was the first film I saw, in the late 1940s, and, yes, I did cry my eyes out). Growing up in the 1950s, I am sure I went to the cinema at least once a week (and, in those days, you saw a double bill). As a student, in the early 1960s, three trips to the cinema in one week was not unusual. On more than one occasion, I went twice in a day and thus saw four films ... And so I continued through into the 1970s, my work in radio and television enabling me to keep up the strike rate.

By the late 1970s, a very significant change came over my film-going habits. Until that time, the only way to see 'old' films and 'classics' (not necessarily the same thing) was to hunt them down when they were revived at art cinemas or at the National Film Theatre in London. There were, of course, showings on the three (yes, only three) TV channels available in Britain in those days – but nothing like the immense choice now available on cable, satellite and terrestrial channels. But then came video. I completely failed to predict how this would catch on with a British public who had been reared to accept films on TV that you did not have to pay for. In no time at all, however, this became very largely my way of 'going to the movies'. While no experience can replace seeing a film properly projected in a decent-sized cinema surrounded by a real and human audience, video does have its compensations – not only in terms of conveni-ence, but also in the ability to skim and skip where called for.

Whatever the method, I think I still view as many movies as ever I did. This book is a small monument to that fact – as well as being a thanksgiving for all the entertainment I have derived from the medium. Thank you to everyone who has given me so much pleasure and interest and excitement. The cinema continues to be one of life's great pleasures.

⊛

In creating this book, I also must thank: the British Library; the British Film Institute; the London Library; and Video City, Notting Hill Gate, London. Among individuals, I would like to thank: Wendy Clay and Lyn Fairhurst, who produced my appearances on BBC Radio's *Movie-Go-Round* in far-off days and enabled me to meet and interview so many great names from the film world; Antony Jay for useful guidance; then my customary colleagues in the pursuit and verification of quotations, phrases and sayings, including: Jaap Engelsman, Wolfgang Mieder, Richard Hollinshead and Jeff Aronson; finally, my wife, Sue, now my partner 'at the video' but also, for a long time to come, I hope, 'at the movies'.

⊛

NOTE TO THE 2002 EDITION

I have taken the opportunity to correct one or two errors that crept into the book when it was first published. Having now seen for myself several films whose quotable lines I had had to rely on others to tell me about, I hope more accurate transcriptions will have resulted. Also, I have been able to make up for some omissions. Some entries have been expanded and these films now have sections devoted to them: *The Addams Family, All That Heaven Allows, American Beauty, Assault on Precinct 13, Blade Runner, The Blob, East of Eden, The Enforcer, Eyes Wide Shut, The Fast Lady, The Fly, O Brother Where Art Thou?, Once Upon a Time In the West, The Outlaw Josey Wales, Son of Ali Baba, Toy Story.*

NIGEL REES

Notting Hill, London, January 2002

F. Murray ABRAHAM

American actor (1939–)

1 You keep getting offered the same role you got the Oscar for. Every time you complain, they don't change the script, they just offer you more money.

QUOTED by Geraldine Page in *Time Out* (June 1986). Abraham won Best Actor for his performance as Salieri in *Amadeus* (US 1984).

ABSENCE OF MALICE

US 1981; screenwriter: Kurt Luedtke; cast: John Harkins (Davidek), Sally Field (Meg Carter), Wilford Brimley (James Wells), Don Hood (Quinn).

2 *Davidek (lawyer, to reporter Carter)*: As a matter of law, the truth of your story is irrelevant. We have no knowledge the story is false, therefore, we're absent malice.

SOUNDTRACK.

3 *Wells (to Quinn)*: A wonderful thing – a subpoena.

SOUNDTRACK.

The ACCIDENTAL TOURIST

US 1988; screenwriters: Frank Galati, Lawrence Kasdan (from Anne Tyler novel); cast: William Hurt (Macon Leary), Kathleen Turner (Sarah Leary), Bill Pulman (Julian), Geena Davis (Muriel Pritchett).

4 *Macon (narrating)*: The business traveller should bring only what fits in a carry-on bag. Checking your luggage is asking for trouble.

SOUNDTRACK.

5 *Sarah (his wife, to Macon)*: There's something so muffled about the way you experience things. It's as if you were trying to slip through life unchanged.

SOUNDTRACK.

6 *Julian (Macon's publisher)*: While armchair travellers dream of going places, travelling armchairs dream of staying put.

SOUNDTRACK.

1 *Macon (to Muriel)*: I really don't care for movies. They make everything seem so close up.

SOUNDTRACK.

The ACCUSED

US 1988; screenwriter: Tom Topor; cast: Jodie Foster (Sarah Tobias).

2 *Sarah (on her rape)*: I heard someone screaming and it was me.

SOUNDTRACK.

3 *Sarah (after her assailants have been convicted)*: I'd like to go home and I'd like to play with my dog.

SOUNDTRACK. Last line of film.

ACE IN THE HOLE

US 1951; screenwriters: Billy Wilder, Lesser Samuels, Walter Newman; cast: Jan Sterling (Lorraine), Kirk Douglas (Tatum).

4 *Lorraine (to Tatum)*: I met a lot of hard-boiled eggs in my life, but you – you're twenty minutes!

SOUNDTRACK.

5 *Lorraine*: I don't go to church. Kneeling bags my nylons.

SOUNDTRACK.

6 *Tatum (dying, to editor)*: How'd you like to make a thousand dollars a day, Mr Boot? I'm a thousand-dollar-a-day newspaperman. You can have me for nothing.

SOUNDTRACK.

Gilbert ADAIR

English critic and novelist (1944–)

7 It is an axiom of cinema history, one admitting of few exceptions, that the longer the film's title the likelier it is to be an outright dud.

ATTRIBUTED remark, in *The Guinness Book of Movie Facts & Feats*, ed. Patrick Robertson (1993 edn).

ADAM'S RIB

US 1949; screenwriters: Ruth Gordon, Garson Kanin; cast: Katharine Hepburn (Amanda Bonner), Spencer Tracy (Adam Bonner), Judy Holliday (Doris Attinger), Marvin Kaplan (Court stenographer), David Wayne (Kip Laurie).

8 *Amanda (to Adam)*: All I'm trying to say is that there's lots of things that a man can do and in society's eyes it's all hunky-dory. A woman does the same thing – the same thing, mind you – and she's an outcast.

SOUNDTRACK.

1 *Amanda (to Doris, accused of shooting her husband)*: And after you shot him – how did you feel?
Doris: Hungry.

SOUNDTRACK.

2 *Amanda (to her father but overheard by Adam)*: A girl named Doris Attinger shot her husband. I'm going to defend her.

SOUNDTRACK. This is the moment Adam realizes that his wife will be opposing his prosecution of Doris. He drops a tray of glasses.

3 *Adam (to Amanda)*: What is marriage? Tell me that … It's a contract. It's the law. Are you going to outsmart that the way you've outsmarted all other laws? That's clever. That's very clever. You've outsmarted yourself and you've outsmarted me and you've outsmarted everything.

SOUNDTRACK.

4 *Adam (to Amanda)*: I'm old-fashioned. I like two sexes.

SOUNDTRACK.

5 *Kip Laurie (to Amanda)*: Lawyers should never marry other lawyers. This is called inbreeding, from which comes idiot children and more lawyers.

SOUNDTRACK.

6 *Adam*: *Vive la différence!*
Amanda: Which means?
Adam: Which means, 'Hooray for that little difference.'

SOUNDTRACK. Last lines of film.

The ADDAMS FAMILY

US 1991; screenwriters: Caroline Thompson, Larry Wilson (after Charles Addams cartoons); cast: Anjelica Huston (Morticia Addams), Raul Julia (Gomez Addams).

7 *Morticia*: Don't torture yourself, Gomez. That's my job.

SOUNDTRACK.

8 *Morticia*: When we first met it was an evening much like this … Magic in the air. A boy.
Gomez: A girl.
Morticia: An open grave.

SOUNDTRACK.

Bill ADLER

American writer

1 The chances of your book being made into a motion picture are about as good as your chances of becoming the president of the United States.

EXTRACTED from *Inside Publishing* (1982).

Warren ADLER

American novelist and executive producer

2 The development guys are very young. No one's over 30, they have absolutely no life experience, they talk in clichés and their reference points are other movies.

QUOTED in *The Observer*, 'Sayings of the Week' (14 April 1991).

The ADVENTURES OF BARON MÜNCHAUSEN

UK/Germany 1989; screenwriters: Terry Gilliam, Charles McKeown; cast: Robin Williams (King of the Moon), Jonathan Pryce (Horatio Jackson), John Neville (Baron Münchausen).

3 *Horatio Jackson (to Münchausen)*: I'm afraid, sir, you have rather a weak grasp of reality.

SOUNDTRACK.

4 *King of the Moon*: No, let me go. I got tides to regulate. Comets to direct. I don't have time for flatulence and orgasms.

SOUNDTRACK.

The ADVENTURES OF DON JUAN

US 1949; screenwriters: George Oppenheimer, Harry Kurnitz; cast: Errol Flynn (Don Juan).

5 *Don Juan*: My dear friend, there's a little bit of Don Juan in every man, but since I am Don Juan, there must be more of it in me.

SOUNDTRACK. Last line of film.

The ADVENTURES OF ROBIN HOOD

US 1938; screenwriters: Seton I. Miller, Norman Reilly Raine; cast: Erroll Flynn (Sir Robin of Locksley), Basil Rathbone (Sir Guy of Gisbourne), Claude Rains (Prince John), Olivia de Havilland (Maid Marian), Alan Hale (Little John), Patric Knowles (Will Scarlet), Eugene Raffles (Friar Tuck), Ian Hunter (King Richard the Lion-Hearted).

6 [Robin Hood – The role that Errol Flynn] was born to play.

SLOGAN. Quoted by C.A. Lejeune in 1938.

1 *Maid Marian*: Why, you speak treason.
Robin Hood: Fluently.

SOUNDTRACK.

2 *Robin Hood (to Prince John)*: I'll organize a revolt, exact a death for a death, and I'll never rest until every Saxon in this shire can stand up free men and strike a blow for Richard and England.

SOUNDTRACK.

3 *Robin Hood (of Maid Marian)*: Hanging would be a small price to pay for the company of such a charming lady.

SOUNDTRACK.

4 *Sir Guy of Gisbourne (to Maid Marian, on her denial of associating with Robin Hood)*: You're very charming, Lady Marian, but not exactly clever.

SOUNDTRACK.

5 *Robin Hood (on being ordered by King Richard to marry Maid Marian)*: May I obey all your commands with equal pleasure, Sire!

SOUNDTRACK. Last line of film.

An AFFAIR TO REMEMBER

US 1957; screenwriters: Leo McCarey, Delmer Daves; cast: Cary Grant (Nickie Ferrante), Deborah Kerr (Terry McKay).

6 *Nickie (to Terry)*: This ship is going much too fast.

SOUNDTRACK.

7 *Terry (reunited with Nickie after being crippled in an accident)*: Oh, darling. Don't .... don't worry, darling. If ... if you can paint, I can walk. Anything can happen.

SOUNDTRACK.

The AFRICAN QUEEN

UK 1951; screenwriter: James Agee (from C.S. Forester novel); cast: Katharine Hepburn (Rose Sayer), Humphrey Bogart (Charlie Allnutt), Peter Bull (Captain of the *Louisa*).

8 *Allnutt*: Never do today what you can put off till tomorrow.

SOUNDTRACK. This comic reversal of the proverbial 'Never put off till tomorrow what you can do today' is of long standing. It occurs, for example, in C.H. Spurgeon, *John Ploughman's Talk* (1869).

9 *Rose (on running the rapids)*: I never dreamed that any mere physical experience could be so stimulating.

SOUNDTRACK.

1 *Allnutt (drunk and losing temper)*: I asked you on board 'cause I was sorry for you on account of your losing your brother and all. That's what you get for feeling sorry for someone. Well, I ain't sorry no more, you crazy psalm-singing, skinny old maid!

SOUNDTRACK.

2 *Allnutt*: A man alone, he gets to living like a hog.

SOUNDTRACK.

3 *Rose (to Allnutt)*: Nature, Mr Allnutt, is what we are put in this world to rise above.

SOUNDTRACK.

4 *Allnutt (giving his impression of Rose)*: Head up, chin out, hair blowing in the wind. The living picture of the heroine.

SOUNDTRACK.

5 *Allnutt*: If there's anything in the world I hate, it's leeches. Filthy little devils.

SOUNDTRACK.

6 *Allnutt (cleaning up the* African Queen *prior to blowing up the German warship* Louisa*)*: She ought to look her best, representing as she does the Royal Navy.

SOUNDTRACK.

7 *Rose (to Allnutt, arguing who is to blow up the* Louisa*)*: Oh, Charlie, we're having our first quarrel.

SOUNDTRACK.

8 *Captain (marrying Allnutt and Rose before their hanging)*: By the authority vested in me by Kaiser Wilhelm II, I pronounce you man and wife. Proceed with the execution.

SOUNDTRACK.

James AGEE

American critic and screenwriter (1909–55)

9 [reviewing *Random Harvest* (US 1942)] I would like to recommend this film to those who can stay interested in Ronald Colman's amnesia for two hours and who could with pleasure eat a bowl of Yardley's shaving soap for breakfast.

QUOTED in Leslie Halliwell, *The Filmgoer's Book of Quotes* (1973).

1 [reviewing *Tycoon* (US 1947)] Several tons of dynamite are set off in this picture; none of it under the right people.

EXTRACTED from journal *The Nation* (14 February 1948).

The AGONY AND THE ECTASY

US 1965; screenwriter: Philip Dunne (from Irving Stone novel); cast: Rex Harrison (Pope Julius II), Charlton Heston (Michelangelo).

2 *Julius II (to Michelangelo)*: You dare to dicker with your pontiff?

SOUNDTRACK.

Anouk AIMÉE

French actress (1932–)

3 You know, you can only perceive real beauty in a person as they get older.

QUOTED in *The Observer*, 'Sayings of the Week' (28 August 1988).

AIRPLANE!

US 1980; screenwriters/directors: Jim Abrahams, David Zucker, Jerry Zucker; cast: Robert Hays (Ted Striker), Leslie Nielsen (Dr Rumack), Kareem Abdul-Jabbar (Murdock), Peter Graves (Captain Oveur), Rossie Harris (Joey), Frank Ashmore (Victor Basta), Julie Hagerty (Elaine), White Lady (Barbara Billingsley), Lloyd Bridges (McCroskey), Robert Stack (Kramer).

4 NO SMOKING/EL NO A YOU SMOKO
FASTEN SEATBELTS/PUTANA DA SEATBELTZ.

SIGN in plane.

5 *Murdock (a co-pilot)*: We have clearance, Clarence.
Captain Oveur: Roger, Roger. What's our vector, Victor?

SOUNDTRACK.

6 *Elaine (flight attendant, making in-flight announcement)*: By the way, is there anyone on board who knows how to fly a plane?

SOUNDTRACK.

7 *Striker*: Surely you can't be serious!
Dr Rumack: I am serious. And don't call me Shirley.

SOUNDTRACK. And in various other situations.

8 *Kramer (air-traffic controller after he has brought plane down safely)*: Ted, that was probably the lousiest landing in the history of the airport, but some of us here, particularly me, would like to buy you a drink and shake your hand.

SOUNDTRACK.

ALADDIN

US 1992; screenwriters: Ron Clements and others; lyrics/music: Howard Ashman, Alan Menken; voices: Jonathan Freeman (Jafar), Scott Weinger (Aladdin), Robin Williams (The Genie).

1 I come from a land, from a faraway place
Where the caravan camels roam.
Where they cut off your ear if they don't like your face.
It's barbaric, but – hey – it's home.

SOUNDTRACK. From the opening song 'Arabian Nights' in the Disney cartoon film. When the film opened in Britain, in order not to offend Arab sensibilities, the lyrics had become: 'Where it's flat and immense and the heat is intense / It's barbaric but – hey – it's home.' The amendment was written by Peter Schneider.

2 *Jafar (to Aladdin)*: You've heard of the golden rule? He who has the gold, makes the rules.

SOUNDTRACK.

3 *The Genie (to Aladdin)*: Hang on to your turban, kid. We're going to make you a star.

SOUNDTRACK.

4 *The Genie (after saving Aladdin's life)*: I'm getting fond of you, kid. Not that I want to pick out curtains or anything.

SOUNDTRACK.

5 *The Genie (leaving)*: I'm history! No, I'm not, I'm mythology! I don't care what I am. I'm free!

SOUNDTRACK.

6 *The Genie (picking up last frame of movie and winking at audience)*: Made you look!

SOUNDTRACK. Last line of film.

The ALAMO

US 1960; screenwriter: James Edward Grant; cast: John Wayne (Col. David Crockett).

7 *Crockett*: Republic. I like the sound of the word. It means people can live free, talk free, go or come, buy or sell, be drunk or sober, however they choose. Some words give you a feeling. Republic is one of those words that makes me tight in the throat – the same tightness a man gets when his baby takes his first step or his first baby shaves and makes his first sound like a man. Some words can give you a feeling that makes your heart warm. Republic is one of those words.

SOUNDTRACK.

1 *Crockett*: Kind of a shame kids have to grow up to be people.

SOUNDTRACK.

ALFIE

UK 1966; screenwriter: Bill Naughton (after his radio and stage plays); cast: Michael Caine (Alfie Elkins), Shelley Winters (Ruby).

2 *Alfie*: The thing I like about Ruby, she's a mature woman. When she gets hold of you, you can feel a lifetime of experience in her fingers. Know what I mean? I find I'm going in more for that sort of woman these days. Here, don't you dig your nails in again like you did last Thursday night. I got scratches all down me back.

SOUNDTRACK.

3 *Alfie*: My understanding of women only goes as far as the pleasures. When it comes to the pain, I'm like every other bloke. I don't want to know.

SOUNDTRACK.

4 *Alfie*: So what's the answer? That's what I keep asking meself. What's it all about? Know what I mean?

SOUNDTRACK. Last line of film. The phrase 'What's it all about, Alfie?' was chiefly popularized by Burt Bacharach and Hal David's song 'Alfie'. This was not written for the film, which had a jazz score, with no songs, by Sonny Rollins, but Cher recorded it and her version was added to the soundtrack for the American release of the picture. Cilla Black then recorded it in Britain and Dionne Warwick in the US.

When Michael Caine published his autobiography in 1992, it was naturally entitled *What's It All About?*

ALGIERS

US 1938; screenwriter: John Howard Lawson, James M. Cain (from novel and film *Pépé le Moko*); cast: Joseph Calleia (Slimane), Charles Boyer (Pépé Le Moko).

5 *Slimane*: I'm sorry, Pépé. He thought you were going to escape.
Pépé le Moko (dying): And so I have, my friend.

SOUNDTRACK. Last lines of film.

6 Come with me to the Casbah.

APOCRYPHAL LINE associated with Charles Boyer (1899–1978), though he does not say it in *Algiers*. He is supposed to have said it to Hedy Lamarr. Boyer impersonators used it and the film was laughed at because of it, but it was simply a Hollywood legend that grew up. Boyer himself denied he had ever said it, and thought it had been invented by a press agent.

Nelson ALGREN

American novelist (1909–81)

1 I went out there [Hollywood] for a thousand a week, and I worked Monday, and I got fired Wednesday. The guy that hired me was out of town Tuesday.

INTERVIEWED in *Writers at Work*, First Series, ed. Malcolm Cowley (1958).

ALICE IN WONDERLAND

US 1951; screenwriters: various (after Lewis Carroll's story); voices: Bill Thompson (The White Rabbit), Kathryn Beaumont (Alice), Sterling Holloway (The Cheshire Cat), Verna Felton (The Queen of Hearts).

2 *White Rabbit*: Don't just do something, stand there!

SOUNDTRACK. This was in the Walt Disney cartoon version. An early appearance of a modern proverb. It was revived in a speech by George Shultz, US Labor Secretary (1920–), when objecting to government meddling (1970). *Compare* Clint **EASTWOOD** 148:1.

ALIENS

US 1986; screenwriter/director: James Cameron; cast: Sigourney Weaver (Ripley), Paul Reiser (Burke), Bill Paxton (Private Hudson), William Hope (Lieutenant Gorman), Michael Biehn (Corporal Hicks), Carrie Henn (Newt).

3 *Ripley (to Burke, on aliens)*: You're going out there to destroy them, right? Not to study, not to bring back, but to wipe them out?

SOUNDTRACK.

4 *Hicks*: I say we take off, nuke the site from orbit. It's the only way to be sure.

SOUNDTRACK.

5 *Ripley*: Sleep tight.
Newt: Affirmative.

SOUNDTRACK.

ALL ABOUT EVE

US 1950; screenwriter: Joseph L. Mankiewicz; cast: Bette Davis (Margo Channing), George Sanders (Addison de Witt), Ann Baxter (Eve Harrington), Marilyn Monroe (Miss Caswell), Thelma Ritter (Birdie), Celeste Holm (Karen Richards), Hugh Marlowe (Lloyd Richards), Gary Merrill (Bill Sampson), Barbara Bates (Phoebe).

6 *Addison (narrating)*: And no brighter light has ever dazzled the eyes than Eve Harrington. Eve. But more of Eve later – all about Eve, in fact.

SOUNDTRACK.

1 *Addison (narrating)*: Margo Channing is a star of the theatre. She made her first stage appearance at the age of four in *A Midsummer Night's Dream*. She played the fairy and entered quite unexpectedly, stark naked. She has been a star ever since. Margo is a great star, a true star. She never was nor ever will be anything else.
SOUNDTRACK.

2 *Birdie (to Margo, her boss)*: I haven't got a union. I'm slave labour.
SOUNDTRACK.

3 *Addison (on being a critic)*: My native habitat is the theatre. I toil not, neither do I spin. I am a critic and a commentator. I am essential to the theatre – as ants to a picnic, as the boll weevil to a cotton field.
SOUNDTRACK.

4 *Margo (to party group)*: Fasten your seat belts. It's going to be a bumpy night.
SOUNDTRACK.

5 *Addison*: Dear Margo, you were an unforgettable Peter Pan, you must play it again soon.
SOUNDTRACK.

6 *Addison (introducing Miss Caswell to Margo)*: You remember Miss Caswell ... Miss Caswell is an actress, a graduate of the Copacabana School of Dramatic Arts.
SOUNDTRACK. This was also Marilyn Monroe's introduction to the screen.

7 *Miss Caswell (of theatrical producers)*: Why do they always look like unhappy rabbits?
SOUNDTRACK.

8 *Eve (to Karen)*: So little, did you say? Why, if there's nothing else, there's applause. I've listened backstage to people applaud. It's like, like waves of love coming over the footlights and wrapping you up.
SOUNDTRACK.

9 *Addison (to Eve, on her calmness at her theatrical debut)*: The mark of a true killer. Sleep tight, rest easy, and come out fighting.
SOUNDTRACK.

10 *Margo (to Eve)*: Nice speech, Eve, but I wouldn't worry too much about your heart. You can always put that award where your heart ought to be.
SOUNDTRACK.

1 *Phoebe (to her idol, Eve)*: Well, lots of actresses come from Brooklyn. Barbara Stanwyck and Susan Hayward. Of course, they're just movie stars.

SOUNDTRACK.

ALL THAT HEAVEN ALLOWS

US 1955; screenwriter: Peggy Fenwick; cast: Jane Wyman (Cary Scott), Rock Hudson (Ron Kirby), Virginia Grey (Alida Anderson).

2 All That Heaven Allows.

TITLE OF FILM. Fenwick's script has widow Cary falling for her gardener Ron to the consternation of her class-conscious friends. Despite Wyman's quoting a hefty chunk from Thoreau's *Walden* (see below), no hint is given as to where the title of the film comes from. In fact, it comes from the poem 'Love and Life' by John Wilmot, Earl of Rochester (1647–80). This was included in Quiller-Couch's *Oxford Book of English Verse* (1900) – that great repository of quotations later to be used as film titles: 'Then talk not of inconstancy, / False hearts, and broken vows; / If I by miracle can be / This live-long minute true to thee, / 'Tis all that Heaven allows.'

3 *Cary (reading from Thoreau's* Walden*)*: 'The mass of men lead lives of quiet desperation ... Why should we be in such desperate haste to succeed? ... If a man does not keep pace with his companions, perhaps it is because he hears a different drummer. Let him step to the music which he hears, however measured or far away.'

SOUNDTRACK. These are edited sentences from different parts of the book.

4 *Alida (on whether Ron has ever read Thoreau's* Walden*)*: Oh, I don't think Ron's ever read it. He just lives it.

SOUNDTRACK.

5 *Society matron*: Haven't I seen you somewhere before?
Ron: Well, Mrs Humphrey, probably in your garden. I've been pruning your trees for the last three years.

SOUNDTRACK.

6 *TV salesman (to Cary)*: All you have to do is turn that dial and you have all the company you want. Right there on the screen. Drama, comedy, life's parade at your fingertips.

SOUNDTRACK.

ALL THAT JAZZ

US 1979; screenwriters: Robert Alan Arthur, Bob Fosse (director); cast: Roy Scheider (Gideon), Wallace Shawn (Businessman).

7 *Gideon*: It's show time, folks!

SOUNDTRACK. His stock phrase – almost a mantra before a performance or to enable him to get on with his life.

1 *Gideon*: Do you suppose Stanley Kubrick ever gets depressed?

SOUNDTRACK.

2 *Gideon*: I don't get married again because I can't find anyone I dislike enough to inflict that kind of torture on.

SOUNDTRACK.

3 *Businessman*: You could be the first show on Broadway to make a profit without really opening.

SOUNDTRACK.

4 *Gideon (to God, as his health rapidly deteriorates)*: What's the matter? Don't you like musical comedy?

SOUNDTRACK.

ALL THAT MONEY CAN BUY

(also known as *The Devil and Daniel Webster* and *Daniel and the Devil*) US 1941; screenwriter: Daniel Toteroh (from a Stephen Vincent Benét story); cast: Walter Huston (Mr Scratch, the Devil), Edward Arnold (Daniel Webster), James Craig (Jabez Stone), Jane Darwell (Ma Stone).

5 *Mr Scratch (to Webster)*: You're only wasting your time writing speeches like that. Why worry about the people and their problems? Think of your own.

SOUNDTRACK. First line of film.

6 *Jabez Stone (just before two pennies appear in his hand)*: That's enough to make a man sell his soul to the Devil! And I would for about two cents!

SOUNDTRACK.

7 *Mr Scratch (to Stone)*: A soul – a soul is nothing. Can you see it, smell it, touch it? No. This soul – your soul – are nothing against seven years of good luck! You'll have money, and all that money can buy.

SOUNDTRACK.

8 *Mr Scratch (to Stone, when he sells his soul)*: A firm, fair signature. One that will last till doomsday.

SOUNDTRACK.

9 *Ma Stone (to Stone)*: Well, thank God, you can always depend on New England for weather. We've got enough for the whole of the United States.

SOUNDTRACK.

1 *Ma Stone (to Stone)*: A man can always change things. That's what makes him different from the barnyard critters.

SOUNDTRACK.

2 *Mr Scratch (to Webster)*: Who has a better right? When the first wrong was done to the first Indian, I was there. When the first slave was put off from the Congo, I stood on the deck. Am I not still spoken of in every church in New England? It's true the North claims me for a Southerner, and the South for a Northerner, but I'm neither. Tell the truth, Mr Webster, though I don't like to boast of it, my name is older in the country than yours.

SOUNDTRACK.

3 *Webster (defending Stone to the jury of the damned)*: Gentlemen of the jury, I ask you to give Jabez Stone another chance to walk upon this earth, among the trees, the growing corn, and the smell of grasses in the spring.

SOUNDTRACK.

4 *Webster (defending Stone to the jury of the damned)*: Gentlemen of the jury, don't let this country go to the Devil! Free Jabez Stone! God bless the United States and the men who made her free!

SOUNDTRACK.

ALL THE KING'S MEN

US 1949; screenwriter: Robert Rossen (from Robert Penn Warren novel); cast: John Ireland (Jack Burden), Broderick Crawford (Willie Stark).

5 *Burden (to Stark, about voters)*: Make them cry. Make them laugh. Make them mad, even mad at you. Stir them up and they'll love it, and come back for more, but, for heaven's sake, don't try to improve their minds.

SOUNDTRACK.

Fred ALLEN

American comedian (1894–1956)

6 Hollywood is a place where people from Iowa mistake themselves for movie stars.

QUOTED in Maurice Zolotow, *No People Like Show People*, Chap. 8 (1951). Said in about 1941.

1 Hollywood is no place for a professional comedian; the amateur competition is too great.

QUOTED in *The Treasury of Humorous Quotations*, eds. Esar & Bentley (1951 edn).

2 An associate producer is the only guy in Hollywood who will associate with a producer.

QUOTED in *The Treasury of Humorous Quotations*, eds. Esar & Bentley (1951 edn).

3 You can take all the sincerity in Hollywood, put it in a flea's navel, and still have room left over for three caraway seeds and an agent's heart.

QUOTED in Silver & Haiblum, *Faster Than a Speeding Bullet* (1980). Quoted earlier in J.R. Colombo, *Wit and Wisdom of the Moviemakers* (1979) as, '... place it in the navel of a fruit fly and still have room enough for three caraway seeds and a producer's heart'.

Woody ALLEN

American actor, screenwriter and director (1935–)

4 If I had my life to live over I would do everything the exact same way – with the possible exception of seeing the movie remake of *Lost Horizon*.

ATTRIBUTED remark in *The Guinness Book of Movie Facts & Feats*, ed. Patrick Robertson (1993 edn). Referring to the musical version (US 1973).

5 I don't mean much to the Rambo crowd.

QUOTED in *The Observer*, 'Sayings of the Week' (14 August 1988).

6 I've never been an intellectual, but I have this look.

QUOTED in *The Observer*, 'Sayings of the Week' (22 March 1992).

7 I don't want to achieve immortality through my work. I want to achieve it through not dying.

QUOTED in Eric Lax, *Woody Allen and His Comedy*, Chap. 12 (1975). Sometimes coupled with 'I don't want to live on in the hearts of my countrymen. I would rather live on in my apartment' – quoted in *Woody Allen on Woody Allen: In Conversation with Stig Björkman* (1995).

8 [accepting an award] I recently turned sixty. Practically a third of my life is over.

QUOTED in *The Observer*, 'Sayings of the Week' (10 March 1996).

9 [on his other career as a jazz clarinettist] If the audience like it, they like it. If they don't, then I say, 'Please folks, I'm a film-maker, don't judge me too harshly.'

QUOTED in *Independent on Sunday*, 'Overheard' (17 March 1996).

1 If Woody Allen were a Muslim, he'd be dead by now.

COMMENT by Salman Rushdie, quoted in *The Independent* (18 February 1989).

2 The only thing Woody Allen has in common with Ingmar Bergman is Sven Nykvist.

COMMENT by Joe Queenan (referring to the director of photography who has worked for them both).

3 [on love scenes with Woody Allen] He did not just keep his clothes on under the sheet, but he kept his shoes on, too. When I asked him why, he said it was in case there was a fire.

COMMENT by Helena Bonham Carter, quoted in *Independent on Sunday*, 'Quotes of the Week' (12 November 1995).

See also ***ANNIE HALL***; ***BROADWAY DANNY ROSE***; ***BULLETS OVER BROADWAY***; ***CRIMES AND MISDEMEANORS***; ***EVERYTHING YOU ALWAYS WANTED TO KNOW ABOUT SEX ...***; ***HANNAH AND HER SISTERS***; ***HUSBANDS AND WIVES***; ***LOVE AND DEATH***; ***MANHATTAN***; ***MANHATTAN MURDER MYSTERY***; ***PLAY IT AGAIN SAM***; ***RADIO DAYS***; ***SLEEPER***; ***TAKE THE MONEY AND RUN***.

Robert ALTMAN

American director (1925–)

4 After all, what's a cult? It just means not enough people to make a minority.

INTERVIEWED in *The Guardian* (11 April 1981).

5 Nobody has ever made a good movie. Someday, someone will make a half good one.

ATTRIBUTED remark.

AMERICAN BEAUTY

US 1999; screenwriter: Alan Ball; cast: Kevin Spacey (Lester Burnham).

6 *Lester (narrating)*: This is my street. This is my life. I'm forty-two years old. In less than a year I'll be dead. Of course, I don't know that yet. And, in a way, I'm dead already.

SOUNDTRACK.

7 *Lester(narrating)*: Look at me – jerking off in the shower. This will be the highpoint of my day. It's all downhill from here.

SOUNDTRACK.

AMERICAN GRAFFITI

US 1973; screenwriters: George Lucas (director) and others; cast: Ron Howard (Steve Bolander), Richard Dreyfuss (Curt Henderson).

1 Where were you in '62?
SLOGAN.

2 *Steve (to Curt, on Curt's ambivalence about leaving town for college)*: You just can't stay seventeen forever.
SOUNDTRACK.

An AMERICAN IN PARIS

US 1951; screenwriter: Alan Jay Lerner; music/lyrics: George & Ira Gershwin; cast: Gene Kelly (Jerry Mulligan), Oscar Levant (Adam Cook), Nina Foch (Milo Roberts), Leslie Caron (Lise Bouvier), Georges Guétary (Henri Baurel).

3 *Jerry (narrating)*: For a painter, the Mecca of the world for study, for inspiration, and for living is here on this star called Paris. Just look at it. No wonder so many artists have come here and called it home. Brother, if you can't paint in Paris, you'd better give up and marry the boss's daughter.
SOUNDTRACK.

4 *Jerry*: Back home everyone said I didn't have any talent. They might be saying the same thing over here, but it sounds better in French.
SOUNDTRACK.

5 *Adam*: It's not a pretty face, I grant you, but underneath its flabby exterior is an enormous lack of character.
SOUNDTRACK.

6 *Henri*: Let's just say I'm old enough to know what to do with my young feelings.
SOUNDTRACK.

7 *Jerry (to Milo)*: That's quite a dress you almost have on. What holds it up?
SOUNDTRACK.

8 *Jerry (to Lise)*: With a binding like you've got, people are going to want to know what's in the book.
SOUNDTRACK.

AND THEN THERE WERE NONE

(also known as *Ten Little Niggers* in the UK) US 1945; screenwriter: Dudley Nichols (from Agatha Christie novel); cast: Judith Anderson (Emily Brent), Barry Fitzgerald (Judge Quincannon), Richard Haydn (Rogers).

1 *Rogers*: Never in my life have I been accused of any crime, sir – and if that's what you think of me, I shan't serve any dinner.

SOUNDTRACK.

2 *Emily Brent*: Very stupid to kill the only servant in the house. Now we don't even know where to find the marmalade.

SOUNDTRACK.

Lindsay ANDERSON

English director (1923–94)

3 Perhaps the tendency is to treat the films of one's own country like the prophets – with less than justice.

QUOTED in Ian Christie, *Arrows of Desire*: *The Films of Michael Powell & Emeric Pressburger* (1985). Remark made in 1947.

4 As film-makers we believe that: No film can be too personal. The image speaks. Sound amplifies and comments. Size is irrelevant. Perfection is not an aim. An attitude means a style. A style means an attitude.

STATEMENT of belief written by Anderson in 1956 on behalf of Free Cinema, a group of British documentarists.

5 I am seeing if I can shake off this reputation for integrity.

QUOTED in *The Independent* (1 April 1989).

6 I suppose I'm the boy who stood on the burning deck whence all but he had fled. The trouble is I don't know whether the boy was a hero or a bloody idiot.

ATTRIBUTED remark.

7 He was a loner. There was an absoluteness of stance about him, an uncompromising quality which gave him many disciples, but also hundreds of enemies.

COMMENT attributed to Karel Reisz.

Ursula ANDRESS

Swiss-born actress (1936–)

8 I'm finished with men, but I have a very full memory.

QUOTED in *The Observer* (7 January 1996). Andress is believed to have had relationships with Marlon Brando, James Dean, Elvis Presley and Ryan O'Neal.

(Dame) Julie ANDREWS

English actress and singer (1935–)

1 I'd like to thank all those who made this possible – especially Jack L. Warner.

SPEECH accepting 'Best Actress' Oscar for her performance in *Mary Poppins* (1964), having been turned down for the Warner Bros. version of the musical *My Fair Lady*, in which she had made her name on stage. Quoted in Leslie Halliwell, *The Filmgoer's Book of Quotes* (1973).

2 Working with her is like being hit over the head by a Valentine's Day card.

COMMENT by Christopher Plummer, Canadian actor (1927–), after he had made *The Sound of Music* (1965) with Andrews. Quoted in Leslie Halliwell, *The Filmgoer's Book of Quotes* (1973).

3 Julie Andrews is like a nun with a switchblade.

COMMENT by Anon., quoted in Leslie Halliwell, *The Filmgoer's Book of Quotes* (1973).

4 She has that wonderful British strength that makes you wonder why they lost India.

COMMENT by Moss Hart.

ANIMAL CRACKERS

US 1930; screenwriters: Morrie Ryskind, George S. Kaufman; music/lyrics: Harry Ruby, Bert Kalmar; cast: Groucho Marx (Capt. Spaulding), Margaret Dumont (Mrs Teasdale), Zeppo Marx (Jamison).

5 *Spaulding (to Teasdale)*: Why, you're one of the most beautiful women I've ever seen, and that's not saying much for you.

SOUNDTRACK.

6 *Spaulding (sings)*: Hello, I must be going.

SOUNDTRACK.

7 *Guests*: Hooray for Captain Spaulding, the African explorer!
Spaulding: Did someone call me schnorrer?
Guests: Hooray, hooray, hooray!

SOUNDTRACK.

8 *Spaulding*: Are we all going to get married?
Teasdale: ... But that's bigamy.
Spaulding: Yes, and it's bigame too.

SOUNDTRACK.

1 *Spaulding*: We must remember that art is art. Still, on the other hand, water is water, isn't it? – and east is east and west is west, and if you take cranberries and stew them like apple sauce, it tastes much more like prunes than rhubarb does.

SOUNDTRACK.

2 *Spaulding*: Well, you go Uruguay, and I'll go mine.

SOUNDTRACK.

3 *Spaulding*: One morning I shot an elephant in my pyjamas. How he got in my pyjamas I dunno ... But that's entirely irrelephant to what I'm talking about.

SOUNDTRACK.

4 *Jamison (reading from letter Spaulding has dictated)*: Quotes, unquotes and quotes.
Spaulding: That's three quotes ... And another quote'll make it a gallon.

SOUNDTRACK.

ANNA CHRISTIE

US 1930; screenwriter: Frances Marion (from play by Eugene O'Neill);
cast: Greta Garbo (Blanche Sweet), Chris Christopherson (George F. Marion).

5 Garbo Talks!

SLOGAN. Said to have been coined by Howard Dietz. A film with the title *Garbo Talks* (US 1984) was directed by Sidney Lumet and concerned a woman whose dying wish is to meet her idol Garbo.

6 *Blanche (to barman)*: Gimme a viskey. Ginger ale on the side. And don't be stingy, baby.

SOUNDTRACK. Garbo's first spoken line in films.

7 *George F. Marion*: Fog, fog all time. You can't tell where you was going. Only that old devil sea, she knows.

SOUNDTRACK. Last line of film.

Princess ANNE (Princess Royal)

British royal (1950–)

8 Cinema managers are nice and let you pop in to see a film without telling. My mother has seen quite a few films that way recently.

QUOTED in Noel St George, *Royal Quotes* (1981).

ANNIE HALL

US 1977; screenwriters: Woody Allen, Marshall Brickman; cast: Woody Allen (Alvy/Max), Diane Keaton (Annie), Joan Newman (Alvy's mother), Tony Roberts (Rob), Marshall McLuhan (himself).

1 *Alvy*: I would never want to belong to any club that would have someone like me for a member. That's the key joke of my adult life, in terms of my relationships with women.

SOUNDTRACK. Alvy states that although usually attributed to Groucho Marx this joke originally appears in Freud's *Wit and its Relation to the Unconscious. Compare* Groucho **MARX** 277:2.

2 *Alvy (to Rob, giving evidence of anti-Semitism)*: You know, I was having lunch with some guys from NBC, so I said, 'Did you eat yet or what?' and Tom Christie said, 'No, jew.'

SOUNDTRACK.

3 *Alvy (on Los Angeles)*: I don't want to live in a city where the only cultural advantage is that you can make a right turn on a red light.

SOUNDTRACK.

4 *Alvy (refusing to see a movie when he has missed the opening credits)*: I've gotta see a picture exactly from the start to the finish – because I'm anal.

SOUNDTRACK. Annie comments: 'But they're in Swedish.'

5 *Marshall McLuhan (to bore in movie line)*: I heard what you were saying. You know nothing of my work. You mean my whole fallacy is wrong. How you ever got to teach a course in anything is totally amazing.

SOUNDTRACK.

6 *Annie*: Well, la-di-da.

SOUNDTRACK. Stock expression.

7 *Alvy (to Annie, who has just parked the motor somewhat casually)*: That's OK, we can walk to the curb from here.

SOUNDTRACK.

8 *Alvy (after sex)*: As Balzac said, there goes another novel.

SOUNDTRACK.

9 *Alvy (to Annie, on sex with her)*: That was the most fun I've ever had without laughing.

SOUNDTRACK. Has also been attributed to Humphrey Bogart in the form 'It was the most fun I ever had without laughing.' However, H.L. Mencken was recording, 'Love [he probably meant sex] is the most fun you can have without laughing' in 1942.

1 *Alvy (to Annie)*: Love is, is too weak a word for the way, I feel – I lurve you, you know, I loave you, I luff you.

SOUNDTRACK.

2 *Alvy*: I was thrown out of NYU in my freshman year for cheating on my metaphysics final, you know. I looked into the soul of the boy sitting next to me.

SOUNDTRACK. Part of stand-up comedy act.

3 *Alvy*: Hey! Don't knock masturbation. It's sex with someone I love.

SOUNDTRACK.

4 *Alvy (on penis envy)*: I'm one of the few males who suffers from that.

SOUNDTRACK.

5 *Alvy*: Darling, I've been killing spiders since I was thirty. OK?

SOUNDTRACK.

6 *Alvy (on Los Angeles)*: They don't throw their garbage away. They make it into television shows.

SOUNDTRACK.

7 *Alvy*: A relationship, I think, is, is like a shark, you know, it has to constantly move forward or it dies, and I think what we got on our hands is a dead shark.

SOUNDTRACK.

8 *Alvy*: Well, I guess that's pretty much now how I feel about relationships. You know, they're totally irrational and crazy and absurd and – but, uh, I guess we keep goin' through it because most of us need the eggs.

SOUNDTRACK. Last lines of film.

ANONYMOUS

9 The always interesting moving pictures in the biograph at Keith's will include this week four new scenes.

NEWS ITEM in the *New York Tribune* (30 October 1898) – containing one of the earliest uses of the term 'moving pictures' (but see Queen **VICTORIA** 435:5).

10 The amusing thing about moving pictures is the enormous number of nonentities who work together to make something any normal half-wit would prefer not to make in the first place.

COMMENT attributed to 'American writer' by C.A. Lejeune in *The Observer* (1945).

1 As the Talkies grow to maturity, one terrible, tragic fact has been learned. Love scenes that were tender and impressive in the silent days now get the succulent and vulgar raspberry in dialogue. John Gilbert has been a victim. The same amorous technique that made Jack adored and famous in the dear old days is inclined to raise a storm of titters in the new.

COMMENT in *Photoplay* (January 1930).

2 The camera does not lie.

COMMENT – almost a modern proverb – as used, for example, by W.H. Auden in a script for a film commentary ('Six Commissioned Texts', No. 1, 1962): 'The camera's eye / Does not lie, / But it cannot show / The life within.'

3 DON'T TRY TO BECOME AN ACTOR. FOR EVERY ONE WE EMPLOY, WE TURN AWAY THOUSANDS.

SIGN above door of Central Casting in the 1930s.

4 The face on the cutting-room floor.

TERM referring to an actor or actress cut out of a film after it has been completed and edited. Used as the title of a novel by Cameron McCabe in 1937 and possibly related to the ballad known as 'The Face on the Bar-room Floor' by H. Antoine d'Arcy (though he insisted the title was simply 'The Face on the Floor'). Now the 'cutting-room floor' tends to be invoked as the place where any unwanted material ends up – and not only in reference to media matters. From Josephine Tey, *A Shilling for Candles* (1936): 'Treating me like bits on the cutting-room floor.'

5 Films are never completed. They're only abandoned.

COMMENT by 'famous film-maker', quoted by George Lucas in introduction to video of *Star Wars*: *Special Edition* (1997).

6 [popular Hollywood joke as said by producers, 1928] I don't care if he can act; can he talk?

COMMENT quoted by Stuart Berg Flexner in *Listening to America* (1982).

7 [on historical films] My dear, they have a certain social value. Until I saw Anna Neagle and Anton Walbrook in the film about Queen Victoria [*Sixty Glorious Years*, UK 1938] I had no idea that the Prince Consort married beneath him!

COMMENT by woman at luncheon party, quoted in James Agate, *Ego 6* (diary entry for 17 August 1943).

8 [on the movies] It is probable that the fad will die out in the next few years.

EXTRACTED from the *Independent* (US) (17 March 1910).

9 The son-in-law also rises.

QUOTED in Leslie Halliwell, *The Filmgoer's Book of Quotes* (1973). Possibly when Louis B. Mayer promoted his daughter's husband William Goetz to a key position at MGM. In J.R. Colombo, *Wit and Wisdom of the Moviemakers* (1979), the line is credited to Edwin H. Knopf.

1 STICKS NIX HICKS PIX.

HEADLINE in *Variety* (17 July 1935), meaning that filmgoers in rural areas were not attracted to films with bucolic themes. Has been credited to Sime Silverman (1873–1933), also to Abel Green (1900–73).

2 [on Jean Cocteau's *The Seashell and the Clergyman* (France 1929)] [This film] is so cryptic as to be almost meaningless. If there is a meaning, it is doubtless objectionable.

COMMENT by British Board of Film Censors, banning the film. Quoted in J.C. Robertson, *Hidden Cinema* (1989).

3 This is where we came in.

TERM used by filmgoers in the days when programmes ran continuously (from the 1920s to the 1970s). Quoted, for example, by C.A. Lejeune in 'My Story' in *Good Housekeeping* (about 1954). In *Punch* (9 March 1938), there is a cartoon of a couple at a boxing match. The ring is covered with bodies and the caption is, 'Isn't this where we came in?' – which rather suggests that the expression was well enough established even then for it to be used in a transferred situation. From 'Cato', *Guilty Men* (1940): 'When the news of the appointment [of Sir Samuel Hoare, re-appointed as Minister of Air in 1940] became known, an aged opponent of the administration rose from his seat; "This is where I came in," he said.'

4 A tree is a tree – a rock is a rock.

COMMENT. An 'old studio motto', quoted in Mae West, *Goodness Had Nothing To Do With It*, Chap. 15 (1959) – meaning that it does not matter much what location you use for a film.

5 Who do I fuck to get off this picture?

COMMENT attributed to 'Hollywood starlet (circa 1930)' in Steve Bach, *Final Cut* (1985). In Bob Chieger, *Was It Good For You Too?* (1983), the line 'Who do you have to fuck to get out of show business?' is specifically credited to one Shirley Wood, talent coordinator of NBC TV's *Tonight* show in the 1960s. 'Who do I have to sleep with to get *out* of this picture?' appears in Carolyn Kenmore, *Mannequin* (1969). *Compare* Terry **SOUTHERN** 390:5.

Michelangelo ANTONIONI

Italian director (1912–)

6 I see the actor (generally) as part of the composition. I do not want the actor to become his own director. I never explain to the actors the characters they are playing. I want them to be passive.

QUOTED in Alexander Walker, *The Celluloid Sacrifice* (1966).

1 I feel like a father towards my old films. You bring children into the world, then they grow up and go off on their own. From time to time you get together, and it's always a pleasure to see them again.

ATTRIBUTED remark.

2 It can happen that films acquire meanings: that is to say, that the meanings appear afterwards.

REMARK quoted in J.R. Colombo, *Wit and Wisdom of the Moviemakers* (1979).

The APARTMENT

US 1960; screenwriters Billy Wilder, I.A.L. Diamond; cast: Shirley Maclaine (Fran Kubelik), Jack Lemmon (C.C. Baxter), David Lewis (Mr Kirkeby), Fred MacMurray (J.D. Sheldrake).

3 *Baxter (narrating)*: You see, I have this little problem with my apartment.

SOUNDTRACK.

4 *Mr Kirkeby*: Premium-wise and billing-wise we are eighteen per cent ahead, October-wise.

SOUNDTRACK.

5 *Sheldrake*: You see a girl a couple of times a week and sooner or later she thinks you'll divorce your wife. Not fair, is it?
Baxter: No, especially to your wife.

SOUNDTRACK.

6 *Fran (to Baxter)*: Just because I wear a uniform doesn't mean I'm a Girl Scout.

SOUNDTRACK.

7 *Fran (to Baxter, after crying over Sheldrake)*: When you're in love with a married man, you shouldn't wear mascara.

SOUNDTRACK.

8 *Fran*: Why can't I ever fall in love with someone nice like you?
Baxter: Yeah, well, that's the way it crumbles, cookie-wise.

SOUNDTRACK.

9 *Baxter*: You hear what I said, Miss Kubelik?
I absolutely adore you.
Fran: Shut up and deal.

SOUNDTRACK. Last lines of film.

APOCALYPSE NOW

US 1979; screenwriters: John Milius, Francis Ford Coppola (director); cast: Robert Duvall (Lieut. Col. Kilgore), Marlon Brando (Col. Kurtz), Martin Sheen (Capt. Benjamin Willard), Jerry Ziesmer (Civilian), Dennis Hopper (Photojournalist).

1 *Willard (narrating)*: Everyone gets everything he wants. I wanted a mission, and for my sins they gave me one.

SOUNDTRACK.

2 *Civilian (ordering the killing of Kurtz)*: Terminate with extreme prejudice.

SOUNDTRACK. This phrase had been in the parlance of the US Central Intelligence Agency since at least 1972.

3 *Willard (on Kilgore)*: He was one of those guys that had that weird light around him. You just knew he wasn't gonna get so much as a scratch here.

SOUNDTRACK.

4 *Kilgore*: I love the smell of napalm in the morning … Smells like victory.

SOUNDTRACK.

5 *Kurtz*: Are my methods unsound?
Willard: I don't see any method at all, sir.

SOUNDTRACK.

6 *Kurtz (recalling incident from his time with Special Forces)*: We left the camp after we had inoculated the children for polio, and this old man came running after us and he was crying, he couldn't see. We went back there, and they had come and hacked off every inoculated arm. There they were in a pile, a pile of little arms.

SOUNDTRACK.

7 *Kurtz (on why he needs men who can kill without judgement)*: Because it's judgement that defeats us.

SOUNDTRACK.

8 *Willard (on Kurtz)*: Even the jungle wanted him dead, and that's who he really took his orders from anyway.

SOUNDTRACK.

9 *Kurtz (dying)*: The horror, the horror!

SOUNDTRACK. Last words, as in Joseph Conrad's story 'Heart of Darkness', upon which the film is based.

Roscoe 'Fatty' ARBUCKLE

American comic and actor (1887–1933)

1 My father [lawyer Earl Rogers] had said at once that, though he was innocent, beyond question he would be publicly castigated because it was repulsive to think of a fat man in the role of a rapist.

COMMENT in Adela Rogers St John, *The Honeycomb* (1969). After initially being suspected of rape and murder, Arbuckle was charged with the manslaughter of a young model in 1921. Although acquitted, his career was effectively ended by the case.

2 In spite of his suet he was an agile man … and became a superb pie pitcher … He could throw two pies at once in different directions, but he was not precise in this feat.

COMMENT by Mack Sennett in his book *King of Comedy* (1954).

ARISE MY LOVE

US 1940; screenwriters: Charles Brackett, Billy Wilder; cast: Walter Abel (Mr Phillips).

3 *Mr Phillips (as harassed editor)*: I'm not happy. I'm not happy at all …

SOUNDTRACK.

George ARLISS

English actor (1868–1946)

4 The talking picture is like a dress rehearsal in the theatre. It never gets those moments of inspiration when an audience lifts an actor out of himself. So I say that no player can ever be seen at his best.

ATTRIBUTED remark.

ARSENIC AND OLD LACE

US 1944; screenwriters: Julius J. & Philip G. Epstein and others (from Joseph Kesselring play); cast: Cary Grant (Mortimer Brewster), Jean Adair (Martha Brewster), Priscilla Lane (Elaine Harper).

5 *Elaine*: But, Mortimer, you're going to love me for my mind, too?
Mortimer: One thing at a time.

SOUNDTRACK.

6 *Mortimer*: Insanity runs in my family. It practically gallops.

SOUNDTRACK.

7 *Martha*: One of our gentlemen found time to say, 'How delicious!' before he died …

SOUNDTRACK.

ARTHUR

US 1981; screenwriter/director: Steve Gordon; cast: Dudley Moore (Arthur Bach), John Gielgud (Hobson).

1 *Arthur*: I'm going to take a bath.
Hobson (butler): I'll alert the media.

SOUNDTRACK.

ASH WEDNESDAY

US 1973; screenwriter: Jean Claude Tramont; cast: Elizabeth Taylor (Barbara Sawyer).

2 *Barbara*: Look at these breasts, Mike, aren't they beautiful?

SOUNDTRACK.

The ASPHALT JUNGLE

US 1950; screenwriters: Ben Maddow, John Huston (from W.R. Burnett novel; cast: Sam Jaffe (Doc Erwin Reidenschneider).

3 *Reidenschneider*: Crime is a left-handed form of human endeavour.

SOUNDTRACK.

ASSAULT ON PRECINCT 13

US 1976; screenwriter/director: John Carpenter; cast: Darwin Joston (Napoleon Wilson).

4 *Wilson (recalling what a preacher said to him as a kid)*: Son, there is something about you. You got something to do with death..

SOUNDTRACK. *Compare* ***ONCE UPON A TIME IN THE WEST*** 316:4.

Fred ASTAIRE

American dancer and actor (1899–1987)

5 I suppose I made it look easy, but gee whiz, did I work and worry.

ATTRIBUTED remark.

6 [of Astaire's first screen test] Can't act, can't sing, slightly bald. Can dance a little.

COMMENT attributed to a 'Hollywood executive' in Leslie Halliwell, *The Filmgoer's Book of Quotes* (1973).

7 *Top Hat* is a vehicle … for Mr Fred Astaire's genius. It doesn't really matter that the music and lyrics are bad. Mr Astaire is the nearest approach we are ever likely to have to a human Mickey Mouse.

COMMENT by Graham Greene in *The Spectator* (25 October 1935).

1 I have never met anyone who did not like Fred Astaire. Somewhere in his monkey-sad face, his loose legs, his shy grin, or perhaps the anxious diffidence of his manner, he has found the secret of persuading the world.

COMMENT by C.A. Lejeune.

2 [It was] Fred Astaire who made envy legitimate. You wouldn't have minded being in his shoes, so to speak.

COMMENT by Jeffrey Bernard in *More Low Life*, 'Who's Coming to Dinner?' (1986).

See also Katharine **HEPBURN** 213:1; Gene **KELLY** 238:4.

Alexandre ASTRUC

French critic, writer and director (1923–)

3 The cinema is quite simply becoming a means of expression, just as all the other arts have been before it, and in particular painting and the novel. After having been successively a fairground attraction, an amusement analogous to boulevard theatre, or a means of preserving the images of an era, it is gradually becoming a language. By a language, I mean a form in which and by which an artist can express his thoughts, however abstract they may be, or translate his obsessions, exactly as he does in the contemporary essay or a novel. That is why I would like to call this new age of cinema the age of *caméra-stylo* [camera-pen].

COMMENT (translated) from article 'The Birth of a New Avant-Garde: La Caméra-Stylo' in *Écran Français* (30 March 1948). This became the programme of the New Wave film-makers ten years later.

4 The film will gradually break free from the tyranny of what is visual, from the image for its own sake, from the immediate and concrete, to become a means of writing as flexible and supple as written language … The fundamental problem of the cinema is how to express thought … What interests us is the creation of this new language.

COMMENT. From the same article.

5 We have come to realize that the meaning which the silent cinema tried to give birth to through symbolic association exists within the image itself, in the development of the narrative, in every gesture of the characters, in every line of dialogue, in those camera movements which relate objects to objects and characters to objects. All thought, like all feeling, is a relationship between one human being and another human being.

COMMENT. From the same article.

AT THE CIRCUS

US 1939; screenwriter: Irving Brecher; cast: Groucho Marx (J. Cheever Loophole), Chico Marx (Antonio), Margaret Dumont (Mrs D.).

1 *Loophole (to Antonio)*: You know, if you hadn't sent for me, I'd probably be home now in a nice warm bedroom, in a comfortable bed with a hot toddy ... That's a drink!

SOUNDTRACK.

2 *Loophole*: I bet your father spent the first year of your life throwing rocks at the stork.

SOUNDTRACK.

ATLANTIC CITY

US 1981; screenwriter: John Guare; cast: Burt Lancaster (Lou), Susan Sarandon (Sally), Robert Joy (Dave).

3 *Lou (to Dave, on mobsters he knew)*: I worked for the people who worked for the people.

SOUNDTRACK.

4 *Sally*: Teach me things.
Lou: You want information or you want wisdom?
Sally: Both.

SOUNDTRACK.

5 *Lou (to Dave)*: The Atlantic Ocean was something then. Yes, you should have seen the Atlantic Ocean in those days.

SOUNDTRACK.

Richard ATTENBOROUGH (Lord Attenborough)

English actor and director (1923–)

6 If Gandhi were alive today he would approve of the SDP.

ATTRIBUTED remark in *The Guardian* (June 1983). The film *Gandhi* had opened in 1982 shortly after the launch of the Social Democratic Party in the UK.

See also ***EASY RIDER*** 149:1.

AUNTIE MAME

US 1958; screenwriters: Betty Comden, Adolph Green (from Patrick Dennis novel and Jerome Lawrence play); cast: Rosalind Russell (Auntie Mame Dennis), Peggy Cass (Agnes Gooch), Jan Handzlik (Patrick Dennis as child).

7 *Patrick (to Mame)*: Karl Marx – is he one of the Marx Brothers?

SOUNDTRACK.

1 *Auntie Mame*: Oh, Agnes! Here you've been taking my dictations for weeks and you haven't gotten the message of my book: live!
Agnes: Live?
Auntie Mame: Yes! Live! Life's a banquet and most poor suckers are starving to death!

SOUNDTRACK.

AUSTIN POWERS: INTERNATIONAL MAN OF MYSTERY

US 1997; screenwriter: Mike Myers; cast: Mike Myers (Austin Powers/Dr Evil).

2 *Dr Evil (holding his cat Bigglesworth)*: When Dr Evil gets angry, Mr Bigglesworth gets upset. And when Mr Bigglesworth gets upset … people die!

SOUNDTRACK.

3 *Austin Powers*: Oh, behave!

SOUNDTRACK. Stock phrase.

4 *Austin Powers*: Shall we shag now, or shall we shag later?

SOUNDTRACK. Also used as slogan for the film.

5 *Austin Powers*: Shagadelic!

SOUNDTRACK. Stock phrase.

6 *Austin Powers*: Yeah, baby, yeah!

SOUNDTRACK. Stock phrase.

AUSTIN POWERS: THE SPY WHO SHAGGED ME

US 1999; screenwriter: Mike Myers; cast: Mike Myers (Austin Powers/ Dr Evil); Heather Graham (Felicity Shagwell).

7 *Felicity (introducing herself)*: Shagwell by name, shag very well by reputation.

SOUNDTRACK.

Daniel AUTEUIL

French actor (1950–)

8 In France we tried to make films like *The Full Monty* but they were just boring. It was people on the dole eating soup.

QUOTED in *The Independent*, 'Quotes of the Week' (22 August 1998).

Gene AUTRY

American actor (1907–98)

1 Autry used to ride off into the sunset. Now he owns it.

COMMENT by Anon. A version has been attributed to Pat Buttram and quoted in J.R. Colombo, *Wit and Wisdom of the Moviemakers* (1979).

The AWFUL TRUTH

US 1937; screenwriter: Vina Delmar (from a play); cast: Cary Grant (Jerry Warriner), Irene Dunne (Lucy Warriner).

2 *Jerry*: In the spring a young man's fancy lightly turns to what he's been thinking about all winter.

SOUNDTRACK. *See also* ***MILDRED PIERCE*** 282:4.

Lauren BACALL

American actress (1924–)

1 The problem in my life has been that people have a concept that I'm a kind of female Bogart ... I'm not like that.

QUOTED in *The Independent* (25 January 1992).

2 Bette Davis was my heroine. She used cigarettes so dramatically.

QUOTED in *The Observer*, 'Sayings of the Week' (8 March 1992).

3 Stardom isn't a profession; it's an accident.

QUOTED in *The Observer*, 'Sayings of the Week' (19 March 1995).

Hilary BAILEY

English critic

4 [reviewing Malcolm Bradbury, *Cuts* (1987)] Writers love the theme of other writers, erotically, selling their virtue to the wicked film producer – it gives them a *frisson*.

COMMENT in *The Guardian* (27 April 1987).

BAISERS VOLÉS

(also known as *Stolen Kisses*) France 1968; screenwriters: François Truffaut (director), Claude de Givray; cast: Delphine Seyrig (Fabienne Tabard).

5 *Baisers Volés* [Stolen Kisses].

TITLE OF FILM. Taken from the song '*Que reste-t-il de nos amours?*' (1943) by Charles Trenet (used in the film).

6 *Fabienne*: I was once taught the difference between tact and politeness – if a man surprises a naked lady in the bathroom, politeness is to say 'Sorry', tact is to say 'Sorry, *sir*.'

SUB-TITLE translation.

Bela BALAZS

Hungarian writer (1884–1949)

1 Film art has a greater influence on the minds of the general public than any other art.

EXTRACTED from *Theory of the Film: Character and Growth of a New Art* (1953).

(Sir) Michael BALCON

English producer (1896–1977)

2 In the absence of money, we'll have to make do with talent.

QUOTED in David Puttnam, *Michael Balcon: The Pursuit of British Cinema*, Preface (1984).

3 Well, if you fellows feel so strongly in favour, on my head be it.

QUOTED in the same book.

4 We made films at Ealing that were good, bad and indifferent, but they were indisputably British. They were rooted in the soil of the country.

QUOTED in *Halliwell's Filmgoer's Companion*, 11th edn (1995).

BALL OF FIRE

US 1941: screenwriters: Charles Brackett, Billy Wilder; cast: Gary Cooper (Professor Bertram Potts), Barbara Stanwyck (Sugarpuss O'Shea), Kathleen Howard (Miss Bragg), Dana Andrews (Joe Lilac), Oscar Homolka (Professor Gurkakoff), Richard Haydn (Professor Oddly).

5 *Sugarpuss (to Potts, on agreeing to participate in his study of slang)*: Well, I got to thinking it over, and pooh, I said to myself, who am I to give science the brush?

SOUNDTRACK.

6 *Potts*: 'Slang,' as the poet Carl Sandburg has said, 'is language which takes off its coat, spits on its hands, and goes to work.' Let us, too, then get down to work.

SOUNDTRACK.

7 *Sugarpuss (defining 'corn' for Potts)*: Or when a guy comes to see a girl and says, 'Let's turn off the lights, it hurts my eyes' – brother, that's corn.

SOUNDTRACK.

8 *Miss Bragg (on Sugarpuss)*: That is the kind of woman that makes whole civilizations topple.

SOUNDTRACK.

9 *Sugarpuss (to Potts)*: Do you know what this means – 'I'll get you on the Ameche'? ... An 'Ameche' is the telephone, on account of he invented it ... in the movies.

SOUNDTRACK. A charming piece of dated slang for 'telephone'. The American actor Don Ameche (1909–93) played the title role in a 1939 biopic about the inventor of the telephone, *The Story of Alexander Graham Bell*. It very definitely did become an expression, though long since abandoned.

1 *Potts (to Sugarpuss)*: No mistake, I shall regret the absence of your keen mind. Unfortunately it is inseparable from an extremely disturbing body.

SOUNDTRACK.

2 *Potts (on himself, to Sugarpuss)*: People like that just ... Well, you see, dust piles up on their hearts, and it took you to blow it away.

SOUNDTRACK.

3 *Sugarpuss*: Who's 'Richard ill'?
Potts: Richard the Third.

SOUNDTRACK.

4 *Potts's colleague (on Sugarpuss marrying Potts)*: We feel that you are marrying all of us, a little.

SOUNDTRACK.

5 *Potts (disagreeing with Oddly's assertion that sex should not be part of the honeymoon)*: Why, the very idea that I should have to spend my honeymoon watching her paint in watercolours just because she's like somebody from the buttercup family – I – I'm a man in love.

SOUNDTRACK.

6 *Potts (to Sugarpuss)*: You've given us all a fine course in the theory and practice of being a sucker.

SOUNDTRACK.

7 *Sugarpuss (to Joe Lilac, about Potts)*: Yes, I love him. I like those hick shirts he wears with the boiled cuffs and the way he always has his vest buttoned wrong. Looks like a giraffe and I love him. I love him because he's the kind of guy that gets drunk on a glass of buttermilk, and I love the way he blushes right up over his ears. I love him because he doesn't know how to kiss – the jerk! I love him, Joe. That's what I'm trying to tell you.

SOUNDTRACK.

8 *Potts (on learning that Sugarpuss loves him)*: I feel like yodelling.

SOUNDTRACK.

1 *Oddly (trying to say 'stickup')*: I think it is known as an upstick.

SOUNDTRACK.

BAMBI

US 1942; screenwriters: Perce Pearce, Larry Morey; voices: Peter Behn (Thumper), Bobby Stewart (Bambi).

2 *Bambi*: What happened, Mother? Why did we all run?
Bambi's mother: Man was in the forest.

SOUNDTRACK.

3 *Bambi (when mother is killed by a hunter)*: Mother! Mother, where are you? Mother!

SOUNDTRACK.

The BAND WAGON

US 1953; screenwriters: Adolph Green, Betty Comden; lyrics/music: Howard Dietz, Arthur Schwarz; cast: Fred Astaire (Tony Hunter), Oscar Levant (Lester Marton), Jack Buchanan (Jeffrey Cordova), Cyd Charisse (Gaby Gerard), Nanette Fabray (Lily Marton).

4 *Train passenger (about Hunter, who is listening in on the conversation)*: Well, he was good twelve to fifteen years ago, but the columnists out there say he's through.

SOUNDTRACK.

5 *Lester (after having his foot stepped on in 42nd Street)*: I can stand anything but pain.

SOUNDTRACK.

6 *Cordova*: I tell you, if it moves you, if it stimulates you, if it entertains you – it's theatre. When the right combination gets together and it spells theatre – well, I got to be right in there up to my armpits.
Lester: That's higher than usual.

SOUNDTRACK.

7 *Cordova (on the Martons' idea for a musical comedy about a children's book illustrator)*: This story's a modern version of Faust.

SOUNDTRACK.

8 *Cordova*: Just like Faust, this man is tempted by the devil. And his compromise, his sell-out, must end in eternal damnation.
Lester: That'll leave them laughing.

SOUNDTRACK.

1 That's Entertainment.

SOUNDTRACK. Title of song – hence *That's Entertainment*, title of compilation movie (1974) of clips from MGM musicals.

2 The world is a stage,
The stage is a world of entertainment.

SOUNDTRACK. Song, 'That's Entertainment'.

3 It might be a fight like you see on the screen;
A swain getting slain for the love of a Queen,
Some great Shakespearean scene
Where a Ghost and a Prince meet
And everyone ends in mincemeat …

SOUNDTRACK. Song, 'That's Entertainment'.

4 *Lily Marton (about Lester)*: We're not quarrelling! We're in complete agreement! We hate each other!

SOUNDTRACK.

5 *Lester (when the Faust version of* The Band Wagon *flops)*: I can stand anything but failure.

SOUNDTRACK.

6 *Hunter (to Gerard, in parody)*: Say, who's the pretty girl? … Miss Gerard, you've been with the firm for years and I've never seen you with your glasses on. Say, you're beautiful!

SOUNDTRACK. *Compare* **CLICHÉS** 104:5.

7 *Hunter (as 'Rod Riley', on Gerard as 'The Girl', in ballet 'Girl Hunt')*: She came at me in sections. More curves than the scenic railway …
I wouldn't trust her any farther than I could throw her.

SOUNDTRACK. The narration for this ballet was written by an uncredited Alan Jay Lerner.

8 *Hunter (as 'Rod Riley', solving crime in ballet 'Girl Hunt')*: Suddenly, all the pieces fitted together. I knew how the crime had been done. The high note on the trumpet that shattered the glass … The glass with the nitroglycerine!

SOUNDTRACK.

9 *Hunter (as 'Rod Riley', at end of ballet 'Girl Hunt')*: She was bad. She was dangerous. I wouldn't trust her any farther than I could throw her. But she was my kind of woman.

SOUNDTRACK.

1 *Lily/Cordova/Lester*: Tony, Gaby, may we say something?

SOUNDTRACK. Last line of film, before breaking into a reprise of 'That's Entertainment'.

2 The best musical of the month, the year, the decade, or for all I know of all time.

COMMENT by Archer Winsten.

The BANK DICK

US 1940; screenwriter: Mahatma Kane Jeeves (W.C. Fields); cast: W.C. Fields (Egbert Sousè)(*sic*).

3 *Character*: Egbert, is it true that married people live longer?
Sousè: No, it just seems longer.

SOUNDTRACK.

4 *Sousè*: I never smoked a cigarette until I was nine.

SOUNDTRACK.

5 *Sousè*: Elusive spondulicks.

SOUNDTRACK. 'Spondulicks' or 'spondoolicks' or 'spondulacks' is an Americanism, current by the 1850s, for money, cash.

Tallulah BANKHEAD

American actress (1903–68)

6 [to Tennessee Williams at premiere of film based on his play *Orpheus Descending*, 1957] Darling, they've absolutely ruined your perfectly dreadful play!

QUOTED in Peter Hay, *Broadway Anecdotes* (1989).

7 They used to photograph Shirley Temple through gauze. They should photograph me through linoleum.

QUOTED in Leslie Halliwell, *The Filmgoer's Book of Quotes* (1973).

See also Howard **DIETZ** 136:1.

Theda BARA

American actress (1890–1955)

8 [Bara] made voluptuousness a common American commodity, as accessible as chewing gum.

COMMENT by Lloyd Morris, *Not So Long Ago* (1949).

9 She was divinely, hysterically, insanely, malevolent.

COMMENT attributed to Bette Davis.

BARBARELLA

France/Italy 1968; screenwriters: Roger Vadim (director), Terry Southern and others; cast: Jane Fonda (Barbarella), Milo O'Shea (Duran Duran).

1 *Barbarella (on learning that Duran Duran has devised a positronic ray)*: Weapon? Why would anyone want to invent a weapon?

SOUNDTRACK.

Brigitte BARDOT

French actress (1934–)

2 I really am a cat transformed into a woman.

QUOTED in Tony Crawley, *Bébé: The Films of Brigitte Bardot* (1975).

3 For twenty years I was cornered and hounded like an animal. I didn't throw myself off my balcony only because I knew people would photograph me lying dead.

ATTRIBUTED remark.

4 The cinema means nothing to me. I cannot remember it.

ATTRIBUTED remark in 1994.

5 Brigitte was inimitable and … her faults might sometimes be qualities. She needed a gardener more than a professor. She was the type of flower that one waters but does not cut.

COMMENT by Roger Vadim in *Bardot, Deneuve and Fonda: The Memoirs of Roger Vadim* (1986).

6 It was the first time on the screen that a woman was shown as really free on a sexual level, with none of the guilt attached to nudity or carnal pleasure.

COMMENT attributed to Roger Vadim.

7 Her boots reach up her thighs like twin chalices for her beauty.

COMMENT attributed to Roger Vadim.

The BAREFOOT CONTESSA

US 1954; screenwriter/director: Joseph L. Mankiewicz; cast: Humphrey Bogart (Harry Dawes), Edmond O'Brien (Oscar Muldoon), Warren Stevens (Kirk Edwards).

8 *Harry*: Life, every now and then, behaves as if it had seen too many bad movies, when everything fits too well – the beginning, the middle, the end – from fade-in to fade-out.

SOUNDTRACK.

1 *Oscar (to Kirk)*: Just this once, Kirk, why don't you empty your own ashtrays?

SOUNDTRACK.

BAREFOOT IN THE PARK

US 1967; screenwriter: Neil Simon (from his play); cast: Jane Fonda (Corie Bratter), Robert Redford (Paul Bratter), Herb Edelman (Harry Pepper), Mildred Natwick (Ethel Banks), Charles Boyer (Victor Velasco).

2 *Mrs Banks (to daughter Corie, after climbing many stairs to her apartment)*: I remember when you were a little girl. You said you wanted to live on the moon. I thought you were joking.

SOUNDTRACK.

3 *Corie*: You know what you are, Paul? You're a watcher. There are watchers in this world and there are doers. And the watchers sit around watching the doers do. Well, tonight, you watched and I did.

SOUNDTRACK.

4 *Corie*: You have absolutely no sense of the ridiculous. Like last Thursday night, you wouldn't walk barefoot with me in Washington Square Park. Why not?
Paul: Simple answer. It was seventeen degrees.
Corie: Exactly, it's very logical. It's very sensible, but it's no fun.

SOUNDTRACK.

5 *Ethel*: I feel like we've died and gone to heaven – only we had to climb up.

SOUNDTRACK.

6 *Ethel*: Oh, good, they made up.

SOUNDTRACK. Last line of film.

Iris BARRY

English writer and film librarian (1895–1969)

7 The film is a machine for seeing more than meets the eye.

ATTRIBUTED remark.

John BARRYMORE

American actor (1882–1942)

8 [Katharine Hepburn, sighing with relief after she had completed filming *A Bill of Divorcement* with Barrymore in 1932, said, 'Thank goodness I don't have to act with you any more.' Replied he:] I didn't know you ever had, darling.

QUOTED in Leslie Halliwell, *The Filmgoer's Book of Quotes* (1973).

1 I like to be introduced as America's foremost actor. It saves the necessity of further effort.

ATTRIBUTED remark.

2 He moved through a movie scene like an exquisite paper knife.

COMMENT by Heywood Broun, quoted in Leslie Halliwell, *The Filmgoer's Book of Quotes* (1973).

Roland BARTHES

French semiologist (1915–80)

3 The face of Garbo is an Idea, that of Hepburn an Event.

EXTRACTED from his book *Mythologies* (1957, translated 1972).

Kim BASINGER

American actress (1953–)

4 The more flesh you show, the higher up the ladder you go.

QUOTED in *The Independent* (13 March 1993).

5 [in speech accepting Oscar] I just want to thank everyone I met in my entire life.

QUOTED in *The Observer*, 'Sayings of the Week' (29 March 1998).

BATMAN

US 1989; screenwriters: Sam Hamm, Warren Skaaren; cast: Jack Nicholson (Joker/Jack Napier), Michael Keaton (Bruce Wayne/Batman).

6 *Joker (to Batman)*: Did you ever dance with the devil in the pale moonlight?

SOUNDTRACK. Refrain.

BATMAN RETURNS

US 1992; screenwriters: Daniel Waters, Sam Hamm; cast: Michelle Pfeiffer (Selina Kyle/Catwoman); Michael Keaton (Bruce Wayne/Batman).

7 *Catwoman (to cat, having just changed from Selina)*: I don't know about you, Miss Kitty, but I feel – so much yummier … I'm Catwoman. Hear me roar.

SOUNDTRACK.

1 *Catwoman (gaining the upper hand in fight with Batman)*: As I was saying, I'm a woman and can't be taken for granted. Life's a bitch. Now so am I.

SOUNDTRACK.

The BATTLESHIP POTEMKIN

Soviet Union 1925; screenwriter/director: Sergei Eisenstein.

2 Part I MEN AND MAGGOTS.

SCREEN TITLE in translation.

3 'Revolution is the only lawful, equal, effectual war. It was in Russia that this war was declared and begun.'

SCREEN TITLE in translation – citing Lenin.

4 We, the sailors of the *Potemkin*, must stand in the first lines of the revolution with our brothers, the workers.

SCREEN TITLE in translation. Seamen Matyushenko and Vakulinchuk talking on deck.

5 Comrades, the time has come to act. / What are we waiting for? All Russia is rising. Are we to be the last?

SCREEN TITLES in translation. Seaman Vakulinchuk calling comrades to mutiny.

6 We've had enough garbage to eat! / A dog wouldn't eat this.

SCREEN TITLES in translation – as sailors refuse to eat maggot-ridden food.

7 Part IV THE ODESSA STEPS.

SCREEN TITLE in translation.

8 Ring up the signal: Don't fight – join us!

SCREEN TITLE in translation. Seaman Matyushenko's call to other ships in the Black Sea fleet.

9 BROTHERS!

SCREEN TITLE in translation, as the mutinous seamen are victorious. Penultimate line of film.

10 The Odessa-steps sequence in *Potemkin* ... is the classic sequence of silent cinema and possibly the most influential six minutes in cinema history.

COMMENT by Roger Manvell in *Film* (1944)

See also A.J.P **TAYLOR** 407:3.

Vicki BAUM

Austrian novelist (1896–1960)

1 What I like about Hollywood is that one can get along by knowing two words of English – *swell* and *lousy*.

ATTRIBUTED remark of about 1933, quoted in *H.L. Mencken's Dictionary of Quotations* (1942).

André BAZIN

French critic (1918–58)

2 The cinema gives us a substitute world which fits our desires.

QUOTED in James Monaco, *The New Wave*, Chap. 7 (1976). Also used in the opening credits of Jean-Luc Godard's film *Le* ***MÉPRIS*** 281:3.

Emmanuelle BÉART

French actress (1965–)

3 There is no Hollywood now.

ATTRIBUTED remark.

4 I could never become a slave to the movie machine. I must be captain of my own ship. That to me is the only imperative.

ATTRIBUTED remark.

BEAT THE DEVIL

UK 1953; screenwriters: Truman Capote, John Huston (director) (from James Helvick novel); cast: Humphrey Bogart (Bill Dannreuther), Peter Lorre (O'Hara), Jennifer Jones (Gwendolen Chelm).

5 *Gwendolen*: Harry, we must beware of those men. They're desperate characters … Not one of them looked at my legs.

SOUNDTRACK.

6 *O'Hara*: Time! Time! What is time? The Swiss manufacture it. The French hoard it. Italians want it. Americans say it is money. Hindus say it does not exist. Do you know what I say? I say time is a crook …

SOUNDTRACK.

(Sir) Cecil BEATON

English photographer and designer (1904–80)

7 Hollywood is a suburb of Los Angeles, or vice versa, depending on your point of view.

EXTRACTED from his book *It Gives Me Great Pleasure* (1955).

Warren BEATTY

American actor and director (1937–)

1 [personal phrase] What's new, pussycat?

QUOTED in Sheilah Graham, *Scratch an Actor* (1969): 'He uses the telephone as a weapon of seduction. He curls up with it, cuddles it, whispers into it, "What's new, pussycat?" (He coined the phrase, and the picture was originally written for him.)' The film with the title (and the Tom Jones song) came out in 1965.

2 [of marriage] I'm not going to make the same mistake once.

QUOTED in Bob Chieger, *Was It Good For You Too?* (1983). In fact, this is a line from *North West Mounted Police* (US 1940), in which Texas Ranger Gary Cooper says to Madeleine Carroll, 'I've always held that a bachelor is a feller who never made the same mistake once.'

3 The difference between directing yourself and being directed is the difference between masturbating and making love.

QUOTED in *Independent on Sunday* (5 January 1992) from *Premiere.*

4 You're so vain, you probably think this song is about you.

COMMENT by Carly Simon, American singer and songwriter (1945–), in song, 'You're So Vain' (1972). It is usually assumed that the subject of the song is, in fact, Beatty.

5 He was insatiable. Three, four, five times a day was not unusual for him, and he was able to accept telephone calls at the same time.

COMMENT attributed to Joan Collins.

6 All presidents want to be Warren Beatty.

COMMENT by Alec Baldwin when Beatty indicated that he might run for the White House. Quoted in *The Mail on Sunday* (25 August 1999).

BEAU GESTE

US 1939; screenwriter: Robert Carson; cast: Brian Donleavy (Sergeant Markoff).

7 'The love of a man for a woman waxes and wanes like the moon, but the love of brother for brother is steadfast as the stars and endures like the word of the prophet' – Arabian proverb.

SCREEN TITLE.

8 *Sergeant Markoff*: Keep shooting, you scum! You'll get a chance yet to die with your boots on!

SOUNDTRACK.

BEAUTY AND THE BEAST

US 1991; screenwriter: Linda Woolverton; voice: David Ogden Stiers (Cogsworth).

1 *Cogsworth (making tour of castle)*: This is yet another example of the late neo-classical baroque period and, as I always say, if it's not baroque, don't fix it!

SOUNDTRACK.

(Sir) Thomas BEECHAM

English orchestral conductor (1879–1961)

2 Movie music is noise. It's even more painful than my sciatica.

QUOTED in *Time* Magazine (24 February 1958).

BEING THERE

US 1980; screenwriter: Jerzy Kosinski (from his novel); cast: Peter Sellers (Chance/Chauncey Gardener).

3 Getting there is half the fun. Being there is all of it.

SLOGAN.

4 *Chance (sagely)*: In a garden, growth has its season. First comes spring and summer but then we have fall and winter. And then we get spring and summer again.

SOUNDTRACK.

5 *Chance (to TV reporter who asks what newspapers he reads)*: I like to watch TV.

SOUNDTRACK.

BELLE OF THE NINETIES

US 1934; screenwriter: Mae West; cast: Mae West (Ruby Carter).

6 *Ruby*: It's better to be looked over than overlooked.

SOUNDTRACK.

7 *Ruby*: A man in the house is worth two in the street.

SOUNDTRACK.

Jean-Paul BELMONDO

French actor (1933–)

8 Hell, everybody knows that an ugly guy with a good line gets the chicks.

ATTRIBUTED remark.

1 Wrong or right, I suppose he represents France.

COMMENT by Daniel Boulander.

BEN HUR

US 1959; screenwriter: Karl Tunberg (based on Lew Wallace novel); cast: Charlton Heston (Judah Ben-Hur).

2 *Ben-Hur (on The Christ)*: And I felt His voice take the sword out of my hand.

SOUNDTRACK. Last line of film.

Robert BENCHLEY

American humorist, critic and performer (1889–1945)

3 [suggested epitaph for an unnamed movie queen] She sleeps alone at last.

ATTRIBUTED remark in *The Book of Hollywood Quotes* (about 1980).

Stephen Vincent BENÉT

American poet and novelist (1898–1943)

4 Of all the Christbitten places and businesses on the two hemispheres, this one [Hollywood] is the last curly kink on the pig's tail ... Jesus, the movies! ... Nowhere have I seen such shining waste, stupidity and conceit as in the business end of this industry.

EXTRACTED from *Selected Letters of Stephen Vincent Benét*, ed. Charles A. Fenton (1960).

Roberto BENIGNI

Italian actor and director (1952–)

5 [accepting BAFTA Best Actor award] This is my first prize in England. I am full of joy like a watermelon. I will explode. I cannot restrain this joy.

SPEECH in London (11 April 1999). Shortly before this, Benigni had won two Oscars for his film *Life Is Beautiful* and leapt over the seats to pick them up.

Alan BENNETT

English playwright and screenwriter (1934–)

6 There is no such thing as a good script, only a good film, and I'm conscious that my scripts often read better than they play.

EXTRACTED from introduction to published screenplay of *A Private Function* (1984).

1 Film is drama at its most impatient, 'What happens next?' the perpetual nag. One can never hang about, thinks the writer, petulantly.

QUOTED in *The Independent* (12 February 1995).

Nicolas BENTLEY

English cartoonist and writer (1907–78)

2 Cecil B. DeMille,
Rather against his will,
Was persuaded to leave Moses
Out of 'The Wars of the Roses'.

ATTTRIBUTED. Appeared anonymously in *Clerihews*, ed. J.W. Carter (1938).

Ingmar BERGMAN

Swedish screenwriter and director (1918–)

3 Film as dream, film as music. No art passes our conscience in the way film does, and goes directly to our feelings, deep down into the dark rooms of our souls.

QUOTED by John Berger in *Sight and Sound* (June 1991).

4 The theatre is like a faithful wife. The film is the great adventure – the costly, exacting mistress.

ATTRIBUTED remark.

Ingrid BERGMAN

Swedish-born actress (1915–82)

5 [Hitchcock's method of dealing with Bergman's objections during the filming of *Under Capricorn*] Since I can't stand arguments, I would say to her, 'Ingrid, it's only a movie!' You see, she only wanted to appear in masterpieces.

COMMENT by Alfred Hitchcock, quoted in François Truffaut, *Hitchcock* (English version, 1968). Hence *It's Only a Movie, Ingrid* – the title of a book (1988) by Alexander Walker, 'encounters on and off screen'. *Compare* Carrie **FISHER** 162:7, Alfred **HITCHCOCK** 217:6.

Busby BERKELEY

American director (1895–1976)

6 In an era of breadlines, depressions and wars, I tried to help people get away from all the misery ... to turn their minds to something else. I wanted to make people happy, if only for an hour.

ATTRIBUTED remark.

Sarah BERNHARDT

French actress (1844–1923)

1 [of her three-reel *La Dame aux Camélias* (1911)] I rely upon these films to make me immortal.

QUOTED by C.A. Lejeune in article 'Looking Back' (January 1943).

John BERRYMAN

American poet (1914–72)

2 I seldom go to films. They are too exciting, said the Honourable Possum.

EXTRACTED from his 77 *Dream Songs*, no. 53 (1964).

Bernardo BERTOLUCCI

Italian director and screenwriter (1940–)

3 If New York is the Big Apple, tonight Hollywood is the Big Nipple.

SPEECH at the Academy Awards ceremony, Los Angeles, quoted in *The Guardian* (13 April 1988). His film *The Last Emperor* had won nine awards. In an attempt at clarification, he went on: 'It is a big suck for me.'

The BEST MAN

US 1964; screenwriter: Gore Vidal (from his play); cast: Henry Fonda (William Russell), Cliff Robertson (Joe Cantwell), Lee Tracy (Art Hockstader), Edie Adams (Mabel Cantwell), Ann Sothern (Mrs Gamadge), John Henry Faulk (T.T. Claypoole).

4 *Russell (of Joe Cantwell)*: Tomorrow we'll buy a used car from that man.

SOUNDTRACK.

5 *Hockstader (to Joe Cantwell)*: I don't object to your headline-grabbing and your crying wolf all the time – that's standard stuff in politics. What disturbs me is your taking your own phoney stuff so seriously. It's par for the course, trying to fool the people, but it's downright dangerous when you start fooling yourself.

SOUNDTRACK.

6 *Hockstader*: There is nothing like a dirty low-down political fight to put the roses in your cheeks.

SOUNDTRACK.

1 *Mrs Gamadge*: The women are solidly behind Bill Russell.
Mabel Cantwell: Under him is their more usual position.

SOUNDTRACK.

2 *Hockstader*: I personally do not care if Joe Cantwell enjoys carnal knowledge of a McCormick reaper.

SOUNDTRACK.

3 *T.T. Claypoole (to Joe Cantwell)*: Nice thing about you, Joe, is that you can sound like a liberal, but at heart you're an American.

SOUNDTRACK.

4 *Russell*: T.T. Claypoole has all the characteristics of a dog except loyalty.

SOUNDTRACK.

5 *Russell*: Men without faces tend to get elected President, and power or responsibility or personal honour fill in the features. Usually, pretty well.

SOUNDTRACK.

BEYOND THE FOREST

US 1949; screenwriter: Lenore Coffee; cast: Bette Davis (Rosa Moline), Joseph Cotten (Dr Louis Moline).

6 *Rosa (to Louis)*: What a dump! … If I don't get out of here, I'll just die! Living here is like waiting for the funeral to begin.

SOUNDTRACK. The opening moments of the play and film of Edward Albee's ***WHO'S AFRAID OF VIRGINIA WOOLF?*** are devoted to a discussion as to which film Bette Davis said this in. 'What a dump!' had earlier been spoken by Dana Andrews of a seedy San Francisco hotel in *Fallen Angel* (US 1945).

The BIG CHILL

US 1983; screenwriter: Lawrence Kasdan, Barbara Benedek; cast: Jeff Goldblum (Michael), William Hurt (Nick).

7 The Big Chill.

TITLE OF FILM. Hence, 'the Big Chill generation', a term alluding to those who grew up in the 1960s. The film is 'the story of eight old friends searching for something they lost, and finding that all they needed was each other'. Accordingly, the *Washington Post* for 1 August 1985 talked of: 'A performance by the Temptations or the Four Tops is always a big thrill for the "Big Chill" generation.' A report of Douglas Ginsburg's rejected nomination as a member of the US Supreme Court in *Time* Magazine (16 November 1987) contained the following: 'Although Ginsburg's indiscretion may have been common among members of the Big Chill generation, his confessions fatally undermined his support among the Capitol Hill conservatives who had lobbied so hard for his nomination.'

1 *Michael (to Nick, at funeral lunch for their friend Alex)*: Amazing tradition. They throw a great party for you on the day they know you can't come.

SOUNDTRACK.

The BIG HEAT

US 1953; screenwriter: Sydney Boehm; cast: Gloria Grahame (Debby Marsh).

2 *Debby*: I've been rich and I've been poor; believe me rich is better.

SOUNDTRACK. Later, this saying came to be associated with Sophie Tucker, the Russian-born American entertainer (1884–1966).

The BIG SLEEP

US 1946; screenwriters: William Faulkner and others (from Raymond Chandler novel); cast: Humphrey Bogart (Philip Marlowe), Charles Waldron (General Sternwood), Lauren Bacall (Vivian Sherwood Rutledge), Martha Vickers (Carmen Sternwood), Bob Steele (Canino), Elisha Cook Jr (Jones), John Ridgley (Eddie Mars), Charles D. Brown (Norris), Louis Jean Heydt (Joe Brody).

3 *Carmen (to Marlowe)*: You're not very tall, are you?

SOUNDTRACK.

4 *Sternwood*: You may smoke, too. I can still enjoy the smell of it. Nice state of affairs when a man has to indulge his vices by proxy.

SOUNDTRACK.

5 *Sternwood*: You like orchids?
Marlowe: Not particularly.
Sternwood: Nasty things! Their flesh is too much like the flesh of men. Their perfume has the rotten sweetness of corruption.

SOUNDTRACK.

6 *Marlowe (to Sternwood, on Carmen)*: Then she tried to sit on my lap while I was standing up.

SOUNDTRACK.

7 *Sternwood (on his daughters Vivian and Carmen)*: They're alike only in having the same corrupt blood. Vivian is spoiled, exacting, smart and ruthless. Carmen is still a little child who likes to pull the wings off flies. I assume they have all the usual vices besides those they've invented for themselves.

SOUNDTRACK.

8 *Sternwood*: If I seem a bit sinister as a parent, Mr Marlowe, it's because my hold on life is too slight to include any Victorian hypocrisy.

I need hardly add that any man who has lived as I have and indulges for the first time in parenthood at my age deserves all he gets.

SOUNDTRACK.

1 *Norris*: Are you attempting to tell me my duties, sir?
Marlowe: No, just having fun trying to guess what they are.

SOUNDTRACK.

2 *Vivian*: So you're a private detective. I didn't know they existed, except in books. Or else they were greasy little men snooping around hotel corridors. My, you're a mess, aren't you?

SOUNDTRACK.

3 *Marlowe*: I don't mind if you don't like my manners. I don't like them myself. They're pretty bad. I grieve over them long winter evenings.

SOUNDTRACK.

4 *Vivian (to Marlowe)*: So you do get up. I was beginning to think you worked in bed, like Marcel Proust.
Marlowe: Who's he?

SOUNDTRACK.

5 *Marlowe (to Joe Brody)*: My, my, my, such a lot of guns around town and so few brains.

SOUNDTRACK.

6 *Marlowe (comparing Vivian to a horse)*: You've got a touch of class, but, uh … I don't know how – how far you can go.
Vivian: A lot depends on who's in the saddle. Go ahead Marlowe. I like the way you work. In case you don't know it, you're doing all right.

SOUNDTRACK.

7 *Vivian (when Marlowe kisses her)*: I liked that. I'd like more.

SOUNDTRACK.

8 *Canino (as hired killer, threatening Jones)*: You want me to count three or something, like a movie?

SOUNDTRACK. Later repeated by Marlowe to Mars.

9 *Marlowe (explaining why he stayed on the case)*: Too many people told me to stop.

SOUNDTRACK.

10 *Marlowe*: What's wrong with you?
Vivian: Nothing you can't fix.

SOUNDTRACK. Last lines of film.

The BIG STORE

US 1941; screenwriters: Sid Kuller, Hal Fimberg, Ray Golden; cast: Groucho Marx (Wolf J. Flywheel), Chico Marx (Ravelli), Harpo Marx (Wacky), Margaret Dumont (Martha Phelps), Tony Martin (Tommy Rogers), Douglas Dumbrille (Mr Grover).

1 *Ravelli (bodyguard to Tommy)*: From now on, you and me is going to be insufferable.

SOUNDTRACK.

2 *Grover*: How do you do?
Flywheel: That's rather a personal question, isn't it, old man? How I do and what I do is my concern.

SOUNDTRACK.

3 *Flywheel (store detective to Martha, store owner)*: If you marry me, you're concern will be my concern.

SOUNDTRACK.

4 *Flywheel*: Martha, dear, there are many bonds that will hold us together through eternity.
Martha: Really, Wolf? What are they?
Flywheel: Your government bonds, your savings bonds, your liberty bonds …

SOUNDTRACK.

5 *Martha (on marriage proposal)*: I'm afraid after we're married awhile, a beautiful young girl will come along and you'll forget all about me.
Flywheel: Don't be silly. I'll write you twice a week.

SOUNDTRACK.

6 Tenement Symphony.

TITLE of song. Music and lyrics by Hal Borne, Sid Kuller and Ray Golden. Sung by Tommy Rogers. One of the most excruciating of all musical interludes in Marx Brothers films.

Juliette BINOCHE

French actress (1964–)

7 When international cinema is discussed in cockney rhyming slang, an overheated melodrama is referred to as a 'Juliette' (Juliette Binoche equals tosh). This likeable actress has appeared in a number of worthwhile films, but also in utter stinkers such as *Damage* and now *The Horseman on the Roof*.

COMMENT by Adam Mars-Jones, English novelist and critic (1954–), in review in *The Independent* (4 January 1996).

Antonia BIRD

English director (1959–)

1 If you're a woman living in Los Angeles and you don't weigh eight stone and have long, brown legs and blonde hair, you're f––d basically.

QUOTED in *The Observer*, 'Soundbites' (14 September 1997).

The BLACK SHIELD OF FALWORTH

US 1954; screenwriter: Oscar Brodney; cast: Tony Curtis (Myles Falworth).

2 *Myles*: Yonda is the castle of my fodda [Yonder is the castle of my father].

APOCRYPHAL LINE – 'or something like it', according to Leslie Halliwell, *The Filmgoer's Book of Quotes* (1978 edn). The imputation was that Curtis's Brooklyn accent survived intact in Medieval England. *See* ***SON OF ALI BABA***.

BLADE RUNNER

US 1982 (Director's Cut, 1991): screenwriters: Hampton Fancher, David Peoples (from Philip K. Dick novel *Do Androids Dream of Electric Sheep*); cast: Brion James (Leon), Harrison Ford (Deckard), Rutger Hauer (Roy Batty), Joe Turkel (Dr Eldon Tyrell), Joanna Cassidy (Zhora).

3 *Batty (to old Oriental who designs eyes)*: 'Fiery the angels fell; dark thunder rolled around their shoes, burning with the fires of orc . . . '

SOUNDTRACK. This is an actual quotation – from William Blake's *America* (1793): 'Fiery the Angels rose, & as they rose deep thunder roll'd / Around their shores: indignant burning with the fires of Orc.'

4 *Batty*: I've seen things you people wouldn't believe. Attack ships on fire off the shoulder of Orion. I watched C-beams glitter in the dark near the Tannhauser Gate. All those moments will be lost in time. Like tears in rain. Time to die.

SOUNDTRACK.

5 Rutger Hauer's final speech in the rain in *Blade Runner* always seemed like a quote from *Paradise Lost* to me.

COMMENT by Neil Jordan in *The Observer* Magazine (6 February 2000).

BLAZING SADDLES

US 1974; screenwriters: Mel Brooks and others; cast: Mel Brooks (Governor William J. Le Petomane), Madeleine Kahn (Lili von Shtüpp), Cleavon Little (Bart), Harvey Korman (Hedley Lamarr), Gene Wilder (The Waco Kid).

6 *Le Petomane (turning to his bikini-clad secretary and finding he is* *faced with her cleavage)*: Hello boys. Have a good night's rest? I missed you.

SOUNDTRACK. (On the concluding credits the name is spelt Lepetomane).

1 *Lamarr (correcting pronunciation of his name)*: It's not Hedy, it's Hedley. Hedley Lamarr.
Le Petomane: What the hell are you worried about? This is 1874. You'll be able to sue her.

SOUNDTRACK.

2 *Bart (about to take out his speech)*: Excuse me while I whip this out.

SOUNDTRACK.

3 *Bart (threatening to shoot himself)*: Hold it. The next man makes a move, the nigger gets it.

SOUNDTRACK.

4 *The Waco Kid (to Bart)*: You've got to remember that these are just simple farmers. These are people of the land. The common clay of the New West. You know – morons.

SOUNDTRACK.

5 *Lili*: Hello, handsome, is that a ten-gallon hat – or are you just enjoying the show?

SOUNDTRACK.

6 *Mexican bandit (to Lamarr)*: Badges? We don't need no stinking badges!

SOUNDTRACK. *Compare The* ***TREASURE OF THE SIERRA MADRE*** 430:1.

7 *Lamarr*: 'Head 'em off at the pass'? I hate that cliché.

SOUNDTRACK. *Compare* **CLICHÉS** 108:1.

8 *Bart (before attempting to blow up township)*: Hold your ears, folks. It's showtime!

SOUNDTRACK. *Compare* ***ALL THAT JAZZ*** 21:7.

BLITHE SPIRIT

UK 1945; screenwriter: Noël Coward (from his play); cast: Rex Harrison (Charles Condomine).

9 *Charles*: If you wish to make an inventory of my sex life, dear, I think it only fair to tell you that you've missed out several episodes. I'll consult my diary and give you a complete list after lunch.

SOUNDTRACK.

The BLOB

US 1958; screenwriters: Theodore Simonson and others; cast: Steven McQueen (Steve Andrews), Earl Rowe (Lieut. Dave).

1 It crawls! It creeps! It eats you alive! Run – don't walk from *The Blob.*

SLOGAN.

2 *Dave (on his superior officer's dislike for Steve)*: Just because some kid smashes into his wife on the turnpike doesn't make it a crime to be 17.

SOUNDTRACK. McQueen was 28 and playing a 17 year old.

BLONDE CRAZY

US 1931; screenwriters: Kubec Glasmon, John Bright; cast: James Cagney (Bert Harris).

3 *Bert*: You dirty, double-crossing rat.

SOUNDTRACK. Although Cagney impersonators always have him saying 'You dirty rat!' it may be that he never said it like that himself. However, in Joan Wyndham's wartime diaries (*Love Lessons*, 1985) her entry for 1 October 1940 begins: 'Double bill at the Forum with Rupert. *Elizabeth and Essex*, and a gangster film where somebody actually *did* say "Stool on me would ya, ya doity rat!"' What film could this have been? Note her surprise that the line was uttered at all.

The nearest Cagney seems to have got to uttering the phrase with which he is most associated was in *Blonde Crazy* (as here) and ***TAXI!*** 407:1. In the Cagney film *Each Dawn I Die* (US 1939), Ed Pawley as Dale gets to say, 'Listen, you dirty rats in there!'

During a speech to an American Film Institute banquet on 13 March 1974, Cagney said to Frank Gorshin, a well-known impersonator: 'Oh, Frankie, just in passing: I never said [in any film] "Mmm, you dirty rat!" What I actually did say was "Judy! Judy! Judy!"' *See also* Cary **GRANT** 200:4.

The BLUE ANGEL

Germany 1930; screenwriters: Robert Liebmann, Karl Zuckmayer, Karl Volmoeller (from Heinrich Mann novel *Professor Unrath*); cast: Marlene Dietrich (Lola Frohlich); Emil Jannings (Professor Immanuel Rath).

4 *Lola (to Rath)*: They call me Lola.

SOUNDTRACK.

BLUE STEEL

US 1990; screenwriters: Kathryn Bigelow, Eric Red; cast: Ron Silver (Eugene Hunt).

5 *Eugene*: Death is the greatest kick of all. That's why they save it for last.

SOUNDTRACK. As psychopathic Wall Street commodities trader.

The BLUES BROTHERS

US 1980; screenwriters: John Landis, Dan Aykroyd; cast: Dan Aykroyd (Elwood Blues), John Belushi (Jake Blues).

1 *Elwood (to Jake)*: They're not gonna catch us. We're on a mission from God.

SOUNDTRACK. The last phrase is spoken frequently as the eponymous brothers attempt to justify their various activities with the suggestion that they are working on behalf of a Mother Superior who has been robbed.

2 *Woman at boarding house*: Are you the police?
Elwood: No, ma'am. We're musicians.

SOUNDTRACK.

BODY HEAT

US 1981; screenwriter/director: Lawrence Kasdan; cast: Kathleen Turner (Matty Walker), William Hurt (Ned Racine).

3 *Matty (to Ned)*: You're not too smart, are you? I like that in a man.

SOUNDTRACK.

(Sir) Dirk BOGARDE

English actor (1921–99)

4 There's something wrong with actors, we've always been a suspect breed. Socially, I find myself more admissible now in England because I've written books.

QUOTED in *Ritz* (April 1983).

5 [to TV interviewer Russell Harty] I'm still in the shell, and you're not going to crack it, ducky.

ATTRIBUTED remark in 1986.

6 [on corseted starlets of the 1950s] To hold one in one's arms was like holding a pillar-box.

QUOTED in *The Observer*, 'Sayings of the Week' (14 August 1994).

7 [to Bogarde at Rank Organization audition] Nice of you to come, but your head's too small for the camera, you are too thin, and ... I don't know what it is exactly about the neck ... but it's not right.

COMMENT by Earl St John, English executive, quoted in Dirk Bogarde, *Snakes and Ladders* (1978).

Humphrey BOGART

American actor (1899–1957)

1 You're not a star until they can spell your name in Karachi.

ATTRIBUTED remark in David Brown, *Star Billing* (1985). However, as 'You're famous when they can spell your name in Karachi' this is merely described as an American showbiz observation in Steve Aronson, *Hype* (1983).

2 He had the damnedest façade of any man I ever met in my life. He was playing Bogart all the time, but he was really just a big, sloppy bowl of mush.

COMMENT by Stanley Kramer, quoted in Leslie Halliwell, *The Filmgoer's Book of Quotes* (1973).

3 Like Edward G. Robinson, all Bogart has to do to dominate a scene is to enter it.

COMMENT by Raymond Chandler, quoted in J.R. Colombo, *Wit and Wisdom of the Moviemakers* (1979).

4 He decided to exploit his mouth.

COMMENT by Louise Brooks, quoted by Kenneth Tynan in *The New Yorker* (11 June 1979).

5 Bogart's a helluva a nice guy till 11.30 p.m. After that he thinks he's Bogart.

COMMENT by Dave Chasen, American restaurateur (1899–1973), quoted in Leslie Halliwell, *The Filmgoer's Book of Quotes* (1973).

Helena BONHAM CARTER

English actress (1966–)

6 If you're pretty and you're working class you have an easier time.

QUOTED in *Independent on Sunday*, 'Quotes of the Week' (6 October 1996).

7 People imagine I'm so cultured. The truth is I drink a lot of Diet Coke and belch, tell dirty jokes and arm wrestle. A double-barrelled name merely makes it hell signing autographs.

QUOTED in *The Observer* (5 September 1999).

8 I never was the demure woman people imagined. I guess I am petite, but what can I do about that? Go on a rack?

QUOTED in *The Independent* (25 September 1999).

9 As a life-long member of the non-pretty working classes, I would like to say to Helena Bonham Carter: shut up you stupid c---.

COMMENT by actress Kathy Burke in letter to *Time Out* replying to 66:6 above, quoted in *The Observer*, 'Soundbites' (20 October 1996).

See also Woody **ALLEN** 25:3.

BONNIE AND CLYDE

US 1967; screenwriters: David Newman, Robert Benton; cast: Warren Beatty (Clyde Barrow), Faye Dunaway (Bonnie Parker).

1 They're young ... they're in love ... and they kill people!

SLOGAN.

2 *Clyde*: I'm Clyde Barrow and this is Miss Bonnie Parker. We rob banks!

SOUNDTRACK.

John BOORMAN

English director (1933–)

3 It [film-making] is the business of turning money into light and then back into money again.

QUOTED by Tom Stoppard in *The Sunday Times* (20 January 1980). *Money into Light: The Emerald Forest, a Diary* was used as the title of a book by Boorman in 1985.

4 [of his film ***HOPE AND GLORY*** at the Montreal festival] All movie-making is seeing with a child's eye.

QUOTED in *The Guardian* (3 September 1987).

Ernest BORGNINE

American actor (1915–)

5 Acting is a matter of calculated instinct.

QUOTED in J.R. Colombo, *Wit and Wisdom of the Moviemakers* (1979).

BORN YESTERDAY

US 1950; screenwriter: Garson Kanin (from his own play); cast: Judy Holliday (Billie Dawn), Broderick Crawford (Harry Brock).

6 *Harry (to hotel official)*: Look, when I say I want a whole floor, I don't want one wing and I don't want two wings. I want the whole bird.

SOUNDTRACK.

7 *Billie (to Harry)*: You're just not couth!

SOUNDTRACK.

1 *Billie*: Will ya do me a favour, Harry? Drop dead.

SOUNDTRACK.

Clara BOW

American actress (1905–65)

2 [written on photograph that she gave to her fiancé, Harry Richman] To my gorgeous lover, Harry. I'll trade all my It for your that.

QUOTED in Bob Chieger, *Was It Good For You Too?* (1983). Bow became known as the 'It Girl' – to describe her vivacious sex appeal – after appearing in the film *It* (1928).

3 Being a sex symbol is a heavy load to carry, especially when one is tired, hurt and bewildered.

QUOTED in Clyde Jeavons & Jeremy Pascal, *A Pictorial History of Sex in the Movies* (1975).

BRAM STOKER'S DRACULA

US 1992; screenwriter: James V. Hart (from Bram Stoker novel); cast: Gary Oldman (Dracula), Winona Ryder (Mina Murray), Keanu Reeves (Jonathan Harker).

4 *Dracula (serving Jonathan)*: You will, I trust, excuse me if I do not join you. But I have already dined and I never drink – wine.

SOUNDTRACK. Compare ***DRACULA*** 143:4.

5 *Dracula (to Mina)*: I am the monster that greedy men would kill. I am Dracula.

SOUNDTRACK.

Marlon BRANDO

American actor (1924–)

6 An actor's a guy who, if you ain't talking about him, ain't listening.

QUOTED in *The Observer* (January 1956). In fact, Brando appears to have been quoting George Glass (1910–84) (source: Bob Thomas, *Brando*, Chap. 8, 1973.)

7 [on playing in Westerns] Sometimes you just get the feeling that here it is 11 o'clock in the morning and you're not in school.

QUOTED in *New York Post* (11 May 1959).

8 In my own behaviour with people, if I didn't trust or like someone, I would either say nothing or mumble. I got to be awfully good at mumbling.

QUOTED in J.R. Colombo, *Wit and Wisdom of the Moviemakers* (1979).

1 [Of *A Dry White Season*, US 1989] After this I'm retiring. I just wish I hadn't finished with a stinker.

QUOTED in *The Observer*, 'Sayings of the Week' (3 September 1989). It was not his last film.

2 I don't mind that I'm fat. You still get the same money.

QUOTED in *The Observer*, 'Sayings of the Week' (15 October 1989).

3 [on being told by TV interviewer Connie Chung that he might have been wasting his talent in *A Dry White Season*] That is like putting fried eggs in your armpit.

QUOTED in *The Guardian* (5 February 1990).

4 [when his son Christian faced murder charges] The messenger of misery has come to my house.

QUOTED in *The Independent* (24 May 1990).

5 I have the eyes of a dead pig.

QUOTED in *Screen International* (18 January 1991).

6 Democracy is a fine way to run a country, but it's a hell of a way to make pictures.

COMMENT by Lillian Hellman on working with Brando on *The Chase.*

7 He [Brando] is our greatest actor, our noblest actor, and he is also our national lout.

COMMENT by Norman Mailer, quoted in *The Observer* (1 January 1989).

8 Most of the time he sounds like he has a mouth full of wet toilet paper.

COMMENT by Rex Reed. It was said that Brando, in fact, put orange peel in his mouth to play Don Corleone in *The Godfather.*

BRAZIL

UK 1985; screenwriters: Terry Gilliam (director), Tom Stoppard, Charles McKeown; cast: Robert De Niro (Richard Tuttle), Jonathan Pryce (Sam Lowry), Kim Greist (Jill Layton), Barbara Hicks (Mrs Terrain), Michael Palin (Spoor).

9 *Spoor (on killing the wrong man)*: The wrong man was delivered to me as the right man. I accepted him in good faith as the right man. Was I wrong?

SOUNDTRACK.

10 *Jill Layton (appearing in a dream to Lowry after she has been killed)*: Care for a little necrophilia?

SOUNDTRACK.

1 *Mrs Terrain*: Can you do something about these terrorists?
Lowry: It's my lunch hour. Besides, it's not my department.
SOUNDTRACK.

BREAKFAST AT TIFFANY'S

US 1961; screenwriter: George Axelrod (from Truman Capote novella); cast: Audrey Hepburn (Holly Golightly), George Peppard (Paul Varjak), Martin Balsam (O.J. Berman), Mickey Rooney (Mr Yunioshi), Dorothy Whitney (Mag Wildwood), Buddy Ebsen (Doc Golightly), John McGiver (Tiffany clerk), José da Silva Perriera (Villalonga).

2 *Mr Yunioshi (to Holly, his frequent complaint about being awakened)*: Miss Go-Lightly, I protest!
SOUNDTRACK.

3 *Holly*: *Quel* rat!
SOUNDTRACK.

4 *Holly (to Paul)*: You know those days when you get the mean reds? … No, the blues are because you're getting fat or maybe it's raining too long, that's all. The mean reds are horrible. Suddenly you're afraid and you don't know what you're afraid of … Well, when I get it, the only thing that does any good is to jump into a cab and go to Tiffany's.
SOUNDTRACK.

5 *Holly (to Paul)*: I mean, a girl just can't go to Sing-Sing with a green face.
SOUNDTRACK.

6 *Holly (to Paul)*: I mean, any gentleman with the slightest chic will give a girl a fifty-dollar bill for the powder room.
SOUNDTRACK.

7 *O.J. Berman (to Paul, about Holly)*: You're wrong, ha. But on the other hand you're right. Because she's a real phoney. You know why? Because she honestly believes all this phoney junk that she believes in.
SOUNDTRACK.

8 *Holly (to Doc Golightly)*: It's a mistake you always made, Doc, trying to love a wild thing … You mustn't give your heart to a wild thing.
SOUNDTRACK.

9 *Holly (to Paul)*: Of course, personally, I think it's a bit tacky to wear diamonds before I'm forty.
SOUNDTRACK.

1 *Tiffany clerk (to Holly, on merchandise under ten dollars)*: Well, frankly, madam, within that price range, the variety of merchandise is rather limited.

SOUNDTRACK.

2 *Holly (to Paul)*: There are certain shades of limelight that can wreck a girl's complexion.

SOUNDTRACK.

3 *Paul*: I love you. You belong to me.
Holly: No, people don't belong to people.
Paul: Of course they do.

SOUNDTRACK.

4 *Holly (on finding her cat)*: Cat, cat!

SOUNDTRACK. Last line of film.

5 Well, I can tell you one thing, Blake: the song has got to go.

COMMENT by Marty Rackin, head of production at Paramount, to director Blake Edwards, on the song *Moon River* by Henry Mancini and Johnny Mercer. It won the Oscar for Best Song.

BREATHLESS [À BOUT DE SOUFFLE]

France 1960; screenwriters: Jean-Luc Godard (director), François Truffaut; cast: Jean-Paul Belmondo (Michel Poiccard/Laszlo Kovacs), Jean Seberg (Patricia Franchini).

6 *Michel (to Patricia)*: Killers kill, squealers squeal.

SUB-TITLE translation.

7 *Michel*: *La vie – c'est dégueulasse* [life's a bitch].

SOUNDTRACK. Dying words.

Claude BRESSON

French director

8 Cinema is the art of showing nothing.

EXTRACTED from *Encountering Directors,* ed. Samuels (1973).

Robert BRESSON

French director (1907–99)

9 A film is not a spectacle, it is pre-eminently a style.

ATTRIBUTED remark.

André BRETON

French poet, essayist and critic (1896–1966)

1 It is at the movies that the only absolutely modern mystery is celebrated.

QUOTED in J.H. Mathews, *Surrealism and Film* (1971).

Marshall BRICKMAN

American screenwriter (1941–)

2 The director of a film is treated by his staff the way a group of passengers would treat a psychotic ship's captain during a typhoon: namely, with respect and apprehension.

INTERVIEWED in *The Guardian* (13 September 1980).

The BRIDE OF FRANKENSTEIN

US 1935; screenwriters: William Hurlbut, John L. Balderston (from Mary Shelley novel); cast: Colin Clive (Henry Frankenstein), Ernest Thesiger (Dr Pretorius), Boris Karloff (The Monster).

3 *Henry*: I've been cursed for delving into the mysteries of life!

SOUNDTRACK.

4 *Pretorius*: Do you like gin? It's my only weakness.

SOUNDTRACK. *Compare The* ***OLD DARK HOUSE*** 314:1.

5 *Pretorius*: To a new world of gods and monsters!

SOUNDTRACK. Proposing a toast to fellow monster-maker, Henry Frankenstein. Hence, *Gods and Monsters*, title of a film (US 1998) about James Whale, director of *Bride*.

6 *The Monster (to blind hermit)*: Alone bad. Friend good. Friend good!

SOUNDTRACK.

7 *The Monster (on Dr Frankenstein, his creator)*: Made me from dead. I love dead. Hate living.

SOUNDTRACK.

8 *The Monster (preparing to blow up laboratory)*: Yes – go. You live. Go. You stay. We belong dead.

SOUNDTRACK.

The BRIDGE ON THE RIVER KWAI

UK 1957; screenwriters: Carl Foreman, Michael Wilson, Pierre Boulle (from Boulle's novel); cast: Alec Guinness (Colonel Nicholson), William Holden (Shears), James Donald (Major Clipton), Sessue Hayakawa (Colonel Saito), Ann Sears (Nurse).

1 *Saito (quoting a motto for the inmates of his prisoner-of-war camp)*: Be happy in your work.

SOUNDTRACK.

2 *Nicholson (to Shears, on Saito)*: I must say, he seems quite a reasonable type.

SOUNDTRACK.

3 *Nicholson (to Saito)*: It's essential for an officer to have that respect, I'm sure you agree. If he loses it, he ceases to command. And what happens then? Demoralization and chaos. A pretty poor commander I would be if I allowed that to happen to my men.

SOUNDTRACK.

4 *Saito*: I hate the British. You are defeated but you have no shame. You are stubborn but have no pride. You endure but you have no courage. I hate the British!

SOUNDTRACK.

5 *Nicholson (stock response to question)*: I haven't the foggiest.

SOUNDTRACK.

6 *Shears (to nurse)*: You give me powders, pills, baths, injections and enemas … when all I need is love.

SOUNDTRACK.

7 *Shears (to bearer, in jungle)*: What's a nice girl like you doing in a place like this?

SOUNDTRACK. *Compare* **CLICHÉS** 108:3.

8 *Shears*: This is just a game, this war. You and that Colonel Nicholson, you're two of a kind. Crazy with courage. For what? How to die like a gentleman.

SOUNDTRACK.

9 *Nicholson (to Saito, standing on the completed bridge)*: But there are times when suddenly you realize you're nearer the end than the beginning … I don't know whether that kind of thinking's very healthy, but I must admit I've had some thoughts on those lines from time to time.

SOUNDTRACK.

1 *Nicholson (realizing he has betrayed the Allied plan to blow up the bridge)*: What have I done?

SOUNDTRACK.

2 *Clipton (viewing corpses round destroyed bridge)* Madness! Madness!

SOUNDTRACK. Closing line of film.

A BRIDGE TOO FAR

US/UK 1977; screenwriter: William Goldman (from Cornelius Ryan book); cast: Dirk Bogarde ('Boy' Browning), Sean Connery (Roy Urquhart).

3 *Browning*: I've just been on to Monty. Very proud and pleased.
Urquhart: Pleased?
Browning: Of course. He thinks that [Operation] Market Garden was ninety per cent successful.
Urquhart: But what do *you* think?
Browning: Well, as you know, I've always thought that we tried to go a bridge too far.

SOUNDTRACK. Although this is key dialogue from the film (and provides its title) debate has raged over whether the words were ever actually spoken. Operation Market Garden was designed to capture eleven bridges needed for the Allied invasion of Germany – an attempt that came to grief at Arnhem, with the Allies suffering more casualties than in the landings at Normandy. On 10 September 1944, in advance of the action, Lieutenant-General 'Boy' Browning, Corps Commander, is said to have protested to Montgomery, who was in overall command: 'But, sir, we may be going a bridge too far.' This incident was recorded by Major-General Roy Urquhart in his (ghost-written) memoir, *Arnhem* (1958). The remark was hardly noticed when the book was published and remained so until Cornelius Ryan picked it up and used it for the title of his book. There is now a strong reason to doubt that Browning ever said any such thing.

The BRIDGES AT TOKO-RI

US 1954; screenwriter: Valentine Davies (from James Michener novel); cast: William Holden (Lieut. Harry Brubaker), Fredric March (Rear-Admiral George Tarrant)

4 *Tarrant (on carrier waiting for pilots he knows will never return)*: Where do we get such men?

SOUNDTRACK. Frequently quoted by President Reagan (by 1985) as 'Where do/did we find such men?' and not always with attribution.

BRIEF ENCOUNTER

UK 1945; screenwriters: Noël Coward (from his play) and others; cast: Celia Johnson (Laura Jesson), Trevor Howard (Alec Harvey), Cyril Raymond (Fred Jesson), Everley Gregg (Dolly Messiter), Stanley Holloway (Albert Godby), Joyce Carey (Myrtle Bagot).

1 *Dolly (interrupting tryst)*: I've been shopping till I'm dropping.
SOUNDTRACK.

2 *Laura (narrating, as though addressing her husband who does not hear)*: This is my home. You're my husband. And my children are upstairs in bed. I'm a happily married woman – or, rather, I was until a few weeks ago. This is my whole world, and it's enough – or, rather, it was until a few weeks ago. But, oh, Fred, I've been so foolish. I've fallen in love. I'm an ordinary woman. I didn't think such violent things could happen to ordinary people.
SOUNDTRACK.

3 *Alec*: I apologize for boring you with long medical words.
Laura: I feel dull and stupid not to be able to understand more.
SOUNDTRACK.

4 *Laura (narrating)*: I stood there and watched his train draw out of the station. I stared after it until its tail light had vanished into the darkness.
SOUNDTRACK.

5 *Laura (narrating)*: I wondered if he'd say, 'I met such a nice woman at the Kardomah: we had lunch and went to the pictures.' And then suddenly I knew he wouldn't. I knew beyond a shadow of a doubt that he wouldn't say a word – and at that moment the first awful feeling of danger swept over me.
SOUNDTRACK.

6 *Albert (to Myrtle)*: Oh, you look wonderful when you're angry.
SOUNDTRACK. *Compare* **CLICHÉS** 108:8.

7 *Laura*: We must be sensible.
Alec: It's too late now to be sensible and all that.
SOUNDTRACK.

8 *Laura (narrating)*: All the silly dreams disappeared and … [I] walked home as usual, quite soberly and without wings, without any wings at all.
SOUNDTRACK.

9 *Laura*: Dolly Messiter! Poor, well-meaning, irritating Dolly Messiter, crashing into those last few precious minutes we had together. She chattered and fussed but I didn't hear what she said. I felt dazed and bewildered.
SOUNDTRACK.

1 *Fred*: Whatever your dream was, it wasn't a very happy one, was it? ... You've been a long way away – thank you for coming back to me.

SOUNDTRACK. Last lines of film.

'Joe Bob BRIGGS' (pseudonym of John Bloom)

American critic

2 Joe Bob says check it out.

STOCK PHRASE. 'Briggs' was the drive-in movie critic of the *Dallas Times Herald* from 1982 to 1985. His reviews represented the views of a self-declared redneck. They frequently caused offence, not least because they tended to rate movies according to the number of 'garbonzas' (breasts) on display. Joe Bob had a battery of stock phrases (not all original to him, by any means), including: 'no way, José'; 'if you know what I mean, and I think you do'; and the inevitable closing comment: 'Joe Bob says check it out'. The column was eventually dropped when Briggs poked fun at efforts to raise money for starving Africans. The columns were published in book form as *Joe Bob Goes to the Drive-In* (1989).

BRIGHTON ROCK

(also known as *Young Scarface* in the US) UK 1947; screenwriters: Graham Greene (from his novel), Terence Rattigan; cast: Richard Attenborough (Pinkie Brown), Wylie Watson (Spicer), Alan Wheatley (Fred Hale).

3 *Spicer (reading from newspaper)*: 'A prize of ten guineas will be awarded to the first person carrying a copy of the *Daily Messenger* who challenges him in the following words: "You are Kolley Kibber and I claim the *Daily Messenger* prize"'.

SOUNDTRACK. While Fred Hale is playing Kibber in a newspaper stunt of the 1930s, he is being pursued by Pinkie Brown and his gang. The stunt (exactly as in Greene's novel) is based on an actual campaign dating from the 1920s in which newspaper readers were encouraged to challenge a man they were told would be in a certain place (usually a seaside resort) on a particular day. His description and a photograph were given in the paper and 'You are so-and-so and I claim my £10' (or whatever the prize was) became the formula. The reader had, of course, to be carrying a copy of that day's paper. The first in the field was the *Westminster Gazette* in August 1927 and the correct challenge was: 'You are Mr Lobby Lud – I claim the *Westminster Gazette* prize' (which was initially £50, though if it was unclaimed it increased weekly). The name 'Lobby Lud' came from the Gazette's telegraphic address – 'Lobby' because of the Westminster connection and 'Lud' from Ludgate Circus off Fleet Street. The stunt did nothing for the paper, which closed the following year, but the idea was taken up by the *Daily News* and the *News Chronicle* and ran on for several years. Colly Cibber (1671–1757) was an English playwright, famous for the 'improvements' he made to Shakespeare's plays.

BRINGING UP BABY

US 1938; screenwriters: Dudley Nicholls (and others); cast: May Robson (Aunt Elizabeth), Cary Grant (David).

1 *Aunt Elizabeth (of the woman's nightgown David is wearing)*: Why are you wearing those clothes?
David: Because I just went gay all of a sudden.

SOUNDTRACK. Thought by some to be the moment when the meaning of the word 'gay' changed.

BROADWAY DANNY ROSE

US 1984; screenwriter/director: Woody Allen; cast: Woody Allen (Danny Rose), Nick Apollo Forte (Lou Canova), Mia Farrow (Tina Vitale).

2 *Rose (as personal manager, of one of his acts)*: I let you have her now at the old price, OK? Which is anything you want to give her.

SOUNDTRACK.

3 *Rose (to balloon-folding act)*: Before you go out on stage, you got to look in the mirror, and you got to say your three S's: star, smile, strong.

SOUNDTRACK.

4 *Rose (to Canova, on adultery)*: Take my Aunt Rose, not a beautiful woman at all. She looked like something you'd buy in a live bait store. But why? She had wisdom. And she used to say, 'You can't ride two horses with one behind.'

SOUNDTRACK.

5 *Rose (defending bird act with no bird, to theatrical manager)*: What do you mean, you don't want to pay? A cat ate his bird. That comes under the act of God clause.

SOUNDTRACK

6 *Rose (defending Canova to Vitale, Canova's mistress)*: I promise you. He's cheating you. He's got integrity. He cheats with one person at a time only. That's his style.

SOUNDTRACK.

7 *Rose (to Vitale)*: My father, may he rest in peace, said, 'In business, friendly, but not familiar.'

SOUNDTRACK.

8 *Rose (to Vitale)*: I'm never going to be Cary Grant. I don't care what anybody says.

SOUNDTRACK.

1 *Rose (to Vitale)*: You know what my philosophy of life is? That it's important to have some laughs, no question about it, but you got to suffer a little, too, because otherwise you miss the whole point of life.

SOUNDTRACK.

2 *Rose (to Vitale)*: The man has an axe. There's two of us. There'll be four of us in no time.

SOUNDTRACK.

Steve BROIDY

American executive (1905–91)

3 The most positive thing in the motion picture business is the negative.

ATTRIBUTED remark when President of Monogram Pictures and before becoming President of its successor Allied Artists (from 1945 to 1965).

Louise BROOKS

American actress (1906–85)

4 The great art of films does not consist of descriptive movement of face and body, but in the movements of thought and soul, transmitted in a kind of intense isolation.

QUOTED by Kenneth Tynan in *The New Yorker* (11 June 1979).

5 [suggesting her own epitaph] I never gave away anything without wishing I had kept it; nor kept anything without wishing I had given it away.

QUOTED in the same article.

6 Every actor has a natural animosity toward every other actor, present or absent, living or dead.

EXTRACTED from her book *Lulu in Hollywood* (1982).

Mel BROOKS

American screenwriter, producer and actor (1926–)

7 Never shoot a film in Belgrade, Yugoslavia! The whole town is illuminated by a 20-watt night light and there's nothing to do. You can't even go for a drive. Tito is always using the car.

QUOTED in *Newsweek* Magazine (17 February 1975).

8 Bad taste is simply saying the truth before it should be said.

ATTRIBUTED remark, quoted in J.R. Colombo, *Wit and Wisdom of the Moviemakers* (1979).

1 The death of Hollywood is Mel Brooks and special effects. If Mel Brooks had come up in my time he wouldn't have qualified to be a busboy.

COMMENT attributed to Joseph L. Mankiewicz.

Richard BROOKS

American director (1912–92)

2 People in Hollywood can't face the truth in themselves or in others. This town is filled with people who make adventure pictures and who have never left this place. They make religious pictures and they haven't been in a church or synagogue in years. They make pictures about love and they haven't been in love – ever.

QUOTED in *A Treasury of Humorous Quotations*, eds. Prochnow & Prochnow (1969).

Yul BRYNNER

American actor (1915–85)

3 People don't know my real self and they're not about to find out.

REMARK quoted in Leslie Halliwell, *The Filmgoer's Book of Quotes* (1973).

BULLETS OVER BROADWAY

US 1994; screenwriters: Woody Allen, Douglas McGrath; cast: Dianne Wiest (Helen Sinclair), John Cusack (David Shayne).

4 *Helen (to David who wishes to profess his devotion)*: Don't speak!

SOUNDTRACK. Stock phrase.

Luis BUÑUEL

Spanish director (1900–83)

5 *Soy ateo gracias a Dios* [I am still an atheist, thank God.]

INTERVIEWED in *Le Monde* (16 December 1959).

Billie BURKE

American actress (1885–1970)

6 [on Hollywood] To survive there, you need the ambition of a Latin-American revolutionary, the ego of a grand opera tenor, and the physical stamina of a cow pony.

QUOTED in Leslie Halliwell, *The Filmgoer's Book of Quotes* (1973).

Kathy BURKE

English actress (1964–)

1 When you are called a character actor, it's because you're too ugly to be called a leading lady.

QUOTED in *The Independent* (24 May 1997).

See also Helena **BONHAM CARTER** 66:9.

George BURNS

American comedian (1896–1996)

2 If it's a good script, I'll do it. And if it's a bad script, and they pay me enough, I'll do it.

QUOTED in the *International Herald Tribune* (9 November 1988).

3 The secret of acting is sincerity – and if you can fake that, you've got it made.

ATTRIBUTED remark – as, for example, in Michael York, *Travelling Player* (1991). Fred Metcalf in *The Penguin Dictionary of Modern Humorous Quotations* (1987) has Burns saying, rather: 'Acting is about honesty. If you can fake that, you've got it made.' However, Kingsley Amis in a devastating piece about Leo Rosten in his *Memoirs* (1991) has the humorist relating 'at some stage in the 1970s' how he had given a Commencement address including the line: 'Sincerity. If you can *fake that* ... you'll have the world at your feet.' So perhaps the saying was circulating even before Burns received the credit. Or perhaps Rosten took it from him? An advertisement in *Rolling Stone*, in about 1982, offered a T-shirt with the slogan (anonymous): 'The secret of success is sincerity. Once you can fake that you've got it made.' Fred MacMurray was quoted in *Variety* (15 April 1987): 'I once asked Barbara Stanwyck the secret of acting. She said: "Just be truthful – and if you can fake that, you've got it made".'

Richard BURTON

Welsh actor (1925–84)

4 [reply when Laurence Olivier said/cabled, 'Make up your mind dear heart. Do you want to be a great actor or a household word'] Both.

ATTRIBUTED remark during the making of *Cleopatra*, in about 1962.

5 [when asked by Gabriel Byrne why he had made so many films instead of going back to the theatre] Because I couldn't bear not to have somewhere to go in the mornings.

QUOTED in *The Observer* Magazine (6 March 1988).

1 There's nothing the British like better than a bloke who comes from nowhere, makes it, and then gets clobbered.

COMMENT by Melvyn Bragg, quoted in *The Observer*, 'Sayings of the Week' (25 September 1988).

2 [of his performance in *The Assassination of Trotsky*] In general, Mr Burton resembles a stuffed cabbage.

COMMENT by Harry Medved & Randy Dreyfuss, *The Fifty Worst Films of All Time (*1978).

BUTTERFIELD 8

US 1960; screenwriters: Charles Schnee, John Michael Hayes (from John O'Hara novel); cast: Elizabeth Taylor (Gloria Wandrous), Mildred Dunnock (Mrs Wandrous).

3 *Gloria (to her mother)*: Mama, face it. I was the slut of all time.

SOUNDTRACK.

BY ROCKET TO THE MOON

(original title *Frau im Mond* [The Woman in the Moon]) Germany 1928; screenwriter: Thea von Harbou; director: Fritz Lang.

4 Five – four – three – two – one.

SCREEN TITLE. It is said that the backward countdown to a rocket launch was first thought of by Lang. He considered it would make things more suspenseful if the count was reversed – 5-4-3-2-1 – so in this silent film he established the routine for future real-life space shots.

C

CABARET

US 1972; screenwriter: Jay Presson Allen (from Masteroff, Kander & Ebb stage musical); cast: Joel Grey (Master of Ceremonies).

1 *Master of Ceremonies*: Where are your troubles now? Forgotten. I told you so. We have no troubles here. Here life is beautiful. The girls are beautiful. Even the orchestra is beautiful.

SOUNDTRACK. Last line of film. *Compare* **TITLES OF FILMS** 421:2.

CABIN IN THE COTTON

US 1932; screenwriter: Paul Green (from novel by Harry Harrison Knoll); cast: Bette Davis (Madge).

2 *Madge*: I'd like to kiss you, but I just washed my hair. Bye!

SOUNDTRACK. This line is also quoted in *Get Shorty* (US 1995).

CADILLAC MAN

US 1990; screenwriter: Ken Friedman; cast: Robin Williams (Joey O'Brien), Judith Hoag (Molly).

3 *Molly*: You know what your problem is, Joey? You're a pig. And you're a chauvinist. And you have no respect for women.
Joey: Oh … well, I guess dinner and a blow job is out of the question then, huh?

SOUNDTRACK.

James CAGNEY

American actor (1899–1986)

4 There's not much to say about acting but this: Never settle back on your heels. Never relax. If you relax, the audience relaxes. And always mean everything you say.

REMARK quoted in Leslie Halliwell, *The Filmgoer's Book of Quotes* (1978 edn).

1 He can't even put a telephone receiver back on the hook without giving the action some special spark of life.

COMMENT by anonymous critic in *Time* Magazine, quoted in Leslie Halliwell, *The Filmgoer's Book of Quotes* (1978 edn).

2 He can do nothing which is not worth watching.

COMMENT by Graham Greene.

(Sir) Michael CAINE

English actor (1933–)

3 Not many people know that.

CATCHPHRASE. It is rare for a personal catchphrase to catch on (as opposed to phrases in entertainment, films and advertising that are engineered to do so). But this one is a notable exception. Peter Sellers started the whole thing off when he appeared on BBC TV's *Parkinson* show on 28 October 1972. The edition in question was subsequently released on disc ('Michael Parkinson Meets the Goons'), thus enabling confirmation of what Sellers said: '"Not many people know that" … this is my Michael Caine impression … You see Mike's always quoting from *The Guinness Book of Records*. At the drop of a hat he'll trot one out. "Did you know that it takes a man in a tweed suit five and a half seconds to fall from the top of Big Ben to the ground? Now there's not many people know that"!'

It was not until 1981–2 that the remark really caught on. Caine was given the line to say as an in-joke (in the character of an inebriated university lecturer) in the film *Educating Rita* (UK 1983), and he put his name to a book of trivial facts for charity with the slight variant *Not a Lot of People Know That!* in 1984.

4 British films are box-office poison.

QUOTED in *Screen International* (29 July 1978).

5 [film acting] is not so much acting as reacting, doing nothing with tremendous skill.

QUOTED in *City Limits* (28 February–6 March 1986).

6 When you're hot, casting directors say: The part's actually for a midget but we think you're perfect for it. But when you're cold, they'll say: Michael, we're doing The Michael Caine Story but unfortunately you're a bit too short.

QUOTED in *Sunday Today*, 'Quotes of the Week' (31 May 1987).

7 Theatre is like operating with a scalpel. Film is operating with a laser.

REMARK in BBC TV *Acting* master class (28 August 1987).

8 The British film industry is alive and well and living in Los Angeles.

QUOTED in *The Observer*, 'Sayings of the Week' (20 March 1994).

1 [collecting Golden Globe award in Beverly Hills] Oh, what a shock. My career must be slipping. This is the first time I've been available to pick up an award.

QUOTED in *The Independent* (26 January 1999).

2 You get paid the same for a bad film as you do for a good one.

ATTRIBUTED remark.

The CAINE MUTINY

US 1954; screenwriter: Stanley Roberts (from Herman Wouk novel); cast: Humphrey Bogart (Captain Queeg), Fred MacMurray (Lieut. Tom Keefer).

3 *Keefer*: There is no escape from the *Caine*, save death. We are all doing penance, sentenced to an outcast ship, manned by outcasts, and named after the greatest outcast of them all.

SOUNDTRACK.

4 *Queeg*: There are four ways of doing things on board my ship. The right way, the wrong way, the navy way and my way. If they do things my way, we'll get along.

SOUNDTRACK.

5 *Queeg*: Ah, but the strawberries! That's … that's where I had them. They laughed and made jokes, but I proved beyond a shadow of a doubt, and with geometric logic, that a duplicate key to the wardroom icebox did exist. And I'd have produced that key if they hadn't pulled the *Caine* out of action. I know now they were only trying to protect some fellow officer.

SOUNDTRACK.

CALIFORNIA SUITE

US 1978; screenwriter: Neil Simon (from his play); cast: Alan Alda (Bill Warren), Jane Fonda (Hannah Warren).

6 *Bill (to Hannah)*: New York is not the centre of the goddamn universe. I grant you it's an exciting, vibrant, stimulating, fabulous city, but it is not Mecca. It just smells like it.

SOUNDTRACK.

James CAMERON

Canadian-born director and screenwriter (1954–)

7 [welcoming cast members to set of *Titanic* in September 1996] Welcome to my nightmare!

QUOTED in Martin Jarvis, *Acting Strangely* (1999).

1 Film-making is a battle between business and aesthetics.

QUOTED in *The Observer*, 'Soundbites' (23 November 1997).

See also ***TITANIC*** 417:5.

CAMILLE

US 1936; screenwriters: Zoë Akins, Frances Marion, James Hilton (after Alexandre Dumas novel and play, *La Dame aux camélias*); cast: Laura Hope Crews (Prudence), Greta Garbo (Marguerite Gauthier), Robert Taylor (Armand Duvall), Henry Daniell (Baron de Varville), Lionel Barrymore (General Duvall).

2 *Prudence (to Marguerite)*: It's a great mistake for any woman to have a heart bigger than her purse.

SOUNDTRACK.

3 *Marguerite (to Duvall)*: I'm afraid of nothing except being bored.

SOUNDTRACK.

4 *Marguerite (to her husband, Baron de Varville, when he returns unexpectedly)*: I learned not to believe a man when he says he's leaving town.

SOUNDTRACK.

5 *Marguerite (to Armand)*: How can one change one's entire life and build a new one on one moment of love? And yet, that's what you make me want to close my eyes and do.

SOUNDTRACK.

6 *Prudence*: Wine used to go to my head, and make me gay. And now it goes to my legs, and makes me old.

SOUNDTRACK.

7 *General Duvall (to Marguerite)*: What you probably feel is the melancholy of happiness. That mood that comes over all of us when we realize that even love can't remain at flood tide forever.

SOUNDTRACK.

8 *Marguerite (to Armand, on her deathbed)*: It's my heart. It's not used to being happy.

SOUNDTRACK.

9 *Marguerite (to Armand, as she dies)*: Perhaps it's better if I live in your heart, where the world can't see me.

SOUNDTRACK.

The CANDIDATE

US 1972; screenwriter: Jeremy Larner; cast: Robert Redford (Bill McKay).

1 *McKay (to campaign manager, on winning election unexpectedly)*: What do we do now?

SOUNDTRACK. Last words of film.

Eddie CANTOR

American comedian (1892–1964)

2 [hearing that Norma Shearer, actress wife of Irving Thalberg, had produced a son, he sent a telegram of the utmost point to the noted Jewish film producer] CONGRATULATIONS ON YOUR LATEST PRODUCTION. AM SURE IT WILL LOOK BETTER AFTER IT'S BEEN CUT.

QUOTED in Max Wilk, *The Wit and Wisdom of Hollywood* (1972).

Frank CAPRA

American director (1897–1991)

3 I made mistakes in drama. I thought drama was when actors cried. But drama is when the audience cries.

ATTRIBUTED remark on French TV (February 1983).

4 There are no rules in film-making. Only sins. And the cardinal sin is dullness.

QUOTED at his death in *People* (16 September 1991).

5 The obligatory scene in most Capra films is the confession of folly in the most public manner possible.

COMMENT by Andrew Sarris.

See also Garson **KANIN** 237:3.

Claudia CARDINALE

Italian actress (1939–)

6 To know women deeply, you have to like them or love them. Our movie profession is filled with men who *don't* like women.

QUOTED in J.R. Colombo, *Wit and Wisdom of the Moviemakers* (1979).

CARRY ON CAMPING

UK 1969; screenwriter: Talbot Rothwell; cast: Kenneth Williams (Dr Soaper); Hattie Jacques (Matron, Miss Haggard); Barbara Windsor (Barbara).

1 *Soaper*: Oooh, matron! Take them away!

SOUNDTRACK. As Barbara is doing her exercises at finishing school, her bra flies off into the face of the principal. Outraged, Soaper says this to Miss Haggard of the revealed breasts.

CARRY ON CLEO

UK 1964; screenwriter: Talbot Rothwell; cast: Kenneth Williams (Julius Caesar).

2 *Julius Caesar (fending off assassination attempt)*: Infamy, infamy – they've all got it in for me!

SOUNDTRACK. Line borrowed (with permission) from a *Take It From Here* radio script by Frank Muir and Denis Norden. In *A Kentish Lad* (1997), Muir says it was first uttered by Dick Bentley as Caesar, attacked by Brutus and Co. He had written to *The Guardian* (22 July 1995) quietly asserting that it was indeed a product of the joint pen. Moreover, Talbot Rothwell, screenwriter of *Carry On Cleo* had very properly asked their permission to use the line, so it was a bit much always hearing Rothwell praised for writing it. Muir's letter concluded, 'Please may we have our line back.'

CARRY ON NURSE

UK 1959; screenwriter: Norman Hudis; cast: Leslie Phillips (Jack Bell), Shirley Eaton (Nurse Dorothy Denton), Wilfrid Hyde White (Colonel), Charles Hawtrey (Hinton), Matron (Hattie Jacques), Kenneth Connor (Bernie Bishop).

3 *Nurse (to Bernie Bishop)*: What a fuss about such a little thing!

SOUNDTRACK. Bernie, a boxer, has hurt his hand in a fight. The nurse has just removed his trousers despite protests from him.

4 *Hinton (having been listening to wireless in hospital bed)*: I say, you don't know what you've missed – the most marvellous recipe ... camp as Jamboree Folly.

SOUNDTRACK. An interesting early use of the word 'camp' in a popular context. The 'Carry On' films – and in particular the contributions of Hawtrey and Kenneth Williams – became particularly associated with the concept.

5 *Nurse Denton (to patient arriving in ward)*: Mr Bell?
Jack Bell (beholding Nurse Denton's charms): Ding dong, you're not wrong!

SOUNDTRACK.

6 *Colonel (prone on hospital bed)*: Come, come, matron, surely you've seen a temperature taken like this before?
Matron: Yes, Colonel, many times – but never with a daffodil.

SOUNDTRACK. Last words of film.

CARRY ON SPYING

UK 1964; screenwriters: Talbot Rothwell, Sid Colin; cast: Jim Dale (Carstairs)

1 *Carstairs*: Café Mozart, eight o'clock.

SOUNDTRACK. This was the time and place of Harry Lime's fatal appointment in *The* ***THIRD MAN***, though not spoken in that film.

CARRY ON UP THE KHYBER

UK 1968; screenwriter: Talbot Rothwell; cast: Kenneth Williams (Khazi of Kalabar), Joan Sims (Lady Ruff-Diamond).

2 *Khazi (to Ruff-Diamond)*: I do not make love … I am extremely rich. I have servants to do everything for me.

SOUNDTRACK.

CARVE HER NAME WITH PRIDE

UK 1958; screenwriters: Vernon Harris, Lewis Gilbert (based on R.J. Minney book); cast: Virginia McKenna (Violette Szabo), Paul Scofield (Tony Fraser), Alain Saury (Etienne Szabo).

3 Carve Her Name With Pride.

TITLE OF FILM. This is taken from the book (1956) by R.J. Minney (1895–1979), but where did he get it from? As Michael Powell comments in *Million-Dollar Movie* (1992), it 'sounds like a quotation, and probably is'. But I think not. Minney makes no reference to the title in his somewhat soupy biography of Violette Szabo, the wartime agent who was executed by the Germans and became the first British woman to receive the George Cross (gazetted posthumously in 1946). The notion of carving an epitaph is, of course, an old one. Robert Browning has 'If ye carve my epitaph aright' in his poem 'The Bishop Orders His Tomb' (1845).

4 *Etienne*: The life that I have is all that I have,
And the life that I have is yours.
The love that I have of the life that I have
Is yours and yours and yours.

A sleep I shall have,
A rest I shall have,
Yet death will be but a pause,
For the peace of my years in the long green grass
Will be yours and yours and yours.

SOUNDTRACK. This 'Code Poem for the French Resistance' was written by Leo Marks (1920–2000), who wrote it to be used as the basis for codes used by Special Operations Executive agents in the Second World War. In the film, it becomes Violette's code poem, she is interrogated about it by the Germans, and it is spoken by her as the last words of the film.

CASABLANCA

US 1942; screenwriters: Julius J. Epstein, Philip G. Epstein, Howard Koch (based on unproduced play *Everybody Comes to Rick's*); cast: Humphrey Bogart (Rick Blaine), Ingrid Bergman (Ilsa Lund), Dooley Wilson (Sam), Claude Rains (Capt. Louis Renault), Conrad Veidt (Major Strasser), Paul Henreid (Victor Laszlo).

1 They had a date with fate in ... Casablanca.

SLOGAN.

2 *Louis*: Everybody comes to Rick's.

SOUNDTRACK.

3 *Rick*: I came to Casablanca for the waters.
Louis: The waters? What waters? We're in the desert.
Rick: I was misinformed.

SOUNDTRACK.

4 *Rick*: I stick my neck out for nobody ...

SOUNDTRACK.

5 *Rick (to Strasser, Renault and others)*: Your business is politics. Mine is running a saloon.

SOUNDTRACK.

6 *Louis*: I'm only a poor corrupt official.

SOUNDTRACK.

7 *Louis (to Ilsa, of Rick)*: Well, mademoiselle, he is the kind of man that – well, if I were a woman, and I were not around, I should be in love with Rick.

SOUNDTRACK.

8 *Ilsa*: Play it once, Sam, for old time's sake.
Sam: I don't know what you mean, Miss Ilsa.
Ilsa: Play it, Sam. Play, 'As Time Goes By.'

SOUNDTRACK. *See also below* 90:1.

9 *Ilsa*: That was the day the Germans marched into Paris.
Rick: ... I remember every detail. The Germans wore grey. You wore blue.

SOUNDTRACK.

10 *Rick*: Of all the gin joints in all the towns in all the world, she walks into mine!

SOUNDTRACK.

1 *Rick*: You know what I want to hear.
Sam: No, I don't.
Rick: You played it for her, you can play it for me.
Sam: Well, I don't think I can remember it.
Rick: If she can stand it, I can. Play it.

SOUNDTRACK. Of course, Rick never actually says 'Play it again, Sam' in the film when talking to the nightclub pianist and reluctant performer of the sentimental song 'As Time Goes By'. Compare Ilsa's earlier exchange with him at 89:8. The catchphrase was well established by the time Woody Allen thus entitled his play *Play It Again Sam* (1969; film US, 1972) about a film critic who is abandoned by his wife and obtains the help of Bogart's 'shade'. By listing it under Allen's name, *Bartlett's Familiar Quotations* (1980 and 1992) might be thought to suggest that Allen coined the phrase. It would be interesting to know by which year it had really become established. In 1943, Jack Benny went to North Africa to entertain the troops. When he returned, two editions of his radio show were based on the idea of a reporter asking him, 'When you toured North Africa, were you in Algiers?' and 'Were you in Casablanca?' Each led to a film parody. In that of *Casablanca*, Benny played the Bogart part and 'Rochester' (Eddie Anderson) played Dooley Wilson. As has now been confirmed with a recording of the original broadcast on 17 October 1943, 'Ricky' (increasingly inebriated) keeps on saying: 'Go ahead, Sam, play that song. Sam, sing it, boy. Sing it, Sam. Sing it, Sam, sing that song that keeps breaking my heart.' Above all, he exclaims: 'Sam, Sam, play that song for me again, will you?' This is certainly closer to the catchphrase than anything uttered in the film and seems reasonable proof that Jack Benny really did help create the phrase. Presumably, rather more people heard the radio show than had seen the film at that point.

2 *Sam*: You must remember this, a kiss is still a kiss,
A sigh is just a sigh;
The fundamental things apply,
As time goes by.

SOUNDTRACK. Song, 'As Time Goes By' by Herman Hupfeld (1894–1951).

3 *Rick (to Ilsa)*: Here's looking at you, kid.

SOUNDTRACK. Stock phrase.

4 *Ilsa (to Rick, in Paris flashback)*: Was that cannon fire or is it my heart pounding?

SOUNDTRACK.

5 *Rick (to Bulgarian woman asking his advice)*: Yes, well, everybody in Casablanca has problems. Yours may work out.

SOUNDTRACK.

6 *Louis*: I'm shocked, *shocked* to find that gambling is going on in here.

SOUNDTRACK. Spoken in mock horror on being informed that there is gambling on the premises at the same time as he is pocketing his share of the evening's take.

1 *Rick*: Drop the gun, Louis!

APOCRYPHAL LINE – another one not uttered in the film. Alastair Cooke writing in *Six Men* (1977) remarked of Bogart: 'He gave currency to another phrase with which the small fry of the English-speaking world brought the neighbourhood sneak to heel: "Drop the gun, Looey!" But we have Bogart's word for it: "I never said, 'Drop the gun, Louie"' (Cooke alludes to a quotation in Ezra Goodman, *Bogey*: *The Good-Bad Guy*, 1965). Towards the end of the film what Rick does say is: 'Not so fast, Louis.' Ironically, it is *Louis* who in fact says: 'Put that gun down.'

2 *Rick (to Ilsa, of Victor)*: If that plane leaves the ground and you're not with him, you'll regret it. Maybe not today, and maybe not tomorrow, but soon and for the rest of your life.

SOUNDTRACK.

3 *Ilsa*: What about us?
Rick: We'll always have Paris.

SOUNDTRACK.

4 *Rick*: Ilsa, I'm no good at being noble, but it doesn't take much to see that the problems of three little people don't amount to a hill of beans in this crazy world.

SOUNDTRACK.

5 *Victor (to Rick)*: Welcome back to the fight. This time I know our side will win.

SOUNDTRACK.

6 *Louis*: Major Strasser has been shot. Round up the usual suspects.

SOUNDTRACK. In the final scene, Renault, the Vichy French police chief in the Moroccan city, is, in his cynical way, appearing to act responsibly following the shooting of a German officer, Major Strasser. Strasser was in fact shot before Renault's very eyes. It is remarkable that, of all the many memorable lines from *Casablanca*, it took until the early 1990s for this one to catch on. Indeed, as meaning 'the people you would expect, the customary lot', it almost became a cliché – as was perhaps confirmed by the release of a film called *The Usual Suspects* (US, 1995), which involved a police identity parade. Examples of the catchphrase in use range from straightforward quotation in 1983 to more recent unattributed allusions: 'All the usual suspects will be out at Fontwell tomorrow, when the figure-of-eight chase course will throw up its usual quota of specialist [horse-racing] winners' – *Independent on Sunday* (17 January 1993). A BBC Radio Scotland discussion show was called *The Usual Suspects* in 1993 – a rather revealing title given that the journalists who take part are inevitably just the sort of people you would expect to hear invited on to such a show.

In a 1992 interview, Howard Koch appeared to concede the coining of the phrase to his co-scriptwriters Julius J. Epstein and Philip G. Epstein.

1 *Rick (walking off into fog)*: Louis, I think this is the beginning of a beautiful friendship.

SOUNDTRACK. Last line of film.

John CASSAVETES

American actor and director (1929–89)

2 I never know what my movies are about until I finish them.

REMARK quoted in J.R. Colombo, *Wit and Wisdom of the Moviemakers* (1979).

3 As a director, too much of the time he is groping when he should be gripping.

COMMENT by Andrew Sarris.

The CAT AND THE CANARY

US 1939; screenwriters: Walter de Leon, Lynn Starling; cast: Bob Hope (Wally Campbell), Nydia Westman (Cicily).

4 *Cicily*: Do you believe people come back from the dead?
Wally: You mean like Republicans?

SOUNDTRACK.

5 *Cicily*: Don't big empty houses scare you?
Wally: Not me. I used to be in vaudeville.

SOUNDTRACK.

6 *Wally*: I get goose pimples. Even my goose pimples get goose pimples.

SOUNDTRACK.

CAT ON A HOT TIN ROOF

US 1958; screenwriters: Richard Brooks (director), James Poe (from Tennessee Williams play); cast: Burl Ives (Big Daddy), Elizabeth Taylor (Maggie), Paul Newman (Brick).

7 *Big Daddy*: Truth is pain and sweat and paying bills and making love to a woman you don't love any more. Truth is dreams that don't come true and nobody prints your name in the paper until you die.

SOUNDTRACK.

8 *Maggie*: Win what? What is the victory of a cat on a hot tin roof?
Brick: Just staying on it, I guess.

SOUNDTRACK. Lines almost as in play.

CAT PEOPLE

US 1942; screenwriter: Dewitt Bodeen; cast: Tom Conway (Louis Judd), Simone Simon (Irene Dubrovna), Kent Smith (Oliver Reed).

1 'Even as fog continues to lie in the valleys, so does ancient sin cling to the low places, the depressions in the world consciousness.'

SCREEN TITLE at start of film, quoting from *The Anatomy of Atavism* by Dr Louis Judd.

2 *Louis Judd (on Dubrovna's periodical changes into a panther)*: These things are very simple for a psychiatrist.

SOUNDTRACK.

3 *Louis Judd*: What does one tell a husband? One tells him nothing.

SOUNDTRACK.

4 *Dubrovna (on her husband telling another woman of their marital problems)*: There are some things a woman doesn't want other women to understand.

SOUNDTRACK.

CATCHPHRASES

5 And so we say farewell …

In commentaries to travelogues directed by James A. Fitzpatrick (1902–80), a supporting feature of cinema programmes from 1925 onwards. With the advent of sound, the commentaries to 'Fitzpatrick Traveltalks' became noted for their closing words: 'And it's from this paradise of the Canadian Rockies that we reluctantly say farewell to Beautiful Banff … And as the midnight sun lingers on the skyline of the city, we most reluctantly say farewell to Stockholm, Venice of the North … With its picturesque impressions indelibly fixed in our memory, it is time to conclude our visit and reluctantly say farewell to Hong Kong, the hub of the Orient … ' Frank Muir and Denis Norden's notable parody of the genre – 'Balham – Gateway to the South' – first written for radio *c.* 1948 and later performed on a record album by Peter Sellers (1958), accordingly contained the words, 'And so we say farewell to the historic borough …'

6 And the winner is …

Customary line of guest presenters when opening envelope and announcing Oscar winners.

7 Cut 'em off at the pass/Head 'em off at the pass

See **CLICHÉS** 108:1.

8 Don't get me mad, see?

Phrase inevitably used by impersonators of James Cagney, but source, if any, unverified. Alternatively, 'Just don't make me mad, see?'

1 Here's another nice mess you've gotten me into.

Oliver Hardy (1892–1957) to Stan Laurel (1890–1965), and spoken in several of their films – notably in *The Laurel and Hardy Murder Case* (US 1930) and *The Sons of the Desert* (US 1933). Oddly, both *The Oxford Dictionary of Modern Quotations* (1991) and *The Oxford Dictionary of Quotations* (1992) place the saying under Laurel's name while acknowledging that it was always said *to* him. Perhaps they are trying to reflect that Laurel was the prime mover in the partnership. John P. Fennell in *Film Quotes: Great Lines from Famous Films* (1991) goes one step further and even has 'Another fine mess you've got us in, *Ollie*.' It is one of the few film catchphrases to register because there was a sufficient number of Laurel and Hardy features for audiences to become familiar with it. Latterly, it has often been remembered as 'another fine mess', possibly on account of one of Laurel and Hardy's thirty-minute features (released in 1930) being entitled *Another Fine Mess. The Independent* (21 January 1994) carried a letter from Darren George of Sheffield – clearly a Laurel and Hardy scholar – which stated that 'nice mess' was what was 'invariably' spoken and that in *Another Fine Mess* 'the duo inexplicably misquote themselves'.

2 Honey, I love ya! *or* [Name], I love ya!

Clark Gable in several films of the 1930s, but unverified. Another putative phrase of his, is – slapping a woman's rear – 'Now beat it.' The woman on one occasion actually replies, 'Thank you.'

3 I'm a ba-a-a-ad-boy!

Lou Costello (1906–59) to Bud Abbott (1895–1974) in their many films of the 1940s, including *Abbott and Costello Meet Frankenstein* (US 1948).

4 It seemed like a good idea at the time.

Possibly first spoken by Richard Barthelmess (1895–1963) in *The Last Flight* (US 1931). American airmen linger on in Europe after the First World War. One of them is gored to death when he leaps into the ring at a bullfight. This is the response of one of his friends when journalists ask why he might have done such a thing. *See also The* ***MAGNIFICENT SEVEN*** 265:2.

5 Let's put on a show!

Variously exclaimed by Mickey Rooney (1920–) and/or Judy Garland (1922–69) in films together from 1939 onwards. The expression took several forms – 'Hey! I've got it! Why don't we put on a show?' / 'Hey kids! We can put on the show in the backyard!' / 'Let's do the show right here in the barn!' – though the duo seems never to have said the catchphrase precisely as it is remembered. In *Babes in Arms* (1939) Rooney and Garland play the teenage children of retired vaudeville players who decide to put on a big show of their own. Alas, they do not actually say any of the above lines, though they do express their determination to 'put on a show'. In *Strike Up the Band* (1940), Rooney has the line: 'Say, that's not a bad idea. We could put on our own show!' – though he does not say it to Garland. He also gets to say: 'Hey, kids! Let's start a band.' In whatever form, the line has become a film cliché, now used only with amused affection.

1 Lights! Camera! Action!

Used more in movies about movies than in actual film-making. According to Stuart Berg Flexner, *Listening to America* (1982), early directors shouted 'Ready! … Start your action!' Then, when cameras no longer needed cranking up ahead of time, this became, 'Ready! Action! Camera! Go!' By the late 1950s, the equipment was so smoothly functional that the cry was merely 'Action! Roll 'em!'

2 Not tonight, Josephine.

Further popularized in *I Cover the Waterfront* (US 1933), this expression of Napoleon's lack of interest in his wife seems to have arisen in drama and vaudeville in the early 1900s. At the same time, there was an early American phonograph record with the title (a song about a stenographer).

3 That's all, folks!

Stammered sign-off line of Porky Pig in the Warner Bros. cartoon series *Merrie Melodies* and *Looney Tunes*. Coinage variously ascribed to Fritz Frelang, cartoon director (1906–) and Rudolf C. Ising (recalled at his death in 1992). Voiced by Mel Blanc (1908–89) who, apparently, has it on his gravestone in Los Angeles.

4 What's up, Doc?

Characteristic inquiry of Bugs Bunny to (Dr) Elmer Fludd in Warner Bros. cartoon series (US 1937–63). Coinage has been attributed to 'Tex' Fred Avery. Voiced by Mel Blanc. Itself became the title of a film (US 1972) – *see* ***WHAT'S UP, DOC?*** 445:7.

5 Yer darn tootin'.

General catchphrase taken to himself by George 'Gabby' Hayes in almost all the films he made with William Boyd (Hopalong Cassidy), e.g. *Hills of Old Wyoming* (US 1937). The phrase also occurs in ***DESTRY RIDES AGAIN*** (US 1939). An early allusion is in P.G. Wodehouse's Hollywood story 'The Nodder' (1933), where its meaning is made clear in this exchange: '"Spurned your love, did she?" "You're dern tooting she spurned my love," said Wilmot. "Spurned it good and hard".'

See also Michael **CAINE** 83:3; **CLICHÉS** 104:5–109:2.

The CATERED AFFAIR

US 1956; screenwriter: Gore Vidal (from Paddy Chayefsky TV play); cast: Bette Davis (Agnes Hurley), Debbie Reynolds (Jane Hurley), Barry Fitzgerald (Uncle Jack Conlon).

6 *Agnes (to her daughter Jane)*: You're going to have a big wedding whether you like it or not. And if you don't like it, you don't have to come.

SOUNDTRACK.

7 *Agnes (to Jane)*: I want you to have this one fine thing with all the trimmings. Something to remember when … well, when the bad days come and you're all wore out and growing old like me.

SOUNDTRACK.

1 *Uncle Jack*: I belong to a long line of bachelors. That is to say, my uncles were all bachelors.

SOUNDTRACK.

2 *Agnes (to Jane)*: And then one day, you'll find out a lot of time's gone by. And you'll wake up knowing this is the way it's always going to be. Just like this. Day after day, year after year. Just the same. And that's why being married is such a big thing.

SOUNDTRACK.

Claude CHABROL

French director (1930–)

3 [on Hollywood films] I'm fascinated by the technology and the huge amount of money that goes into making them – and by their unbelievable stupidity.

QUOTED in *The Observer*, 'Sayings of the Week' (9 May 1993)

Raymond CHANDLER

American novelist (1888–1959)

4 The challenge of screenwriting is to say much in little and then take half of that little and still preserve an effect of leisure and natural movement.

EXTRACTED from *Atlantic Monthly* (November 1945).

5 If my books had been any worse, I should not have been invited to Hollywood, and if they had been any better, I should not have come.

EXTRACTED from a letter to Charles W. Morton (12 December 1945), in D. Gardiner & K.S. Walker, *Raymond Chandler Speaking* (1962).

6 The Bible … is a lesson in how not to write for the movies. The worst kind of overwriting. Whole chapters that could have been said in one paragraph. And the dialogue!

EXTRACTED from a letter to Edgar Carter (28 March 1947).

7 The motion picture made in Hollywood, if it is to create art at all, must do so within such strangling limitations of subject and treatment that it is a blind wonder it ever achieves any distinction beyond the purely mechanical slickness of a glass and chromium bathroom.

EXTRACTED from *Atlantic Monthly (March* 1948).

1 [on Los Angeles] A big hard-boiled city with no more personality than a paper cup.

EXTRACTED from his novel *The Little Sister*, Chap. 26 (1949).

2 Real cities have something else, some bony structure under the muck. Los Angeles has Hollywood – and hates it. It ought to consider itself damn lucky. Without Hollywood it would be a mail-order city. Everything in the catalogue you could get better somewhere else.

EXTRACTED from the same book.

3 They don't want you until you've made a name, and by the time you've made a name, you have developed some kind of talent they can't use. All they will do is spoil it, if you let them.

EXTRACTED from a letter to Dale Warren (7 November 1951).

(Sir) Charles CHAPLIN

English actor, writer and director (1889–1977)

4 The cinema is little more than a fad. It's canned drama. What audiences really want to see is flesh and blood on the stage.

ATTRIBUTED remark in about 1916.

5 [of the advent of talking pictures] They are spoiling the oldest art in the world – the art of pantomime. They are ruining the great beauty of silence.

INTERVIEWED in *Motion Picture Magazine* (May 1929).

6 I remain just one thing and one thing only – and that is a clown. It places me on a far higher plane than any politician.

QUOTED in *The Observer*, 'Sayings of the Week' (17 June 1960).

7 [on his Tramp character] A tramp, a gentleman, a poet, a dreamer, a lonely fellow, always hopeful of romance and adventure.

EXTRACTED from *My Autobiography*, Chap. 10 (1964).

8 [on film-making in about 1916] All I need to make a comedy is a park, a policeman and a pretty girl.

EXTRACTED from the same book.

9 I am known in parts of the world by people who have never heard of Jesus Christ.

QUOTED in Lita Grey Chaplin, *My Life With Chaplin* (1966).

1 Comedy is tragedy in long shot.

ATTRIBUTED in film *Swingers* (US 1996). 'Life is tragedy when seen in close-up but a comedy in long-shot' was quoted in his obituary in *The Guardian* (28 December 1977).

2 [on the universality of silent films] Words are cheap. The biggest thing you can say is 'elephant'.

QUOTED in Barry Norman, *The Movie Greats* (1981).

3 The Tramp is as centrally representative of humanity, as many-sided and as mysterious as Hamlet, and it seems unlikely that any dancer or actor can ever have excelled him in eloquence, variety or poignancy of emotion.

COMMENT by James Agee, quoted in Theodore Huff, *Charles Chaplin* (1951).

4 The Zulus know Chaplin better than Arkansas knows Garbo.

COMMENT by Will Rogers in *Atlantic Monthly* (August 1939).

5 [of Chaplin's work] The son of a bitch is a ballet dancer ... He's the best ballet dancer that ever lived ... and if I get a good chance I'll kill him with my bare hands.

COMMENT by W.C. Fields, quoted by Kenneth Tynan in *Sight and Sound* (February 1951).

6 Chaplin is no business man – all he knows is that he can't take anything less.

COMMENT by Samuel Goldwyn, quoted in Charles Chaplin, *My Autobiography*, Chap. 19 (1964).

7 People never sat at his feet. He went to where people were sitting and stood in front of them.

COMMENT by Herman J. Mankiewicz, quoted by Louise Brooks in Kenneth Tynan, 'Louise Brooks' in *The New Yorker* (11 June 1979).

8 I can't once remember him *still*. He was always standing up as he sat down, and going out as he came in.

COMMENT by Louise Brooks, quoted by Kenneth Tynan in *The New Yorker* (11 June 1979).

9 The audience didn't realize how odd he was because he was so near to reality in his madness.

COMMENT by (Sir) Ralph Richardson, English actor (1902–83), on BBC TV *Parkinson* (13 December 1980) (unverified).

10 Chaplin's genius was in comedy. He had no sense of humour.

COMMENT by ex-wife Lita Grey, quoted in Richard Lamparski, *Whatever Became of ---?* (1983).

CHARADE

US 1963; screenwriter: Peter Stone; cast: Audrey Hepburn (Regina Lambert), Cary Grant (Peter Joshua).

1 *Regina (to Peter)*: I don't bite, you know – unless it's called for.

SOUNDTRACK.

2 *Regina*: Do you know what's wrong with you?
Peter: No, what?
Regina: Nothing.

SOUNDTRACK.

CHARIOTS OF FIRE

UK 1981; screenwriter: Colin Welland; cast: Ian Charleson (Eric Liddell).

3 *Eric*: I believe that God made me for a purpose. For China. But he also made me fast. And when I run, I feel his pleasure.

SOUNDTRACK.

See also Colin **WELLAND** 443:1.

CHARLIE BUBBLES

UK 1968; screenwriter: Shelagh Delaney; cast: Albert Finney (Charlie Bubbles), Joe Gladwin (Waiter).

4 *Waiter*: Do you just do your writing now – or are you still working?
Charlie: No ... I just do the writing.

SOUNDTRACK.

Alexander CHASE

American journalist (1926–)

5 The movie actor, like the sacred king of primitive tribes, is a god in captivity.

EXTRACTED from *Perspectives* (1966).

CHER

American actress and singer (1946–)

6 Mother told me a couple of years ago, 'Sweetheart, settle down and marry a rich man.' I said, 'Mom, I am a rich man.'

INTERVIEWED in *The Observer* Review (November 1995).

Maurice CHEVALIER

French actor and singer (1888–1972)

1 Love the public the way you love your mother.

ATTRIBUTED remark.

2 An artist carries on throughout his life a mysterious, uninterrupted conversation with his public.

QUOTED in J.R. Colombo, *Wit and Wisdom of the Moviemakers* (1979).

3 The 70-odd years young Maurice Chevalier takes his place beside children and animals as one of the great scene stealers of all times.

COMMENT by Mike Connelly.

The CHILDREN'S HOUR

US 1962; screenwriter John Michael Hayes (from Lillian Hellman play); cast: Shirley Maclaine (Martha Dobie), Miriam Hopkins (Lily Mortar).

4 *Martha (on her Aunt Lily)*: Well, I suppose we'll have to feed the duchess. Even vultures have to eat.

SOUNDTRACK.

5 [when Goldwyn was told by the head of his script department that they could not film Hellman's play because it dealt with lesbians] OK, so we make them Albanians.

COMMENT by Samuel Goldwyn. Re-told by Philip French in *The Observer* (10 May 1992). Sounds pretty unlikely. This anecdote made an early appearance in Edmund Fuller, *2500 Anecdotes for All Occasions* (1943) with the contentious script being, rather, Radclyffe Hall's *The Well of Loneliness* and the reply: 'All right – where they got lesbians, we'll use Austrians.'

CHINATOWN

US 1974; screenwriter: Robert Towne; cast: Faye Dunaway (Evelyn Mulwray), Jack Nicholson (J.J. Gittes), Roman Polanski (Thug), John Huston (Noah Cross), Bruce Glover (Duffy).

6 *Mulwray (to Gittes)*: I don't get tough with anyone, Mr Gittes. My lawyer does.

SOUNDTRACK.

7 *Thug (to Gittes, before slitting a nostril)*: You're a very nosy fellow, kitty-cat, huh?

SOUNDTRACK.

1 *Cross*: Politicians, ugly buildings, and whores all get respectable if they last long enough.

SOUNDTRACK.

2 *Gittes*: He passed away two weeks ago and he bought the land a week ago. That's unusual.

SOUNDTRACK.

3 *Gittes*: I said I want the truth!
Mulwray: She's my sister *and* my daughter.

SOUNDTRACK.

4 *Cross*: See, Mr Gittes, most people never have to face the fact that at the right time and the right place they are capable of anything.

SOUNDTRACK.

5 *Duffy*: Forget it, Jake. It's Chinatown.

SOUNDTRACK. Last line of film.

Julie CHRISTIE

English actress (1940–)

6 Suddenly you start to get these roles as the mother of the ingenue you'd have been playing five years ago – it happens in a very swift moment.

QUOTED in *The Independent* (16 September 1987).

CHRISTMAS IN JULY

US 1940; screenwriter/director: Preston Sturges; cast: Dick Powell (Jimmy MacDonald).

7 *Jimmy*: 'If you can't sleep at night, it isn't the coffee, it's the bunk!'

SOUNDTRACK. Quoting his prize-winning coffee slogan.

CITIZEN KANE

US 1941; screenwriters: Herman J. Mankiewicz, Orson Welles; cast: Orson Welles (Kane), Dorothy Comingore (Susan), George Couloris (Thatcher), Everett Sloane (Mr Bernstein), William Alland (Thompson), Joseph Cotten (Jedediah Leland).

8 Everybody's Talking About It! It's terrific!

SLOGAN.

9 *Kane*: Rosebud!

SOUNDTRACK. Kane's dying word, first word spoken in the film, and referred to throughout – as finding out what it meant to him is a theme of the picture. It is finally glimpsed written on the side of a sledge – a powerful talisman of childhood innocence, or a 'symbol of maternal affection, the loss of which deprives him irrecoverably of the power to love or be loved' (Kenneth Tynan). Orson Welles himself issued a statement (14 January 1941) explaining: '"Rosebud" is the trade name of a cheap little sled on which Kane was playing on the day he was taken away from his home and his mother. In his subconscious it represented the simplicity, the comfort, above all the lack of responsibility in his home, and also it stood for his mother's love which Kane never lost.'

1 'I am, have been, and will be only one thing – an American.' – Charles Foster Kane.

SCREEN TITLE. In newsreel highlights of Kane's life.

2 *Kane (in newsreel highlights of life, relating to 1935)*: I've talked with the responsible leaders of the Great Powers – England, France, Germany, and Italy. They're too intelligent to embark on a project which would mean the end of civilization as we now know it. You can take my word for it: there'll be no war!

SOUNDTRACK.

3 *Newsreel announcer*: As it must to all men, death came to Charles Foster Kane.

SOUNDTRACK.

4 *Thatcher (reading letter from Kane)*: 'I think it would be fun to run a newspaper.'

SOUNDTRACK.

5 *Kane*: I don't know how to run a newspaper, Mr Thatcher. I just try everything I can think of.

SOUNDTRACK.

6 *Kane (replying to a war correspondent's message, 'Could send you prose poems about scenery but … there is no war in Cuba')*: Dear Wheeler, you provide the prose poems. I'll provide the war.

SOUNDTRACK. Based on an 1898 exchange between Frederic Remington and William Randolph Hearst (1863–1951). *Compare* ***TOMORROW NEVER DIES*** 428:3.

7 *Bernstein*: A fellow will remember a lot of things you wouldn't think he remembers. You take me. One day, back in 1896, I was crossing over to Jersey on the ferry, and, as we pulled out, there was another ferry pulling in, and on it there was a girl waiting to get off. A white dress she had on. She was carrying a white parasol. I only saw her for one second. She didn't see me at all, but I'll bet a month hasn't gone by since that I haven't thought of that girl.

SOUNDTRACK.

1 *Kane (on his paper's readers)*: They're going to get the truth in *The Inquirer* – quickly and simply and entertainingly.

SOUNDTRACK. Declaration of principles for *The Inquirer*.

2 *Bernstein (about 'Rosebud')*: Maybe that was something he lost. Kane was a man who lost almost everything he had.

SOUNDTRACK.

3 *Bernstein (on old age)*: It's the only disease, Mr Thompson, that you don't look forward to being cured of.

SOUNDTRACK.

4 *Kane (to Susan)*: I run a couple of newspapers – what do you do?

SOUNDTRACK.

5 *Susan (of her forced career as an opera singer)*: I'm the one who's got to do the singing. I'm the one who gets the raspberries.

SOUNDTRACK.

6 *Susan (to Thompson)*: Well, if you're smart you'll get in touch with Raymond – he's the butler. You'll learn a lot from him. He knows where all the bodies are buried.

SOUNDTRACK. An early citation of the 'bodies are buried' expression.

7 *Thompson*: Mr Kane was a man who got everything he wanted and then lost it. Maybe Rosebud was something he couldn't get or something he lost ... I don't think any word can explain a man's life. No, I guess Rosebud is just a piece in a jigsaw puzzle, a missing piece.

SOUNDTRACK.

8 [*Citizen Kane*] is probably the most exciting film that has come out of Hollywood for twenty-five years. I am not at all sure that it isn't the most exciting film that ever came out of anywhere.

COMMENT by C.A. Lejeune in *The Observer* (12 October 1941).

9 It's as though you had never seen a movie before.

COMMENT by Cecilia Ager.

10 Fiction is the great virus waiting to do away with fact – that is one of the most ominous meanings of the film.

COMMENT by David Thomson in *Rosebud: the Story of Orson Welles* (1996).

René CLAIR

French director (1898–1981)

1 That which makes the cinema is not to be discussed.

QUOTED in Penelope Houston, *Contemporary Cinema* (1963) – '[Said] forty or so years ago'.

CLASH OF THE TITANS

UK 1981; screenwriter: Beverley Cross; cast: Laurence Olivier (Zeus).

2 *Zeus*: Even if we, the gods, are abandoned or forgotten, the stars will never fade, never. They will burn till the end of time.

SOUNDTRACK. Last lines of film.

CLEOPATRA

US 1963; screenwriters: Joseph L. Mankiewicz and others; cast: Elizabeth Taylor (Cleopatra), Marc Antony (Richard Burton).

3 *Member of crowd*: Nothing like this has come to Rome since Romulus and Remus.

SOUNDTRACK.

4 *Cleopatra (on Antony's death)*: There has never been such a silence …

SOUNDTRACK.

See also Joseph L. **MANKIEWICZ** 273:4.

CLICHÉS

5 But Miss ---, you're beautiful!

Boss to secretary when she removes her spectacles. Or 'Why, Miss ---, without your glasses, you're … beautiful!' or 'You look beautiful without your glasses.' *Compare The* ***BAND WAGON*** 46:6, though a parody of the line. Someone says it to Twiggy in *The Boy Friend* (1971), but that is also in parody. There is an allusion in *Strictly Ballroom* (Australia 1992). Cited by Dick Vosburgh as cliché in 'I Love a Film Cliché' in musical play *A Day in Hollywood, A Night in the Ukraine* (1980).

6 Daddy, why is momma crying?

Cited as cliché in Vosburgh (as above).

7 Dr ---, must you tamper with forces unknown?!

Cited as cliché in Vosburgh (as above).

8 The end of civilization as we know it.

The End of Civilization As We Know It was the title of an announced but unreleased film (US 1977). 'Once again, we have saved civilization as we know it' appears in *Star Trek VI: The Undiscovered Country* (US 1991). *Compare* ***CITIZEN KANE*** 102:2.

1 Fire mountain say you have broken our island taboo!

Cited as cliché in Vosburgh (as above).

2 Follow that cab!

Said to driver when in pursuit, e.g. in *Top Hat* (US 1935) and *Mr Deeds Goes to Town* (US 1936); James Stewart says it jokily in *The Philadelphia Story* (US 1940); Fred Astaire says it in *Let's Dance* (US 1950) in order to chase Betty Hutton. In *Sabotage* (UK 1936), there is a 'Follow that taxi!' In *Song of the Thin Man* (US 1947), a taxi driver says to William Powell and Myrna Loy, 'Follow that cab?' 'Hmmm,' says she. 'A movie fan.' In *The Moon Is Blue* (US 1953), William Holden is pursuing a girl who gets into an elevator. He tells the elevator operator, 'Follow that car!' In *Arabesque* (US 1966), Gregory Peck says, 'Follow that car!' and the cab driver replies: 'All my life I've waited for somebody to say that!' In *A Fine Pair* (Italy 1969), Claudia Cardinale says, 'Follow that car!' and the cabby replies: 'I gave up my career as a stockbroker just to hear someone say, "Follow that car".'

3 I could help get you into films.

Cliché of seduction (in real life, that is).

4 I couldn't, ---, I'd only feel cheap.

Woman rejecting pass. Cited as cliché in Vosburgh (as above).

5 I'm giving you till sundown to get out of town.

See The ***VIRGINIAN*** 437:1.

6 It's quiet out there – too quiet.

In *Attack!* (US 1956), Jack Palance as a Second World War lieutenant in France identifies this as a cliché of cowboy movies: 'There's always one joker that says … ' In British stiff-upper-lip contexts, often cited as 'too damned quiet', and as addressed to one 'Carruthers'.

7 I've given you the best years of my life.

What the female half of a sparring couple usually says. *See* ***MR AND MRS SMITH*** 284:3.

8 I've never believed in anything so much in all my life.

As in *Dangerous Moonlight* (UK 1941); 'Mary, I was never more sure of anything in my life', Rooney to Garland in *Strike Up the Band* (US 1940); 'I was never so sure of anything in my life', Astaire to Hayworth in *You'll Never Get Rich* (US 1941); 'I've never believed in anything so much in my life' – *That Night in Rio* (US 1941).

9 --- Is ---.

Cliché of sloganeering, e.g. 'Michael Caine is Alfie is wicked!' (*Alfie*, UK 1966); 'Sean Connery *is* James Bond' (*You Only Live Twice*, UK 1967); 'Paul Hogan *is* Crocodile Dundee' (*Crocodile Dundee*, Australia 1986).

1 Is that a crime, Inspector?

Suggested by Jeremy Nicholas (1999) – a B-movie dialogue cliché: 'Look here, Johnny Martin asked me to take the Lagonda for a spin down to Monte Carlo. On the way back I dropped into the club for a drink. Is that a crime, Inspector?' (taps untipped Navy Cut on back of cigarette case and lights up).

2 The killer's name, Inspector, is – Aaaaahhh!

Compare The ***THIRTY-NINE STEPS*** 413:8 – Mr Memory (Wylie Watson) is cut short by a bullet when he tells Richard Hannay (Robert Donat): 'The Thirty-Nine Steps is the name of an organization of foreign spies collecting information for ...'

3 Let's get outta here!

Used in 81% of US films surveyed between 1938 and 1985, as reported in Patrick Robertson, *The Guinness Book of Movie Facts and Feats* (1995 edn).

4 Men of the Middle Ages, tomorrow sees the beginning of the Hundred Years' War.

Untraced example of screenwriter's fatuousness quoted by Chris Langham on BBC Radio *Quote ... Unquote* (5 June 1998). However, it may be no more than a development of a suggested joke ending for a play, as suggested by Max Beerbohm to his actor brother Herbert Beerbohm Tree, recorded in Hesketh Pearson, *Lives of the Wits* (1962): 'Herbert ... howled with laughter when Max suggested an effective line to bring the curtain down on a play, "Where are you going?" asks the sorrowful heroine. "I am going to the Thirty Years' War", answers the distraught hero.'

5 The natives are restless tonight.

Compare ***ISLAND OF LOST SOULS*** 229:5.

6 Nice little place you got here. Be too bad if somethin' was to happen to it.

Cited as cliché in Vosburgh (as above).

7 No trial for us. We're for stringing him up right away.

Cited as cliché in Vosburgh (as above).

8 Please, blackmail is such an ugly word.

Cited as cliché in Vosburgh (as above).

9 Please don't shoot my dog! Lassie couldn't have eaten those sheep.

Cited as cliché in Vosburgh (as above).

10 She'll pull through, but she's gonna be a mighty sick little lady for a while.

Cited as cliché in Vosburgh (as above).

11 There is no reason to be frightened. Can't you see I'm offering you eternal life?

Cited as cliché in Vosburgh (as above).

1 These are modern times ... 1804.

Example of thumping time-setter line, from *Forever and a Day* (US 1943). *See also* ***JEZEBEL*** 234:2.

2 This thing is bigger than both of us.

Where 'this thing' is 'our love'. *Compare* ***KING KONG*** 241:1.

3 This town ain't big enough for the both of us!

Villain to opposer in Westerns, e.g. baddy Charles King to Tex Ritter in *Boots and Saddles* series (US 1936); Yosemite Sam to Bugs in *Bugs Bunny Rides Again* (US 1948).

4 Those drums are driving me mad!

Cited as cliché in Vosburgh (as above).

5 Time has passed by this ---.

Cliché of travelogue commentary. Memorably completed in the commentary to Muir and Norden's sketch 'Balham, Gateway to the South' (1948) thus: 'Time has passed by this remote corner. So shall we.'

6 Try to get some sleep now.

Said to participants in any sort of disturbance. Cited by critic David McGillivray, as reported in Patrick Robertson, *The Guinness Book of Movie Facts and Feats* (1995 edn). 'Try and get some rest' rivals it. The latter is spoken in *Deceived* (US 1992).

7 Walk this way – [*exit, with the addressee mimicking the other's gait*].

As in *After the Thin Man* (US 1936). Did the Marx Brothers use it? Not sure that it was in their films, but in the introduction to *The Groucho Letters* (1967), Arthur Sheekman wrote: 'If in a mood to parody the small-time comedians, [Marx] might say to a waiter – or waitress – "Have you got frog legs?" And no matter what the reply, Groucho will look painfully disappointed and say, "That's the wrong answer. You were supposed to say, 'No; it's rheumatism that makes me walk this way.'"'

An even earlier use of the cliché is in *The Laurel and Hardy Murder Case* (US 1930). The pair enter a weird, frightening old house, to be greeted by the hideously deformed butler who invites them to 'Walk this way.' Stanley takes this literally, and follows him imitating his Quasimodo-like gait until thumped by Olly.

8 We could make beautiful music together.

Gary Cooper said it (perhaps first) to Madeleine Carroll in *The General Died At Dawn* (US 1936).

9 We'd better call the police. / I am the police.

This is in *Dirty Harry* (US 1971) and *Magnum Force* (US 1973) and much earlier in *Laura* (US 1944) and *Ask a Policeman* (UK 1938): Moore Marriott (telephoning): 'Help! Help! Help! Police! Police!' Will Hay: 'Shut up, you old idiot. We are the police.'

1 We'll head 'em off at Eagle Pass.

Said by villain in Westerns – Charles Bickford (1889–1967) held that he had said it regularly for more than fifteen years. His remark was quoted, sometime after 1954, by C.A. Lejeune in an article entitled 'Head 'em off at Eagle Pass' in *Good Housekeeping* Magazine. *Compare* ***BLAZING SADDLES*** 63:7. Also in the form 'cut 'em off at the pass' (meaning 'intercept, ambush'). This resurfaced as one of the milder sayings in the transcripts of the Watergate tapes (published as *The White House Transcripts*, 1974). As used by President Nixon it meant simply 'we will use certain tactics to stop them'. The phrase occurred in a crucial exchange in the White House Oval Office on 21 March 1973 between the President and his Special Counsel, John Dean:

P: You are a lawyer, you were a counsel … What would you go to jail for?
D: The obstruction of justice.
P: The obstruction of justice?
D: That is the only one that bothers me.
P: Well, I don't know. I think that one … I feel it could be cut off at the pass, maybe, the obstruction of justice.

2 What do we do now? / We wait.

In *Rough Cut* (US 1980), *Beverley Hills Cop* (US 1984) and *Ghost* (US 1990) (where the line is changed to 'Just wait'). It seems to have been routinely written into episodes of TV crime series for decades. It was used in *The Professionals* and in a 1967 episode of *The Champions.*

3 What's a nice girl like you doing in a place like this?

May have arisen in Hollywood Westerns of the 1930s. It was certainly established as a film cliché by the 1950s when Frank Muir and Denis Norden included this version in a BBC radio *Take It From Here* parody: 'Thanks, Kitty. Say, why does a swell girl like you have to work in a saloon like this?' *See also The* ***BRIDGE ON THE RIVER KWAI*** 73:7; ***KISS ME STUPID*** 242:1 and ***YOU ONLY LIVE TWICE*** 458:2.

4 White man speak with forked tongue.

Supposedly the way a Red Indian chief would pronounce on the duplicitous ways of the White man in Western movies. In *Yukon Vengeance* (US 1954), Carol Thurston as Princess Yellow Flower gets to say: 'White man's tongue is forked.'

5 Why can't I make you see – I've got music inside of me, Pa?

Cited as cliché in Vosburgh (as above).

6 You can't be that same freckle-faced little tomboy with the braces in her teeth!

Cited as cliché in Vosburgh (as above).

7 You keep him busy … I'm gonna work round behind him.

Cited as cliché in Vosburgh (as above).

8 You're beautiful when you're angry.

Clark Gable says it to Lana Turner in *Betrayed* (US 1954). Nelson Eddy as

Charles, Duc de Villiers, says it to Jeanette MacDonald in *New Moon* (US 1940). *Compare* ***BRIEF ENCOUNTER*** 75:6, *The* ***CONQUEROR*** 114:1.

1 You're gonna throw the fight in round two!

Cited as cliché in Vosburgh (as above).

2 You're just like all the others! They too think I'm mad.

Cited as cliché in Vosburgh (as above) – usually said by a mad scientist. *Compare* ***FRANKENSTEIN*** 169:7; *The* ***VAMPIRE BAT*** 435:1.

See also The ***LIVES OF A BENGAL LANCER*** 256:6; ***MUTINY ON THE BOUNTY*** 296:4; ***NO WAY TO TREAT A LADY*** 308:4; ***ODETTE*** 313:1.

Montgomery CLIFT

American actor (1920–66)

3 He's the only person I know who's in worse shape than I am.

COMMENT by Marilyn Monroe, his co-star in *The Misfits* (1961).

4 He acts like he's got a Mixmaster up his ass and doesn't want anyone to know it.

COMMENT by Marlon Brando, quoted in Maria Leach, *The Ultimate Insult* (1996).

A CLOCKWORK ORANGE

UK 1972; screenwriter/director: Stanley Kubrick (from Anthony Burgess novel); cast: Malcolm McDowell (Alex), Paul Farrell (tramp), Patrick Magee (Mr Alexander), Adrienne Corri (Mrs Alexander), Madge Ryan (Dr Branom), Carl Duering (Dr Brodsky), Anthony Sharp (Minister of the Interior).

5 Being the adventures of a young man whose principal interests are rape, ultra-violence and Beethoven.

SLOGAN.

6 *Alex (narrating)*: There was me, that is Alex, and my three droogs, that is Pete, Georgy, and Dim, and we sat in the Korova Milkbar trying to make up our rassoodocks what to do with the evening. The Korova Milkbar sold Milkplus, Milkplus Vellocet, or Synthemesc or Drencrom, which is what we were drinking. This would sharpen you up and make you ready for the bit of the old ultra-violence.

SOUNDTRACK.

7 *Alex (narrating how a rival gang was attempting to rape a woman)*: They were getting ready to perform a little of the old in-out in-out on a weepy young devotchka they had there.

SOUNDTRACK.

1 *Alex (telling Mr Alexander to watch as he rapes his wife)*: Viddy well, little brother, viddy well.

SOUNDTRACK.

2 *Alex (hearing woman in Milkbar sing part of Beethoven's Ninth Symphony)*: It was a bit from the Glorious Ninth by Ludwig van.

SOUNDTRACK.

3 *Dr Branom (on Alex's Ludovico treatment)*: You're becoming healthy, that's all. By this time tomorrow, you'll be healthier still.

SOUNDTRACK.

4 *Dr Brodsky (on teaching Alex to hate Beethoven's Ninth)*: Can't be helped. Here's the punishment element, perhaps. Governor ought to be pleased.

SOUNDTRACK.

5 *Minister (on moral objections to Alex's treatment)*: These are subtleties. We're not concerned with motives, with the higher ethics. We are concerned only with cutting down crime.

SOUNDTRACK.

6 *Alex (to the Minister, as to whether he is clear about the terms of their collaboration)*: As an unmuddied lake, Fred. As clear as an azure sky of deepest summer. You can rely on me, Fred.

SOUNDTRACK.

7 *Alex (narrating, on his return to violence)*: I was cured, all right.

SOUNDTRACK. Last line of film.

CLOSE ENCOUNTERS OF THE THIRD KIND

US 1977; screenwriter/director: Steven Spielberg; cast: Richard Dreyfuss (Roy Neary).

8 Close Encounters of the Third Kind.

TITLE OF FILM. Said to be taken from the categories used in the American forces to denote UFOs. A 'close encounter 1' would be a simple UFO sighting; a 'close encounter 2', evidence of an alien landing; and a 'close encounter 3', actual contact with aliens. The categories were devised by a UFO researcher called J. Allen Hynek (source: Rick Meyers, *The Great Science Fiction Films*).

9 We are not alone.

SLOGAN.

10 Watch the skies.

SLOGAN. *See also The* ***THING*** 410:7.

1 *Neary (making model of Devil's Tower out of mashed potatoes)*: This means something. This is important.

SOUNDTRACK.

The COCOANUTS

US 1929; screenwriters: George S. Kaufman, Morrie Ryskind; cast: Groucho Marx (Hammer), Chico Marx (Chico), Margaret Dumont (Mrs Potter), Oscar Shaw (Bob).

2 *Hammer*: Three years ago I came to Florida without a nickel in my pocket. And now I've got a nickel in my pocket.

SOUNDTRACK.

3 *Hammer*: Do you know that this is the biggest development since Sophie Tucker?

SOUNDTRACK.

4 *Chico*: We want a room, and no bath.
Hammer: Oh, I see. You're just here for the winter.

SOUNDTRACK.

5 *Hammer (to Potter, indicating sofa)*: Won't you – lie down?

SOUNDTRACK.

6 *Hammer (to Potter)*: I mean – your eyes – your eyes, they shine like the pants of a blue serge suit.

SOUNDTRACK.

7 *Hammer (to Potter)*: I'll meet you tonight under the moon. Oh, I can see you now, you and the moon. You wear a necktie so I'll know you.

SOUNDTRACK.

8 *Hammer (to Chico)*: Say, the next time I see you, remind me not to talk to you, will you?

SOUNDTRACK.

9 *Hammer*: I say here is a little peninsula, and here's a viaduct leading over to the mainland.
Chico: All right. Why a duck?

SOUNDTRACK.

10 *Hammer*: Believe me, you've to get up early if you want to get out of bed.

SOUNDTRACK.

1 *Hammer*: I'll wrestle anybody in the crowd for five dollars. Be free, my friends. One for all and all for me – me for you and three for five and six for a quarter.

SOUNDTRACK.

2 *Bob*: Oh, Mr Hammer, there's a man outside wants to see you, with a black moustache.
Hammer: Tell him I've got one.

SOUNDTRACK.

Jean COCTEAU

French poet, screenwriter and director (1889–1963)

3 The cinema – that temple of sex, with its goddesses, its guardians and its victims.

SPEECH at 1959 Cannes Festival (in translation). Quoted in Alexander Walker, *The Celluloid Sacrifice* (1966).

4 A film is a petrified fountain of thought.

REMARK in *Esquire* (February 1961).

5 [on the size of the CinemaScope screen] The next time I write a poem I'll use a big sheet of paper.

QUOTED in Penelope Houston, *Contemporary Cinema* (1963).

6 [of Henri Langlois, founder of the Cinémathèque Française (1914–77)] *Ce dragon qui veille sur nos trésors* [This dragon who guards our treasures].

QUOTED on Langlois's gravestone in Montparnasse cemetery, Paris.

Harry COHN

American producer (1891–1958)

7 [how to rate a film] If my fanny squirms, it's bad. If my fanny doesn't squirm, it's good. It's as simple as that.

ATTRIBUTED remark.

See also George **JESSEL** 233:5.

Joan COLLINS

English actress (1933–)

8 I've never yet met a man who could look after me. I don't need a husband. What I need is a wife.

QUOTED in *The Observer* 'Sayings of the Week' (26 July 1987). After her fourth marriage had gone bust.

1 Glamour is on a life-support machine and not expected to live.

QUOTED in *The Independent* (24 April 1999).

Ronald COLMAN

English actor (1891–1958)

2 [to his agent] Before God I'm worth 35 dollars a week. Before the motion picture industry I'm worth anything you can get.

ATTRIBUTED remark.

3 He is as ingratiating when he talks as when he was silent.

COMMENT in *The New York Times* (1929).

See also James **AGEE** 15:9.

Robbie COLTRANE

Scottish actor (1950–)

4 If anyone asked me what I was doing, I'd say 'I've come 1500 miles to a foreign country to pretend to be someone else in front of a machine.'

INTERVIEWED in *Arena* (1991).

(Sir) Sean CONNERY

Scottish actor (1930–)

5 [on being called 'the sexiest man alive'] Well, there are very few sexy ones that are dead.

QUOTED in *The Independent* (15 June 1991).

6 [accepting Cecil B. DeMille award at Golden Globe ceremony] I prefer my audiences stirred, not shaken.

QUOTED in *The Observer* (28 January 1996).

7 With the exception of Lassie, he's the only person I know who's never been spoiled by success.

COMMENT attributed to Terence Young (director).

8 As long as actors are going into politics, I wish, for Christ's sake, that Sean Connery would become king of Scotland.

COMMENT by John Houston, quoted by John Millar in *From Limelight to Satellite*, ed. Eddie Dick (1990).

The CONQUEROR

US 1955; screenwriter: Oscar Millard; cast: John Wayne (Temujin/Genghis Khan), Susan Hayward (Bortai).

1 *Bortai*: For me there is no peace while you live, Mongrel!
Temujin: You're beautiful in your wrath! I shall keep you, Bortai! I shall keep you, and, in responding to my passions, your hatred will kindle into love.

SOUNDTRACK.

2 *Temujin*: This Tartar woman is for me, and my blood says, take her!

SOUNDTRACK.

3 *Temujin (after sexual encounter with Bortai)*: All other women are like the second pressing of the grape.

SOUNDTRACK.

Joseph CONRAD

Polish-born novelist (1857–1924)

4 All things considered, I prefer cinema to stage. The movie is just a silly stunt for silly people – but the theatre is more compromising since it is capable of falsifying the very soul of one's work.

EXTRACTED from a letter (18–23 August 1920).

CONTEMPT *See Le* ***MÉPRIS****.*

CONTINENTAL DIVIDE

US 1981; screenwriter: Lawrence Kasdan; cast: John Belushi (Ernie Souchak).

5 *Souchak (in the wild)*: It's so quiet up here, you can hear a mouse get a hard-on.

SOUNDTRACK.

COOL HAND LUKE

US 1967; screenwriters: Donn Pearce, Frank Pierson; cast: Strother Martin (Captain), Paul Newman (Luke), George Kennedy (Dragline).

6 *Captain (to Luke)*: What we've got here is failure to communicate. Some men you just can't reach.

SOUNDTRACK. 'What We've Got Here Is A [*sic*] Failure To Communicate' was a line used to promote the film.

1 *Dragline*: Old Luke, he was some boy. Cool Hand Luke, hell, he's a natural-born world-shaker.

SOUNDTRACK. Last line of film.

Gary COOPER

American actor (1901–61)

2 In Westerns you were permitted to kiss your horse but never your girl.

QUOTED in *Saturday Evening Post* (17 March 1958).

3 Gary Cooper comes to join us … He is a nice shy quiet modest young man, devoid of any brains.

COMMENT by Harold Nicolson, in *Harold Nicolson's Diaries and Letters* (entry for 25 March 1933 at Los Angeles) (1966).

4 He was a poet of the real.

COMMENT by Clifford Odets, quoted in Leslie Halliwell, *The Filmgoer's Book of Quotes* (1973).

5 One of the best loved illiterates this country has ever known.

COMMENT by Carl Sandburg, quoted in Leslie Halliwell, *The Filmgoer's Book of Quotes* (1973).

6 He's got a reputation as a great actor just by thinking hard to remember his next line.

COMMENT attributed to King Vidor, American director (1894–1982).

7 The fellow is the world's greatest actor. He can do with no effort what the rest of us spent years trying to learn; to be perfectly natural.

COMMENT by John Barrymore, quoted in Jane Mercer, *Great Lovers of the Movies* (1975).

8 Gary is an embodiment of the old saying that art consists in concealing its own artfulness. After seeing him on the screen, any young man might say, 'Shucks, I could do that.' The young man would be wrong.

COMMENT by Cecil B. DeMille, in his *Autobiography* (1960).

9 When he puts his arms round me I feel like a horse.

COMMENT attributed to Clara Bow.

See also ***GONE WITH THE WIND*** 195:5.

Aaron COPLAND

American composer (1900–90)

1 Film music is like a small lamp that you place below the screen to warm it.

QUOTED in Nat Shapiro, *An Encyclopedia of Quotations about Music* (1978).

Francis Ford COPPOLA

American screenwriter and director (1939–)

2 I bring to my life a certain amount of mess.

ATTRIBUTED remark.

3 I probably have genius. But no talent.

ATTRIBUTED remark.

4 He is his own worst enemy. If he directs a little romance, it has to be the biggest most overdone little romance in movie history.

COMMENT by Kenneth Turan.

Roger CORMAN

American producer and director (1926–)

5 Poe writes the first reel or the last reel. Roger does the rest.

COMMENT by James H. Nicholson.

6 He once said, 'Martin, what you have to get is a very good first reel because people want to know what's going on. Then you need a very good last reel because people want to hear how it all turns out. Everything else doesn't really matter.

COMMENT by Martin Scorsese.

The COUNTRY GIRL

US 1954; screenwriter: George Seaton; cast: William Holden (Ernie Dodd), Grace Kelly (Georgie Elgin).

7 *Dodd*: That's what my ex-wife used to keep reminding me of, tearfully. She had a theory that behind every great man there was a great woman.

SOUNDTRACK. An example of the cliché line that had been around since the late 1930s.

The COURT *JESTER*

US 1955; screenwriters/directors: Norman Panama, Melvin Frank; cast: Danny Kaye (Hawkins); Basil Rathbone (Sir Ravenshurst).

1 *Hawkins*: Get it?
Sir Ravenshurst: Got it.
Hawkins: Good.

SOUNDTRACK. The exchange is repeated by others.

2 *Hawkins (correctly repeating instructions as to how to avoid a poisoned drink)*: 'The pellet with the poison's in the vessel with the pestle; the chalice from the palace has the brew that is true.'

SOUNDTRACK. He soon garbles this and, anyway, the instructions are changed when the chalice from the palace gets broken. He has as much difficulty remembering: 'The pellet with the poison's in the flagon with the dragon; the vessel with the pestle has the brew that is true.'

(Sir) Noël COWARD

English actor, director and screenwriter (1899–1973)

3 [in letter to his mother in 1937] I'm not very keen on Hollywood. I'd rather have a nice cup of cocoa really.

QUOTED in Cole Lesley, *The Life of Noël Coward* (1976).

4 [to William Fairchild, who wrote dialogue for the part of Coward in the film *Star!* (US 1968), after Coward had checked the script] Too many Dear Boys, dear boy.

QUOTED in same book.

5 [of Jeanette MacDonald and Nelson Eddy in Technicolor version of his *Bitter Sweet*] An affair between a mad rockinghorse and a rawhide suitcase.

ATTRIBUTED remark.

6 [on the short-lived career of actor Keir Dullea when they were making the film *Bunny Lake Is Missing* in 1965] Keir Dullea, gone tomorrow.

ATTRIBUTED by Sheridan Morley on BBC Radio *Quote ... Unquote* (7 November 1989).

7 [on Peter O'Toole in *Lawrence of Arabia*] If it had been any prettier, it would have been *Florence of Arabia*.

ATTRIBUTED remark.

See also **TITLES OF FILMS** 422:2.

Joan CRAWFORD

American actress (1904–77)

1 I never go out unless I look like Joan Crawford the movie star. If you want to see the girl next door, go next door.

ATTRIBUTED remark.

2 I found that incredible thing, a public.

QUOTED in Alexander Walker, *Joan Crawford*: *The Ultimate Star* (1983).

3 Joan Crawford was the perfect image of the movie star, and, as such, [was] largely the creation of her own indomitable will.

COMMENT by George Cukor, quoted in same book.

4 Why can't Joan ever forget for a single second that she's Joan Crawford?

COMMENT by Alexander Kirkland, quoted in J.R. Colombo, *Wit and Wisdom of the Moviemakers* (1979).

5 Joan Crawford is the only actress to read the whole script. Most actresses just read their own lines to find out what clothes they're going to wear.

COMMENT by Anita Loos.

6 The best time I ever had with Joan Crawford was when I pushed her down the stairs in *Whatever Happened to Baby Jane*?

COMMENT by Bette Davis, attributed in Doug McLelland, *Star Speak* (1987).

7 Joan [Crawford] always cries a lot. Her tear ducts must be very close to her bladder.

COMMENT by Bette Davis, quoted in Shaun Considine, *Bette and Joan*: *The Divine Feud* (1989).

Charles CRICHTON

English director (1910–99)

8 People think that if you're directing comedy you've got to be funny. On the contrary, you've got to be serious.

QUOTED in *The Independent* (15 September 1999). Apparently, this was said to the cast during the making of ***A FISH CALLED WANDA***.

CRIMES AND MISDEMEANORS

US 1989; screenwriter: Woody Allen; cast: Martin Landau (Judah Rosenthal), Anjelica Huston (Dolores Paley), Mia Farrow (Halley Reed), Jerry Orbach (Jack Rosenthal), Alan Alda (Lester), Woody Allen (Cliff Stern), Martin Bergmann (Professor Louis Levy).

1 *Cliff*: The last time I was inside a woman was when I visited the Statue of Liberty.

SOUNDTRACK.

2 *Lester (on New York City)*: It's like thousands of straight lines just looking for a punch line.

SOUNDTRACK.

3 *Judah*: God is a luxury I can't afford.

SOUNDTRACK.

4 *Cliff (to his wife, on the date she stopped sleeping with him)*: April 20. I remember the date exactly 'cause it was Hitler's birthday.

SOUNDTRACK.

5 *Lester*: Showbusiness is dog eat dog. It's worse than dog eat dog. It's dog doesn't return other dog's phone calls.

SOUNDTRACK.

6 *Lester (on comedy)*: If it bends, it's funny. If it breaks, it isn't.

SOUNDTRACK.

7 *Cliff (to Halley, about Lester)*: What is the guy so upset about? He's not the first person to be compared to Mussolini.

SOUNDTRACK.

8 *Cliff (in tuxedo at formal party)*: I'm so self-conscious. Every single thing on me is rented.

SOUNDTRACK.

9 *Cliff (to Halley, when she returns a love letter to him)*: It's probably just as well. I plagiarized most of it from James Joyce. You probably wondered about all the references to Dublin.

SOUNDTRACK.

10 *Professor Levy*: Human happiness does not seem to have been included in the design of creation. It is only we, with our capacity to love, that give meaning to the indifferent universe. And yet most human beings seem to have the ability to keep trying and even to find joy from simple things, like their family, their work, and from the hope that future generations might understand more.

SOUNDTRACK. Last speech of film.

David CRONENBERG

Canadian director (1943–)

1 More blood! More blood!

ATTRIBUTED remark on set of horror films. Quoted in Neil Gaiman & Kim Newman, *Ghastly Beyond Belief* (1985).

Bing CROSBY

American singer and actor (1903–77)

2 Once or twice I've been described as a light comedian. I consider this the most accurate description of my abilities I've ever seen.

REMARK quoted in J.R. Colombo, *Wit and Wisdom of the Moviemakers* (1979).

The CROWD

US 1928; screenwriter/director: King Vidor.

3 Marriage isn't a word … it's a sentence!

SCREEN TITLE.

Tom CRUISE

American actor (1962–)

4 A lot of the time, what acting is really about is meeting someone's eye.

INTERVIEWED in *The Guardian* (28 February 1989).

5 [on her divorce from him] At least I can wear high heels now.

COMMENT by Nicole Kidman. Quoted in *The Independent* (11 August 2001).

The CRYING GAME

UK 1992; screenwriter/director: Neil Jordan; cast: Chris Rea (Fergus), Forest Whitaker (Jody), Jaye Davidson (Dil).

6 *Fergus (reporting what the scorpion said to the frog in story)*: I can't help it. It's in my nature.

SOUNDTRACK. He has been told it earlier by Jody. He is now explaining why he is doing time for Dil. The Orson Welles film *Mr Arkadin* (1962) was based on his own novel (1956). Early on in it, the eponymous character holds a party in his castle and tells a fable: 'A scorpion, who could not swim, begged a frog to carry him to the other side. The frog complained that the scorpion would sting him. This was impossible, said the scorpion, because he would then drown with the frog. So the pair set forth. Halfway over, the scorpion stung the frog. Is that logical?" asked the frog. "No, it's not," answered the scorpion, as they both sunk to the bottom, "but I can't help it, it's my nature."' Recalled in Frank Brady, *Citizen Welles* (1989).

Billy CRYSTAL

American actor and comic (1947–)

1 [when yet another Oscar went to the British-made film *The English Patient*] Aside from wheat and auto parts, America's biggest export is now the Oscar.

REMARK as MC of Academy Awards ceremony (March 1997).

Jamie Lee CURTIS

American actress (1958–)

2 I don't want to become a caricature of myself in my fifties. The problem with being in the movies is that it's all about how you look.

QUOTED in *The Independent* (6 August 1984).

Richard CURTIS

English screenwriter (1956–)

3 Whatever your script is like, no matter how much stewing and rewriting – if the punters don't want to sleep with the star, you may never be asked to write another one.

EXTRACTED from introduction to published script of *Four Weddings and a Funeral* (1994).

Tony CURTIS

American actor (1925–)

4 Hollywood ... the most sensational merry-go-round ever built.

QUOTED in J.R. Colombo, *Wit and Wisdom of the Moviemakers* (1979).

5 I don't act on the screen. I *be* on the screen.

QUOTED in *The Observer*, 'Sayings of the Week' (28 May 1995).

Michael CURTIZ

Hungarian-born director (1888–1962)

6 [during filming of *The Charge of the Light Brigade* (US 1936), Curtiz ordered the release of a hundred riderless steeds by shouting] Bring on the empty horses!

QUOTED in David Niven, *Bring On the Empty Horses*, 'Errol' (1975) – hence Niven's title.

1 [following the above utterance, Niven and Errol Flynn promptly fell about with laughter; Curtiz rounded on them and said] You and your stinking language … you think I know fuck nothing … well, let me tell you – I know FUCK *ALL*!

QUOTED in Niven's book. It is not clear how original this remark is. 'You think I know damn nothing – I tell you I know damn all' is said to have appeared as caption to a *Punch* cartoon at some time between 1900 and 1933.

Serge DANEY

French critic (1944–92)

1 If you can't *believe* a little in what you see on the screen, it's not worth wasting your time on cinema.

QUOTED in *Sight and Sound* (July 1992).

DANIEL AND THE DEVIL See *ALL THAT MONEY CAN BUY.*

The DARK CORNER

US 1946; screenwriters: Jay Dratler and others; cast: Clifton Webb (Hardy Cathcart).

2 *Hardy*: How I detest the dawn. The grass always looks like it's been left out all night.

SOUNDTRACK.

DARLING

UK 1965; screenwriter: Frederic Raphael; cast: Dirk Bogarde (Robert Gold), Julie Christie (Diana Scott).

3 *Robert (to Diana)*: Your idea of fidelity is not having more than one man in the bed at the same time … You're a whore, baby, that's all, just a whore, and I don't take whores in taxis.

SOUNDTRACK.

DAVID COPPERFIELD

US 1935; screenwriters: Howard Easterbrook, Hugh Walpole (after Charles Dickens novel); cast: W.C. Fields (Mr Micawber).

4 *Micawber*: Young friend, I counsel you. Annual income twenty pounds, annual expenditure nineteen pounds, result – happiness. Annual income twenty pounds, annual expenditure twenty-one pounds, result – misery. That advice is so far worth taking, I have never taken it myself and am the miserable creature you behold.

SOUNDTRACK. More or less as in the novel, though the sentences have been rearranged.

Terence DAVIES

English director (1945–)

1 The great thing in life is to be very beautiful and very stupid.

QUOTED in *The Observer*, 'Sayings of the Week' (17 May 1992).

Bette DAVIS

American actress (1908–89)

2 Valentino silently acted out the fantasies of women all over the world. Valentino and his world were a dream. A whole generation of females wanted to ride off into a sandy paradise with him. At thirteen I had been such a female.

EXTRACTED from her book *The Lonely Life* (1962).

3 If Hollywood didn't work out I was prepared to be the best secretary in the world.

EXTRACTED from the same book.

4 [on a starlet] I see – she's the original good time that was had by all.

QUOTED in Leslie Halliwell, *The Filmgoer's Book of Quotes* (1973). In the form, 'There, standing at the piano, was the original good time who had been had by all', it has also been attributed to Kenneth Tynan at an Oxford Union debate in the late 1940s.

5 MOTHER OF THREE – 10, 11 & 15 – DIVORCÉE. AMERICAN. THIRTY YEARS EXPERIENCE AS AN ACTRESS IN MOTION PICTURES. MOBILE STILL AND MORE AFFABLE THAN RUMOR WOULD HAVE IT. WANTS STEADY EMPLOYMENT IN HOLLYWOOD. (HAS HAD BROADWAY). REFERENCES UPON REQUEST.

ADVERTISEMENT placed by Davis in 'Situation Wanted, Women – Artists' column of the *Hollywood Reporter* and other trade papers (1962).

6 I was never beautiful like Miss Hayworth or Miss Lamarr. I was known as the little brown wren. Who'd want to get me at the end of the picture?

INTERVIEWED in *Films Illustrated* (December 1979).

7 I think that people need something to look up to, and Hollywood was the only Royalty that America ever had.

QUOTED by Katharine Whitehorn in *The Observer* (20 September 1987).

8 I was the only star they allowed to come out of the water looking wet.

ATTRIBUTED remark.

1 The kid may be all right for certain roles, but what audience would ever believe that the hero would want to get *her* at the fade-out?

COMMENT by anonymous in studio report, quoted by Davis in *The Lonely Life* (1962).

2 She would probably have been burned as a witch if she had lived two or three hundred years ago. She gives the curious feeling of being charged with power which can find no ordinary outlet.

COMMENT by E. Arnot Robertson in 1935.

3 Bette Davis is my bloody idol. I admire her more than any film star.

COMMENT by George C. Scott in *Playboy* (December 1980).

See also ***GONE WITH THE WIND*** 195:6.

Sammy DAVIS Jr

American entertainer (1925–90)

4 Being a star has made it possible for me to get insulted in places where the average Negro could never hope to get insulted.

ATTRIBUTED remark.

Doris DAY

American singer and actress (1924–)

5 The really frightening thing about middle age is the knowledge that you'll grow out of it.

QUOTED in A.E. Hotchner, *Doris Day* (1978).

6 *Romance on the High Seas* was Doris Day's first picture; that was before she became a virgin.

COMMENT by Oscar Levant in *Memoirs of an Amnesiac* (1965).

7 I've been around so long, I knew Doris Day before she was a virgin.

COMMENT by Groucho Marx, quoted in Leslie Halliwell, *The Filmgoer's Book of Quotes* (1973).

8 Doris Day is as wholesome as a bowl of cornflakes and at least as sexy.

COMMENT by Dwight Macdonald, American writer and critic (1906–82), quoted in J.R. Colombo, *Wit and Wisdom of the Moviemakers* (1979).

9 She thinks she doesn't get old. She told me once it was her cameraman who was getting older. She was going to fire him.

COMMENT by Joe Pasternak. *Compare* Hal **MOHR** 288:6.

A DAY AT THE RACES

US 1937; screenwriters: Robert Pirosh, George Seaton, George Oppenheimer; cast: Groucho Marx (Dr Hackenbush), Chico Marx (Tony), Harpo Marx (Stuffy), Allan Jones (Gil), Esther Muir (Flo); Margaret Dumont (Mrs Emily Upjohn), Sig Rumann (Dr Steinberg).

1 *Hackenbush (on his medical training)*: Oh, well, to begin with I took four years at Vassar.
Mrs Upjohn: Vassar? But that's a girls' college.
Hackenbush: I found that out the third year. I'd've been there yet, but I went out with the swimming team.

SOUNDTRACK.

2 *Tony*: One dollar and you remember me all your life.
Hackenbush: That's the most nauseating proposition I ever had.

SOUNDTRACK.

3 *Hackenbush*: Have the florist send some roses to Mrs Upjohn and write 'Emily I love you' on the back of the bill.

SOUNDTRACK. *Compare* ***TROUBLE IN PARADISE*** 430:4.

4 *Hackenbush (taking Stuffy's pulse)*: Either he's dead or my watch has stopped.

SOUNDTRACK.

5 *Flo*: I've never been so insulted in my life.
Hackenbush: Well, it's early yet.

SOUNDTRACK.

6 *Tony (disguised as hotel detective)*: Have you got a woman in here?
Hackenbush: If I haven't, I've wasted thirty minutes of valuable time.

SOUNDTRACK.

7 *Flo*: Oh, hold me closer! Closer! Closer!
Hackenbush: If I hold you any closer, I'll be in back of you!

SOUNDTRACK.

8 *Hackenbush (to Mrs Upjohn)*: It's the old, old story. Boy meets girl – Romeo and Juliet – Minneapolis and St Paul!

SOUNDTRACK.

9 *Gil*: Are you a man or a mouse?
Hackenbush: You put a piece of cheese down there and you'll find out.

SOUNDTRACK.

1 *Hackenbush (to Steinberg)*: And don't point that beard at me – it might go off!

SOUNDTRACK.

2 *Hackenbush (to Mrs Upjohn)*: Emily, I have a little confession to make. I really am a horse doctor. But marry me and I'll never look at any other horse.

SOUNDTRACK. Last lines of film.

DAY FOR NIGHT [LA NUIT AMÉRICAINE]

France/Italy 1973; screenwriters: François Truffaut and others; cast: François Truffaut (Ferrand), Jean-Pierre Léaud (Alphonse).

3 Day for Night [*La Nuit Américaine*].

TITLE OF FILM. 'Day for night' is a film-maker's term for shooting a scene during the day and then tinting it dark to make it look like night. Hence, the English title given to Truffaut's film about film-making whose original title *La Nuit Américaine* ('American night'), is the French equivalent.

4 *Ferrand*: *La cinéma règne.* [Cinema is king!]

SOUNDTRACK.

5 *Ferrand (film director, to Alphonse, actor with personal problems)*: Films are smoother than life. They don't just grind to a halt. They glide on, like trains in the night. For people like you and me, our happiness lies in the cinema.

SUB-TITLE translation.

C(ecil) DAY-LEWIS

Anglo-Irish poet and critic (1904–72)

6 Enter the dream-house, brothers and sisters, leaving
Your debts asleep, your history at the door:
This is the home for heroes, and this loving
Darkness a fur you can afford.

EXTRACTED from poem 'Newsreel'.

Daniel DAY-LEWIS

Anglo-Irish actor (1957–)

7 Being at the centre of a film is a burden one takes on with innocence – the first time. Thereafter, you take it on with trepidation.

INTERVIEWED in *City Limits* (7 April 1988).

1 This has provided me with the makings of one hell of a weekend in Dublin.

SPEECH accepting Oscar for *My Left Foot,* quoted in *Today* (28 March 1990).

2 I hardly ever work. I have an inverse theory that you get worse at acting the more you do it.

QUOTED in *The Observer*, 'Soundbites' (9 February 1997).

3 Daniel Day Lewis has what every actor in Hollywood wants: talent. And what every actor in England wants: looks.

COMMENT by (Sir) John Gielgud, quoted in *The Independent* (13 May 1995).

Olivia DE HAVILLAND

British-born actress (1916–)

4 The one thing that you simply have to remember all the time that you are here is that Hollywood is an Oriental city. As long as you do that you might survive. If you try to equate it with anything else you'll perish.

QUOTED in Dirk Bogarde, *Snakes and Ladders* (1978).

Cecil B. DeMILLE

American director (1881–1959)

5 [of a script] What I have crossed out I didn't like. What I haven't crossed out I'm dissatisfied with.

QUOTED in Leslie Halliwell, *Filmgoer's Book of Quotes* (1973).

6 [to Adolph Zukor, who had protested at the escalating costs of *The Ten Commandments*] What do you want me to do? Stop shooting now and release it as *The Five Commandments*?

QUOTED in Mervyn LeRoy, *Take One* (1974).

7 The trouble with Cecil is that he always bites off more than he can chew – and then chews it.

COMMENT by William DeMille (1878–1955), brother of Cecil, quoted in Leslie Halliwell, *The Filmgoer's Book of Quotes* (1973).

8 DeMille made small-minded pictures on a big scale.

COMMENT by Pauline Kael in *Kiss Kiss Bang Bang*, 'Epics' (1968).

Robert DE NIRO

American actor (1943–)

9 [Being] a Hollywood star is death as far as acting is concerned. I don't want people to recognize me in the streets. I don't want to do what real stars have to do – repeat themselves in film after film, always being themselves.

INTERVIEWED in *Screen International* (May 1976).

1 As a screen presence, he's as threatening and ungraspable as a sweet-faced madman who pours a torrent of talk over you on the subway, trapped in the tunnel between Bellevue and Groucho.

COMMENT by David Thomson in *A Biographical Dictionary of Film* (1994 edn).

Brian DE PALMA

American director (1940–)

2 Any movie that makes you a little uncomfortable is good news to me, because it means you're experiencing things that you are not familiar with.

INTERVIEWED in *Sight and Sound* (December 1992).

Vittorio DE SICA

Italian actor and director (1901–74)

3 A fine actor, a polished hack, and a flabby whore – not necessarily in that order.

COMMENT by Stanley Kauffman.

DEAD MEN DON'T WEAR PLAID

US 1982; screenwriters: Carl Reiner (director), George Gipe, Steve Martin; cast: Rachel Ward (Juliet Forrest), Steve Martin (Rigby Reardon).

4 *Juliet (to Rigby)*: If you need me, just call. You know how to call, don't you? You just put your finger in the hole and make tiny little circles.

SOUNDTRACK. *Compare* ***TO HAVE AND HAVE NOT*** 426:5.

James DEAN

American actor (1931–55)

5 Mr Dean appears to be wearing my last year's wardrobe and using my last year's talent ...

COMMENT by Marlon Brando, quoted in *James Dean in His Own Words*, ed. Mick St Michael (1989).

6 [Dean enshrined] the glamour of delinquency ... When the delinquent becomes the hero in our films, it is because the image of instinctive rebellion expresses something in many people that they don't dare express.

COMMENT by Pauline Kael in *I Lost It At the Movies* (1964).

1 The main thing you felt about him is hurt. And the main thing the girls felt and the boys felt and the faggots felt about him was that you'd want to put your arm around him and protect him and look after him ... Don't cry kid, I'm on your side.

COMMENT by Elia Kazan, quoted in Peter Lewis, *The Fifties* (1978).

DEATH OF A SALESMAN

US 1951; screenwriter: Stanley Roberts (from play by Arthur Miller); cast: Royal Beal (Ben), Fredric March (Willy Loman), Mildred Dunnock (Linda Loman).

2 *Ben*: A salesman's gotta dream, boy. It comes with the territory.

SOUNDTRACK.

3 *Linda Loman*: Attention must finally be paid to such a man. He's not to be allowed to fall into his grave like an old dog.

SOUNDTRACK.

4 *Willy Loman*: A salesman is someone way up there in the blue, riding on a smile and a shoeshine.

SOUNDTRACK.

DEATH ON THE NILE

UK 1978; screenwriter: Anthony Shaffer (based on Agatha Christie novel); cast: Peter Ustinov (Hercule Poirot), David Niven (Colonel Race).

5 *Poirot*: I was thinking of Molière – '*La grande ambition des femmes est d'inspirer l'amour*'.
Race: I do wish you'd speak some known language.
Poirot: 'The great ambition of women is to inspire love.'

SOUNDTRACK.

Shelagh DELANEY

English playwright and screenwriter (1939–)

6 *Jo*: You never go to the pictures.
Helen: I used to but the cinema has become more and more like the theatre, it's all mauling and muttering, can't hear what they're saying half the time and when you do it's not worth listening to.

EXTRACTED from her play *A Taste of Honey*, Act 1 Sc. 2 (1958).

Bernard DELFONT (Lord Delfont)

Russian-born British producer (1910–94)

1 I do allow four-letter words and nudity in my films, if they are in the right context, if it has integrity.

QUOTED in Hunter Davies, *The Grades* (1981).

DELIVERANCE

US 1972; screenwriter: James Dickey (from his novel); cast: Burt Reynolds (Lewis).

2 *Lewis (on shooting rapids)*: Oh, it's the best … well, the second best sensation I've ever known.

SOUNDTRACK.

(Dame) Judi DENCH

English actress (1934–)

3 I'm squeamish about seeing myself on screen. I don't like it.

QUOTED in *The Observer*, 'Soundbites' (4 January 1998).

Catherine DENEUVE

French actress (1943–)

4 She is the man I would have liked to be.

COMMENT by Gérard Depardieu.

Gérard DEPARDIEU

French actor (1948–)

5 Cinema is there for eternity and that's incredible.

QUOTED in *Time* Magazine (6 February 1984).

6 I sometimes think I shall never view
A French film lacking Gérard Depardieu.

COMMENT by John Updike.

Bo DEREK

American actress (1957–)

7 I guess a film in which I didn't end up in bed, in the sea, or in a hot tub, would have the same appeal as a Clint Eastwood movie in which nobody got shot.

QUOTED in *The Independent* (25 March 1995).

DESPERATE JOURNEY

US 1942; screenwriter: Arthur T. Horman; cast: Errol Flynn (Flight Lieut. Terence Forbes).

1 *Forbes*: Now for Australia and a crack at those Japs!

SOUNDTRACK. Last words of film.

DESTRY RIDES AGAIN

US 1939; screenwriters: Felix Jackson, Gertrude Purcell, Henry Myers (from Max Brand novel); music/lyrics: Frank Loesser/Frederick Hollander; cast: Marlene Dietrich (Frenchy), James Stewart (Thomas Jefferson Destry Jr).

2 There's gold in them thar hills.

APOCRYPHAL LINE. Although Dietrich was allowed by the Hays Office to drop coins down her cleavage, this accompanying line was cut.

3 *Frenchy (of saloon customers and her singing)*: The longer they wait, the better they like it.

SOUNDTRACK.

4 *Destry (on trial of kid who killed his parents)*: And the kid said [to the judge], 'Well, I just hope that your honor has some regard for the feelin's of a poor orphan.'

SOUNDTRACK. The classic definition of *chutzpah*.

5 *Frenchy (singing)*: See what the boys in the backroom will have. And tell them I'm having the same.

SOUNDTRACK.

6 Dietrich singing the Boys in the Backroom is a greater work of art than the Mona Lisa.

COMMENT by Max Aitken (Lord Beaverbrook), quoted in A.J.P. Taylor, *Beaverbrook* (1972).

Adolph DEUTSCH

American composer (1897–1980)

7 A film musician is like a mortician – he can't bring the body back to life, but he's expected to make it look better.

QUOTED in Tony Thomas, *Music for the Movies* (1973).

The DEVIL AND DANIEL WEBSTER *See* ***ALL THAT MONEY CAN BUY***.

DEVOTION

US 1946; screenwriter: Keith Winter; cast: Sydney Greenstreet (William Thackeray), Uncredited actor (Charles Dickens).

1 *Dickens*: Morning, Thackeray.
Thackeray: Morning, Dickens.
SOUNDTRACK.

I.A.L. DIAMOND

Romanian-born American screenwriter (1915–88)

2 [of the screenwriter] If Ernest Lehman had written *The Sound of Music* a little dirtier and if he had written *Who's Afraid of Virginia Woolf?* a little cleaner, he would not have the money he has today.
COMMENT attributed by Denis Norden on BBC Radio *Quote ... Unquote* (13 September 1999).

DIAMONDS ARE FOREVER

UK 1971; screenwriter: Richard Maibaum, Tom Mankiewicz (after Ian Fleming novel); cast: Sean Connery (James Bond), Jill St John (Tiffany Case), Charles Gray (Victor Blofeld), Lana Wood (Plenty O'Toole), Putter Smith (Mr Kidd), Bruce Glover (Mr Wint).

3 *Mr Kidd (having just exploded a helicopter)*: If God had intended man to fly ...
Mr Wint: ... Would have given him wings, Mr Kidd.
SOUNDTRACK.

4 *Tiffany*: I'll finish dressing.
Bond: Oh, please, don't. Not on my account.
SOUNDTRACK.

5 *Plenty*: Hi, I'm Plenty.
Bond: Of course you are.
Plenty: Plenty O'Toole.
Bond: Named after your father, perhaps?
SOUNDTRACK.

DICK TRACY

US 1990; screenwriters: Jim Cash, Jack Epps Jr (from strip cartoons); cast: Warren Beatty (Dick Tracy), Glenne Headly (Tess Trueheart), Al Pacino (Big Boy Caprice), Madonna (Breathless Mahoney), Charlie Korsmo (Kid).

6 *Tracy (into wrist radio)*: I'm on my way.
SOUNDTRACK. Stock phrase.

1 *Tracy (to Truehart)*: Tess, there's about as much chance of me getting behind a desk as there is of me getting a new girlfriend.

SOUNDTRACK.

2 *Caprice*: 'All's fair in love and business' – Benjamin Franklin.

SOUNDTRACK. Caprice is always quoting people throughout the film. This may be one of his more accurate attributions, though Franklin originated very few of the proverbs he published.

3 *Caprice*: Around me, if a woman don't wear mink, she don't wear nothing.
Mahoney: Well, I look good both ways.

SOUNDTRACK.

4 *Mahoney (when asked if she is grieving for her recently rubbed-out boyfriend)*: I'm wearing black underwear.

SOUNDTRACK.

5 *Tracy*: You know it's legal for me to take you down to the station, and sweat it out of you under the lights.
Mahoney: I sweat a lot better in the dark.

SOUNDTRACK.

6 *Mahoney (to Tracy)*: I know how you feel. You don't know if you want to hit me or kiss me. I get a lot of that.

SOUNDTRACK.

7 *Caprice (to Tracy)*: You mind if I call you Dick?

SOUNDTRACK.

8 *Caprice (exhorting henchmen to kill Tracy)*: What's the matter?
You bums forgot how to kill people? Doesn't your work mean anything
to you any more? Have you no sense of pride in what you do?
No sense of duty? No sense of destiny? I'm looking for generals.
What do I get? Foot soldiers.

SOUNDTRACK.

9 *Caprice*: I'm having a thought! ... It's coming! It's gone!

SOUNDTRACK.

10 *Kid (about Trueheart)*: You know something, Tracy, I kind of like that dame.

SOUNDTRACK. Last words of film.

DIE HARD

US 1988; screenwriters: Jeb Stuart, Steven E. de Souza; cast: Bruce Willis (John McClane), Alan Rickman (Hans Gruber).

1 *McClane*: If this is their idea of Christmas, I gotta be here for New Year's.

SOUNDTRACK.

Marlene DIETRICH

German-born actress and singer (1901–92)

2 The relationship between the make-up man and the film actor is one of accomplices in crime.

ATTRIBUTED remark.

3 She has sex, but no particular gender, her masculinity appeals to women, and her sexuality to men.

COMMENT by Kenneth Tynan in *Sight and Sound* (April 1954), quoting an earlier remark of his.

4 Age does not wither her, nor custom stale her infinite sameness.

COMMENT by David Shipman in *The Great Movie Stars*, Vol. 1 (1970).

See also ***DESTRY RIDES AGAIN*** 132:6.

Howard DIETZ

American studio executive and lyricist (1896–1983)

5 Leo the Lion, with the Latin *Ars Gratia Artis* (Art for Art's Sake) decorating his proud dome, was my idea.

EXTRACTED from his book *Dancing in the Dark* (1974). On the famous trademark and motto of the Metro-Goldwyn-Mayer company, which he devised in about 1916. Dietz, director of publicity and advertising with the original Goldwyn Pictures company, had left Columbia University not long before. He based his idea on the university's lion and added the Latin words underneath. The trademark and motto were carried over when Samuel Goldwyn retired to make way for the merger of Metropolitan with the interests of Louis B. Mayer. 'Goldwyn Pictures Griddle The Earth' is the no doubt apocryphal slogan said to have been suggested by Samuel Goldwyn himself.

6 Goldwyn had formed a partnership with Selwyn. When Goldwyn changed his name, he took the first syllable of his 'Goldfish' and the second syllable of 'Selwyn' to make Goldwyn. Had he taken the first syllable of 'Selwyn' and the second of 'Goldfish', he would have had Selfish.

EXTRACTED from the same book.

1 Tallulah [Bankhead] could wear one out. I said, 'A day away from Tallulah is like a month in the country.'

EXTRACTED from the same book. Quoted, as by Anon., in *Show Business Illustrated* (17 October 1961).

DINNER AT EIGHT

US 1933; screenwriters: Frances Marion, Herman J. Mankiewicz; cast: Jean Harlow (Kitty Packard), Wallace Beery (Dan Packard), Marie Dressler (Carlotta Vance); Louise Closser Hale (Woman).

2 *Woman*: Ed hates anything that keeps him from going to the movies every night. I guess I'm what you call a Garbo widow.

SOUNDTRACK.

3 *Kitty (to husband Dan)*: Politics? You couldn't get into politics. You couldn't get in anywhere. You couldn't get into the men's room at the Astor.

SOUNDTRACK.

4 *Kitty*: You know, I was reading a book the other day.
Carlotta: Reading a book!
Kitty: Yes. It's all about civilization or something – a nutty kind of book. Do you know that the guy said that machinery is going to take the place of every profession?
Carlotta: Oh my dear, that's something you need never worry about.

SOUNDTRACK.

DIRTY HARRY

US 1971; screenwriters: Harry Julian Fink and others; cast: Clint Eastwood (Harry Callahan).

5 *Callahan (holding .44 magnum to bank robber's temples)*: I know what you're thinking. Did he fire six shots or only five? Well, to tell you the truth, in all this excitement, I've kind of lost track myself. But being as this is a .44 Magnum, the most powerful handgun in the world, and would blow your head clean off, you've got to ask yourself one question: 'Do I feel lucky?' Well, do ya, punk?

SOUNDTRACK.

Walt DISNEY

American animator and studio executive (1901–66)

1 [to his animators after the Second World War, heralding a move to cheap compilations] We're through with caviar … from now on it's mashed potato and gravy!

QUOTED in Brian Sibley & Richard Holliss, *The Disney Studio Story* (1988).

2 Having adapted Beethoven's Sixth Symphony for *Fantasia*, Walt Disney commented: 'Gee! This'll make Beethoven.'

QUOTED in Marshall McLuhan, *Culture Is Our Business* (1970).

3 Girls bored me – they still do. I love Mickey Mouse more than any woman I've ever known.

QUOTED in Walter Wagner, *You Must Remember This* (1975).

4 [on Ray Bradbury's suggestion that he run for Mayor of Los Angeles] Why should I run for Mayor when I'm already King?

QUOTED in *The Listener* (7 October 1982).

5 [to wife during his last illness] Fancy being remembered around the world for the invention of a mouse!

QUOTED in Leonard Mosley, *Disney's World* (1985).

6 I do not know whether he [Disney] draws a line himself. I hear that at his studio he employs hundreds of artists to do the work. But I assume his is the direction, the constant aiming after improvement in the new expression … it is the direction of a real artist. It makes Disney, not as a draughtsman but as an artist who uses his brains, the most significant figure in graphic art since Leonardo.

COMMENT by (Sir) David Low, New Zealand-born cartoonist (1891–63), quoted in Richard Schickel, *The Disney Version*, Chap. 20 (1986).

DIVA

France 1982; screenwriters: Jean-Jacques Beineix, Jean Van Hamme (from a novel); cast: Wilhelmenia Wiggins Fernandez (Cynthia Hawkins).

7 *Cynthia (on the name 'Jules')*: It suits you so badly, that it suits you very well.

SUB-TITLE translation.

8 *Cynthia (on not recording her music)*: Music. It comes and goes. Don't try to keep it.

SOUNDTRACK. Spoken in English.

DOCTOR DOLITTLE

US 1967; screenwriter/songwriter: Leslie Bricusse (after Hugh Lofting novels); cast: Rex Harrison (Dr Dolittle), Richard Attenborough (Albert Blossom).

1 *Blossom*: I've never seen anything like it in my life!

SOUNDTRACK. Blossom, a circus owner, has been given a pushmi-pullyu (a two-headed llama) by a well-meaning friend. This exclamation is incorporated in a song.

DR NO

UK 1962; screenwriters: Richard Maibaum, Johanna Harwood, Berkley Mather (from Ian Fleming novel); cast: Sean Connery (James Bond), Joseph Wiseman (Dr No), Lois Maxwell (Miss Moneypenny), Bernard Lee (M), Ursula Andress (Honeychile Rider), Eunice Gayson (Sylvia Trench), Anthony Dawson (Professor Dent).

2 *Bond*: Bond – James Bond.

SOUNDTRACK. Introducing himself to fellow gambler Sylvia Trench.

3 *Bond*: Moneypenny? What gives?
Moneypenny: Me – given an ounce of encouragement.

SOUNDTRACK.

4 *M*: When do you sleep, 007?
Bond: Never on the Crown's time, sir.

SOUNDTRACK.

5 *M*: If you carry a double-0 number, it means you're licensed to kill, not get killed.

SOUNDTRACK.

6 *Servant*: One medium dry vodka Martini – mixed like you said, sir, and not stirred.

SOUNDTRACK. First reference in a Bond film to his peculiar requirement. Dr No also mentions the fad – see below 139:3, though the words are not spoken by Bond himself. In the third film, ***GOLDFINGER*** 188:9, Bond does get to say 'a Martini, shaken not stirred' – he needs a drink after just escaping a laser death-ray – and there are also references to the fad in *You Only Live Twice* (1967) and *On Her Majesty's Secret Service* (1969), among others.

This example of would-be sophistication became a running-joke in the early Bond films. However, the *idea* stems from the very first book in the series, *Casino Royale* (1953), in which Bond orders a cocktail of his own devising. It consists of one dry Martini 'in a deep champagne goblet', three measures of Gordon's gin, one of vodka – 'made with grain instead of potatoes' – and half a measure of Kina Lillet. 'Shake it very well until it's ice-cold.' Bond justifies this fussiness a page or two later: 'I take a ridiculous pleasure in what I eat and drink. It comes partly from being a bachelor, but mostly from a habit of taking a lot of trouble over details. It's very pernickety and old-maidish really, but when I'm working I generally have to eat all my meals alone and it makes them more interesting when one takes trouble.'

The phrase was taken up in all the numerous parodies of the Bond phenomenon on film, TV and radio, though – curiously enough – it may be a piece of absolute nonsense. According to one expert, shaking a dry Martini 'turns it from something crystal-clear into a dreary frosted drink. It should be stirred quickly with ice in a jug.'

The *Oxford Dictionary of Modern Quotations* (1991) claimed to have discovered the source of the catchphrase actually in one of Fleming's novels – *Dr No* (1958) ('Bond said ... Martini – with a slice of lemon peel. Shaken and not stirred, please'), and this was taken up by *Bartlett's Familiar Quotations* (1992). But the catchphrase appears in the novels earlier than that: 'The waiter brought the Martinis, shaken and not stirred, as Bond had stipulated' (*Diamonds are Forever*, 1956).

1 *Bond (to Dent, who has just tried to shoot him with empty pistol)*: That's a Smith and Wesson, and you've had your six.

SOUNDTRACK.

2 *Bond (to Honeychile, in spectacular white bikini)*: I can assure you my intentions are strictly honourable.

SOUNDTRACK.

3 *Dr No (handing Bond a drink)*: A medium dry Martini, lemon peel, shaken not stirred.
Bond: Vodka?
Dr No: Of course.

SOUNDTRACK.

4 *Dr No (when Bond grabs bottle as weapon)*: That's a Dom Perignon '55. It would be a pity to break it.
Bond: I prefer the '53 myself.

SOUNDTRACK.

5 *Bond (to Dr No)*: Tell me, does the toppling of American missiles really compensate for having no hands?

SOUNDTRACK.

6 *Dr No*: I'm a member of SPECTRE ... Special Executive for Counterintelligence, Terrorism, Revenge, Extortion. The four great cornerstones of power, headed by the greatest brains in the world.

SOUNDTRACK.

7 *Bond*: World domination! Same old dream. Our asylums are full of people who think they're Napoleon or God.

SOUNDTRACK.

8 *Dr No (to Bond)*: Unfortunately, I misjudged you. You are just a stupid policeman whose luck has run out.

SOUNDTRACK.

1 *Dr No*: I never fail, Mr Bond.
SOUNDTRACK.

DR STRANGELOVE: OR HOW I LEARNED TO STOP WORRYING AND LOVE THE BOMB

US 1963; screenwriters: Stanley Kubrick (director), Terry Southern, Peter George; cast: Peter Sellers (Dr Strangelove/Mandrake/President Muffley), George C. Scott (Gen. 'Buck' Turgidson), Sterling Hayden (Gen. Jack D. Ripper).

2 *Ripper*: I can no longer sit back and allow Communist infiltration, Communist indoctrination, Communist subversion, and the international Communist conspiracy to sap and impurify all of our precious bodily fluids.
SOUNDTRACK.

3 *Turgidson*: Mr President, I'm not saying we wouldn't get our hair mussed. But I do say no more than ten to twenty million people killed, tops, depending on the breaks.
SOUNDTRACK.

4 *President Muffley*: Gentlemen, you can't fight in here. This is the war room!
SOUNDTRACK.

5 *Strangelove (rising from his wheelchair as the world is about to be destroyed)*: *Mein Führer!* I can walk!
SOUNDTRACK.

DR ZHIVAGO

UK 1965; screenwriter: Robert Bolt (from Boris Pasternak novel); cast: Rod Steiger (Victor Komarovsky), Julie Christie (Lara), Omar Sharif (Yuri), Tom Courtenay (Pasha).

6 *Victor (to Lara, before he rapes her)*: There are two kinds of men, and only two. And that young man is one kind. He is high-minded. He is pure. He is the kind of man that the world pretends to look up to, and, in fact, despises … There is another kind. Not high-minded. Not pure, but alive.
SOUNDTRACK.

7 *Yuri (to Pasha)*: I hate everything you say, but not enough to kill you for it.
SOUNDTRACK.

DOG DAY AFTERNOON

US 1975; screenwriter: Frank Pierson; cast: Al Pacino (Sonny).

1 *Sonny (leading crowd chant against police)*: Attica! Attica!

SOUNDTRACK.

La DOLCE VITA

Italy/France 1960; screenwriter: Federico Fellini (director) and others; cast: Marcello Mastroianni (Marcello Rubini), Anita Ekberg (Sylvia Rank), Alain Cuny (Steiner), Walter Santesso (Paparazzo).

2 La Dolce Vita.

TITLE OF FILM – meaning 'The Sweet Life'. The title of Fellini's film passed into the English language as a phrase suggesting a high-society life of luxury, pleasure and self-indulgence – a precursor of the Swinging Sixties. It is not clear how much of a set phrase it was in Italian before it was taken up by everyone else. Compare the long-established Italian phrase *dolce far niente* [sweet idleness].

3 *Sylvia (film-star running up staircase in Vatican, disguised as a priest)*: This is the right way to lose weight. I must remember to tell Marilyn.

SOUNDTRACK.

4 *Marcello (to Sylvia, as they dance together)*: You are the first woman on the first day of creation. You are mother, sister, lover, friend, angel, devil, earth, home.

SUB-TITLE in translation.

5 *Marcello*: Leave her alone, Paparazzo.
Paparazzo: It's a great picture, Marcello!

SUB-TITLE in translation. The sensation-seeking photographer called Paparazzo in this movie soon had his name applied to all such photographers who snatch photographs of celebrities. The collective name *paparazzi* is similar to *papagalli*, the word for 'parrots' – who also hang around in trees making a racket. Whether Fellini really took this name from a character in George Gissing's travel book *By the Ionian Sea* (1900), as has been suggested, is not confirmed.

6 *Steiner (to Marcello)*: Don't be like me. Salvation doesn't lie within four walls. I'm too serious to be a dilettante and too much of a dabbler to be a professional. Even the most miserable life is better than a sheltered existence in an organized society where everything is calculated and perfected.

SUB-TITLE in translation.

7 *Transvestite (at final party)*: By 1965, there'll be total depravity. How squalid everything will be.

SUB-TITLE in translation.

Robert DONAT

English actor (1905–58)

1 A half-Greek god who has winged his way from Olympus.

COMMENT by anonymous critic in the 1930s. Donat's response was to sigh, 'Actually, I'm a half-Pole who's winged his way from Withington, Manchester.' Quoted in Emlyn Williams in *George* (1973).

A DOUBLE LIFE

US 1947; screenwriters: Ruth Gordon, Garson Kanin; cast: Ronald Colman (Anthony John), Signe Hasso (Brita).

2 *Anthony John (to Brita)*: Strike me pink!

SOUNDTRACK. An expression of mock surprise.

Bill DOUGLAS

Scottish director (1934–91)

3 For as long as I remember I always liked the pictures … That was my real home, my happiest place when I was lucky enough to be there. Outside, whether in the village or the city, whether I was seven or seventeen, it always seemed to be raining or grey and my heart would sink to despairing depths. I hated reality. Of course I had to go to school – sometimes. And I had to go and apply myself to the things one has to do. But the next picture, how to get in, was the thing that occupied my mind.

QUOTED by Andrew Noble in *Bill Douglas: A Lanternist's Account* (1993).

4 [on scriptwriting] When you write, write only what you see, what you want the audience to see. Nothing more. Every shot is a sentence.

QUOTED in the above book.

5 Never show the audience anything they can imagine better than you can show it.

ATTRIBUTED remark.

Kirk DOUGLAS

American actor (1916–)

6 My children didn't have my advantages: I was born into abject poverty.

REMARK in several interviews, early 1980s. Quoted again in *Sunday Today*, 'Quotes of the Week' (26 April 1987).

1 He's wanted to be Burt Lancaster all his life.

COMMENT by John Frankenheimer.

DRACULA

US 1931; screenwriter: Garrett Fort (based on play by Hamilton Deane and John Balderston and on Bram Stoker novel); cast: Bela Lugosi (Count Dracula).

2 *Dracula*: Ay yam Drak-ku-lah … Ay bid you velcome!

SOUNDTRACK. *Reprised in* ***BRAM STOKER'S DRACULA*** 68:5.

3 *Dracula (on howling wolves)*: Listen to them. Children of the night. What music they make!

SOUNDTRACK.

4 *Dracula*: I never drink …. wine.

SOUNDTRACK. *Reprised in* ***BRAM STOKER'S DRACULA*** 68:4.

5 *Dracula*: To die, to be really dead, that might be glorious.

SOUNDTRACK.

The DRESSER

UK 1983; screenwriter: Ronald Harwood (from his play); cast: Albert Finney (Sir), Tom Courtenay (Norman).

6 *Sir (loudly, to train pulling out of station)*: STOP THAT TRAIN!

SOUNDTRACK. It works.

7 *Sir (after tumultuous and thunderous noises have been produced by backstage staff)*: Where was the storm?

SOUNDTRACK.

Marie DRESSLER

Canadian-born actress (1869–1934)

8 You're only as good as your last picture.

QUOTED in Leslie Halliwell, *The Filmgoer's Book of Quotes* (1973) – suggesting that Dressler was the first to utter this famous maxim. *Compare* Murray **KEMPTON** 238.6.

DRIVING MISS DAISY

US 1989; screenwriter: Alfred Uhry (from his play); cast: Dan Aykroyd (Boolie Werthan), Jessica Tandy (Daisy Werthan), Morgan Freeman (Hoke Colburn), Patti Lupone (Florine Werthan), Ray McKinnon (Trooper No. 1).

1 *Boolie (to Daisy, when she blames her car for an accident)*: Mama, cars don't behave. They are behaved upon.

SOUNDTRACK.

2 *Boolie (to Hoke, about Daisy)*: She's all there. Too much there is the problem.

SOUNDTRACK.

3 *Hoke (to Daisy)*: I just love the smell of a new car. Don't you, Miss Daisy?

SOUNDTRACK.

4 *Hoke (to Boolie, on how long it took Daisy to let him drive her)*: It only took me six days. Same time it took the Lord to make the world.

SOUNDTRACK.

5 *Daisy (to Boolie, on his wife)*: If I had a nose like Florine, I wouldn't go around saying Merry Christmas to anybody.

SOUNDTRACK.

6 *Trooper No. 1*: An old nigger and an old Jew woman taking off down the road together. That is one sorry sight.

SOUNDTRACK.

7 *Daisy (to Hoke)*: You're my best friend.

SOUNDTRACK.

DUCK SOUP

US 1933; screenwriters: Bert Kalmar, Harry Ruby, Arthur Sheekman, Nat Perrin; cast: Groucho Marx (Rufus T. Firefly), Chico Marx (Chicolini), Harpo Marx (Pinkie), Margaret Dumont (Mrs Teasdale), Raquel Torres (Vera Marcal), Louis Calhern (Ambassador Trentino), Zeppo Marx (Minister of Finance Bob Roland), Edwin Maxwell (Minister of War).

8 Duck Soup.

TITLE OF FILM. This is an American phrase meaning 'anything simple or easy, a cinch' or 'a gullible person, easily victimised, a pushover'. Groucho Marx admitted that he did not understand it. Nevertheless, he explained: 'Take two turkeys, one goose, four cabbages, but no duck, and mix them together. After one taste, you'll duck soup for the rest of your life.' The film's director Leo McCarey had earlier made a Laurel and Hardy picture with the same title.

9 *Mrs Teasdale*: As chairwoman of the reception committee, I welcome you with open arms.
Firefly: Is that so? How late do you stay open?

SOUNDTRACK.

1 *Firefly (to Mrs Teasdale)*: Well, that covers a lot of ground. Say, you cover a lot of ground yourself. You better beat it. I hear they're going to tear you down and put up an office building where you're standing. You can leave in a taxi. If you can't leave in a taxi you can leave in a huff. If that's too soon, you can leave in a minute and a huff. You know, you haven't stopped talking since I came here. You must have been vaccinated with a phonograph needle.

SOUNDTRACK.

2 *Mrs Teasdale (of her husband)*: Why, he's dead.
Firefly: I'll bet he's just using that as an excuse.
Mrs Teasdale: I was with him to the very end.
Firefly: No wonder he passed away.
Mrs Teasdale: I held him in my arms and kissed him.
Firefly: So it was murder!

SOUNDTRACK.

3 *Mrs Teasdale (gushingly)*: Oh, your Excellency!
Firefly: You're not so bad yourself.

SOUNDTRACK.

4 *Firefly (to Latin temptress Vera Marcal)*: I could dance with you till the cows come home. On second thoughts, I'd rather dance with the cows and you come home.

SOUNDTRACK.

5 *Firefly (to Minister of Finance)*: Why a four-year-old child could understand this report. Run out and find me a four-year-old child. I can't make head or tail out of it.

SOUNDTRACK.

6 *Minister of War*: Sir, you try my patience!
Firefly: I don't mind if I do. You must come over and try mine sometime.

SOUNDTRACK.

7 *Firefly (to Chicolini)*: I've got a good mind to join a club and beat you over the head with it.

SOUNDTRACK.

8 *Firefly*: What is it that has four pair of pants, lives in Philadelphia, and it never rains but it pours?

SOUNDTRACK.

1 *Firefly (as Pinkie rides off on his motorbike leaving him stationary in the sidecar)*: This is the fifth trip I've made today, and I haven't been anywhere yet.

SOUNDTRACK.

2 *Firefly (to Trentino)*: Go, and never darken my towels again!

SOUNDTRACK.

3 JOIN THE ARMY AND SEE THE NAVY.

SIGN carried by Pinkie.

4 *Firefly*: Remember, you're fighting for this woman's honour ... which is probably more than she ever did.

SOUNDTRACK.

Faye DUNAWAY

American actress (1941–)

5 A star today has to take charge of every aspect of her career. There are no studios left to do it for you.

ATTRIBUTED remark.

John Gregory DUNNE

American screenwriter and novelist (1932–)

6 The truly absorbing aspect of the motion picture ethic, of course, is that it affects not only motion picture people but almost everyone alive in the United States today. By adolescence, children have been programmed with a set of responses and life lessons learned almost totally from motion pictures, television and the recording industry.

ATTRIBUTED remark.

Deanna DURBIN

Canadian singer and actress (1921–)

7 Just as a Hollywood pin-up represents sex to dissatisfied erotics, so I represented the ideal daughter millions of fathers and mothers wished they had.

REMARK quoted in Leslie Halliwell, *The Filmgoer's Book of Quotes* (1973).

8 She is one of those personalities the world will insist on regarding as its private property.

COMMENT by Joe Pasternak.

E.T. THE EXTRA-TERRESTRIAL

US 1982; screenwriter: Melissa Matthison; cast: Henry Thomas (Elliott), Robert MacNaughton (Mike), K.C. Martel (Greg).

1 *Elliott (to Mike)*: How do you explain school to a higher intelligence?

SOUNDTRACK.

2 *E.T. (wanting to contact his home planet)*: E.T. phone home.

SOUNDTRACK. Tearful refrain.

3 *Elliott (to E.T.)*: You must be dead because I don't know how to feel … I'll believe in you all my life … E.T., I love you.

SOUNDTRACK. When E.T. is apparently dead.

4 *Mike*: I've never driven forward before!

SOUNDTRACK. When driving E.T. off in a van that belongs to the scientists. Previously Mike, Elliott's elder brother, has merely reversed the family car down the driveway for his mother.

5 *Greg (on being told that E.T. has to be taken to his spaceship)*: Well, can't he just beam up?
Elliott: This is reality, Greg.

SOUNDTRACK.

6 *E.T. (pointing to his heart, as he is about to leave)*: Ouch.

SOUNDTRACK.

7 *E.T. (touching his head, to Elliott, quoting what Elliott has said to him before)*: I'll be right here.

SOUNDTRACK. Last line of film.

See also Steven **SPIELBERG** 391:7.

EAST OF EDEN

US 1955; screenwriter: Paul Osborn (from John Steinbeck novel); cast: James Dean (Cal Trask), Julie Harris (Abra).

8 *Cal (to Abra)*: I don't have to explain anything to anybody.

SOUNDTRACK.

Clint EASTWOOD

American actor and director (1930–)

1 My old drama coach used to say: 'Don't just do something, stand there.' Gary Cooper wasn't afraid to do nothing.

QUOTED in *Newsweek* (23 September 1985). *Compare* ***ALICE IN WONDERLAND*** 19:2.

2 My involvement goes deeper than acting or directing. I love every aspect of the creation of motion pictures and I guess I'm committed to it for life.

ATTRIBUTED remark.

EASY RIDER

US 1969; screenwriters: Peter Fonda, Dennis Hopper, Terry Southern; cast: Peter Fonda (Wyatt/Captain America), Dennis Hopper (Billy); Jack Nicholson (George Hanson).

3 A man went looking for America and couldn't find it anywhere!

SLOGAN.

4 *George (on his town's dislike of longhaired men)*: Well, they got this here, see, scizzor-happy 'Beautify America' thing going on around here. They're trying to make everybody look like Yul Brynner.

SOUNDTRACK.

5 *George (after taking a drink)*: Nic-nic-nic-f-f-f – Indians!

SOUNDTRACK.

6 *George*: You know, this used to be a hell of a good country. I can't understand what's gone wrong with it.

SOUNDTRACK.

7 *George*: They're not scared of you. They're scared of what you represent to them … What you represent to them is freedom … But talking about it and being it, that's two different things … It's real hard to be free when you are bought and sold in the marketplace … Don't ever tell anybody they're not free, 'cause then they're gonna get real busy killin' and maimin' to prove to you that they are.

SOUNDTRACK.

8 *Wyatt*: You know, Billy, we blew it … We blew it. Goodnight, man.

SOUNDTRACK. Last words before they are killed. Peter Biskind, *Easy Riders, Raging Bulls,* Chap. 2 (1998) comments: 'There was a spirited debate in the press over what Captain America actually meant when he said, "We blew it".'

Biskind also quotes Peter Fonda thinking at that time: 'What's my motivation? My motivation is "Hello, [Hopper], you fascist fuck, you've blown our big chance".'

1 Then came *Easy Rider*, a disaster in the history of film to set beside the loss of Technicolor, the invention of gross participation, the early death of Murnau, and the longevity of Richard Attenborough.

COMMENT by David Thomson in *A Biographical Dictionary of the Cinema* (1975).

EATING RAOUL

US 1982; screenwriters: Paul Bartel, Richard Blackburn; cast: Paul Bartel (Paul Bland), Mary Woronov (Mary Bland), Robert Beltran (Raoul), Susan Saiger (Doris the Dominatrix), Don Steele (Host), Richard Blackburn (James).

2 *Mary (to Paul)*: You could think you could buy another frying pan? I'm just a little squeamish about cooking in the one we're using to kill people.

SOUNDTRACK.

3 *Doris (disguised as a nun)*: You have been very wicked and you are in terrible danger.
Raoul: So is everybody who eats here.

SOUNDTRACK.

4 *Host (welcoming Paul and Mary to party)*: Hi, swingers! I'm Howard Swine, your hearty host that's hung with the most. Though I hate to boast, I'm as big as a post and warm as toast.

SOUNDTRACK.

5 *James (eating Raoul)*: I hope you make this a permanent item on your menu. It's French?
Mary: No. Actually, it's more Spanish.

SOUNDTRACK.

6 *Paul (on dish of human meat he is serving)*: It's amazing what you can do with a cheap piece of meat if you know how to treat it.

SOUNDTRACK. Almost last line of film.

Jake EBERTS

Canadian-born executive (1941–)

7 My Indecision Is Final.

TITLE of book (1990) on 'The Rise and Fall of Goldcrest Films', written with Terry Ilott.

Thomas Alva EDISON

American inventor (1847–1931)

1 The talking motion picture will not supplant the regular motion picture … There is such a tremendous investment in pantomime pictures that it would be absurd to disturb it.

ATTRIBUTED remark in March 1913.

2 I have determined that there is no market for talking pictures.

REMARK in 1926, quoted in Stuart Berg Flexner, *Listening to America* (1982).

EDUCATING RITA

UK 1983; screenwriter: Willy Russell (from his play); cast: Michael Caine (Dr Frank Bryant), Julie Walters (Rita), Michael Williams (Brian).

3 *Bryant*: Of course, I'm drunk. You don't really expect me to teach this when I'm sober.

SOUNDTRACK.

4 *Rita (to Bryant)*: *Howard's End*? Sounds filthy, doesn't it?

SOUNDTRACK.

5 *Brian (to Rita about Bryant)*: Needs you? Most of the time he can hardly see you!

SOUNDTRACK.

6 *Bryant (reading inscription on pen, a gift from Rita)*: 'Must only be used for poetry, by strictest order – Rita.'

SOUNDTRACK.

See also Michael **CAINE** 83:3.

Sergei EISENSTEIN

Russian director (1898–1948)

7 A collar button under a lens and thrown on the screen may become a radiant planet.

QUOTED in J.R. Colombo, *Wit and Wisdom of the Moviemakers* (1979).

8 Cinema has only ever produced one giant, a genius of talent, and that's Eisenstein. Nobody else has ever come remotely near him. You can put Eisenstein up with Michelangelo and da Vinci.

COMMENT by Peter Greenaway in journal *Transcript*, quoted in *Independent on Sunday*, 'Overheard' (8 January 1995).

Michael EISNER

American studio executive (1942–)

1 If you're not part of the steamroller, you're part of the road.

QUOTED in *Screen International* (late 1993). Eisner was CEO of the Walt Disney Corporation at the time.

Britt EKLAND

Swedish-born actress (1942–)

2 Men like long nails – in old movies couples were always scratching each others' backs.

QUOTED in *The Observer*, 'Sayings of the Week' (12 February 1984).

The ELECTRIC HORSEMAN

US 1979; screenwriter: Robert Garland; cast: Valerie Perrine (Charlotta), Robert Redford (Sonny Steele).

3 *Charlotta (to Sonny, on his pointless existence)*: You're just walking around to save funeral expenses.

SOUNDTRACK. To John Huston is attributed the similar (undated) remark: 'Peter O'Toole looks like he's walking around just to save funeral expenses.'

The ELEPHANT MAN

US 1980; screenwriters: David Lynch (director) and others; cast: John Hurt (John Merrick).

4 *Merrick (shouting to crowd that is bothering him)*: I am not an elephant, I am not an animal. I am a man!

SOUNDTRACK. The slogan used on posters was slightly different: 'I am not an animal! I am a human being! I … am … a man!'

Denholm ELLIOTT

English actor (1922–92)

5 'Never work with children, dogs, or Denholm Elliott', British actors are said to advise one another.

COMMENT in *The Guardian* (29 April 1989). This view has also been attributed to actor Gabriel Byrne.

The EMPIRE STRIKES BACK

US 1980; screenwriters: Leigh Brackett, Lawrence Kasdan; cast: Carrie Fisher (Princess Leia), Harrison Ford (Han Solo).

1 The Empire Strikes Back.

TITLE OF FILM – the first sequel to George Lucas's *Star Wars* – alluding to the 'evil empire' (*see* ***STAR WARS*** 397:3). The phrase caught on in other ways, too. In about 1981, the proprietors of an Indian restaurant in Drury Lane, London, considered it as a name before rejecting it in favour of 'The Last Days of the Raj'.

2 The Adventure Continues …

SLOGAN.

3 *Leia (to Han when he can't get his spaceship off the ground)*: Would it help if I got out and pushed?

SOUNDTRACK.

4 *Leia (softening towards to Han)*: You do have your moments. Not many of them, but you do have them.

SOUNDTRACK.

Les ENFANTS DU PARADIS

France 1945; screenwriter: Jacques Prévert; cast: Arletty (Garance), Jean-Louis Barrault (Baptiste Dubureau).

5 *Garance (to Baptiste)*: *C'est tellement simple, l'amour* [It's so simple, love].

SOUNDTRACK.

The ENFORCER

US 1951 (known elsewhere as *Murder, Inc.*); screenwriter: Martin Rackin; cast: Humphrey Bogart (Martin Ferguson), Everett Sloane (Albert Mendoza).

6 *Mendoza*: I'll have a better memory: you looking like a chump in that courtroom today.
Ferguson: If you think you can get away with this, you're crazy. You think you can shut people up by killing them, but you're wrong. Even the dead can talk. Maybe not in a courtroom, but they'll be talking to you, Mendoza. At night when you're trying to sleep …
Mendoza: I don't have to listen to this.

SOUNDTRACK. 'Even the dead can talk' is quoted in the Clive James/Pete Atkin song 'Driving Through Mythical America' (1971).

St John ERVINE

Irish playwright and novelist (1883–1971)

1 American motion pictures are written by the half-educated for the half-witted.

QUOTED in *The Treasury of Humorous Quotations*, eds. Esar & Bentley (1951 edn).

(Dame) Edith EVANS

English actress (1888–1976)

2 People always ask me the most ridiculous questions. They want to know, 'How do you approach a role?' Well, I don't know. I approach it by first saying yes, then getting on with the bloody thing.

REMARK quoted in J.R. Colombo, *Wit and Wisdom of the Moviemakers* (1979).

3 Acting with her was heaven. It was like being in your mother's arms.

COMMENT by (Sir) Michael Redgrave.

EVERY DAY'S A HOLIDAY

US 1937; screenwriter: Mae West; cast: Mae West (Peaches O'Day), Charles Butterworth (Larmadou Graves), Charles Winninger (Van Reighle Van Pelter Van Doon).

4 *Van Reighle*: Now tell me, Peaches, do you keep a diary?
Peaches: I always say, keep a diary and some day it'll keep you.

SOUNDTRACK.

5 *Larmadou*: What do you think of Inspector Quade?
Peaches: Mmm, that's a guy so crooked he uses a corkscrew for a ruler.

SOUNDTRACK.

EVERYTHING YOU ALWAYS WANTED TO KNOW ABOUT SEX (BUT WERE AFRAID TO ASK)

US 1972; screenwriter/director: Woody Allen; cast: Woody Allen (Victor/Fabrizio/The Fool/Sperm), Lynn Redgrave (Queen), Tony Randall (In-body operator).

6 *Queen (to Fool)*: Didst I feel aright – or didst I feel that thy two hands did upon my royal body cop a feel?

SOUNDTRACK.

7 *Fool (unable to unlock Queen's chastity belt)*: I must think of something quickly because before you know it, the Renaissance will be here and we'll all be painting.

SOUNDTRACK.

1 More fun than laughing.

SUB-TITLE in translation (during Italian episode). *Compare* ***ANNIE HALL*** 30:9.

2 *In-body operator (on sexual act from the inside)*: Fatigue reading four and a half. Looks good! We're going for seconds. Attention, gonads, we're going for a record.

SOUNDTRACK. Last lines of film.

EXCALIBUR

US 1981; screenwriters: Rospo Pallenberg, John Boorman (director) (after Thomas Malory, *Le Morte d'Arthur*); cast: Nicol Williamson (Merlin), Nigel Terry (King Arthur).

3 Forged by a God! Foretold by a wizard! Found by a king!

SLOGAN.

4 No mortal could possess it! No kingdom could command it!

SLOGAN.

5 *Merlin (when Arthur is conceived)*: The future has taken root in the present. It is done.

SOUNDTRACK.

6 *King Arthur*: What is the secret of the Grail? Who does it serve?

SOUNDTRACK.

The EXORCIST

US 1973; screenwriter: William Peter Blatty (from his novel); voice of: Mercedes McCambridge (Demon); cast: Jason Miller (Father Karras).

7 *Demon (possessing girl)*: Your mother sucks cocks in hell, Karras.

SOUNDTRACK.

EYES WIDE SHUT

US 1999; screenwriter: Frederic Raphael (from Arthur Schnitzler story); cast: Tom Cruise (Dr William Harford), Nicole Kidman (Alice Harford).

8 Eyes Wide Shut.

TITLE OF FILM. Basil Copper wrote to *The Observer* (19 Sepember 1999): 'I have a close friend who appears in the film and over many weeks on the shoot he came to know [Stanley Kubrick, the director]. He told me that the director often repeated to friends and colleagues an aphorism of his own coinage: "Governments, politicians and generals are leading the world with their eyes wide shut".'

9 *Alice*: Why haven't you ever been jealous about me?
William: I don't know. Maybe because you're my wife.

SOUNDTRACK.

The FACE OF FU MANCHU

UK 1965; screenwriter: Peter Welbeck; cast: Christopher Lee (Fu Manchu).

1 *Fu Manchu*: The world shall hear from me again!

SOUNDTRACK. Last words of film, Fu Manchu having been blown up. This is a reprise of Boris Karloff's line at the end of *The Mask of Fu Manchu* (US 1932).

William FADIMAN

American writer and producer (1909–99)

2 Hollywood is bounded on the north, south, east, and west by agents.

EXTRACTED from his book *Hollywood Now* (1972).

Douglas FAIRBANKS

American actor (1883–1939)

3 In his private life Douglas had always faced a situation in the only way he knew how, by running away from it.

COMMENT by Mary Pickford in *Sunshine and Shadow* (1956).

FAREWELL MY LOVELY

(also known as *Murder My Sweet* in US) US 1944; screenwriter: John Paxton (from Raymond Chandler novel); cast: Dick Powell (Philip Marlowe); Anne Shirley (Ann).

4 *Marlowe (narrating)*: I caught the blackjack right behind my ear. A black pool opened up at my feet. I dived in. It had no bottom.

SOUNDTRACK.

5 *Marlowe*: He gave me a hundred bucks to take care of him, and I didn't. I'm just a small businessman in a very messy business, but I like to follow through on a sale.

SOUNDTRACK.

6 *Marlowe (narrating)*: They were just a bunch of bananas that looked like fingers.

SOUNDTRACK.

1 *Marlowe (narrating)*: 'Okay Marlowe,' I said to myself. 'You're a tough guy. You've been sapped twice, choked, beaten silly with a gun, shot in the arm until you're crazy as a couple of waltzing mice. Now let's see you do something really tough – like putting your pants on.

SOUNDTRACK.

2 *Marlowe (to Ann)*: The cops always like to solve murders done with my gun.

SOUNDTRACK.

FAREWELL, MY LOVELY

(US 1975); screenwriter: David Zelag Goodman (from Raymond Chandler novel); cast: Robert Mitchum (Philip Marlowe).

3 *Marlowe (narrating)*: Her hair was the colour of gold in old paintings. She had a full set of curves which nobody had been able to improve on. She was giving me the kind of look I could feel in my hip pocket.

SOUNDTRACK. But what does this line ('She gave me a *smile* I could feel in my hip pocket' in Chandler's novel) mean? A winning smile, presumably – but is the reference to the hip pocket meant to suggest something about money (where the wallet might be kept), or about guns or about the other things that men keep in their trousers?

FARGO

US 1996; screenwriter: Joel & Ethan Coen; cast: Frances McDormand (Marge Gunderson).

4 *Marge Gunderson*: I guess that was your accomplice in the wood chipper.

SOUNDTRACK.

Frances FARMER

American actress (1914–70)

5 The nicest thing I can say about Frances Farmer is that she is unbearable.

COMMENT attributed to William Wyler.

Mia FARROW

American actress (1945–)

6 [to Jim Broadbent when he told her he was to be in a film directed by

Woody Allen] Congratulations! He's a great director. Just don't have babies by him ...

QUOTED by Broadbent on BBC Radio *Quote ... Unquote* (10 June 1997). He added that this was advice he heeded.

Rainer Werner FASSBINDER

German director (1946–82)

1 I hope to build a house with my films. Some of them are the cellar, some are the walls, and some are the windows. But I hope in time there will be a house.

ATTRIBUTED remark.

2 He was a genius. And geniuses are notoriously loony, because it's a very fine line between madness and genius.

COMMENT by (Sir) Dirk Bogarde.

The FAST LADY

UK 1962; screenwriters: Jack Davies, Henry Blyth; cast: Leslie Phillips (Freddie Fox).

3 *Freddie (to himself in mirror, after spraying himself and smoothing his moustache before meeting girl)*: Oh, you sexy beast!

SOUNDTRACK. Sometimes recalled as 'You gorgeous beast!'

FATAL ATTRACTION

US 1987; screenwriter: James Dearden; cast: Michael Douglas (Dan Gallagher), Glenn Close (Alex Forrest).

4 *Alex*: I'm not gonna be ignored, Dan.

SOUNDTRACK.

The FATAL GLASS OF BEER

US 1933; screenwriter: W.C. Fields; cast: W.C. Fields (Mr Snavely).

5 *Mr Snavely*: 'T'ain't a fit night out for man nor beast.

SOUNDTRACK. Repeated phrase. In a letter (8 February 1944) quoted in *W.C. Fields by Himself* (1974), Fields states that the catchphrase was first used by him in a sketch in Earl Carroll's *Vanities* and then as the title of the picture he made for Mack Sennett. He concluded: 'I do not claim to be the originator of this line as it was probably used long before I was born in some old melodrama.'

6 *Mr Snavely*: I think I'll go milk the elk.

SOUNDTRACK.

William FAULKNER

American novelist and screenwriter (1897–1962)

1 [to Irving Thalberg] Ah don't believe Ah know which pictures are yours. Do you make the Mickey Mouse brand?

QUOTED in Max Wilk, *The Wit and Wisdom of Hollywood* (1972).

Federico FELLINI

Italian director (1920–93)

2 [on Nino Rota] He hasn't got the presumption of so many composers, who want their music to be heard in the film. He knows that, in a film, music is something marginal and secondary, something that cannot occupy the foreground except in a few rare moments … and must be content to support the rest of what's happening.

EXTRACTED from book *Fellini on Fellini* (1976).

3 The cinema is very much like the circus; and in fact, if it didn't exist, I might well have become a circus director. The circus, too, is an exact mixture of technique, precision and improvisation. While the rehearsed spectacle is on, you are still taking risks: that is, simultaneously, you live. I love this way of creating and living at the same time, without the limits set to a writer or a painter, through being plunged into action.

QUOTED in David Thomson, *A Biographical Dictionary of Film* (1994 edn).

4 Although my father wanted me to become an engineer and my mother a bishop, I myself am quite content to have succeeded in becoming an adjective.

ATTRIBUTED remark.

The FEMALE ON THE BEACH

US 1955; screenwriters: Robert Hill (from his play) and others; cast: Joan Crawford (Lynn Markham), Jeff Chandler (Drummond Hall), Jan Sterling (Amy Rawlinson).

5 *Lynn (to Drummond)*: I wouldn't have you if you were hung with diamonds – upside down!

SOUNDTRACK.

6 *Lynn (to Amy)*: I know it's considered noble to accept apologies, but I'm afraid I'm not the noble type.

SOUNDTRACK.

Marco FERRERI

Italian director (1928–)

1 *Per essere considerato un classico un film deve riuscire a far sbadigliare almeno tre generazoni di spetattori* [To be considered a classic, a film must succeed in making at least three generations of moviegoers yawn].

ATTRIBUTED remark.

FERRIS BUELLER'S DAY OFF

US 1986; screenwriter/director: John Hughes; cast: Matthew Broderick (Ferris Bueller).

2 *Ferris*: Cameron's so tight, if you stuck a piece of coal up his ass in two weeks you'd have a diamond.

SOUNDTRACK.

FIELD OF DREAMS

US 1989; screenwriter/director: Phil Alden Robinson (from W.P. Kinsella novel *Shoeless Joe*); cast: Kevin Costner (Ray Kinsella), Himself (Voice).

3 *Voice*: If you build it, he will come.

SOUNDTRACK. Costner portrays an Iowa farmer who hears a voice that gives this advice repeatedly. Accordingly, Kinsella creates a baseball pitch in his field so that 'Shoeless Joe' Jackson, the discredited Chicago White Sox player of 'Say it ain't so, Joe' fame, can come back from the dead and be rehabilitated. The Voice's other messages are: 'Go the distance' and 'Ease his pain'.

W.C. FIELDS

American comedian (1879–1946)

4 [when asked why he did not drink water] Fish fuck in it.

QUOTED in Leslie Halliwell, *The Filmgoer's Book of Quotes* (1973).

5 Never act with animals or children.

ATTRIBUTED remark, quoted by Phyllis Hartnoll in *Plays and Players* (1985). Fields was possibly the first person to make this observation.

6 Someone has stolen the cork out of my lunch!

QUOTED in Mae West, *Goodness Had Nothing To Do With It*, Chap. 16 (1959), as having been exclaimed by Fields during the making of *My Little Chickadee*.

7 I'm afraid Bill has slipped off the wagon this morning. He's telling the kid actors to go out and play in the traffic.

COMMENT by an assistant director on *My Little Chickadee* and quoted by Mae West in the same book as above.

1 His main purpose seemed to be to break as many rules as possible and cause the maximum amount of trouble for everybody.

COMMENT by Robert Lewis Taylor (his biographer), quoted in Leslie Halliwell, *The Filmgoer's Book of Quotes* (1973).

2 The only thing I can say about W.C. Fields, whom I have admired since the day he advanced upon Baby LeRoy with an ice pick, is this: any man who hates dogs and babies can't be all bad.

COMMENT by Leo Rosten in speech (16 February 1939) at a Masquer's Club dinner. Sometimes quoted as 'Any man who hates children and dogs can't be all bad' and often ascribed to Fields himself (for example, by *Radio Times*, 12 August 1965).

See also Mae **WEST** 445:5.

Albert FINNEY

English actor (1936–)

3 [on making films in the early 1960s] In love scenes on beds you had to keep one foot on the floor at all times, which made it rather like playing snooker or pool. If you lifted that one foot off the floor, it was a foul shot.

ATTRIBUTED remark in 1981, quoted in Bob Chieger, *Was It Good For You Too?* (1983).

4 If we'd known he was going to be an actor, we'd have given him a fancier name.

COMMENT attributed to his mother, Mrs Alice Finney.

Ronald FIRBANK

English novelist (1886–1926)

5 'She reads at such a pace,' she complained, 'and when I asked her *where* she had learnt to read so quickly, she replied, "On the screens at cinemas".'

EXTRACTED from his novel *The Flower Beneath the Foot* (1923).

FIRE OVER ENGLAND

UK 1937; screenwriters: Clemence Dane and others; cast: Flora Robson (Queen Elizabeth I).

6 *Elizabeth*: I know I have the body of a weak and feeble woman, but I have the heart and valour of a king, and of a king of England too; not Spain nor any prince of Europe shall dare to invade the borders of my realm. Pluck up your hearts, by your peace in camp and your valour in the field we shall shortly have a famous victory.

SOUNDTRACK. Based loosely on the reported speech by the historical Elizabeth before the Spanish Armada in 1588. In particular, note how the traditional 'heart and stomach' of the original has become 'heart and valour'.

A FISH CALLED WANDA

UK 1988; screenwriters: John Cleese, Charles Crichton (director); cast: Jamie Lee Curtis (Wanda Gerschwitz), Kevin Kline (Otto), John Cleese (Archie Leach), Maria Aitken (Wendy Leach), Michael Palin (Ken), Tom Georgeson (George).

1 *Otto*: Oh, that's quite a stutter you've got there, Ken.

SOUNDTRACK.

2 *Otto (customary method of seeking clarification)*: What was the middle thing?

SOUNDTRACK.

3 *Otto (stock threat)*: Don't ever call me stupid!

SOUNDTRACK.

4 *George*: So, 'Next week we won't have to look for work. And it won't have to look for us' – Oscar Wilde.

SOUNDTRACK.

5 *Otto (about animals)*: You know what Nietzsche said about that? He said they were God's second blunder.

SOUNDTRACK.

6 *Otto*: It's a Buddhist meditation technique. Focuses your aggression. The monks used to do it before they went into battle.
Wanda: What kind of Buddhism is this, Otto?

SOUNDTRACK.

7 *Otto (to Wendy)*: Oh, you English are so superior, aren't you? Well, would you like to know where you'd be without us, the old U.S. of A., to protect you? I'll tell you. The smallest fucking province in the Russian Empire!

SOUNDTRACK.

8 *Archie*: Wanda, do you have any idea what it's like being English? Being so correct all the time, being so stifled by this dread of doing the wrong thing? … You see, Wanda, we're all terrified of embarrassment. That's why we're so … dead.

SOUNDTRACK.

1 *Wanda (to Otto)*: To call you stupid would be an insult to stupid people. I've known sheep that could outwit you. I've worn dresses with higher I.Q.s. But you think you're an intellectual, don't you, ape?

SOUNDTRACK.

2 *Wanda (to Otto)*: Now let me correct you on a couple of things, okay? Aristotle was not Belgian. The central message of Buddhism is not every man for himself ... And the London Underground is not a political movement. Those are all mistakes, Otto. I looked them up.

SOUNDTRACK.

3 *Otto*: The English contribution to world culture: the chip.

SOUNDTRACK.

4 *Otto (when Archie tells him to put his hands up)*: I'll make a deal with you. I'll put one up.

SOUNDTRACK.

5 *Archie (on Otto's view that, unlike Americans, the British don't like winners)*: Winners like ... North Vietnam?

SOUNDTRACK.

Carrie FISHER

American actress (1956–)

6 It struck me today that the people that have had an impact on me are the people who didn't make it. Marilyn Monroe, Judy Garland, Montgomery Clift, Lenny Bruce, Janis Joplin, John Belushi. It's not Making It to be Marilyn Monroe, but it is to me.

EXTRACTED from her novel *Postcards from the Edge*, 'Postcards from the Edge' (1987).

7 'And don't take this movie thing so seriously. Don't they always say, "It's only a movie"?'
'Yeah, Gran, that's what they say,'

EXTRACTED from *Postcards from the Edge*, 'Dreaming Outside Your Head' (1987). *Compare* Ingrid **BERGMAN** 56:5, Alfred **HITCHCOCK** 217:6.

8 Acting engenders and harbours qualities that are best left way behind in adolescence. People-pleasing, going on those interviews and jamming your whole personality into getting the job, ingratiating yourself to people you wouldn't fucking spit on if they were on fire.

INTERVIEWED in *Vanity Fair* (August 1990).

9 I'm a product of Hollywood. Fantasy is not unnatural to me: it's my reality. Hollywood people are like everyone else, only more so. They depict reality as opposed to being it.

INTERVIEWED in *The Weekend Guardian* (12–13 January 1991).

F. Scott FITZGERALD

American novelist (1896–1940)

1 Not half a dozen men have ever been able to keep the whole equation of pictures in their head.

EXTRACTED from his unfinished novel *The Last Tycoon* (1941).

2 Hollywood is a Jewish holiday, a Gentile tragedy.

QUOTED in Matthew J. Bruccoli, *Some Sort of Epic Grandeur* (1962).

FIVE EASY PIECES

US 1970; screenwriter: Adrien Joyce (Carol Eastman); cast: Jack Nicholson (Robert Dupeau).

3 *Robert (to waitress who refuses to serve him plain toast because it is not on the menu)*: Now all you have to do is hold the chicken, bring me the toast, give me a check for the chicken salad sandwich, and you haven't broken any rules.

SOUNDTRACK.

Robert FLAHERTY

American documentary producer and director (1884–1951)

4 First I am an explorer, and only then an artist.

REMARK quoted in J.R. Colombo, *Wit and Wisdom of the Moviemakers* (1979).

5 World-famous and world-loved, his standing in his own profession was nil. You might suppose that a master film-director who would work for a salary normally paid an assistant would be in great demand, but that is not the way of things in the film world.

COMMENT in Richard Griffith, *The World of Robert Flaherty* (1963).

The FLINTSTONES

US 1994: screenwriters: Tom S. Parker, Jim Jennewein, Steven E. de Souza (after TV series).

6 Yabba Dabba Do!

SLOGAN. Making use of the famous catchphrase from the TV series. This gave rise to the following critical comments: 'Yabba Dabba Doo-doo' (*Philadelphia Inquirer*), 'Yabba Dabba Don't' (*USA Today*), 'Yabba Dabba Dud' (*New York Daily Post*), 'Yabba Dabba Poo! (*Empire*).

1 NO DINOSAURS WERE HARMED IN THE MAKING OF THIS MOTION PICTURE.

SCREEN TITLE.

The FLY

US 1986; screenwriters: Charles Edward Pogue, David Cronenburg (director); cast: Jeff Goldblum (Seth Brundle), Geena Davis (Veronice Quaife), Joy Boushel (Tawny).

2 *Veronice (to Tawny, Seth's date)*: No. Be afraid. Be very afraid.

SOUNDTRACK. Also used as a slogan.

Errol FLYNN

Australian-born American actor (1909–59)

3 My problem lies in reconciling my gross habits with my net income.

QUOTED in Jane Mercer, *Great Lovers of the Movies* (1975).

4 A fifty-year trespass against good taste.

COMMENT by Leslie Mallory.

5 The great thing about Errol was – you always knew precisely where you stood with him because he *always* let you down. He let himself down too, from time to time, but that was his prerogative.

COMMENT by David Niven in *Bring On the Empty Horses*, 'Errol' (1975).

6 [when asked whether he resented the popularity of Mikhail Gorbachev] Good Lord, I co-starred with Errol Flynn once.

COMMENT by President Ronald Reagan, quoted in *Time* Magazine (14 December 1987). Reagan was talking to students in Jacksonville, Florida.

The FOG

US 1979; screenwriters: John Carpenter (director), Debra Hill.

7 All that we see or seem
Is but a dream within a dream.

SCREEN TITLE. Quoting Edgar Allan Poe, 'A Dream Within a Dream' (1849). *See also* ***PICNIC AT HANGING ROCK*** 328:1.

Henry FONDA

American actor (1905–82)

8 Acting is putting on a mask. The worst torture that can happen to me is not having a mask to get in back of.

REMARK quoted in J.R. Colombo, *Wit and Wisdom of the Moviemakers* (1979).

1 The best actors do not let the wheels show.

QUOTED in *The Barnes and Noble Book of Quotations*, ed. Robert I. Fitzhenry (1986).

2 I ain't really Henry Fonda. Nobody could have that much integrity.

ATTRIBUTED remark.

Jane FONDA

American actress (1937–)

3 I found out that acting was hell. You spend all your time trying to do what they put people in asylums for.

QUOTED in J.R. Colombo, *Wit and Wisdom of the Moviemakers* (1979).

4 Working in Hollywood does give one a certain expertise in the field of prostitution.

QUOTED in J.R. Colombo, *Wit and Wisdom of the Moviemakers* (1979).

5 [on reading ex-husband Roger Vadim's memoirs] If he needed the money so badly, I'd have given him alimony.

QUOTED in *Sunday Today*, 'Quotes of the Week' (17 August 1986).

FOR WHOM THE BELL TOLLS

US 1943; screenwriter: Dudley Nicholls (from Ernest Hemingway novel); cast: Ingrid Bergman (Maria), Gary Cooper (Robert Jordan).

6 *Maria*: I don't know how to kiss, or I would kiss you. Where do the noses go?

SOUNDTRACK.

7 *Robert*: A man fights for what he believes in, Fernando.

SOUNDTRACK.

Bryan FORBES

English actor, screenwriter, director and studio executive (1926–)

8 We shall find life tolerable once we have consented to be always ill at ease.

QUOTING Gustave Flaubert in *The Times* (23 June 1969) when Forbes was the newly appointed head of production at Elstree Studios. 'As an everyday working rule for anybody contemplating an existence in the British film industry,' he added, 'it is not without a certain valid cold comfort.'

1 By treating violence as a game without cost, certain sections of the film industry display their contempt for anything other than box-office success.

QUOTED in *The Independent* (13 March 1993).

FORBIDDEN PLANET

US 1956; screenwriter: Cyril Hume; cast: Earl Holliman (Cookie), Jack Kelly (Lieut. Farman), Anne Francis (Altaira), Walter Pidgeon (Morbius), Leslie Nielsen (Commander Adams), Warren Stevens (Lieut. 'Doc' Ostrow).

2 *Farman (explaining kissing to Altaira)*: It's an old custom. All the really high civilizations go in for it … It stimulates the whole system. As a matter of fact, you can't be in tip-top health without it.

SOUNDTRACK.

3 *Morbius (to Adams, when the Commander performs badly on an intelligence meter)*: It's all right, sir. A commanding officer doesn't need brains, just a good loud voice.

SOUNDTRACK.

4 *Ostrow (on monsters from the unconscious)*: Monsters, John. Monsters from the Id.

SOUNDTRACK.

5 *Morbius (as Monster from the Id closes in)*: Guilty! Guilty! My evil self is at that door – and I have no power to stop it!

SOUNDTRACK.

Harrison FORD

American actor (1942–)

6 I do movies to stimulate me. I have got more money than I can handle.

QUOTED in *The Independent* (18 September 1993).

John FORD

Irish-American director (1895–1973)

7 Anybody can direct a picture once they know the fundamentals. Directing is not a mystery, it's not an art. The main thing about directing is: photograph the people's eyes.

ATTRIBUTED remark.

8 Don't give them too much extra film, then they can't cut it a different way.

QUOTED by Fred Zinnemann, Austrian-born director (1907–).

1 [when asked which directors he admired] I like the old masters, by which I mean John Ford, John Ford and John Ford.

COMMENT by Orson Welles, quoted in *Hollywood Anecdotes*, eds. Boller & Davis (1988).

Wallace FORD

English film actor (1898–1966)

2 [suggested epitaph] At last I get top billing.

QUOTED in Leslie Halliwell, *The Filmgoer's Book of Quotes* (1973). Ford went to Hollywood in the early 1930s. After a number of 'semi-leads', he was condemned to a succession of supporting roles in Hollywood films and decided that his gravestone epitaph should read thus. According to a story told by Terence Frisby on BBC Radio *Quote ... Unquote* (16 February 1979), this inscription was duly put on his grave and then along came a graffiti artist and chalked above it, 'Clark Gable and Myrna Loy supported by ...'

FOREIGN CORRESPONDENT

US 1940; screenwriters: Charles Bennet, Robert Benchley, James Hilton and others (from novel *Personal History* by Vincent Sheean); cast: Joel McCrea (Haverstock).

3 *Haverstock*: I've been watching a part of the world blown to pieces! I can't read the rest of the speech I had because the lights have gone out. It is as if the lights were out everywhere, except America. Keep those lights burning there! Cover them with steel! Ring them with guns! Build a canopy of battleships and bombing planes around them! Hello, America! Hang on to your lights, they're the only lights left in the world!

SOUNDTRACK.

Milos FORMAN

Czech director (1932–)

4 [on ***ONE FLEW OVER THE CUCKOO'S NEST***] One of the criteria of casting was that we couldn't afford to have a prick in the company.

ATTRIBUTED remark.

FORREST GUMP

US 1994; screenwriter: Eric Ross; cast: Tom Hanks (Forrest Gump).

5 *Forrest*: My momma always said, life was like a box of chocolates ... you never know what you're gonna get.

SOUNDTRACK.

48HRS

US 1983; screenwriters: Walter Hill (director) and others; cast: Eddie Murphy (Reggie Hammond).

1 *Hammond (flashing police credentials at bar full of whites)*: I'm your worst nightmare, a nigger with a badge.

SOUNDTRACK.

49TH PARALLEL

UK 1941; screenwriters: Emeric Pressburger, Michael Acland; cast: Raymond Massey (Andy Brock), Eric Portman (Lieut. Hirth).

2 *Brock (as Canadian soldier, to Nazi)*: When things go wrong, we can take it. We can dish it out, too.

SOUNDTRACK.

3 *Hirth (German U-boat commander)*: Today, Europe … tomorrow the whole world!

SOUNDTRACK.

FORTY-SECOND STREET

US 1933; screenwriters: James Seymour, Rian James; cast: Warner Baxter (Julian Marsh), Ruby Keeler (Peggy Sawyer).

4 *Julian (producer, to chorus girl, Peggy)*: Sawyer, you listen to me and you listen hard. Two hundred people, two hundred jobs, two hundred thousand dollars, five weeks of grind and blood and sweat depend on you. It's the lives of all these people who've worked with you. You've got to go on, and you've got to give and give and give … And, Sawyer, you're going out a youngster – but you've *got* to come back a star!

SOUNDTRACK. The origin of a notable show business cliché. Peggy is given her big break when she has to take over at short notice from the star of the show who has broken her leg.

The FOUR FEATHERS

UK 1939; screenwriters: R.C. Sherriff, Lajos Biro, Arthur Wimperis (from A.E.W. Mason novel); cast: John Clements (Harry Faversham), Ralph Richardson (John Durrance), Frederick Culley (Dr Sutton).

5 THE KHALIFA'S ARMY OF DERVISHES AND FUZZY-WUZZIES MASSES ON THE NILE.

SCREEN TITLE. This film was made in the days before political correctness.

1 *Faversham*: To be a soldier and a coward is to be an impostor, a menace to the men whose lives are in your hands.

SOUNDTRACK.

2 *Faversham*: In England, the white feather is the mark of a coward.

SOUNDTRACK.

3 *Durrance (to Dr Sutton)*: You've always got some confoundedly cold-blooded reason for doing nothing.

SOUNDTRACK.

FOUR WEDDINGS AND A FUNERAL

UK 1994; screenwriter: Richard Curtis; cast: Simon Callow (Gareth), John Hannah (Matthew), Hugh Grant (Charles), Andie MacDowell (Carrie).

4 *Gareth*: A toast before we go into battle. True love – in whatever shape or form it may come – we'll all in our dotage be proud to say, "I was adored once too."

SOUNDTRACK. The final quotation is from Sir Andrew Aguecheek in Shakespeare, *Twelfth Night* (II.iii.181).

5 *Matthew*: Stop all the clocks, cut off the telephone,
Prevent the dog from barking with a juicy bone,
Silence the pianos and with muffled drum
Bring out the coffin, let the mourners come …

SOUNDTRACK. Quoting from W.H. Auden's 'Funeral Blues', originally in *The Ascent of F6* (1937), a play jointly written with Christopher Isherwood. Set to music, a pastiche blues, by Benjamin Britten for the play, the original words mocked the death of a political leader. Auden then rewrote the poem as more of a love-song and it had a separate existence for many years as one of Britten's 'Cabaret Songs'. Then in 1994, the text was spoken at the funeral 'of another splendid bugger' (i.e. Gareth) in *Four Weddings and a Funeral.* Seldom can a poem have become so immediately known and made popular.

6 *Carrie (to Charles)*: Is it still raining? I hadn't noticed.

SOUNDTRACK.

FRANKENSTEIN

US 1931; screenwriters: Garrett Ford and others (from the play by Peggy Webling and the novel by Mary Shelley); cast: Colin Clive (Dr Henry Frankenstein).

7 *Frankenstein*: Crazy am I? Well, see whether I am crazy or not … I have discovered the great ray that first brought life into the world.

SOUNDTRACK.

Arthur FREED

American director (1894–1973)

1 Talk of art grows and the audience diminishes.

QUOTED in Lillian Ross, *Picture* (1952).

Philip FRENCH

English critic (1933–)

2 The movie [*Independence Day*] … has a role I could have played – a character identified in the cast list as 'Intellectual on roof'.

REMARK in *The Observer* (11 August 1996).

Brenda FRICKER

Irish actress (1944–)

3 When you are lying drunk at the airport you're Irish. When you win an Oscar you're British.

QUOTED in T*he Observer*, 'Sayings of the Week' (8 April 1990). Fricker had just been awarded an Oscar as Best Supporting Actress for her role in *My Left Foot.*

FROM RUSSIA WITH LOVE

UK 1963; screenwriters: Richard Maibaum, Johanna Harwood (from Ian Fleming novel); cast: Sean Connery (James Bond), Daniela Bianchi (Tatiana Romanova), Robert Shaw (Red Grant), Lotte Lenya (Rosa Klebb), Bernard Lee (M), Pedro Armendariz (Kerim Bey).

4 From Russia With Love.

TITLE OF FILM. The simple form of wording used to accompany a present, but, when used here, the origin of any number of allusions of the 'from --- with ---' variety. In *Keep Taking the Tabloids* (1983), Fritz Spiegl noted these headline uses: 'From the Rush Hour with Love', 'From Maggie without love!' Compare *To Barcelona, With Love* (book by Clifford King, 1959) and films *To Paris With Love* (UK 1954) and *To Sir With Love* (from book by E.R. Braithwaite, 1959, UK 1967).

5 *Bond (about Tatiana Romanovna who has demanded that he take on a case)*: Suppose when she meets me in the flesh, I don't come up to expectations?
M: Just see that you do.

SOUNDTRACK.

6 *Bond*: She should have kept her mouth shut.

SOUNDTRACK. The 'mouth' is that of Anita Ekberg on a huge poster for *Call Me Bwana* (UK 1962) on a wall in Istanbul. A foe of Bond's has just been shot as he attempted to escape through a door in the mouth.

1 *Kerim*: I like big families myself. In fact, my whole life has been a crusade for larger families.
Bond: So I heard.

SOUNDTRACK.

2 *Bond (on Red Grant's lack of breeding)*: Red wine with fish. That should've told me something.

SOUNDTRACK.

3 *Red Grant (threatening Bond with gun)*: It'll be slow and painful … The first one won't kill you. Not the second. Not even the third. Not till you crawl over here and you kiss my foot.
Bond: How about a cigarette?

SOUNDTRACK.

4 *Bond (on the death of Rosa Klebb, she of the poisoned boots)*: She's had her kicks.

SOUNDTRACK.

The FRONT PAGE

US 1931; screenwriters: Bartlett Cormack, Charles Lederer, Ben Hecht (from Hecht & MacArthur play); cast: Adolphe Menjou (Walter Burns), Pat O'Brien (Hildy Johnson).

5 *Burns*: The son of a bitch stole my watch!

SOUNDTRACK. Last line of film (as of play). Referring to Johnson who thinks he has escaped Burns's clutches. Burns has in fact just presented Johnson with the watch (as Johnson leaves by train) and uses this ruse to get him arrested at the next stop. In the 1931 film, the word 'bitch' was blotted out on the soundtrack. It was said, loud and clear, by Walter Matthau in the 1974 remake.

David FRYE

American impressionist and comedian (1934–)

6 [of President Gerald R. Ford] He looks like the guy in a science fiction movie who is the first to see the Creature.

ATTRIBUTED in 1975 and quoted in Nigel Rees, *Quote … Unquote* (1978).

The FUGITIVE

US 1993; screenwriters: Jeb Stuart, David Twohy (after TV series); cast: Tommy Lee Jones (Deputy Samuel Gerard), Harrison Ford (Dr Richard Kimble), Tom Wood (Newman).

7 *Gerard (finding leg irons of escaped prisoner Kimble)*: You know, we're always fascinated when we find leg irons with no legs in 'em.

SOUNDTRACK.

1 *Gerard*: Listen up, ladies and gentlemen. Our fugitive has been on the run for ninety minutes. Average foot speed over uneven ground, barring injury, is four miles an hour. That gives us a radius of six miles. What I want out of each and every one of you is a hard target search of every gas station, residence, warehouse, farmhouse, henhouse, outhouse and doghouse in that area. Checkpoints go up at fifteen miles. Your fugitive's name is Dr Richard Kimble. Go get 'im.

SOUNDTRACK.

2 *Kimble (holding Gerard at gunpoint)*: I didn't kill my wife.
Gerard: I don't care.

SOUNDTRACK.

3 *Gerard (on finding Kimble alive)*: So he showed up not dead yet. Let that be a lesson to you, boys and girls: Don't ever argue with the big dog. Big dog is always right.

SOUNDTRACK.

4 *Gerard (asking Kimble to surrender)*: Give it up. It's time to stop running.

SOUNDTRACK.

5 *Kimble (when released from handcuffs)*: Thought you didn't care.
Gerard: I don't. Don't tell anybody, okay?

SOUNDTRACK. Last lines of film.

FULL METAL JACKET

US 1987; screenwriters: Stanley Kubrick (director), Michael Herr, Gustav Hasford (from Hasford's novel); cast: Lee Ermey (Gunnery Sgt. Hartman), Matthew Modine (Private Joker), Vincent D'Onofrio (Private Pyle), John Terry (Lieut. Lockhart), Adam Baldwin (Animal Mother), Ngoc Le (Vietnamese sniper).

6 *Hartman (to recruits)*: I am Gunnery Sergeant Hartman, your senior drill instructor. From now on, you will speak only when spoken to, and the first and last words out of your filthy sewers will be 'Sir!' Do you maggots understand this?

SOUNDTRACK.

7 *Lockhart (at editorial meeting of Marine newspaper)*: We have a new directive from M.A.F. on this. In the future, in place of 'search and destroy', substitute the phrase 'sweep and clear'.

SOUNDTRACK.

8 *Joker (on why he wears peace button as well as a helmet labelled*

'BORN TO KILL'): I think I was trying to suggest something about the duality of man, sir.

SOUNDTRACK.

1 *Animal Mother (to Joker)*: You talk the talk. Do you walk the walk?

SOUNDTRACK.

2 *Joker (voice over)*: I'm so happy that I am alive, in one piece and short. I'm in a world of shit, yes. But I am alive. And I am not afraid.

SOUNDTRACK. Last lines of film.

The FULL MONTY

UK/US 1997; screenwriter: Simon Beaufoy; cast: Mark Addy (Dave).

3 *Dave (to audience waiting to see male strippers)*: Ladies and gents, and you buggers at the back – we may not be young, we may not be pretty and we may not be reet good, but for one night and one night only, we are here, we're live and we're going no less than the Full Monty.

SOUNDTRACK. Hence, the title. Originally meaning 'the full amount, everything included', this phrase has been known in British English since the early 1980s. Various theories have been advanced as to its origin. Could it be a corruption of the 'full amount'? Or could it have something to do with 'monty' (from the Spanish *monte*), a card game or the Australian/New Zealand term for a horse considered certain to win a race? Or, again, could it have something to do with bales stuffed full of wool and imported from Montevideo? Or with Field Marshal Montgomery being kitted out with all his medals? Or, most convincingly of all, with being dressed in a full suit (or similar) from the tailors Montague Burton (first established in Chesterfield in 1904)? It was possible to buy or hire a complete outfit – shirt, tie, suit and socks: so when you elected to have the whole lot you were wearing the 'full monty', especially when you were being demobbed from the army.

The film comedy about six unemployed Yorkshire men who take a gamble to hit the jackpot by forming a male strippers group gave the phrase a specific meaning, in that they would give their audience 'the full monty' of full frontal nudity. William Safire's 'On Language' column in *The New York Times* (16 November 1997) revealed how this specific interpretation was the one that caught on in the US: '*The San Diego Union-Tribune* ran a story about the Carlsbad City Council's zoning restrictions to avert garishness: "Carlsbad has reached the point where it can afford to go the full monty – full frontal snobbery". Fox Searchlight Pictures publicity defines the phrase this way: "1. Naked, nude. 2. To go the Full Monty, vb., to take all one's clothes off, to go the whole way, to be totally naked".' Safire also noted how America was taking gleefully to the new phrase and already spawning puns. *Entertainment Week* had referred to a remake of *Wuthering Heights* as 'the full Brontë'.

1 I feel guilty about the success of that film. The serious issues that I wanted to write about were eclipsed by the stripping thing. I tried to put as much misery in as possible, but it was marketed as this big, funny feel-good film.

COMMENT by Simon Beaufoy, interviewed in the *Yorkshire Post* (12 June 1999). *Compare* Daniel **AUTEUIL** 40:8.

FUNNY FACE

US 1957; screenwriter: Leonard Gershe; cast: Kay Thompson (Maggie Prescott).

2 *Maggie*: Lettie, take an editorial. 'To the women of America' – no, make it 'To Women Everywhere: Banish the black, burn the blue and bury the beige. From now on, girls, think pink.'

SOUNDTRACK.

FUNNY GIRL

US 1968; screenwriter: Isobel Lennart (from her play); cast: Barbra Streisand (Fanny Brice).

3 *Fanny (to herself in dressing room mirror)*: Hello, gorgeous!

SOUNDTRACK. Opening line.

4 [when asked, as director, if he had had any trouble with Barbra Streisand as his leading lady] Not really, seeing as it's the first film she ever directed.

COMMENT attributed to William Wyler.

Clark GABLE

American actor (1901–60)

1 I'm no actor and I never have been. What people see on the screen is me.

ATTRIBUTED remark.

2 Hell, if I'd jumped on all the dames I'm supposed to have jumped on – I'd have had no time to go fishing.

ATTRIBUTED remark.

3 [of his first screen test] Ears too big.

COMMENT attributed to 'Hollywood executive'. In the form 'His ears are too big. He looks like an ape' it has been attributed to Samuel Goldwyn, in David Niven, *Bring On the Empty Horses* (1975), and to Darryl F. Zanuck, in J.R. Colombo, *Wit and Wisdom of the Moviemakers* (1979).

4 That man's ears make him look like a taxi-cab with both doors open.

COMMENT by Howard Hughes, quoted in Charles Higham & Joel Greenberg, *Celluloid Muse* (1969).

5 Clark Gable has the best ears of our lives.

COMMENT by Milton Berle, quoted in Leslie Halliwell, *The Filmgoer's Book of Quotes* (1973).

6 [during the filming of *Gone With the Wind*] Oh, Gable has enemies all right – but they all like him!

COMMENT by David O. Selznick, quoted in David Niven, *Bring on the Empty Horses*, 'The King' (1975).

7 If you say 'Hiya, Clark, how are you?' he's stuck for an answer.

COMMENT by Ava Gardner.

Zsa Zsa GABOR

Hungarian-born actress (1919–)

1 [when asked how many husbands she had had] You mean apart from my own?

ATTRIBUTED remark in answer to TV interviewer, by 1976.

See also George **SANDERS** 363:4.

GANDHI

UK 1982; screenwriter: John Briley; cast: Ben Kingsley (Mahatma Gandhi), Martin Sheen (Walker), Ian Charleson (Reverend Charlie Andrews), Roshan Seth (Pandit Nehru), Trevor Howard (Judge Broomfield), John Gielgud (Lord Irwin), Geraldine James (Mirabell).

2 *Gandhi (to Walker)*: If you are a minority of one, the truth is the truth.

SOUNDTRACK.

3 *Gandhi*: They may torture my body, break my bones, even kill me. Then they will have my dead body – not my obedience.

SOUNDTRACK.

4 *Gandhi (to British representatives)*: We think it is time you recognized that you are masters in someone else's home.

SOUNDTRACK.

5 *British general*: You don't think we're just going to walk out of India. *Gandhi*: Yes. In the end you will walk out because 100,000 Englishmen simply cannot control 350 million Indians if those Indians refuse to cooperate.

SOUNDTRACK.

6 *Gandhi*: An eye for an eye only ends up making the whole world blind.

SOUNDTRACK.

7 *Judge Broomfield (to Gandhi)*: It is impossible for me to ignore that you are in a different category from any person I have ever tried or am likely to try.

SOUNDTRACK.

8 *Gandhi (on taking the initiative against opponents)*: They are not in control, we are. That is the strength of civil resistance.

SOUNDTRACK.

9 *Walker (dictating newspaper report over phone)*: Whatever moral ascendancy the West held was lost here today. India is free, for she has taken all that steel and cruelty can give and she has neither cringed nor retreated.

SOUNDTRACK.

1 *Gandhi (to man who has killed Muslim child in retaliation for the death of his own son by Muslims)*: I know a way out of hell. Find a child, a child whose mother and father have been killed, a little boy about this high, and raise him as your own. Only be sure that he is a Muslim and that you raise him as one.

SOUNDTRACK.

2 *Mirabell (on Gandhi)*: I may be blinded by my love for him, but I believe when we most needed it he offered the world a way out of madness. But he doesn't see it. Neither does the world.

SOUNDTRACK.

3 *Gandhi (speaking posthumously as his ashes are scattered)*: When I despair, I remember that all through history the way of truth and love has always won. There have been tyrants and murderers and for a time they can seem invincible, but in the end they always fall. Think of it. Always.

SOUNDTRACK.

4 *Gandhi* was everything the voting membership of the Academy would like to be: moral, tan and thin.

COMMENT by Jan Morgenstern in the *Los Angeles Herald-Examiner* (April 1983).

5 [*Gandhi*] looms over the real world like an abandoned space station – *eternal*, expensive and forsaken.

COMMENT by David Thomson in *A Biographical Dictionary of Film* (1994 edn).

Greta GARBO

Swedish-born actress (1905–90)

6 I want to be alone.

ATTRIBUTED remark. Oddly, as Alexander Walker observes in *Sex in the Movies* (1968): 'Nowhere in anything she said, either in the lengthy interviews she gave in her Hollywood days when she was perfectly approachable, or in the statements on-the-run from the publicity-shy fugitive she later became, has it been possible to find the famous phrase, "I want to be alone". What one can find, in abundance, later on, is "Why don't you let me alone?" and even "I want to be left alone", but neither is redolent of any more exotic order of being than a harassed celebrity. Yet the world prefers to believe the mythical and much more mysterious catchphrase utterance.'

Garbo herself claimed (in *Life* Magazine, 24 January 1955) that 'I only said, "I want to be *let* alone"' – i.e. she wanted privacy rather than solitude.

What complicates the issue is that Garbo herself *did* employ the line several times *on the screen*. 'I like to be alone' appeared as a screen title in the silent *Love* (US 1927). In the 1929 silent film *The Single Standard* she gave the brush-off to a stranger and a title-card declared: 'I am walking alone because I want to be alone.' And, as the ageing ballerina who lost her nerve and fled back to her suite in ***GRAND HOTEL*** (1932), she actually *spoke* it (to John Barrymore). Walker calls this 'an excellent example of art borrowing its effects from a myth that was reality for millions of people'.

The phrase was obviously well established by 1932 when the impressionist Florence Desmond spoke it on record in her sketch 'The Hollywood Party'. In 1935 Groucho Marx uttered it in *A Night at the Opera*. Then Garbo said, 'Go to bed, little father. We want to be alone' in ***NINOTCHKA*** (1939). So it is not surprising that the myth has taken such a firm hold, and particularly since Garbo became a virtual recluse for the second half of her life.

1 I tink I go home [I think I go home].

ATTRIBUTED remark. At one time, spoken in a would-be Swedish accent, this was as much part of the impressionist's view of Garbo as 'I want to be alone.' A caricatured Garbo was shown hugging Mickey Mouse in a cartoon film in the 1930s. She said, 'Ah tahnk ah kees you now' and 'Ah tink ah go home.' One version of how the line came to be spoken is told by Norman Zierold in *Moguls* (1969): 'After such films as *The Torrent* and *Flesh and the Devil*, Garbo decided to exploit her box-office power and asked Louis B. Mayer for a raise – from three hundred and fifty to five thousand dollars a week. Mayer offered her twenty-five hundred. "I tank I go home," said Garbo. She went back to her hotel and stayed there for a full seven months until Mayer finally gave way.'

Alexander Walker in *Garbo* (1980) recalls what Sven-Hugo Borg, the actress's interpreter, said of the time in 1926 when Mauritz Stiller, who had come with her from Sweden, was fired from directing *The Temptress*: 'She was tired, terrified and lost ... as she returned to my side after a trying scene, she sank down beside me and said so low it was almost a whisper, "Borg, I think I shall go home now. It isn't worth it, is it?"'

Walker comments: 'That catchphrase, shortened into "I think I go home", soon passed into the repertoire of a legion of Garbo-imitators and helped publicize her strong-willed temperament.'

2 [when asked by David Niven why she had given up the movies] I had made enough faces.

QUOTED in David Niven, *Bring On the Empty Horses* (1975).

3 One day, there's a hand that goes over the face and changes it. You look like an apple that isn't young any more.

QUOTED in *Vanity Fair* (February 1994).

4 Co-starring with Garbo hardly constituted an introduction.

COMMENT by Fredric March.

1 What, when drunk, one sees in other women, one sees in Garbo sober.

COMMENT by Kenneth Tynan, English critic (1927–80), in *Sight and Sound* (April 1954).

2 I can't make up my mind whether Garbo was a remarkable actor or simply a person so extraordinary that she made everything she did, including acting, seem remarkable.

COMMENT attributed to Isobel Quigley.

3 Every man's harmless fantasy mistress. She gave you the impression that, if your imagination had to sin, it could at least congratulate itself on its impeccable taste.

COMMENT attributed to Alistair Cooke.

4 [on Garbo's appearance] The whole set-up has taken on a very weathered look, dry and draughty, like an abandoned temple, something lost in the jungles at Angkor Wat.

COMMENT by Truman Capote in *Answered Prayers*, III (1986).

5 She gave cinema the sacredness of mass.

COMMENT by Federico Fellini, quoted in *The Independent* (21 April 1990), at Garbo's death.

Ava GARDNER

American actress (1922–90)

6 *On the Beach* is a story about the end of the world, and Melbourne sure is the right place to film it.

ATTRIBUTED remark from 1959. As revealed, however, by *The Dictionary of Australian Quotations* (1984), this was in fact an invention of a Melbourne journalist, Neil Jillett (1933–).

7 There comes a point when every woman has to face up to being an old broad.

QUOTED in *The Observer*, 'Sayings of the Week' (15 July 1984).

8 What I'd really like to say about stardom is that it gave me everything I never wanted.

EXTRACTED from her book *Ava: My Story* (1990).

9 It's the kissiest business in the world. You *have* to keep kissing people.

ATTRIBUTED remark.

Judy GARLAND

American actress (1922–69)

1 If I'm such a legend, then why am I so lonely? If I'm such a legend, then why do I sit at home for hours staring at the damned telephone, hoping it's out of order? ... Let me tell you, legends are all very well if you've got someone around who loves you, some man who's not afraid to be in love with Judy Garland.

QUOTED in John Gruen, *Close-Up* (1968).

2 I was born at the age of twelve on a Metro-Goldwyn-Mayer lot.

QUOTED in *The Observer*, 'Sayings of the Week' (18 February 1951).

3 Hollywood is a strange place when you're in trouble. Everyone is afraid it's contagious.

QUOTED in Simon Rose, *Classic Film Guide* (1995).

4 She's beautiful, an angel – with spurs.

COMMENT by Joe Pasternak, quoted in J.R. Colombo, *Wit and Wisdom of the Moviemakers* (1979).

5 You see that girl? She used to be a hunchback. You see what I've made her into.

COMMENT by Louis B. Mayer.

Greer GARSON

Anglo-Irish actress (1908–)

6 One of the most richly syllabled queenly horrors of Hollywood.

COMMENT by Pauline Kael.

GAY DIVORCEE

(also known as *The Gay Divorce* in the UK) US 1934; screenwriters: various (from musical play); cast: Ginger Rogers (Mimi Glossop), Alice Brady (Aunt Hortense).

7 *Mimi*: A man tore my dress off.
Aunt Hortense: My goodness! Anyone we know?

SOUNDTRACK.

GENEVIEVE

UK 1953: screenwriter: William Rose; cast: Kenneth More (Ambrose Claverhouse), Kay Kendall (Rosalind Peters), Dinah Sheridan (Wendy McKim), John Gregson (Alan McKim), Joyce Grenfell (Hotel proprietress).

1 *Hotel proprietress*: When you want to take a bath, would you be so kind as to sign the little book you'll find inside the bathroom door … Hot water is only provided in the afternoons between the hours of half-past two and six

SOUNDTRACK.

2 *Ambrose*: When that car gets started, you'll be intoxicated by the exuberance of your own velocity. D'you get that? …
Rosalind: I said I'm not drinking anything at all today – nothing at all!

SOUNDTRACK.

3 *Rosalind*: Ambrose seems to think of only two things – that silly old car and the other thing.
Wendy (of Alan): What other thing? Oh, no, my husband only thinks about the car.

SOUNDTRACK.

King GEORGE V

British sovereign (1865–1936)

4 [on being asked which film he would like to see while convalescing] Anything except that damned mouse.

QUOTED in George Lyttelton letter to Rupert Hart-Davis (12 November 1959).

GEORGE WHITE'S SCANDALS

US 1945; screenwriters: Hugh Wedlock and others; cast: Joan Davis (Joan Mason).

5 *Joan*: Champagne! I love it. It tastes like your foot's asleep.

SOUNDTRACK.

GET CARTER

UK 1971; screenwriter/director: Mike Hodges (based on novel *Jack's Return Home* by Ted Lewis); cast: Michael Caine (Jack Carter), Britt Ekland (Anna Fletcher), John Osborne (Cyril Kinnear), Ian Hendry (Eric Paice).

6 *Jack (to Eric)*: I'd almost forgotten what your eyes looked like. They're still the same. Piss-holes in the snow.

SOUNDTRACK.

7 *Jack (to Anna, over phone)*: I want to stroke you and kiss you all over … Take your bra off … Now, hold them gently … Imagine it's me.

SOUNDTRACK.

1 'What would Jesus say?'

SIGN over bed in which Jack lays some woman or other.

GHOST

US 1990; screenwriter: Bruce Joel Rubin; cast: Patrick Swayze (Sam Wheat), Demi Moore (Molly Jensen), Whoopi Goldberg (Oda Mae Brown).

2 *Molly Jensen*: I really love you.
Sam Wheat: Ditto.

SOUNDTRACK. Her wish for him to say not this but 'I love you' is a recurring motif.

3 *Oda Mae Brown (to Sam Wheat, who has demanded she donate an illegally obtained check to charity)*: I know you don't think I'm gonna give this four million dollars to a bunch of nuns.

SOUNDTRACK.

4 *Oda Mae Brown (a medium, to Molly Jensen)*: Don't you see I'm not a fake, not about this.

SOUNDTRACK. She is trying to get over that she really is in touch with Sam Wheat, Molly Jensen's dead lover.

5 *Oda Mae Brown (referring to the afterlife)*: Sam – they're waitin' for you, Sam.

SOUNDTRACK.

The GHOST AND MRS MUIR

US 1947; screenwriter: Philip Dunne; cast: George Sanders (Miles Fairley), Gene Tierney (Lucy).

6 *Miles (to Lucy, in London rainstorm)*: It is easy to understand why the most beautiful poems about England in the spring were written by poets living in Italy at the time.

SOUNDTRACK.

Mel GIBSON

American actor (1956–)

7 I'll tell you what really turns my toes up – love scenes [between] 68-year-old men and young actresses. I promise you, when I get to that age I will say no.

QUOTED in *The Observer* (16 May 1999). Referring to Sean Connery and Catherine Zeta Jones in *Entrapment* (US 1999).

GIGI

US 1958; screenwriter/lyricist: Alan Jay Lerner (from Anita Loos play and Colette novel); cast: Isabel Jeans (Aunt Alicia), Leslie Caron (Gigi), Hermione Gingold (Mme Alvarez), Maurice Chevalier (Honore Lachaille).

1 *Aunt Alicia (to Gigi)*: It doesn't matter who gives them as long as you never wear anything second-rate. Wait for the first-class jewels, Gigi. Hold on to your ideals.

SOUNDTRACK.

2 *Mme Alvarez*: Thank heaven.

SOUNDTRACK. Last line of film. Alluding to the song Honore Lachaille has sung earlier, 'Thank Heaven for Little Girls' (music by Frederick Loewe).

Penelope GILLIATT

English screenwriter and critic (1933–93)

3 Black and white are the most ravishing colours of all in film.

EXTRACTED from her book *Three-Quarter Face* (1980).

4 Film-making has now reached the same stage as sex – it's all technique and no feeling.

ATRIBUTED remark in the 1980s.

Françoise GIROUD

Swiss-born critic (1916–)

5 *Nouvelle vague* [new wave].

REMARK in the newspaper *L'Express* (1958). A term for the new film-making movement originating in France at that time. Rapidly adopted. 'It is a film made by one of the old guard rather than by a member of the *nouvelle vague*' – *The Times* (4 September 1959).

Lillian GISH

American actress (1899–1993)

6 You know, when I first went into the movies, Lionel Barrymore played my grandfather. Later he played my father and finally he played my husband. If he had lived, I'm sure I would have played his mother. That's the way it is in Hollywood. The men get younger and the women get older.

ATTRIBUTED remark.

1 I've never been in style, so I can't go out of style.

ATTRIBUTED remark.

2 Hollywood – an emotional Detroit.

QUOTED in *Hollywood Wits*, ed. K. Madsen Roth (1995).

GLENGARRY GLEN ROSS

US 1992; screenwriter: David Mamet (from his play); cast: Alec Baldwin (Blake), Ed Harris (Dave Morris), Al Pacino (Ricky Roma), Kevin Spacey (John Williamson), Jack Lemmon (Shelley 'The Machine' Levine).

3 *Blake (announcing competition for real estate salesmen)*: First prize is a Cadillac Eldorado. Second prize is a set of steak knives. Third prize is you're fired.

SOUNDTRACK.

GO WEST

US 1940; screenwriter: Irving Brecher; cast: Groucho Marx (S. Quentin Quale), Harpo Marx ('Rusty' Panello), Chico Marx (Joe Panello), June MacCloy (Lulubelle).

4 Go West.

TITLE OF FILM. A screen title derives it from 'Go west, young man' and ascribes that to Horace Greeley, the American editor and politician (1811–72). However, this is an example of a misattribution that refuses to be corrected. The originator of the saying was John Babsone Lane Soule, who first wrote it in the *Terre Haute, Indiana, Express* in 1851 when, indeed, the thing to do in the United States was to head westwards, where gold and much else lay promised. However, Horace Greeley repeated it in his newspaper, the *New York Tribune*, and, being rather more famous, a candidate for the Presidency, and all, it stuck with him. Greeley reprinted Soule's article to show where he had taken it from, but to no avail. The original sentence was, 'Go west, young man, and grow up with the country.' To 'go west' meaning 'die' is a completely separate coinage. It dates back to the 16th century and alludes to the setting of the sun.

5 *Quale*: Lulubelle, it's you! I didn't recognize you standing up!

SOUNDTRACK.

6 *Quale (to Lulubelle)*: Time wounds all heals.

SOUNDTRACK.

7 *Quale*: I was going to thrash them within an inch of their lives but I didn't have a tape measure.

SOUNDTRACK.

8 *Quale (romancing Lulubelle)*: Let's go somewheres where we can be alone. Ah, there doesn't seem to be anyone on this couch.

SOUNDTRACK.

GO WEST YOUNG MAN

US 1936; screenwriter: Mae West; cast: Mae West (Mavis Arden).

1 *Mavis*: Between two evils, I always pick the one I haven't tried before.

SOUNDTRACK. *Compare* ***KLONDIKE ANNIE*** 242:3.

Jean-Luc GODARD

French screenwriter and director (1930–)

2 The cinema is not a craft. It is an art. It does not mean team work. One is always alone; on the set as before the blank page.

EXTRACTED from journal *Cahiers du Cinéma* (July 1958).

3 Cinema is the most beautiful fraud in the world.

EXTRACTED from sketch *Le Grand Escroc* (1963).

4 To me style is just the outside of content, and content the inside of style, like the inside and outside of the human body – both go together, they can't be separated.

QUOTED in Richard Roud, *Jean-Luc Godard*, Introduction (1967).

5 If I had to define myself I'd say I am a 'painter of letters' as one would say that there are 'men of letters'.

QUOTED in Jay Leyda, *Voices of Film Experience* (1977).

6 Every film should have a beginning, a middle and an end – but not necessarily in that order.

QUOTED in Len Deighton, *Close Up* (1972). In *Time* Magazine (14 September 1981), Godard is quoted as making the remark to Georges Franju in the form: 'Movies should have … '

7 *Ceci n'est pas une image juste, c'est juste une image* [This is not a just image, it is just an image].

QUOTED in Colin McCabe, *Godard*: *Images, Sounds, Politics* (1980).

8 Films have become canned goods.

QUOTED in *The Independent* (15 June 1991).

9 All you need for a movie is a gun and a girl.

QUOTED in *Projections*, eds. Boorman & Donohue (1992). Apparently taken from Godard's diary entry for 16 May 1991.

10 I've always had the impression that real militants are like cleaning women, doing a thankless, daily but necessary job. But you, you're the Ursula Andress of militancy, you make a brief appearance, just enough time for the cameras to flash, you make two or three startling remarks and then you disappear again, trailing clouds of self-serving mystery.

COMMENT by François Truffaut in letter to Godard (May–June 1973).

See also Le ***MÉPRIS***; Le ***PETIT SOLDAT***.

Paulette GODDARD

American actress (1911–90)

1 Hollywood is now a place to retire to.

QUOTED in J.R. Colombo, *Wit and Wisdom of the Moviemakers* (1979).

The GODFATHER

US 1972; screenwriters: Francis Ford Coppola, Mario Puzo (from Puzo's novel), Robert Towne; cast: Marlon Brando (Don Vito Corleone), Al Martino (Johnny Fontane), Salvatore Corsitto (Bonasera), Al Pacino (Michael Corleone), John Cazale (Fredo), Al Lettieri (Sollozzo), Robert Duvall (Tom Hagen), Abe Vigoda (Tessio), James Caan (Sonny Corleone), Richard Castellano (Clemenza), John Martino (Paulie), Diane Keaton (Kay Corleone).

2 *Bonasera (to Vito Corleone)*: I believe in America.

SOUNDTRACK. Opening words of film. He is pleading for vengeance against the men who assaulted his daughter.

3 *Vito Corleone (to Bonasera)*: Someday, and that may never come, I'll call upon you to do a service. Until that day, accept this justice as a gift on my daughter's wedding day.

SOUNDTRACK.

4 *Vito Corleone*: In a month from now this Hollywood big shot's going to give you what you want.
Fontane: Too late, they start shooting in a week.
Corleone: I'm gonna make him an offer he can't refuse.

SOUNDTRACK. Johnny Fontane, a singer, desperately wants a part in a movie and goes to see his Godfather, Don Corleone, seeking help. All the contracts have been signed and there is no chance of the studio chief changing his mind. Still, with these words the Godfather promises Fontane he will get him the part.
In Puzo's original novel, the words are: 'He's a businessman. I'll make him an offer he can't refuse.' Thus was given to the language a new expression, which, as far as can be established, was Puzo's own invention. In the film, Michael Corleone, when he takes over as the Godfather, also gets to say: 'I'm gonna make him an offer he can't refuse' – to Fredo, about a rival gangster. In 1973, following the film's release, Jimmy Helms had a hit with the song 'Gonna Make You An Offer You Can't Refuse'.

5 *Tessio (to Sonny, explaining the meaning of a package of fish)*: It's a Sicilian message. It means Luca Brasi sleeps with the fishes.

SOUNDTRACK.

1 *Vito (to Michael)*: I never … I never wanted this for you. I worked my whole life – I don't apologize – to take care of my family. And I refused to be a fool dancing on a string held by all those … big shots. I don't apologize; that's my life. But I thought that … when it was your time that … that you would be the one to hold the strings.

SOUNDTRACK.

2 *Tessio (to Hagen, before being killed for betraying Michael)*: Tell Mike it was only business.

SOUNDTRACK.

3 *Michael (to his wife)*: Don't ask me about my business, Kay.

SOUNDTRACK.

4 *Bonasera*: Young people don't respect anything these days. Times are changing for the worse.

SOUNDTRACK.

The GODFATHER PART II

US 1974; screenwriters: Francis Ford Coppola, Mario Puzo (from Puzo's novel); cast: Al Pacino (Michael Corleone), John Cazale (Fredo).

5 *Michael (kissing his brother while knowing that Fredo had conspire d to kill him)*: I know it was you, Fredo. You broke my heart. You broke my heart.

SOUNDTRACK.

Josef GOEBBELS

German Nazi propagandist (1897–1945)

6 The film … is a cultural bridge between the nations; it promotes understanding among them because it assists them to learn to know each other.

QUOTED in Roger Manvell, *Film* (1944).

7 More than all other forms of art, the film must be popular in the best sense of the word.

SPEECH at International Film Congress (1935), quoted in Roger Manvell & Heinrich Fraenkel, *Doctor Goebbels: His Life and Death* (1960). Films, Goebbels went on, should be strictly contemporary in spirit even when dealing with subjects set in the past; once they achieved this quality they would bridge the nations and become the 'spokesmen of our age'.

1 What a good idea of mine it was to have taken possession of the film industry on behalf of the Reich several years ago!

QUOTED in J.R. Colombo, *Wit and Wisdom of the Moviemakers* (1979).

See also ***MRS MINIVER*** 286:6.

GOLDFINGER

UK 1964; screenwriters: Richard Maibaum, Paul Dehn; cast: Sean Connery (James Bond); Gert Frobe (Goldfinger), Shirley Eaton (Jill Masterson), Honor Blackman (Pussy Galore), Lois Maxwell (Miss Moneypenny), Desmond Llewellyn (Q), Mai Ling (Mei-Lei).

2 *Bond (to telephone caller when he is in bed with Jill)*: Felix ... I'm sorry, I can't. Something big's come up.

SOUNDTRACK.

3 *Bond (to Jill)*: My dear girl, there are some things that just aren't done. Such as drinking Dom Perignon '53 above a temperature of 38 degrees Fahrenheit. That's as bad as listening to the Beatles without earmuffs.

SOUNDTRACK.

4 *Moneypenny (to Bond)*: The only gold I know is the kind you wear – you know, on the third finger of your left hand.

SOUNDTRACK.

5 *Goldfinger*: This is gold, Mr Bond. All my life I've been in love with its colour, its brilliance, its divine heaviness.

SOUNDTRACK.

6 *Goldfinger*: Choose your next witticism carefully, Mr Bond. It may be your last.

SOUNDTRACK.

7 *Bond (as laser beam approaches)*: Do you expect me to talk?
Goldfinger: No, I expect you to die.

SOUNDTRACK.

8 *Pussy (introducing herself)*: My name is Pussy Galore.
Bond: I must be dreaming.

SOUNDTRACK.

9 *Mei-Lei*: Can I do something for you, Mr Bond?
Bond: Just a drink – a Martini, shaken not stirred.

SOUNDTRACK. He needs a drink after just escaping a laser death-ray. There are also references to his fad in ***DR NO*** (*see* 138:6 and 139:3), and others.

1 *Pussy (to Bond)*: You can turn off the charm. I'm immune.

SOUNDTRACK.

2 *Bond (on man buried in crushed car)*: As you said, he had a pressing engagement.

SOUNDTRACK.

William GOLDMAN

American screenwriter and novelist (1931–)

3 Screenwriting is what feminists call 'shit-work': if it's well done, it's ignored. If it's badly done, people call attention to it.

ATTRIBUTED remark, made in 1975.

4 In terms of authority, screenwriters rank somewhere between the man who guards the studio gate and the man who runs the studio (this week).

EXTRACTED from his book *Adventures in the Screen Trade*, 'Author's Note' (1983).

5 As far as the film-making process is concerned, stars are essentially worthless and absolutely essential.

EXTRACTED from same book, Pt 1, Chap. 1, 'Stars'.

6 Today, a million dollars is what you pay a star you don't want.

EXTRACTED from same book and chapter.

7 Studio executives are intelligent, brutally overworked men and women who share one thing in common with baseball managers: They wake up every morning of the world with the knowledge that sooner or later they're going to get fired.

EXTRACTED from same book, 'Studio Executives'.

8 Compounding [the studio executive's] problem of no job security in the decision-making process is the single most important fact, perhaps, of the entire movie industry: NOBODY KNOWS ANYTHING ... Not one person in the entire motion picture field *knows* for a certainty what's going to work.

EXTRACTED from same book and chapter. Jake Eberts comments in *My Indecision Is Final*, Chap. 9 (1990): 'That's true in terms of the ever elusive formula for making hit pictures. But in terms of deal points and properties, of what's around town and who is talking to whom, the opposite is true: everyone knows everything.'

1 [of the screenwriter's problems over the star system] You can't make a 'Hamlet' without breaking a few egos.

QUOTED in *The Observer* (8 April 1984).

Jerry GOLDSMITH

American composer (1929–)

2 No music has ever saved a bad picture, but a lot of good pictures have saved a lot of bad music.

QUOTED in Irwin Bazelon, *Knowing the Score* (1975).

Sam GOLDWYN

Polish-born American producer (1882–1974)

3 Include me out.

ATTRIBUTED remark. This apparently arose when Goldwyn and Jack L. Warner were in disagreement over a labour dispute. Busby Berkeley, who had made his first musical for Goldwyn, was discovered moonlighting for Warner Brothers. Goldwyn said to Warner: 'How can we sit together and deal with this industry if you're going to do things like this to me? If this is the way you do it, gentlemen, include me out!'

Scott Berg, working on the official biography, told *The Sunday Times* (3 May 1981) that he claimed the ability to tell which Goldwynisms are genuine and suggested this one *might* be, as Goldwyn himself appeared to acknowledge when speaking at Balliol College, Oxford, on 1 March 1945: 'For years I have been known for saying "Include me out" but today I am giving it up for ever.' On the other hand, Boller & George, *They Never Said It* (1989) report Goldwyn as having denied saying it, claiming rather to have said to members of the Motion Picture Producers and Distributors of America: 'Gentlemen, I'm withdrawing from the association' (this would have been in 1933).

4 [on it being suggested that he make a film on the life of Bismarck] Who in hell wants to see a picture about a herring?

QUOTED in Reginald Pound, *Their Moods and Mine* (1937).

5 An oral [or verbal] contract isn't worth the paper it's written on.

ATTRIBUTED remark, quoted in Alva Johnston in *The Great Goldwyn* (1937). Samuel Goldwyn Jr (interviewed by Michael Freedland in *TV Times*, 13 November 1982) has commented on the 'twenty-eight' genuine sayings attributed to his father and included this as one. Carol Easton, *Search for Goldwyn* (1976), has of Joseph M. Schenk: 'His verbal contract is worth more than the paper it's written on.' Garson Kanin apparently ruled that this was one of the Goldwynisms dreamt up by the Goldwyn studio's press office.

6 In two words – impossible!

ATTRIBUTED remark in same Johnston book. The joke appeared in a humour magazine late in 1925, and was subsequently imposed upon Goldwyn. *H.L. Mencken's Dictionary of Quotations* (1942) has: 'I can answer in two words – im possible' and ascribes it to 'an American movie magnate, 1930'. However, *Punch* Magazine (10 June 1931) has the following caption to a cartoon by George Belcher: '*Harassed Film-Producer*. This business can be summed up in two words: "IM–POSSIBLE".'

1 That's the way with these directors, they're always biting the hand that lays the golden egg.

ATTRIBUTED remark, in same book.

2 I want a movie that starts with an earthquake and works up to a climax ...

ATTRIBUTED remark, in same book.

3 [of one of his own films] It's greater than a masterpiece, it's mediocre.

ATTRIBUTED remark, in same book.

4 Take away the essentials and what have you got?

ATTRIBUTED remark, in same book.

5 [on films with a 'message'] Messages are for Western Union.

ATTRIBUTED remark, in same book. In the 1978 edition of *The Filmgoer's Book of Quotes*, Leslie Halliwell also attributes to Jack Warner: 'We'll make the pictures: let Western Union deliver the messages.' Arthux Marx, *Goldwyn* (1976) has Goldwyn saying: 'Pictures are for entertainment, messages should be delivered by Western Union.'

6 [on being shown bad reviews of one of his pictures] It runs off my back like a duck.

ATTRIBUTED remark, in same book.

7 The trouble with this business is the dearth of bad pictures.

ATTRIBUTED remark, quoted in Michael Freedland, *The Goldwyn Touch* (1986), but probably apocryphal. Said to have been uttered after making *The Goldwyn Follies* (1937).

8 God makes stars. I just produce them.

QUOTED by Paul Holt in the *Daily Express* (16 May 1939).

9 [to David Niven when he left Hollywood in 1939 to return to Europe and sign up] I'll cable Hitler and ask him to shoot around you.

QUOTED by David Niven in *Bring On the Empty Horses* (1975).

10 [before the opening of his film *The Best Years of Our Lives* (1946)] I don't care if it doesn't make a nickel, I just want every man, woman, and child in America to see it.

QUOTED in Norman Zierold, *Moguls* (1969).

1 [on being told a story was too caustic] Too caustic? To hell with the cost. If it's a sound story, we'll make a picture of it anyway.

ATTRIBUTED remark, in same book.

2 [to James Thurber, who was concerned about the amount of violence that had crept into a film treatment of his story *The Secret Life of Walter Mitty*] I'm sorry you felt it was too bloody and thirsty.

QUOTED in Arthur Marx, *Goldwyn*: *A Biography of the Man Behind the Myth* (1976). Thurber, with commendable presence of mind, replied, 'Not only did I think so, I was horror and struck.' *Mitty* was eventually released in 1947.

3 Hollywood is too much publicized. There are too many people here. Some of them should go back on a slow train.

QUOTED in *News Review* (11 December 1947).

4 Let's have some new clichés.

QUOTED in *The Observer* (24 October 1948).

5 Why should people go out and pay to see bad movies when they can stay at home and see bad television for nothing?

QUOTED in *The Observer* (9 September 1956).

6 We have all passed a lot of water since then.

QUOTED in E. Goodman, *The Fifty Year Decline of Hollywood* (1961), but probably apocryphal.

7 The reason so many people showed up at [Louis B. Mayer's] funeral was because they wanted to make sure he was dead.

QUOTED in Bosley Crowther, *Hollywood Rajah* (1960). Probably apocryphal, if only because Mayer's funeral in 1957 was in fact sparsely attended. *Compare* George **JESSEL** 233:5.

8 You've still only got the mucus of a good idea.

ATTRIBUTED by Terry Wogan on BBC Radio *Quote ... Unquote* (29 May 1980), but probably another invention. In the P.G. Wodehouse story 'The Castaways' (*Strand* Magazine, June 1933) (set in Hollywood), Mr Schnellenhamer, the film mogul, says of a script he has bought, 'It has the mucus of a good story. See what you can do with it.'

9 I seriously object to seeing on the screen what belongs in the bedroom.

QUOTED in Leslie Halliwell, *The Filmgoer's Book of Quotes* (1973).

10 How'm I gonna do decent pictures when all my good writers are in jail? ... Don't misunderstand me, they all ought to be hung.

QUOTED by Dorothy Parker in *Writers at Work*, First Series ed. Malcolm Cowley (1958). This remark was made in the days of McCarthy witch-hunts, Hollywood black lists, etc.

1 Let's bring it up to date with some snappy nineteenth-century dialogue.

QUOTED by King Vidor in *A Tree Is a Tree* (1953). Vidor adds, 'I was there when he said [it].'

2 A wide screen just makes a bad film twice as bad.

QUOTED in *Quote* Magazine (9 September 1956).

3 [on a script treatment] I read part of it all the way through.

QUOTED in Philip French, *The Movie Moguls*, Chap. 4 (1969).

4 [Goldwyn] filled the room with wonderful panic and beat at your mind like a man in front of a slot machine, shaking it for a jackpot.

COMMENT by Ben Hecht in *A Child of the Century* (1954).

5 There are lucky ones whose great hearts, shallow and commonplace as bedpans, beat in instinctive tune with the great heart of the public, who laugh as it likes to laugh, weep the sweet and easy tears it likes to weep – Goldwyn is blessed with that divine confidence in the rightness (moral, aesthetic, commercial) of his own intuition – and that I suppose is the chief reason for his success.

COMMENT by Lindsay Anderson, made in 1974.

See also The **CHILDREN'S HOUR** 100:5.

GONE WITH THE WIND

US 1939; screenwriter: Sidney Howard and others (from Margaret Mitchell's novel); cast: Clark Gable (Rhett Butler), Vivien Leigh (Scarlett O'Hara), Butterfly McQueen (Prissy), Thomas Mitchell (Gerald O'Hara), Olivia de Havilland (Melanie Hamilton), Leslie Howard (Ashley Wilkes).

6 The greatest motion picture ever made.

SLOGAN.

7 [Prologue] There was a land of Cavaliers and Cotton Fields called the Old South. Here in this patrician world the Age of Chivalry took its last bows. Here was the last ever seen of the Knights and their Ladies fair, of Master and Slave. Look for it only in books, for it is no more than a dream remembered, a Civilization gone with the wind.

SCREEN TITLE at opening.

8 *Scarlett (to suitors)*: Fiddle-dee-dee. War, war, war. This war talk's spoiling all the fun at every party this spring.

SOUNDTRACK.

1 *Gerald (to daughter Scarlett)*: Why, land's the only thing in the world worth working for, worth fighting for, worth dying for, because it's the only thing that lasts.

SOUNDTRACK.

2 *Scarlett (at her first meeting with Rhett)*: Sir, you are no gentleman.
Rhett: And you, miss, are no lady.

SOUNDTRACK.

3 *Rhett (to Scarlett)*: I believe in Rhett Butler. He's the only cause I know. The rest doesn't mean much to me.

SOUNDTRACK.

4 *Rhett (to Scarlett)*: You should be kissed, and often, and by someone who knows how.

SOUNDTRACK.

5 *Prissy*: I don't know nothin' about birthin' babies!

SOUNDTRACK.

6 *Scarlett (alone after the war is over)*: As God is my witness, as God is my witness, they're not going to lick me! I'm going to live through this, and when it's all over, I'll never be hungry again – no, nor any of my folks! If I have to lie, steal, cheat, or kill – as God is my witness, I'll never be hungry again!

SOUNDTRACK.

7 *Scarlett (after killing intruder)*: Well, I guess I've done murder. I won't think about that now. I'll think about it tomorrow.

SOUNDTRACK.

8 *Ashley (to Scarlett)*: Yes, there is something. Something you love better than me, though you may not know it. Tara.

SOUNDTRACK.

9 *Scarlett*: Where shall I go? What shall I do?
Rhett: Frankly, my dear, I don't give a damn.

SOUNDTRACK. In Mitchell's novel (Chap. 57), Rhett's reply is simply: 'My dear, I don't give a damn.' In the last scene of the film, these famous words were only allowed on to the soundtrack after months of negotiation with the Hays Office, which controlled film censorship. In those days, the word 'damn' was forbidden in Hollywood under Section V (1) of the Hays Code, even if it was what Mitchell had written in her novel (though she hadn't included the 'frankly'). Sidney Howard's original draft was accordingly changed to: 'Frankly, my dear, I don't care.' The scene was shot with both versions of the line, and the producer, David Selznick, argued at great length with the censors over which was to be used. He did this not least because he thought he would look a fool if the famous line was excluded. He also wanted to show how faithful the film was to the novel. Selznick argued that the *Oxford Dictionary* described 'damn' not as an oath but as a vulgarism, that many women's magazines used the word and that preview audiences had expressed disappointment when the line was omitted. The censors suggested 'darn' instead. Selznick finally won the day – but because he was technically in breach of the Hays Code he was fined $5,000. The line still didn't sound quite right: Clark Gable, as Rhett, had to put the emphasis unnaturally on 'give' rather than on 'damn'.

1 *Scarlett*: Tara! Home! I'll go home, and I'll think of some way to get him back. After all, tomorrow is another day!

SOUNDTRACK. Last lines of film.

2 [declining David O. Selznick's offer of a percentage instead of salary for directing the picture] Don't be a damn fool, David. This picture is going to be one of the biggest white elephants of all time.

COMMENT by Victor Fleming.

3 Forget it, Louis. No Civil War picture ever made a nickel.

COMMENT by MGM production executive Irving Thalberg. He was advising Louis B. Mayer not to bid for the film rights of Margaret Mitchell's novel. Mayer took Thalberg's advice, saying 'Irving knows what's right.'

4 I wouldn't pay fifty thousand bucks for any damn book any damn time.

COMMENT by Jack L. Warner, of Warner Brothers, in 1936.

5 *Gone With the Wind* is going to be the biggest flop in Hollywood history. I'm just glad it'll be Clark Gable who's falling flat on his face and not Gary Cooper.

COMMENT by Gary Cooper (who had turned down the part of Rhett Butler), on Clark Gable, who accepted it, in 1938.

6 I bet it's a pip!

COMMENT by Bette Davis, turning down the part of Scarlett O'Hara, in1938.

7 [on seeing the number of Confederate troops in the film of her novel] If we'd had as many soldiers as that, we'd have won the war!

COMMENT by Margaret Mitchell, quoted in W.G. Harris, *Gable and Lombard* (1976).

8 [after viewing the film] And the next thing they are going to do will be the Bible and it will last for two days.

COMMENT by Lord Berners to Billa Harrod, quoted in Mark Amory, *Lord Berners*, Chap. 14 (1998).

1 You come out of *Gone With the Wind* feeling that history isn't so disturbing after all. One can always make a dress out of a curtain.

COMMENT by Dilys Powell, English critic (1902–95), quoted in *Independent on Sunday* (29 April 1990).

GOODBYE COLUMBUS

US 1969; screenwriter: Arnold Schulman (based on Philip Roth novel); cast: Richard Benjamin (Neal), Brenda (Ali McGraw).

2 *Neal (on what kind of person he is)*: I'm a liver!
Brenda: I'm a pancreas.

SOUNDTRACK.

3 *Brenda (when Neal reaches out for her)*: Later.
Neal: What happens if I can't wait?
Brenda: Start without me.

SOUNDTRACK.

4 *Guest at wedding*: By the way, sweetie, what have you been doing with yourself this summer?
Brenda: Growing a penis.

SOUNDTRACK.

GOODBYE MR CHIPS

UK 1939; screenwriter: R.C. Sherriff and others (from James Hilton novella); cast: Robert Donat (Charles Chipping), Terry Kilburn (Peter Colley III).

5 *Chipping (on his deathbed, on having no children)*: Oh, but I have. Thousands of them. And all boys!

SOUNDTRACK.

6 *Peter Colley III*: Goodbye, Mr Chips. Goodbye.

SOUNDTRACK. Last line of film.

GOODFELLAS

US 1990; screenwriters: Martin Scorsese, Nicholas Pileggi (from his book); cast: Ray Liotta (Henry Hill), Robert De Niro (James Conway), Christopher Serrone (Young Henry Hill), Lorraine Branco (Karen), Joe Pesci (Tommy De Vito), Catherine Scorsese (De Vito's mother), Paul Sorvino (Pauly Cicero).

7 *Henry Hill (narrating)*: As far back as I can remember I always wanted to be a gangster … To me being a gangster was better than being President of the United States.

SOUNDTRACK.

1 *Karen*: What do you do?
Henry Hill: I'm in construction.
Karen: You don't feel like you're in construction.
Henry Hill: Well, I'm a union delegate.
SOUNDTRACK.

2 *Karen (narrating)*: I know there are women like my best friends who would have gotten out of there the minute their boyfriend gave them a gun to hide. But I didn't. I gotta admit the truth. It turned me on.
SOUNDTRACK.

3 *Henry Hill (to Karen)*: Nobody goes to jail unless they want to. Unless they make themselves get caught. They don't have things organized.
SOUNDTRACK.

4 *Tommy De Vito*: I need this knife. I'm gonna take this. OK?
Mother: OK.
Tommy De Vito: I just need it for a little while.
Mother: Bring it back, though, you know.
SOUNDTRACK.

5 *Mother*: Why don't you get yourself a nice girl?
Tommy De Vito: I get a nice one almost every night, Ma.
SOUNDTRACK.

6 *James Conway (about Karen and Henry)*: She'll kill him but she won't divorce him.
SOUNDTRACK.

7 *Henry Hill (narrating)*: You know, we always called each other goodfellas. Like you'd say to somebody, 'You're gonna like this guy, he's all right, he's a goodfella, he's one of us.' You understand? We were goodfellas, wiseguys.
SOUNDTRACK.

8 *Henry Hill (narrating)*: If you're part of a crew, nobody tells you that they're going to kill you … Your murderers come with smiles. They come as your friends.
SOUNDTRACK.

Ezra GOODMAN

American writer

1 Reading a fan magazine is similar to eating a banana under water.

EXTRACTED from his book *The Fifty Year Decline and Fall of Hollywood* (1961).

Paul GOODMAN

American writer and psychoanalyst (1911–)

2 The stultifying effect of the movies is *not* that the children see them but that their parents do, as if Hollywood provided a plausible adult recreation to grow up into.

EXTRACTED from his book *Growing Up Absurd* (1960).

Betty GRABLE

American actress (1916–73)

3 There are two reasons why I'm in show business, and I'm standing on them.

ATTRIBUTED remark, quoted in Barbara Rowes, *The Book of Quotes* (1979).

Lew GRADE (Lord Grade)

Russian-born British producer (1906–99)

4 [to Franco Zeffirelli, who explained that the high cost of the TV film *Jesus of Nazareth* (1977) was partly because there had to be twelve apostles] Twelve! So who needs twelve? Couldn't we make do with six?

ATTRIBUTED remark, quoted in *Radio Times* (October 1983).

5 [on producing the famously expensive and unsuccessful film *Raise the Titanic* (1980)] It would have been cheaper to lower the Atlantic.

ATTRIBUTED remark. Alas, on TV-am's *Frost on Sunday* (23 November 1987), Grade denied ever having said it. All he had actually managed was, 'I didn't raise the Titanic high enough.'

6 [on hearing Pierce Brosnan had only sixteen minutes of dialogue in a Bond film] They could call them something else instead of actors. People today, they don't have to do any acting. Actors are a sideshow. The real movie is about car chases and things being blown up.

QUOTED in *The Independent* (14 December 1998).

The GRADUATE

US 1967; screenwriters: Buck Henry, Calder Willingham; cast: Anne Bancroft (Mrs Robinson), Dustin Hoffman (Ben Braddock), Walter Brooke (Mr Maguire).

1 *Mr Maguire*: Ben – I just want to say one word to you – just one word – plastics.

SOUNDTRACK.

2 *Ben*: Mrs Robinson, you're trying to seduce me. Aren't you?

SOUNDTRACK.

3 *Mrs Robinson*: Do you find me undesirable?
Ben: Oh no, Mrs Robinson. I think … I think you're the most attractive of all my parents' friends. I mean that.

SOUNDTRACK.

Sheilah GRAHAM

British-born Hollywood columnist (1904–88)

4 No one has a closest friend in Hollywood.

EXTRACTED from her book *The Rest of the Story* (1964).

GRAND HOTEL

US 1932; screenwriter: William A. Drake (from play based on Vicki Baum novel); cast: Greta Garbo (Grusinskaya), Lewis Stone (Dr Otternschlag), John Barrymore (Baron Felix von Geigern), Lionel Barrymore (Otto Kringelein), Wallace Beery (General Director Preysing).

5 *Von Geigern*: That's my creed, Kringelein. A short life and a gay one.

SOUNDTRACK. Kringelein has a fatal disease.

6 *Grusinskaya (to von Geigern)*: I want to be alone …

SOUNDTRACK. *See also* Greta **GARBO** 177:6.

7 *Otternschlag (to Kringelein)*: What do you do in the Grand Hotel? Eat. Sleep. Loaf around. Flirt a little. Dance a little. A hundred doors leading to one hall, and no one knows anything about the person next to them. And when you leave, someone occupies your room, lies in your bed, and that's the end.

SOUNDTRACK.

8 *Otternschlag (to Kringelein)*: A man who is not with a woman is a dead man.

SOUNDTRACK.

1 *Otternschlag (to himself)*: The Grand Hotel. Always the same. People come, people go ... nothing ever happens.

SOUNDTRACK.

Stewart GRANGER

English actor (1913–93)

2 I've never done a film I'm proud of.

ATTRIBUTED remark.

Cary GRANT

British-born actor (1904–86)

3 Everybody wants to be Cary Grant. Even *I* want to be Cary Grant.

ATTRIBUTED remark.

4 Judy ... Judy ... Judy!

ATTRIBUTED remark. Impersonators always put this line in Grant's mouth (as alluded to by James **CAGNEY** 64:3), but Grant denied that he had ever said it and had a check made of all his films. According to Richard Keyes, *Nice Guys Finish Seventh* (1992), Grant once said: 'I vaguely recall that at a party someone introduced Judy [Garland] by saying, "Judy, Judy, Judy," and it caught on, attributed to me.'

5 [a magazine writer preparing a profile of Grant sent a cable to his agent inquiring, 'HOW OLD CARY GRANT?' Grant sent the reply himself] OLD CARY GRANT FINE. HOW YOU?

QUOTED in Leslie Halliwell, *The Filmgoer's Book of Quotes* (1973).

6 [when offered the part of Henry Higgins in film of *My Fair Lady*] Not only will I not play it, but if Rex Harrison doesn't do it, I won't even go to see it.

ATTRIBUTED remark in about 1963.

7 I improve on misquotation.

ATTRIBUTED remark.

8 He was the best and most important actor in the history of the cinema. The essence of his quality can be put quite simply: he can be attractive and unattractive simultaneously; there is a light and dark side to him but, whichever is dominant, the other creeps into view.

COMMENT by David Thomson in *A Biographical Dictionary of Film* (1994 edn).

Hugh GRANT

English actor (1960–)

1 They love me in Japan. But unfortunately I don't want their love. I want their money.

QUOTED in *The Observer*, 'Sayings of the Week' (17 July 1994).

The GRAPES OF WRATH

US 1940; screenwriter: Nunnally Johnson (from John Steinbeck novel); cast: Jane Darwell (Ma Joad), Henry Fonda (Tom Joad).

2 *Ma Joad (to Tom)*: You done what you had to do.

SOUNDTRACK. This is as near as the film script gets to the actual phrase 'a man got to do what he got to do' which occurs in Steinbeck's novel – one of the first recorded instances of its use.

3 *Ma Joad*: That's what makes us tough. Rich fellas come up and they die and their kids ain't no good and they die out. But we keep a-comin'. We're the people that live. They can't wipe us out. They can't lick us. We'll go on forever, Pa … 'cause … we're the people.

SOUNDTRACK. Last lines of film.

The GRASSHOPPER AND THE ANTS

US 1934; music/lyrics: Leigh Harline, Larry Morey.

4 *Grasshopper*: Oh! the world owes me a living
Deedle, diedle, doedle, diedledum.

SOUNDTRACK. The expression 'the world owes me a living' was ascribed to Disney when used as the epigraph of Graham Greene's novel *England Made Me* (1935). The cartoon film in question – one of the first 'Silly Symphonies' – is based on the Aesop fable 'Of the ant and the grasshopper' (as it is called in Caxton's first English translation, 1484), which tells of a grasshopper asking an ant for corn to eat in winter. The ant asks, 'What have you done all the summer past?' and the grasshopper can only answer, 'I have sung.' The moral is that you should provide yourself in the summer with what you need in winter. Disney turns the grasshopper into a fiddler and gives him a song to sing.

GREASE

US 1978; screenwriter: Bronte Woodard (based on stage musical by Jim Jacobs and Warren Casey); cast: Eve Arden (Miss McGee).

5 *Miss McGee*: If you can't be an athlete, be an athletic supporter.

SOUNDTRACK.

GREASE 2

US 1982; screenwriter: Ken Finkleman; cast: Michelle Pfeiffer (Stephanie), Maxwell Caulfield (Michael), Eve Arden (Miss McGee).

1 *Female student*: I'm a little worried. I've missed my last two periods.
Miss McGee: That's all right, dear, you can make them up after school!
SOUNDTRACK.

2 *Michael*: Actually, I think you're kind of terrific.
Stephanie: Get out of here! *You're* the terrific one. I mean you know all this deep junk and everything.
SOUNDTRACK.

The GREAT DICTATOR

US 1940; screenwriter/director: Charlie Chaplin; cast: Charlie Chaplin (Jewish barber/Adenoid Hynkel, Dictator of Tomania).

3 *Jewish barber*: We think too much and feel too little. More than machinery we need humanity. More than cleverness, we need kindness and gentleness.
SOUNDTRACK.

The GREAT LIE

US 1941; screenwriter: Lenore Coffee (from a novel by Polan Banks); cast: Mary Astor (Sandra Kovac).

4 *Sandra*: If I didn't think you meant so well, I'd feel like slapping your face.
SOUNDTRACK.

The GREATEST STORY EVER TOLD

US 1965; screenwriters: James Lee Barrett, George Stevens (director); cast: John Wayne (The Centurion)

5 *The Centurion*: Truly, this man was the son of God.

SOUNDTRACK. Wayne's sole line in the film. According to an old story re-told by Brian Viner in *Independent on Sunday* (24 October 1999): 'The director George Stevens, unimpressed by his wooden delivery, is reported to have offered some tactful advice, saying, "You're referring to the son of God here, Duke, you've got to deliver the line with awe." Wayne accepted the advice. On the next take he said, "Aw, truly this was the Son of God!"'

GREEN MANSIONS

US 1959; screenwriter: Dorothy Kingsley (from W.H. Hudson novel); cast: Audrey Hepburn (Rima the Bird Girl).

1 *Rima (narrating)*: If you look in this place tomorrow, and it's gone, you mustn't be sad, because you know it still exists, not very far away.

SOUNDTRACK. Last lines of film.

Peter GREENAWAY

English director and screenwriter (1942–)

2 We don't need books to make films. It's the last thing we want – it turns cinema into the bastard art of illustration.

QUOTED in *Independent on Sunday* (10 July 1994).

See also Sergei **EISENSTEIN** 150:8.

Graham GREENE

English novelist, screenwriter and critic (1904–91)

3 Occasionally a film of truth and tragic value gets somehow out of Hollywood on to the screen. Nobody can explain it – perhaps a stage needs using, all the big executives are in conference over the latest Mamoulian 'masterpiece' – Jehovah is asleep.

REMARK in *Night and Day* (4 November 1937), reviewing *They Won't Forget.* Robert Mamoulian was a director of such films as *Queen Christina. They Won't Forget* was an anti-lynching melodrama.

4 For me it is impossible to write a film play without first writing a story.

EXTRACTED from his book *Ways of Escape* (1980).

5 My books don't make good films. Film companies think they will, but they don't.

INTERVIEWED by Mort Rosenblum in *St Louis Post Dispatch* (12 September 1982).

See also Shirley **TEMPLE** 409:1; Sam **ZIMBALIST** 459:3.

John GRIERSON

Scottish producer of documentaries (1898–1972)

6 Film-making belongs like all show business to that magical world in which two and two can make five, but also three and even less. It is, by that token, not a business to which the Presbyterian mind is natively and nationally attuned.

EXTRACTED from 'A Scottish Film Industry' in journal *Saltire Review* (Summer 1960).

1 Documentary can achieve an intimacy of knowledge and effect impossible to the shimsham mechanics of the studio and the lily-fingered interpretation of the metropolitan actor.

QUOTED by Cliff Hanley in *The Sunday Mail Story of Scotland*, No. 26 (1988).

D.W. GRIFFITH

American director (1875–1948)

2 Viewed as drama, the war is somewhat disappointing.

REMARK from 1918, quoted in Leslie Halliwell, *The Filmgoer's Book of Quotes* (1973).

3 [directing an epic film] Move those ten thousand horses a trifle to the right. And that mob out there, three feet forward.

QUOTED in Josef Von Sternberg, *Fun In a Chinese Laundry* (1965).

4 Speaking movies are impossible. When a century has passed, all thoughts of our so-called 'talking pictures' will have been abandoned. It will never be possible to synchronize the voice with the picture.

REMARK from 1926, quoted in Stuart Berg Flexner, *Listening to America* (1982).

5 I made them *see*, didn't I? … I changed everything. Remember how small the world was before I came along. I made them see it both ways in time as well as space.

QUOTED in Adela Rogers St Johns, *The Honeycomb* (1969).

6 There is no suspense like the suspense of a delayed coition.

ATTRIBUTED remark.

(Sir) Alec GUINNESS

English actor (1914–2000)

7 I don't really know who I am. Quite possibly, I do not exist at all.

REMARK quoted in J.R. Colombo, *Wit and Wisdom of the Moviemakers* (1979).

John GUNTHER

American journalist and author (1901–70)

8 Hollywood is nothing more than a suburb of the Bronx, both financially and from the point of view of talent.

EXTRACTED from his book *Inside U.S.A.* (1947).

GUYS AND DOLLS

US 1955; screenwriter: Joseph L. Mankiewicz (from musical by Jo Swerling and Abe Burrows, based on a Damon Runyon story); cast: Marlon Brando (Sky Masterson), Frank Sinatra (Nathan Detroit), Jean Simmons (Sarah).

1 *Sky (to Nathan)*: No matter who you marry, you wake up married to someone else.

SOUNDTRACK.

GYPSY

US 1962; screenwriter: Leonard Spigelgrass (after stage musical based on memoirs of Gypsy Rose Lee); cast: Rosalind Russell (Rose Hovick), Diane Pace (Baby Louise), Natalie Wood (Louise Hovick/Gypsy Rose Lee), Karl Malden (Herbie), Ann Jillian (Dainty June).

2 *Rose (to Baby Louise)*: Sing out, Louise. Sing out!

SOUNDTRACK. She is prompting the future Gypsy Rose Lee at a children's talent contest.

3 *Rose*: So everything was coming up roses.

SOUNDTRACK. She later sings the song 'Everything's Coming Up Roses' (lyrics by Stephen Sondheim, music by Jule Styne, 1959). But did the expression exist before this? It is possibly adapted from the expression, 'to come out smelling of roses', but there do not seem to be any examples even of *that* before the date of the Sondheim coinage.

4 *Rose*: Was I right or was I right?

SOUNDTRACK. It is not clear when 'Am I right, or am I right?' entered the language. As an expression brooking no debate, one suspects it originated in American show biz. *Compare* ***I'M NO ANGEL*** 225:7.

5 *Gypsy (to Rose)*: I thought you did it for me, Mama!

SOUNDTRACK.

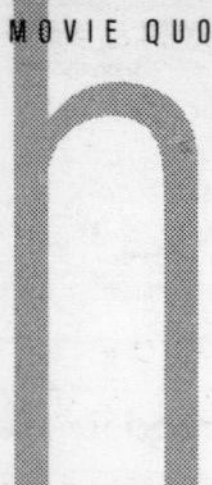

HAMLET

UK 1948; screenwriter: Alan Dent (from Shakespeare's play); cast: Laurence Oliver (Hamlet).

1 *Opening narration*: This is the tragedy of a man who could not make up his mind.

SOUNDTRACK. Olivier spoke Dent's words but did not write them, as is implied by *The Oxford Dictionary of Quotations* (1992). Dent's capsule comment was criticized on the grounds that *Hamlet* is not so much about a man who could not make up his mind as about one who could not bring himself to take the necessary action. Dent was a Scottish critic and writer (1905–78).

Christopher HAMPTON

English playwright and screenwriter (1946–)

2 The secret of being a successful screenwriter is that you have to write very, very badly, *but you also have to write as well as you possibly can.*

EXTRACTED from his book *Tales from Hollywood* (1985).

Helen HANFF

American writer (1916–89)

3 Hollywood isn't a place, it's a way of life.

EXTRACTED from her book *Q's Legacy* (1985).

HANNAH AND HER SISTERS

US 1986; screenwriter/director: Woody Allen; cast: Michael Caine (Elliot), Barbara Hershey (Lee).

4 *Elliot (quoting)*: 'nobody, not even the rain, has such small hands.'

SOUNDTRACK. Elliot buys a book of e.e.cummings's poetry and urges Lee (his wife's sister) to read the poem 'somewhere I have never travelled' (1931) as part of his seduction of her.

(Sir) Cedric HARDWICKE

English actor (1893–1964)

1 God felt sorry for actors, so he gave them a place in the sun and a swimming pool. The price they had to pay was to surrender their talent.

ATTRIBUTED remark.

Jean HARLOW

American actress (1911–37)

2 She perfectly understood the roles she invariably played (even to the point of asking her agent, when he phoned with a new part, 'What kinda whore am I this time?')

QUOTED in Clyde Jeavons & Jeremy Pascall, *A Pictorial History of Sex in the Movies* (1975).

3 Jean Harlow was very soft about her toughness.

COMMENT by George Cukor, quoted in Gavin Lambert, *On Cukor* (1972).

Leslie HARRIS

American director

4 The typical black story is not from 'hood anymore. We are entrenched in American society, dealing more with the politics, money and job pressures, which are what the American dream is all about.

QUOTED in *The Observer* (17 September 1995).

Moss HART

American playwright and director (1904–61)

5 [on Hollywood] The most beautiful slave-quarters in the world.

QUOTED in Leslie Halliwell, *The Filmgoer's Book of Quotes* (1973).

Laurence HARVEY

Lithuanian-born actor (1928–73)

6 He demonstrated conclusively that it is possible to succeed without managing to evoke the least audience sympathy – and to go on succeeding despite unanimous critical antipathy and overwhelming public apathy.

COMMENT by David Shipman in *The Great Movie Stars*, Vol. 2 (1972).

See also ***ROOM AT THE TOP*** 357:6.

HARVEY

US 1950; screenwriters: Oscar Brodney, Mary Chase (from her play); cast: James Stewart (Elwood P. Dowd), Peggy Dow (Miss Kelly), Nana Bryant (Mrs Chumley), Jesse White (Wilson), Charles Drake (Mr Sanderson), Cecil Kellaway (Dr Chumley), Josephine Hull (Veta Louise Simmons), Victoria Horne (Myrtle Mae), Wallace Ford (Lofgren).

1 *Elwood*: Every day's a beautiful day.

SOUNDTRACK.

2 *Wilson*: Pooka. From the old Celtic mythology, a fairy spirit in animal form, always very large. The pooka appears here and there, now and then, to this one and that one. A benign but mischievous creature, very fond of rumpots, crackpots, and how are you Mr Wilson?

SOUNDTRACK.

3 *Elwood (repeating what his mother used to say, to Chumley)*: 'In this world, Elwood, you must be, oh, so smart, or, oh, so pleasant.' For years, I was smart. And you may quote me.

SOUNDTRACK.

4 *Elwood (to Chumley)*: I've wrestled with reality for 35 years and I'm happy, doctor. I finally won out over it.

SOUNDTRACK.

5 *Elwood*: Well, thank you, Harvey. I prefer you, too.

SOUNDTRACK. Last line of film.

Molly HASKELL

American writer and critic

6 There are two cinemas: the films we have actually seen and the memories we have of them.

QUOTED in J.R. Colombo, *Wit and Wisdom of the Moviemakers* (1979).

Henry HATHAWAY

American director (1898–1985)

7 There's a lot of nice guys walking around Hollywood but they're not eating.

QUOTED by Charles Hamblett in *The Times* (22 March 1969).

Frank HAUSER

English stage director and critic (1922–)

1 [on *Another Man's Poison* (UK 1951)] Like reading Ethel M. Dell by flashes of lightning.

COMMENT attributed as written in the *New Statesman*. Ethel M. Dell (1881–1939) was an English writer of light romantic fiction who was much in vogue in the 1920s and 30s. This comment alludes to Coleridge's observation about Edmund Kean: 'To see him act is like reading Shakespeare by flashes of lightning' (*Table-Talk*).

HAYS CODE *See* **PRODUCTION CODE**

Rita HAYWORTH

American actress and dancer (1918–87)

2 Every man I knew had fallen in love with Gilda and wakened with me.

ATTRIBUTED remark. Hayworth's portrayal of the eponymous heroine of *Gilda* (US 1946) was the high spot of her career. *See also* ***NOTTING HILL*** 310:5.

HEAVENS ABOVE!

UK 1963; screenwriters: Frank Harvey, John Boulting; cast: Peter Sellers (Reverend John Smallwood), Eric Sykes (Harry Smith), Bernard Miles (Simpson), Nicholas Phipps (Mr Hughes).

3 *Mrs Smith-Gould (about the vicar)*: And those ghastly boots he wears.
Mr Hughes: Oh, I don't know. I once knew a chap at the BBC who wore boots.
Mrs Smith-Gould: That doesn't surprise me at the very least.

SOUNDTRACK.

4 *Harry Smith (holding up a chicken)*: All legs and breast, just waiting to be stuffed.

SOUNDTRACK. *Compare* ***TO CATCH A THIEF*** 425:8.

5 *Simpson (to Smallwood)*: Now I'm going to give you two bits of the Bible – Matthew 27:5, 'He went and hanged himself'; Luke 10:27, 'Go and do thou likewise'.

SOUNDTRACK.

HEAVEN'S GATE

US 1980; screenwriter/director: Michael Cimino; cast: Kris Kristofferson (James Averill), John Hurt (Billy Irvine).

1 Heaven's Gate.

TITLE OF FILM. There are various contenders for the source of the title of this film, famous for having lost more money than any other film to date – about £34 million. In it, 'Heaven's Gate' is the name of a roller-skating rink used by settlers and immigrants in Wyoming in 1891. Conceivably, the name is meant to be taken as an ironic one for the rough situation many of the characters find themselves in as they arrive to start a new life. The idea of a 'gate to heaven' goes back to the Bible. For example, Genesis 28:17 has: 'This is none other but the house of God, and this is the gate of heaven.' Psalm 78:23 has: 'He commanded the clouds from above, and opened the doors of heaven.' Shakespeare twice uses the phrase. In *Cymbeline* (II.iii.20) there is the song, 'Hark, hark, the lark at heaven's gate sings', and Sonnet 29 has 'Like to the lark at break of day arising / From sullen earth sings hymns at heaven's gate.' William Blake's 'Jerusalem' (1820) has: 'I give you the end of a golden string; / Only wind it into a ball, / It will lead you in at Heaven's gate, / Built in Jerusalem's wall.' Robert Browning also uses the phrase, and Steven Bach in his book *Final Cut* (1985) about the making of the film cites not only Blake as a possible source but also the Wallace Stevens poem with the title 'The Worms at Heaven's Gate'.

2 What one loves about life are the things that fade.

SLOGAN.

3 The most talked about film of the decade!

SLOGAN.

4 *James (to Billy)*: Billy, you're the only son of a bitch worth getting seriously drunk with.

SOUNDTRACK.

Ben HECHT

American playwright and screenwriter (1894–1964)

5 Movies are one of the bad habits that corrupted our century. Of their many sins, I offer as the worst their effect on the intellectual side of the nation. It is chiefly from that viewpoint I write of them – as an eruption of trash that has lamed the American mind and retarded Americans from becoming a cultured people … They have slapped into the American mind more human misinformation in one evening than the Dark Ages could muster in a decade.

EXTRACTED from his book *A Child of the Century*, Bk 5 (1954).

1 The movie-makers are able to put more reality into a picture about the terrors of life at the ocean bottom than into a tale of two Milwaukeeans in love.

ATTRIBUTED remark in news reports (1954).

2 Starlet is a name for any woman under thirty not actively employed in a brothel.

QUOTED in *Hollywood Anecdotes*, eds. Boller & Thompson (1987).

Hein HECKROTH

German art director (1901–70)

3 Movies are the folklore of the twentieth century.

QUOTED in Michael Powell, *A Life in Movies* (1986).

The HEIRESS

US 1949; screenwriters: Ruth & Augustus Goetz (from their play and Henry James novel *Washington Square*); cast: Olivia De Havilland (Catherine Sloper).

4 *Catherine*: Yes, I can be very cruel. I have been taught by masters.

SOUNDTRACK.

HELL'S ANGELS

US 1930; screenwriters: Howard Estabrook, Harry Behn; cast: Jean Harlow (Helen), Ben Lyon (Monte).

5 *Helen (to Monte)*: Would you be shocked if I put on something more comfortable?

SOUNDTRACK. Invariably misquoted – e.g. 'Do you mind if I put on something more comfortable?' or 'Excuse me while I slip into something more comfortable.' 'Pardon me while I slip into something more comfortable' was perpetrated by Denis Gifford in *The Independent* (22 July 1995). What Helen says is, of course, by way of a proposition, and she duly exchanges her fur wrap for a dressing gown.

Lillian HELLMAN

American playwright and writer (1907–84)

6 The convictions of Hollywood and television are made of boiled money.

EXTRACTED from her book *An Unfinished Woman* (1969).

Ernest HEMINGWAY

American novelist (1899–1961)

1 [on seeing the remake of *A Farewell to Arms* (1957)] You write a book like that you're fond of, then you see that happen to it, it's like pissing in your father's beer.

QUOTED in A.E. Hotchner, *Papa Hemingway* (1966).

2 [of adaptations of books for the cinema] Take the money and run.

ATTRIBUTED remark, quoted in William Goldman, *Adventures in the Screen Trade* (1984).

Paul HENREID

Austrian-born actor (1908–92)

3 He looks as if his idea of fun would be to find a cold damp grave and sit on it.

COMMENT by Richard Winnington.

HENRY V

UK 1944; screenwriters: Laurence Olivier (director), Alan Dent (from Shakespeare's play); cast: Laurence Olivier (Henry V), Robert Newton (Pistol).

4 To the Commandos and Airborne troops of Great Britain – the spirit of whose actions it has humbly attempted to recapture in some ensuing scenes – this film is dedicated.

SCREEN TITLE.

5 *Pistol*: Is it not passing brave to be a king,
And ride in triumph through Persepolis?

SOUNDTRACK. Lines appropriated from Christopher Marlowe's *Tamburlaine the Great*, Pt 1, Act 2, Sc 5 (about 1587). Pistol speaks them on leaving the Boar's Head tavern following the similarly interpolated death of Falstaff. In no sense could Pistol have been 'quoting' Marlowe's mighty line because, of course, the events of *Henry V* pre-date the Elizabethan playwright.

Katharine HEPBURN

American actress (1907–)

6 The average Hollywood film star's ambition is to be admired by an American, courted by an Italian, married to an Englishman and have a French boyfriend.

QUOTED in the *New York Journal-American* (22 February 1954).

1 [on what makes the screen partnership of Fred Astaire and Ginger Rogers work] He gives her class and she gives him sex.

QUOTED in Leslie Halliwell, *The Filmgoer's Book of Quotes* (1973), but otherwise unsubstantiated.

2 I don't care what is written about me so long as it isn't true.

QUOTED in *A Treasury of Humorous Quotations*, eds. Prochnow & Prochnow (1969).

3 Acting is the most minor of gifts and not a very high-class way to earn a living. After all, Shirley Temple could do it at the age of four.

ATTRIBUTED remark.

4 I stopped going to see my films when I began to watch what was bad about my face, my neck, my body, my voice.

QUOTED in *The Observer*, 'Sayings of the Week' (20 July 1986).

5 Film was and is still a romantic business, just as life is romantic.

QUOTED in *The Observer*, 'Sayings of the Week' (5 October 1987).

6 Box-office poison.

COMMENT in 1938 attributed to US Independent Motion Picture Theatre Proprietors. Alexander Walker in *Stardom* (1970) refers, however, to 'the notorious red-bordered advertisement placed by a group of exhibitors in a trade paper which listed the stars [*sic*] who were deemed to be "box-office poison"'. So perhaps she was not alone.

7 She has a face that belongs to the sea and the wind, with large rocking-horse nostrils and teeth that you just know bite an apple every day.

COMMENT by Cecil Beaton.

8 At the studio they call her Katherine of Arrogance.

COMMENT attributed to Estelle Winwood, British actress (1882–1984).

Margaret HERRICK

American secretary

9 [on seeing the Academy Awards statuette for the first time in 1931] Why, it looks like my uncle Oscar.

QUOTED in J.R. Colombo, *Wit and Wisdom of the Moviemakers* (1979). Herrick was a secretary at the American Academy of Motion Picture Arts and Sciences where the awards had been made since 1928. The design of the statuette was by Cedric Gibbons, MGM's art director. The nickname became known by 1936.

Werner HERZOG

German director and screenwriter (1942–)

1 You should look straight at a film; that's the only way to see one. Film is not the art of scholars but of illiterates. Film culture is not analysis but agitation of the mind.

QUOTED in *The Guardian* (8 September 1977).

Charlton HESTON

American actor (1924–)

2 I have played three presidents, three saints and two geniuses, If that doesn't create an ego problem I don't know what does.

ATTRIBUTED remark.

3 A graduate of the Mount Rushmore school of acting.

COMMENT attributed to Edward G. Robinson.

See also C. A. **LEJEUNE** 252:2.

HIGH NOON

US 1952; screenwriter: Carl Foreman; cast: Gary Cooper (Marshal Will Kane), Ian MacDonald (Frank Miller), Grace Kelly (Amy Kane), Otto Kruger (Percy Mettrick), Howland Chamberlin (Hotel clerk), Katy Jurado (Helen Ramirez), Lloyd Bridges (Deputy Harvey Pell), Lon Chaney Jr (Martin Howe).

4 When the hands point up – the excitement starts!

SLOGAN.

5 *Kane*: They're making me run. I've never run from anybody before.

SOUNDTRACK.

6 *Amy (arguing with her husband's decision)*: You're asking me to wait an hour to find out if I'm going to be a wife or a widow.

SOUNDTRACK.

7 *Hotel clerk (to Amy, who is planning to miss the confrontation)*: Now, me, I wouldn't leave this town at noon for all the tea in China. No, sir, it's going to be quite a sight to see.

SOUNDTRACK.

8 *Howe (to Kane, on the life of a lawman)*: It's a great life. You risk your skin catchin' killers and the juries turn 'em loose so they can come back and shoot at you again. If you're honest, you're poor your whole life, and in the end you wind up dyin' all alone on some dirty street. For what? For nothin'. For a tin star.

SOUNDTRACK.

1 *Howe*: People gotta talk themselves into law and order before they do anything about it. Maybe just because down deep they don't care. They just don't care.

SOUNDTRACK.

HIS GIRL FRIDAY

US 1940; screenwriter: Charles Lederer (from play *The Front Page* by Ben Hecht and Charles MacArthur); cast: Cary Grant (Walter Burns), Rosalind Russell (Hildy Johnson); Ralph Bellamy (Bruce Baldwin).

2 *Burns (to Johnson)*: I'd know you anytime, anyplace, anywhere.

SOUNDTRACK. Having just re-met his ex-wife, Burns is recalling a line he had used to her on the night he proposed. An early example of the 'anytime, anyplace, anywhere' expression that became quite common in movie scripts. *See also The* **STRAWBERRY BLONDE** 400:4.

3 *Burns (to Baldwin)*: I'm more or less particular about whom my wife marries.

SOUNDTRACK. Baldwin is lined up to be Burns's ex-wife's next husband.

4 *Baldwin (of Burns)*: He's not the man for you. I can see that, but I sorta like him. He's got a lot of charm.
Johnson: He comes by it naturally. His grandfather was a snake.

SOUNDTRACK.

5 *Burns (to Johnson)*: Hildy, this is war!

SOUNDTRACK. He is not referring to their post-divorce relationship but to the exciting events surrounding a condemned man.

HIS KIND OF WOMAN

US 1951; screenwriter: Frank Fenton; cast: Robert Mitchum (Dan Milner), Jane Russell (Lenore Brett), Vincent Price (Mark Cardigan), Raymond Burr (Nick Ferraro).

6 *Man at bar (of film)*: It has a message no pigeon would carry.
Cardigan (film star): At my studio, all messages are handled by Western Union.

SOUNDTRACK. *Compare* Sam **GOLDWYN** 191:5.

7 *Milner (to Brett)*: It's an old habit. Whenever I have nothing to do and I can't think, I always iron my money.

SOUNDTRACK.

8 *Ferraro (pointing pistol at Milner)*: Wake up, I want you to see it coming … I want him to be fully conscious … I want to see the expression on his face when he knows it's coming.

SOUNDTRACK.

(Sir) Alfred HITCHCOCK

English director (1899–1980)

1 Actors are cattle.

REMARK quoted in the *Saturday Evening Post* (22 May 1943). He later denied this: 'What I said was actors should be *treated* like cattle' (quoted in Leslie Halliwell, *The Filmgoer's Book of Quotes*, 1973). In François Truffaut, *Hitchcock* (English version), Chap. 6 (1968), Hitchcock more seriously commented: 'A few years prior to my arrival in Hollywood I had been quoted as saying that all actors are cattle. I'm not quite sure in what context I might have made such a statement. It may have been made in the early days of the talkies in England, when we used actors who were simultaneously performing in stage plays [who did not have much commitment and regarded films as slumming] … I had no use for that kind of actor.'

2 I aim to provide the public with beneficial shocks. Civilization has become so protective that we're no longer able to get our goose bumps instinctively. The only way to remove the numbness and revive our moral equilibrium is to use artificial means to bring about the shock. The best way to achieve that, it seems to me, is through a movie.

REMARK at Hollywood press conference (1947), quoted in François Truffaut, *Hitchcock* (English version, 1968).

3 For me the cinema is not a slice of life, but a piece of cake.

REMARK quoted in *The Sunday Times* Magazine (6 March 1977). This appears to be based on an August 1962 interview published in François Truffaut, *Hitchcock* (English version), Chap. 4 (1968) where the remark is quoted by Truffaut as, 'Some films are slices of life. Mine are slices of cake.' Hitchcock comments: 'I don't want to film a "slice of life" because people can get that at home … They don't have to pay money to see a slice of life.'

4 Making a film means, first of all, to tell a story … What is drama, after all, but life with the dull bits cut out?

QUOTED in François Truffaut, *Hitchcock* (English version), Chap. 4 (1968).

5 [referring to his film *Foreign Correspondent*] That secret clause was our "MacGuffin" … it's the device, the gimmick, if you will … [it's] the term we use to cover all that sort of thing: to steal plans or documents, or discover a secret, it doesn't matter what it is. And the logicians are wrong in trying to figure out the truth of a MacGuffin, since it's beside the point. The only thing that really matters is that in the picture the plans, documents, or secrets must seem to be of vital importance to the characters. To me, the narrator, they're of no importance whatever.

QUOTED in François Truffaut, *Hitchcock* (English version), Chap. 6 (1968). Another way of explaining the MacGuffin is as a distracting device, a red herring, in a thriller upon which the whole plot appears to turn but which, in the end, has no real relevance to the plot or its solution. Hitchcock also cites the example of the uranium in *Notorious* (1946), which turns out to be less important than the notorious woman falling for the US agent.

1 The chief requisite for an actor is the ability to do nothing well.

QUOTED in François Truffaut, *Hitchcock* (English version, 1968).

2 The length of the film should be directly related to the endurance of the human bladder.

ATTRIBUTED remark.

3 In film, murders are always very clean. I show how difficult it is and what a messy thing it is to kill a man.

ATTRIBUTED remark.

4 If I made *Cinderella*, the audience would be looking for the body in the coach.

ATTRIBUTED remark.

5 Hitchcock was shooting on location and bad weather had got him behind schedule. 'What the hell are you going to do about it?' the studio trouble-shooter demanded. 'I shall do whatever is necessary,' said Hitchcock in his measured tones, 'to complete what, in the course of time, you will come to refer to as "our film".'

QUOTED in John Boorman, *Money Into Light* (1985).

6 When I was doing *Vertigo*, poor Kim Novak bless her heart, said, 'Mr Hitchcock, what is my character feeling in relation to her surroundings?' There was silence on the set and Hitch said, 'It's only a movie, for God's sakes.' She never asked another question.

QUOTED by James Stewart. *Compare* Ingrid **BERGMAN** 56:5, Carrie **FISHER** 162:7.

7 Hitchcock is one of the greatest inventors of form in the history of cinema. Perhaps the only film-makers who can be compared with him in this respect are Murnau and Eisenstein ... Here, form does not merely embellish content, but actually creates it.

COMMENT by Eric Rohmer & Claude Chabrol in their book *Hitchcock* (1957).

8 Much of Hitchcock's limitations, I think, but also his greatness within them, are to be found in his heavy body. His way of always working in the studio, using a static camera, not moving about, he has erected it all into a system, using long scenes where he won't have to give himself the trouble of having to move about.

COMMENT by Ingmar Bergman, interviewed in *Bergman on Bergman* (1970).

1 [Hitchcock] thought of himself as looking like Cary Grant. That's tough, to think of yourself one way and look another.

COMMENT by Tippi Hedren, American actress (1935–), interviewed in California (1982) and quoted in *Hollywood Anecdotes*, eds. Boller & Davis (1988).

Abbie HOFFMAN

American radical (1936–)

2 Reality is a movie.

QUOTED in Barbara Rowes, *The Book of Quotes* (1979).

HOLD BACK THE DAWN

US 1941; screenwriters: Charles Brackett, Billy Wilder; cast: Charles Boyer (George Iscovescu), Paulette Godard (Anita Dixon).

3 *George*: Your husband?
Anita: No, no, Shaughnessy was a jockey from Caliente. Five foot three! Once over the border, I went to a judge. I said, a woman wants a man, not a radiator cap! Divorce granted, fifty dollars.

SOUNDTRACK.

William HOLDEN

American actor (1918–81)

4 I'm a whore. All actors are whores. We sell our bodies to the highest bidder.

ATTRIBUTED remark.

HOLIDAY INN

US 1942; music/lyrics: Irving Berlin; cast: Bing Crosby (Jim Hardy).

5 *Hardy (sings)*: I'm dreaming of a white Christmas.

SOUNDTRACK. Song, 'White Christmas'. Reprised in *White Christmas* (US, 1954).

Agnieszka HOLLAND

Polish director (1948–)

6 In Hollywood, they don't feel guilt.

QUOTED in *The Observer*, 'Sayings of the Week' (17 October 1993).

HOLLYWOOD HOTEL

US 1937; music/lyrics: Richard Whiting, Johnny Mercer; cast: Johnny Davis, Frances Langford.

1 Hooray for Hollywood,
That screwy, ballyhooey Hollywood …

SOUNDTRACK. Song, 'Hooray for Hollywood'.

Bob HOPE

British-born American comedian (1903–)

2 They are doing things on the screen now that I wouldn't do in bed, if I could.

ATTRIBUTED remark from 1965

3 They are doing things on the screen these days that the French don't even put on postcards.

REMARK from 1970, quoted in Leslie Halliwell, *The Filmgoer's Book of Quotes* (1973).

4 There'll always be an England … even if it's in Hollywood.

QUOTED in Leslie Halliwell, *The Filmgoer's Book of Quotes* (1973).

5 Bob Hope is still about as funny as he ever was. I just never thought he was that funny in the first place.

COMMENT attributed to Chevy Chase.

HOPE AND GLORY

UK 1987; screenwriter/director: John Boorman; cast: Sebastian Rice Edwards (Bill Rohan).

6 *Bill (narrating)*: All my life nothing ever quite matched the perfect joy of that moment. My school lay in ruins; the river beckoned with a promise of stolen days.

SOUNDTRACK. Last words of film.

See also John **BOORMAN** 67:4.

Hedda HOPPER

American actress and columnist (1890–1966)

7 [of Hollywood] No matter what you say about the town, and anything you say probably is true, there's never been another like it.

EXTRACTED from her book *From Under My Hat* (1952).

1 Smart writers never understand why their satires on our town [Hollywood] are never successful. What they refuse to accept is that you can't satirize a satire.

EXTRACTED from the same book.

2 The geniuses who conduct the motion-picture business killed glamour when they decided that what the public wanted was not dream stuff, from which movies used to be made, but realism.

EXTRACTED from *The Whole Truth and Nothing But*, written with James Brough (1963).

The HORN BLOWS AT MIDNIGHT

US 1945; screenwriters: Sam Hellman, James V. Kern; cast: Jack Benny (Athanael), Alexis Smith (Elizabeth).

3 *Athanael*: Elizabeth, I just had the craziest dream. You know, if you saw it in the movies, you'd never believe it.

SOUNDTRACK.

HORSE FEATHERS

US 1932; screenwriters: Bert Kalmar and others; cast: Groucho Marx (Prof. Wagstaff), Zeppo Marx (Frank Wagstaff), Chico Marx (Baravelli), Harpo Marx (Pinky), Thelma Todd (Connie Bailey).

4 *Prof. Wagstaff (to retiring president of college)*: Why don't you go home to your wife? I'll tell you what, I'll go home to your wife, and outside of the improvement she'll never know the difference.

SOUNDTRACK.

5 *Prof. Wagstaff (to Frank)*: I'm ashamed to be your father. You're a disgrace to our family name of Wagstaff, if such a thing is possible.

SOUNDTRACK.

6 *Prof. Wagstaff (to Frank)*: I'd horsewhip you if I had a horse.

SOUNDTRACK.

7 *Frank*: Anything further, Father?
Prof. Wagstaff: 'Anything further, Father?' That can't be right. Isn't it 'Anything father, further?' The idea! I married your mother because I wanted children. Imagine my disappointment when you arrived.

SOUNDTRACK.

8 *Prof. Wagstaff*: Baravelli, you've got the brain of a four-year-old boy, and I bet he was glad to get rid of it.

SOUNDTRACK.

1 *Prof. Wagstaff (to widow Connie Bailey)*: Oh, I love sitting on your lap. I could sit here all day if you didn't stand up.

SOUNDTRACK.

2 *Prof. Wagstaff (to Baravelli)*: How much would you want to stand at the wrong end of a shooting gallery?

SOUNDTRACK.

3 *Lucille*: What a day! Spring in the air!
Prof. Wagstaff: Who, me? I should spring in the air and fall in the lake.

SOUNDTRACK.

4 *Prof. Wagstaff*: For years before my son was born
I used to yell from night till morn
Whatever it is – I'm against it!
And I've been yelling since I first commenced it –
I'm against it!

SOUNDTRACK.

5 *Staff member*: The Dean is furious. He's waxing wrath.
Prof. Wagstaff: Is Roth out there, too? Tell Roth to wax the Dean for a while.

SOUNDTRACK.

6 *Prof. Wagstaff (putting lamp in window)*: Be a lamp in the window for my wandering boy.

SOUNDTRACK. What is this? Probably a bringing together of two clichés from popular fiction and the parlour songbook. 'Where is my wand'ring boy tonight?' is the first line of a poem/song written and composed by the (presumably American) Rev. R. Lowry in 1877. Under the title 'Where Is Your Boy Tonight?' it is No. 303 in Ira D. Sankey's *Sacred Songs and Solos*. No mention of a lamp in the window, however. Most likely, this allusion is to the silent film entitled *Where Is My Wandering Boy Tonight?* (US, 1922) of which nothing is known to me, however.

Putting a light or lamp in a window is a traditional sign of devotion to or of showing support for a cause. In a speech in Scotland on 29 November 1880 Lord Rosebery said of Gladstone: 'From his home in Wales to the Metropolis of Scotland there has been no village too small to afford a crowd to greet him – there has been no cottager so humble that could not find a light to put in his window as he passed.'

Groucho returned to the theme in *At the Circus* (1939). About to become a ringmaster, he is being helped by Chico into a tail coat that he finds rather tight. 'You'd have to be a wizard to get into this coat,' he says. Chico: 'That's-a-right, it belonged to a wizard.' At this point, a pigeon flies out of the tail pocket. Chico: 'It's a homing pigeon.' And Groucho says: 'Then there'll always be a candle burning in my pocket for my wandering pigeon.'

The HOUND OF THE BASKERVILLES

US 1939; screenwriter: Ernest Pascal (from Conan Doyle novel); cast: Basil Rathbone (Sherlock Holmes), Nigel Bruce (Dr Watson).

1 *Holmes*: Quick, Watson, the needle!

SOUNDTRACK. A line not uttered by Holmes in any of the books but here used to suggest his cocaine habit. It was a line known a good bit before this film, however: P.G. Wodehouse in a letter (22 December 1922) wrote: 'I wonder what an osteopath does if a patient suddenly comes apart in his hands. ("Quick, Watson, the seccotine!")'

Leslie HOWARD

English actor (1893–1943)

2 The great favourite among picture fans is now Leslie Howard. We find that Adonis at tea – he looks like an assistant master at some inferior private school. Glasses and bad teeth.

COMMENT by Harold Nicolson, in *Harold Nicolson's Diaries and Letters* (entry for 26 March 1933 at Pasadena) (1966).

Trevor HOWARD

English actor (1916–88)

3 I believe Trevor Howard has quite a nice, gentle riposte to unwanted attention. Someone saw him in a bar once and said: 'Are you Trevor Howard?' 'Yes,' he replied, 'When I'm working I am.'

COMMENT by fellow actor Charles Dance.

HUD

US 1963; screenwriters: Irving Ravetch, Harriet Frank Jr (from Larry McMurtry novel); cast: Paul Newman (Hud Bannon), Patricia Neal (Alma Brown).

4 *Hud (to Alma)*: The only question I ever ask any woman is, 'What time is your husband coming home?'

SOUNDTRACK.

Rock HUDSON

American actor (1925–85)

5 I can't play a loser. I don't look like one.

ATTRIBUTED remark.

6 I call him Ernie because he's certainly no Rock.

COMMENT by Doris Day.

The HUNCHBACK OF NOTRE DAME

US 1939; screenwriters: Sonya Levien, Bruno Frank (from Victor Hugo novel); cast: Charles Laughton (Quasimodo).

1 *Quasimodo (to a gargoyle)*: Why was I not made of stone like thee?

SOUNDTRACK. Last line of film.

Liz HURLEY

English actress (1966–)

2 [on the dress she wore for the English premiere of *Four Weddings and a Funeral*] You thought you saw a lot more of me than you actually did in That Dress. Although it looked precarious, it didn't shift all night, the pins didn't jab and it was incredibly comfortable.

QUOTED in *The Independent* (7 January 1995).

HUSBANDS AND WIVES

US 1992; screenwriter/director: Woody Allen; cast: Woody Allen (Gabe Roth), Mia Farrow (Judy Roth), Juliette Lewis (Rain).

3 *Gabe*: I've always had this penchant for what I call Kamikaze women … They crash their plane … into you, and you die along with them.

SOUNDTRACK.

4 *Gabe (quoting, with approval, a remark in Rain's story)*: 'Life doesn't imitate art. It imitates bad television.'

SOUNDTRACK.

5 *Gabe*: My heart does not know from logic.

SOUNDTRACK. Later, Allen said of his love for Mia Farrow's adopted daughter, Soon-Yi (whom he was to marry): 'The heart wants what it wants. There's no logic to these things.'

6 *Judy (to Gabe, on their marriage)*: It's over and we both know it.

SOUNDTRACK. The film was generally viewed as prefiguring the break-up of Allen and Farrow's relationship.

John HUSTON

American director, actor and screenwriter (1906–87)

7 I don't try to guess what a million people will like. It's hard enough to know what I like.

REMARK quoted in Leslie Halliwell, *The Filmgoer's Book of Quotes* (1973).

I AM A CAMERA

UK 1955; screenwriter: John Collier (from John van Druten's play based on Christopher Isherwood's stories); cast: Laurence Harvey (Christopher Isherwood).

1 *Isherwood*: I am a camera, with its shutter open, just watching it, quite detached, taking pictures of it all, to be developed sooner or later and printed.

SOUNDTRACK. Opening narration, adapting Isherwood's 'I am a camera with its shutter open, quite passive, recording, not thinking' from 'A Berlin Diary', *Goodbye to Berlin* (1939). Isherwood became irritated with people assuming that this passive approach to writing was intended to describe his own.

2 Me no Leica.

APOCRYPHAL comment. A small joke, but a good one. There was a vogue for dismissive one-line criticisms of plays and films, especially in the 1930s, '40s and '50s, when suitable opportunities presented themselves. It was either when Isherwood's Berlin stories were turned first into a play, *I am a Camera* (1951), or subsequently into a film (1955), that one critic summed up his/her reaction with the words '(Me) no Leica'. This has been variously attributed to C.A. Lejeune, George Jean Nathan, Walter Kerr and Kenneth Tynan. It is a comment on the transitory nature of much criticism that one cannot say for sure who did originate the joke.

Lejeune was film critic for variously *The Observer* and the *News Chronicle* and is remembered for her pithy dismissals of undistinguished films – though few of these lines have been verified. But the chances of the above remark having been written by Miss Lejeune or most of the others have receded since the discovery of a review of the film by the critic of the *Sunday Dispatch* (16 October 1955) wherein appears: 'No Leica, snarled a New York critic.' This may well take us back to the likes of George Jean Nathan, who was ascribed the quote in a book review by Frederic Raphael and who, being a theatre critic, was writing about the *play*.

I'M ALL RIGHT JACK

UK 1959; screenwriters: Frank Harvey, John Boulting (from Alan Hackney novel); cast: Peter Sellers (Fred Kite), Terry-Thomas (Major Hitchcock).

3 *Major Hitchcock (of the workers)*: I can tell you, they're an absolute shower – a positive shower.

SOUNDTRACK.

1 *Major Hitchcock*: We've got men here who can break into a muck sweat merely by standing still.

SOUNDTRACK.

2 *Fred Kite (on Soviet Russia)*: It's the one place I'd like to go to, though – all them cornfields, and ballet in the evening.

SOUNDTRACK. As in the Hackney novel, *Private Life* (1958) – 'Miles of cornfields, and ballet in the evening.'

I'M NO ANGEL

US 1933; screenwriters: Mae West, Harlan Thompson; cast: Mae West (Tira), Gertrude Howard (Beulah).

3 *Tira (to maid after male admirer has just stormed out on her)*:
Oh, Beulah!
Beulah: Yes, ma'am.
Tira: Peel me a grape!

SOUNDTRACK. In Mae West's *Goodness Had Nothing To Do With It*, Chap. 12 (1959) she writes: 'I must confess that while I wrote all my own lines, I owed one of the funniest and best-remembered lines ... to Boogie, a cute pet African woolly monkey I cherished at that time. Boogie loved grapes, but he would always peel the tough skin off each of them with fastidious and exaggerated care before he ate it. He was an expert at it.'

4 *Tira*: It's not the men in my life, but the life in my men.

SOUNDTRACK. She apparently reprised the line in *Sextette* (US 1978).

5 *Tira*: When I'm good, I'm very, very good. But when I'm bad, I'm better.

SOUNDTRACK.

6 *Tira*: I've been things and seen places.

SOUNDTRACK.

7 *Tira*: Is that elegant, or is that elegant?

SOUNDTRACK. *Compare* ***GYPSY*** 205:4.

IF...

UK 1968; screenwriter: David Sherwin (from original script with John Howlett); cast: Peter Jeffrey (Headmaster), Malcolm McDowell (Mick Travis).

8 *Headmaster*: Education in Britain is a nubile Cinderella, sparsely clad and much interfered with.

SOUNDTRACK.

9 *Mick*: One man can change the world with a bullet in the right place.

SOUNDTRACK. Possibly a quotation, but untraced.

IN A LONELY PLACE

US 1950; screenwriter: Andrew Solt; cast: Gloria Grahame (Laurel Gray), Humphrey Bogart (Dixon Steele), Jeff Donnell (Sylvia Nicolai), Art Smith (Mel Lippman).

1 *Sylvia (to husband when he appears in swimsuit)*: My hero!

SOUNDTRACK. The quintessential cry of the female in romantic fiction when her beau has just rescued her or overcome some formidable obstacle to their love. Obviously said in parody here. Raina says it a number of times in Shaw's play *Arms and the Man* (1894), but that is really a parody, too. Burns in *The Jolly Beggars* (1785) has a woman say to a soldier: 'But whilst with both hands I can hold the glass steady / Here's to thee, my hero, my sodger laddie!'

2 *Dixon (quoting from his own script)*: 'I was born when she kissed me. I died when she left me. I lived a few weeks when she loved me.'

SOUNDTRACK. Dixon is a Hollywood scriptwriter. The lines also appear in a slightly different form. After they split up, Laurel's farewell to Dixon – and last line of the film – is 'I lived a few weeks while you loved me. Goodbye, Dix.'

3 *Mel*: I'm the guy who tried to talk Selznick out of *Gone With the Wind*.

SOUNDTRACK. Mel is Dixon's agent. *Compare* ***SUNSET BOULEVARD*** 402:2.

IN THE GOOD OLD SUMMERTIME

US 1949; screenwriters: Robert Z. Leonard and others (from Miklos Laszlo play *The Shop Around the Corner*); cast: Judy Garland (Veronica Fisher).

4 *Veronica*: Psychologically, I'm very confused, but personally I feel just wonderful.

SOUNDTRACK.

IN THE HEAT OF THE NIGHT

US 1967; screenwriter: Stirling Silliphant; cast: Sidney Poitier (Virgil Tibbs).

5 *Tibbs*: They call me *Mr* Tibbs.

SOUNDTRACK. Hence, the title of the subsequent *They Call Me Mister Tibbs* (US 1970).

IN WHICH WE SERVE

UK 1942; screenwriter/director: Noël Coward; cast: Noël Coward (Capt. 'D.'/Kinross), John Mills (Ordinary Seaman Shorty Blake).

6 *Narrator*: This is the story of a ship …

SOUNDTRACK.

7 'Daily Express holds canvass of its reporters in Europe. And ten out of twelve say NO WAR THIS YEAR.'

HEADLINE on newspaper floating in ship's wreckage. This was based on fact.

'Britain will not be involved in a European war this year, or next year either' was an actual front-page headline in the *Daily Express* (30 September 1938). Contrary to popular myth this was the only time the paper predicted as much in a headline though, occasionally, the view that 'There will be no European war' appeared in leading articles. While the statement turned out to be true up to the comma, Lord Beaverbrook, the paper's proprietor, unfortunately insisted on the 'or next year either'. He said: 'We must nail our colours *high* to the mast.' Something like the phrase 'Britain will not be involved in a European war' appeared eight times in the *Express* between September 1938 and August 1939 (A.J.P. Taylor, *Beaverbrook*, 1966). As a result of Coward's use of the headline, Beaverbrook launched a campaign to try to suppress the film.

1 *Kinross (in speech to crew of* HMS Torrin *on commissioning day)*: A happy and efficient ship. A very happy and a very efficient ship … you can't have one without the other. A ship can't be happy unless she's efficient and she certainly won't be efficient unless she's happy.

SOUNDTRACK. Coward based his script on Lord Louis Mountbatten's association with HMS *Kelly* and its sinking during the Battle of Crete. This speech echoed Mountbatten's: 'In my experience, I have always found that you cannot have an efficient ship unless you have a happy ship, and you cannot have a happy ship unless you have an efficient ship. That is the way I intend to start this commission, and that is the way I intend to go on – with a happy and efficient ship.'

2 *Shorty (when Prime Minister Neville Chamberlain on the radio says, 'You can imagine what a bitter blow it is to me' at outbreak of war)*: It's not exactly a bank holiday for us …

SOUNDTRACK.

3 *Narrator*: Here ends the story of a ship. But there will always be other ships for we are an island race. Through all our centuries the sea has ruled our destiny … God bless our ships and all who sail in them.

SOUNDTRACK. Last lines of film.

INDIANA JONES AND THE LAST CRUSADE

US 1989; screenwriter: Jeffrey Boam; cast: Harrison Ford (Indiana Jones).

4 *Jones*: I don't know, but I'll think of something.

SOUNDTRACK. Stock phrase in times of crisis.

INDISCREET

US 1958; screenwriter: Norman Krasna; cast: Ingrid Bergman (Anna Kalman), Cary Grant (Philip Adams).

5 *Anna (on Philip)*: How dare he make love to me and not be a married man?

SOUNDTRACK. He has pretended to be married to another.

Richard INGRAMS

English editor and columnist (1937–)

1 I do pride myself on having a certain instinct about the cinema, a knack of knowing in advance that I am not going to enjoy a particular film – especially if everyone else is saying how brilliant it is.

REMARK in *The Observer* (14 March 1999).

INHERIT THE WIND

US 1960; screenwriters: Nathan E. Douglas, Harold Jacob Smith (from a play by Jerome Lawrence and Robert E. Lee); cast: Gene Kelly (E.K. Hornbeck), Fredric March (Matthew Brady); Claude Akins (Reverend Brown).

2 *Hornbeck (of Brady)*: He hasn't an enemy in the world. Only his friends hate him.

SOUNDTRACK. This appears to be adapted from Oscar Wilde's famous jibe at Bernard Shaw: 'He hasn't an enemy in the world – and none of his friends like him.' Shaw himself quoted this remark in *Sixteen Self Sketches* (1949). An early appearance occurs in Irvin S. Cobb, *A Laugh a Day Keeps the Doctor Away* (1921), in which someone says of Shaw, 'He's in a fair way to make himself a lot of enemies.' 'Well,' replies Wilde, 'as yet he hasn't become prominent enough to have any enemies. But none of his friends like him.' Hesketh Pearson in *The Life of Oscar Wilde* (1946) wonders whether Shaw did not adapt to himself the following from *Dorian Gray*: 'Ernest Harrowden, one of those middle-aged mediocrities so common in London clubs, who have no enemies, but are thoroughly disliked by their friends.'

3 *Hornbeck (to Brady)*: Mr Brady, it's the duty of a newspaper to comfort the afflicted and to flick the comfortable.

SOUNDTRACK.

4 *Revd Brown*: Remember the wisdom of Solomon in the book of Proverbs: 'He that troubleth his own house shall inherit the wind.'

SOUNDTRACK. Hence the title.

INTOLERANCE

US 1916; screenwriter/director: D.W. Griffith.

5 Out of the Cradle Endlessly Rocking.

SCREEN TITLE accompanying a shot of Lillian Gish rocking a cradle and repeated many times during the course of the long silent film. The Gish character is billed as 'The Woman Who Rocks the Cradle'. From the title of a poem (1859) in *Leaves of Grass* by Walt Whitman (1859).

The INVISIBLE MAN

US 1933; screenwriters: R.C. Sherriff, Philip Wylie (from H.G. Wells novel); cast: Claude Rains (Griffin).

1 *Griffin*: We'll begin with a reign of terror – a few murders here and there. Murders of great men, murders of little men – just to show we make no distinction.

SOUNDTRACK.

Eugène IONESCO

Romanian-born French playwright (1912–94)

2 You'll probably say that progress can be good or bad, like Jews or Germans or films!

EXTRACTED from his play *Maid to Marry* (1963) (in translation).

Jeremy IRONS

English actor (1948–)

3 She [his wife, actress Sinead Cusack] doesn't get jealous. When she sees me in sex scenes she says to herself, 'Oh, he is only acting. I know he can't last that long.'

ATTRIBUTED remark.

4 [on a re-make of *Lolita*] I have heard people say that it will not get a distributor to release it. If it does not, I will leave the country.

QUOTED in *The Observer*, 'Soundbites' (22 December 1996).

ISLAND OF LOST SOULS

US 1933; screenwriters: Philip Wylie, Waldemar Young (from H.G. Wells novel *The Island of Dr Moreau*); cast: Charles Laughton (Dr Moreau).

5 *Dr Moreau (on natives of the island)*: They are restless tonight.

SOUNDTRACK. In fact he is speaking of animals he has transformed into humans on a remote South Sea island. *Compare* **CLICHÉS** 106:5.

IT HAPPENED ONE NIGHT

US 1934; screenwriter: Robert Riskin (from a novelette 'Night Bus' by Samuel Hopkins Adams); cast: Claudette Colbert (Ellie Andrews), Clark Gable (Peter Warne), Walter Connally (Alexander Andrews), Harry Holman (Auto Camp Manager), Maidel Turner (Auto Camp Manager's wife).

6 *Ellie (on Peter arranging the room they are to share)*: Darn clever, these Armenians.

SOUNDTRACK. The expression 'damn(ed) clever these Chinese!' became popular during the Second World War. Which was the original nationality named is impossible to tell.

1 *Peter (to Ellie, after night on bus)*: Remember me? I'm the fellow you slept on last night.

SOUNDTRACK.

2 *Ellie*: Your ego is absolutely colossal.
Peter: Yeah. Yep. Not bad. How's yours?

SOUNDTRACK.

3 *Peter*: Behold the walls of Jericho! Maybe not as thick as the ones that Joshua blew down with his trumpet, but a lot safer. You see, I have no trumpet.

SOUNDTRACK. Ellie has been forced to spend the night with Peter in a motel room but he hangs a blanket on a line between their two beds.

4 *Peter*: Perhaps you're interested in how a man undresses? You know, it's a funny thing about that. Quite a study in psychology. No two men do it alike.

SOUNDTRACK.

5 *Peter (on dunking doughnuts in coffee)*: Dunking's an art. Don't let it soak so long. A dip and plop, into your mouth. If you let it hang there too long, it'll get soft and fall off. It's all a matter of timing. I ought to write a book about it.

SOUNDTRACK.

6 *Ellie (after hitching a ride by showing her legs)*: Well, I proved once and for all that the limb is mightier than the thumb.
Peter: Why didn't you take off *all* your clothes? You could have stopped forty cars.

SOUNDTRACK.

7 *Alexander Andrews (on his daughter, Ellie)*: Do you love her?
Peter: Yes! But don't hold that against me. I'm a little screwy myself.

SOUNDTRACK.

8 *Auto Camp Manager's Wife (on honeymooning couple's odd request)*: But what in the world do they want a trumpet for?
Auto Camp Manager: Dunno.

SOUNDTRACK. Last words of film.

IT'S A GIFT

US 1934; screenwriters: Jack Cunningham, W.C. Fields; cast: W.C. Fields (Harold Bissonette).

1 *Real estate agent*: You're drunk!
Bissonette: Yeah, and you're crazy. I'll be sober tomorrow, but you'll be crazy the rest of your life.

SOUNDTRACK. Compare Winston Churchill's (later) response to Bessie Braddock MP who had told him he was drunk: 'And you, madam, are ugly. But I shall be sober in the morning.' Quoted in Sykes & Sproat, *The Wit of Sir Winston* (1965), without naming Braddock. She was named in Leslie Frewin, *Immortal Jester* (1973).

IT'S A MAD, MAD, MAD, MAD WORLD

US 1963; screenwriters: William & Tania Rose; cast: Ethel Merman (Mrs Marcus), Terry-Thomas (J. Algernon Hawthorne).

2 *Mrs Marcus (to Englishman Hawthorne)*: Where did you get that funny accent? Are you from Harvard or something?

SOUNDTRACK.

IT'S A WONDERFUL LIFE

US 1946; screenwriters: Frank Capra and others; cast: James Stewart (George Bailey).

3 *George*: Well, you look about the kind of angel I'd get. Sort of a fallen angel, aren't you? What happened to your wings?

SOUNDTRACK.

The ITALIAN JOB

UK 1969; screenwriter: Troy Kennedy Martin; cast: Michael Caine (Charlie Croker), Professor Peach (Benny Hill).

4 *Professor Peach (referring to Italian women)*: Are they big? I like 'em big.

SOUNDTRACK.

5 *Charlie (when van is completely blown up during dummy run)*: You're only supposed to blow the bloody doors off.

SOUNDTRACK.

6 *Charlie (to Mini drivers about to carry out robbery in Turin)*: Just remember this. In this country, they drive on the wrong side of the road.

SOUNDTRACK.

7 *Charlie (as coach is balanced by stolen gold on edge of cliff)*: Hang on a minute, lads, I've got a great idea … er … er.

SOUNDTRACK. Last line of film.

Glenda JACKSON

English actress and politician (1936–)

1 My old films come up regularly on television and I think: 'What the hell were you doing getting involved in this?'

QUOTED in *The Observer*, 'Sayings of the Week' (30 June 1985).

2 The important thing in acting is to be able to laugh and cry. When I have to cry, I think of my love life. When I have to laugh, I think of my love life.

QUOTED by Kim Basinger in *Playboy* (May 1986).

3 The least erotic experience in one's life is an erotic experience fabricated for the screen.

QUOTED in *The Independent* (29 May 1999).

4 Her face could launch a thousand dredgers.

COMMENT by Jack De Manio, English broadcaster (1914–88), quoted in *The Naff Sex Guide* (1984).

5 I watched *The Music Lovers*. One can't really blame Tchaikowsky for preferring boys. Anyone might become a homosexualist who had once seen Glenda Jackson naked.

COMMENT by Auberon Waugh in *Private Eye* in about 1970.

Clive JAMES

Australian-born critic (1939–)

6 All television ever did was shrink the demand for ordinary movies. The demand for extraordinary movies increased. If any one thing is wrong with the movie industry today, it is the unrelenting effort to astonish.

REMARK in *The Observer* (16 June 1979).

See also Marilyn **MONROE** 292:1, Arnold **SCHWARZENEGGER** 364:7.

JAWS

US 1975; screenwriters: Peter Benchley and others (from his novel); cast: Roy Scheider (Police Chief Martin Brody), Robert Shaw (Quint).

1 *Brody (on sighting the shark they are to chase)*: You're gonna need a bigger boat.

SOUNDTRACK.

The JAZZ SINGER

US 1927; screenwriter: Alfred A. Cohn; cast: Al Jolson (Jakie Rabinowitz/Jack Robin).

2 *Jakie*: Wait a minute, wait a minute, you ain't heard nothin' yet. Wait a minute, I tell ya. You ain't heard nothin'! You wanna hear 'Toot, Toot, Tootsie'? All right, hold on, hold on.

SOUNDTRACK. It seems that when Jolson exclaimed this in the first full-length talking picture, he did not add 'folks' at the end of his mighty line, as *Bartlett's Familiar Quotations* (1992), the *Penguin Dictionary of Modern Quotations* (1980) and the *Oxford Dictionary of Quotations* (1979) all say he did. Nor was he just ad-libbing as is usually supposed. He was promoting the title of one of his songs. He had recorded 'You Ain't Heard Nothing Yet', written by Gus Kahn and Buddy de Sylva, in 1919, and had also used the words as a catchphrase in his act before making the film. He supposedly first said it in a café, competing with the din from a neighbouring building site in about 1906 – at least according to M. Abramson, *The Real Story of Al Jolson* (1950).

Tom JENK

3 Hollywood is a locality where people without reputation try to live up to it.

QUOTED in Dick Richards, *Ginger, Salute to a Star* (1969).

The JERK

US 1979; screenwriters: Steve Martin and others; cast: Steve Martin (Navin R. Johnson).

4 *Navin*: She's going to get me some work – a blow job.

SOUNDTRACK.

George JESSEL

American entertainer (1898–1981)

5 [on the large number of mourners at film producer Harry Cohn's funeral (2 March 1958)] Same old story: you give 'em what they want and they'll fill the theatre.

QUOTED in Lillian Hellman, *Scoundrel Time* (1976). Earlier quoted, as said on TV by Red Skelton (1910–97), in Philip French, *The Movie Moguls* (1969); and, in the form, 'Well, it only proves what they say – give the public something they want to see, and they'll come out for it', in Bob Thomas, *King Cohn* (1967). An unattributed version appears in Oscar Levant, *The Unimportance of Being Oscar* (1968).

JEZEBEL

US 1938; screenwriter: Clements Ripley and others (from a play by Owen Davis Sr); cast: Bette Davis (Julie), George Brent (Buck Cantrell).

1 *Buck*: I like my convictions undiluted, same as I do my bourbon.

SOUNDTRACK.

2 *Julie (on why she can wear red to a ball)*: This is 1852, dumpling. 1852.

SOUNDTRACK. *Compare* **CLICHÉS** 107:1.

Nunnally JOHNSON

American screenwriter, director and producer (1897–1977)

3 [on being asked how he would adjust to writing for the wide screen] Very simple. I'll just put the paper in sideways.

QUOTED in Nora Johnson, *Flashback* (1979).

Erica JONG

American novelist (1942–)

4 Every country gets the circus it deserves. Spain gets bullfights. Italy gets the Catholic Church. America gets Hollywood.

EXTRACTED from book *How To Save Your Own Life* (1977).

5 Where is Hollywood located? Chiefly between the ears. In that part of the American brain lately vacated by God.

EXTRACTED from the same book.

6 People in the land of LaLa look like expensive wax fruit. And they work hard to achieve that look.

EXTRACTED from book *Serenissima* (1987).

JUMBO

US 1962; screenwriter: Sidney Sheldon (based on the 1935 Rodgers–Hart–Hecht–MacArthur stage show); cast: Jimmy Durante (Pop Wonder).

7 *Sheriff*: Where are you going with that elephant?
Pop Wonder: What elephant?

SOUNDTRACK. This joke is specifically credited to Charles Lederer.

Carl Gustav JUNG

Swiss psychologist (1875–1961)

1 The cinema, like the detective story, makes it possible to experience without danger all the excitement, passion and desirousness which must be repressed in a humanitarian ordering of life.

QUOTED in Roger Manvell, *Film* (1944).

The JUNGLE BOOK

US 1967; music/lyrics: Terry Gilkyson; voice of: Phil Harris (Baloo, the Bear)

2 *Baloo, the Bear*: The Bare Necessities.

TITLE of song.

Pauline KAEL

American critic (1919–2001)

1 The words 'Kiss Kiss Bang Bang', which I saw on an Italian movie poster, are perhaps the briefest statement imaginable of the basic appeal of movies. This appeal is what attracts us and ultimately what makes us despair when we begin to understand how seldom movies are more than this.

EXTRACTED from book *Kiss Kiss Bang Bang*, 'A Note on the Title' (1968). Usually, the words are taken to refer to the James Bond movies. Indeed, Bond's creator Ian Fleming himself described his books in a letter (in about 1955) to Raymond Chandler as 'straight pillow fantasies of the bang-bang, kiss-kiss variety'. John Barry, composer of music for most of the Bond films, named one of his themes 'Mr Kiss Kiss Bang Bang' – for *Thunderball* (1965). *Compare* Hortense **POWDERMAKER** 333:1.

2 Movies are so rarely great art that if we cannot appreciate the great trash we have very little reason to be interested in them.

EXTRACTED from book *Kiss Kiss Bang Bang* (1968).

3 [Nicol Williamson] *is* brilliant, he *is* dazzling – yet he's awful … probably the worst major (and greatly gifted) actor on the English-speaking screen today.

REMARK in *The New Yorker* (January 1970).

4 We learn to settle for so little, we moviegoers.

EXTRACTED from *Going Steady* (1970).

5 When I see those ads with the quote 'You'll have to see this picture twice', I know it's the kind of picture I don't want to see once.

EXTRACTED from book *Deeper Into Movies*, 'Waiting for Orgy' (1973).

6 Writers who go to Hollywood still follow the classic pattern: either you get disgusted by 'them' and you leave or you want the money and you become them.

EXTRACTED from the same book.

1 If you're afraid of movies that excite your senses, you're afraid of movies.

ATTRIBUTED remark of 1978, quoted in *Newsweek* Magazine (1991).

2 For a while in the twenties and thirties, art was talked about as a substitute for religion; now B movies are a substitute for religion.

EXTRACTED from book *Movie Love* (1991).

Garson KANIN

American playwright, screenwriter and director (1912–99)

3 I'd rather be Frank Capra than God – if there is a Frank Capra.

QUOTED in his obituary in *The Times* (16 March 1999).

Boris KARLOFF

English actor (1887–1969)

4 You could heave a brick out of the window and hit ten actors who could play my parts. I just happened to be on the right corner at the right time.

ATTRIBUTED remark, quoted in Leslie Halliwell, *The Filmgoer's Book of Quotes* (1973).

5 The monster was the best friend I ever had.

ATTRIBUTED remark, quoted in Leslie Halliwell, *The Filmgoer's Book of Quotes* (1973).

Jeffrey KATZENBERG

American studio executive (1951–)

6 Inside every human being in my opinion is a 12- to 14-year-old.

QUOTED in *The Observer*, 'Sayings of the Week' (17 December 1989). Spoken when President of Walt Disney.

George S. KAUFMAN

American playwright and screenwriter (1889–1961)

7 Excuse me for interrupting but I actually thought I heard a line I wrote.

ATTRIBUTED remark at rehearsal of the Marx Brothers film *Animal Crackers* for which he wrote the script – according to Scott Meredith, *George S. Kaufman and the Algonquin Round Table* (1974). In fact, the remark most probably dates from the days of the *stage* version of *The Cocoanuts*. In *Harpo Speaks* (1961), Harpo recalled: 'We were a hit … But we still didn't know George well enough. He came backstage with his chin on his chest and said that Act One seemed to be all right, but Act Two needed another cut. Somewhere in the middle of Act Two – he wasn't exactly sure where – he could have sworn he heard one of his original lines.'

Buster KEATON

American comic and actor (1895–1966)

1 Keaton's face ranked almost with Lincoln's as an early American archetype; it was haunting, handsome, almost beautiful, yet it was irreducibly funny.

COMMENT by James Agee in *Agee on Film* (1964).

Diane KEATON

American actress (1946–)

2 In real life, Keaton believes in God. But she also believes that the radio works because there are tiny people inside it.

COMMENT by Woody Allen.

3 An acting style that's really a nervous breakdown in slow motion.

COMMENT by John Simon.

Gene KELLY

American dancer and actor (1912–96)

4 Fred Astaire represents the aristocracy when he dances. I represent the proletariat.

ATTRIBUTED remark.

Grace KELLY (Princess Grace of Monaco)

American actress (1929–82)

5 You never meet anyone in Hollywood except by appointment.

QUOTED in Cecil Beaton, *It Gives Me Great Pleasure* (1955).

Murray KEMPTON

American journalist (1917–)

6 Hollywood is a place where there is no definition of your worth earlier than your last picture.

EXTRACTED from his book *Part of Our Time*, 'The Day of the Locust' (1955).
Compare Marie **DRESSLER** 143:8.

Patsy KENSIT

English actress (1968–)

1 I saw several very good actors, and she was by far and away the best. She needed to be very beautiful and very blonde … but above all to understand the stupidity of the character.

COMMENT by A.S. Byatt (whose story *Angels and Insects* was filmed with Kensit in it) in *The Guardian*, quoted in the *Independent on Sunday*, 'Overheard' (31 March 1996).

Deborah KERR

English actress (1921–)

2 All the most successful people these days seem to be neurotic. Perhaps we should stop being sorry for them and start being sorry for me – for being so confounded normal.

ATTRIBUTED remark.

The KILLING FIELDS

UK 1984; screenwriter: Bruce Robinson; cast: Haing S. Ngor (Dith Pran).

3 *Dith Pran (narrating, on the genocide in Cambodia)*: Nothing's forgiven, nothing.

SOUNDTRACK. Last line of film.

See also Haing S. **NGOR** 303:3.

KIND HEARTS AND CORONETS

UK 1949; screenwriters: Robert Hamer, John Dighton (from a novel *Noblesse Oblige* by Roy Horniman); cast: Dennis Price (Louis Mazzini), Alec Guinness (The Revd Lord Henry D'Ascoyne/The Parson), Joan Greenwood (Sibella), Valerie Hobson (Edith D'Ascoyne).

4 *Mazzini (to prison governor who has asked if he has any special requests, on the eve of his proposed execution)*: I hate to disappoint the newspaper-reading public but it will be too early for the conventional hearty breakfast.

SOUNDTRACK.

5 *Mazzini (narrating)*: It is so difficult to make a neat job of killing people with whom one is not on friendly terms.

SOUNDTRACK.

1 *Mazzini (narrating, of first victims)*: I was sorry about the girl, but found some relief in the reflection that she had presumably during the weekend already undergone a fate worse than death.

SOUNDTRACK.

2 *Edith*: Was Lord Tennyson far from the mark when he wrote, 'Kind hearts are more than coronets / And simple faith than Norman blood.'

SOUNDTRACK. Hence, the title of the film. The quotation is from 'Lady Clara Vere de Vere' (1833).

3 *Mazzini (narrating)*: As the Italian proverb says, 'Revenge is the dish which people of taste prefer to eat cold.'

SOUNDTRACK.

4 *The Parson*: I always say that my west window has all the exuberance of Chaucer without, happily, any of the concomitant crudities of his period.

SOUNDTRACK.

5 *Mazzini (narrating)*: I shot an arrow in the air. She fell to earth in Berkeley Square.

SOUNDTRACK. Referring to Lady Agatha, the suffragette. He has shot down the balloon in which she was riding. The lines alludes to Longfellow: 'I shot an arrow in the air, / It fell to earth, I know not where' – from 'The Arrow and the Song'.

6 *Mazzini (explaining his actions in support of his mother, to Ethelred, 8th Duke of Chalfont, his final victim)*: Because she married for love, instead of for rank, or money, or land, they condemned her to a life of poverty and slavery, in a world with which they had not equipped her to deal.

SOUNDTRACK.

7 *Mazzini*: My memoirs. My memoirs. My memoirs. My memoirs!

SOUNDTRACK. Having been reprieved at the last minute from execution, he realises that he has left behind in prison the manuscript detailing all his murders. Last words of film.

KING KONG

US 1933; screenwriters: James Creelman, Ruth Rose (from a story by Edgar Wallace); cast: Robert Armstrong (Carl Denham).

8 *Denham (correcting police officer)*: Oh no, it wasn't the airplanes. It was beauty killed the beast.

SOUNDTRACK. Last line of film.

KING KONG

US 1976; screenwriter: Lorenzo Semple Jr; cast: Jeff Bridges (Jack Prescott), Jessica Lange (Dwan).

1 *Prescott (to Dwan, with the giant ape brushing against the side of the house they are sheltering in)*: He's bigger than both of us, know what I mean?

SOUNDTRACK.

The KING OF COMEDY

US 1983; screenwriter: Paul D. Zimmerman; cast: Robert De Niro (Rupert Pupkin).

2 *Pupkin (to TV audience)*: Tomorrow you'll know I wasn't kidding and you'll think I was crazy, but look, I figure it this way: better to be king for a night than [a] schmuck for a lifetime.

SOUNDTRACK.

KING RICHARD AND THE CRUSADERS

US 1954; screenwriter: John Twist (from Sir Walter Scott's novel *The Talisman*); cast: Virginia Mayo (Lady Edith).

3 *Lady Edith*: Fight, fight, fight! That's all you think of, Dick Plantagenet!

SOUNDTRACK.

KING'S ROW

US 1941; screenwriter: Casey Robinson (from a novel); Ronald Reagan (Drake McHugh), Ann Sheridan (Randy Monaghan).

4 *Drake (to Randy)*: Randy – where's the rest of me?

SOUNDTRACK. A famous moment occurs when Drake, on waking to find that his legs have been amputated by a sadistic doctor, poses this pained question. *Where's the Rest of Me?* was used by Reagan as the title of an early autobiography (1965).

Miles KINGTON

English humorist (1941–)

5 Cinemas and theatres are always bigger inside than they are outside.

REMARK in *The Independent* (29 March 1989). 'Albanian proverb'.

KISS ME STUPID

US 1964; screenwriters: Billy Wilder, I.A.L. Diamond; cast: Dean Martin (Dino), Ray Walston (Orville J. Spooner), Kim Novak (Polly the Pistol).

1 *Dino (telling a joke to Orville and Polly)*: There was the one about this doctor, you see. He was examining a girl's knee and he said, 'What's a joint like this doing in a pretty girl like you?'

SOUNDTRACK. 'Reducing the age-old seducer's spiel, while telling the same old story', as Walter Redfern comments in *Puns* (1984). *See also* **CLICHÉS** 108:3.

KLONDIKE ANNIE

US 1936; screenwriter: Mae West and others; cast: Mae West (Annie).

2 *Annie*: Give a man a free hand and he'll try to put it all over you.

SOUNDTRACK.

3 *Annie*: Between two evils, I always pick the one I never tried before.

SOUNDTRACK. *Compare* ***GO WEST YOUNG MAN*** 185:1.

KNOCK ON ANY DOOR

US 1949; screenwriters: Daniel Taradash, John Monks Jr (from novel by Willard Motley); cast: John Derek (Romano).

4 *Romano*: Live fast, die young and have a good-looking corpse.

SOUNDTRACK.

KNUTE ROCKNE, ALL AMERICAN

US 1940; screenwriter: Robert Buckner; cast: Pat O'Brien (Knute Rockne), Ronald Reagan (George Gipp).

5 *Knute*: And the last thing he said to me, 'Rock,' he said, 'sometimes when the team is up against it and the breaks are beating the boys, tell them to go out there with all they've got and win just one for the Gipper!'

SOUNDTRACK. Bridging his film and political careers, Reagan adopted the slogan 'Win this one for the Gipper' in his post-Hollywood life. George Gipp was a real-life football star who died young. At half-time in a 1928 Army game, Rockne, the team coach, had recalled something Gipp had said to him: 'Rock, someday when things look real tough for Notre Dame, ask the boys to go out there and win one for me' – and the above is how it was included in the film script. Reagan used the political slogan countless times. One of the last was at a campaign rally for Vice-President George Bush in San Diego, California, on 7 November 1988. Reagan's peroration included these words: 'So, now we come to the end of this last campaign … And I hope that someday your children and grandchildren will tell of the time that a certain President came to town at the end of a long journey and asked their parents and grandparents to join him in setting America on the course to the new millennium ... So, if I could ask you just one last time. Tomorrow, when mountains greet the dawn, would you go out there and win one for the Gipper? Thank you, and God bless you all.'

(Sir) Alexander KORDA

Hungarian-born British producer (1893–1956)

1 [on the preponderance of Hungarians at his Denham Studios in the 1930s] It's not enough to be Hungarian, you must have talent, too.

ATTRIBUTED remark.

Norman KRASNA

American screenwriter (1909–84)

2 [to Jack Warner, who imposed a strict 9–5.30 schedule on his writers] I can't tell you [the perfect ending to a script] ... I thought of the answer after 5.30.

QUOTED in Michael Freedland, *Warner Brothers* (1983).

Stanley KUBRICK

American director (1928–99)

3 [On comic method in ***DR STRANGELOVE*** ...] Confront a man in his office with a nuclear alarm, and you have a documentary. If the news reaches him in his living room, you have a drama. If it catches him in the lavatory, the result is comedy.

QUOTED in Alexander Walker, *Stanley Kubrick Directs* (1972).

4 He gives new meaning to the word meticulous.

COMMENT attributed to Jack Nicholson.

Akira KUROSAWA

Japanese director (1910–99)

5 I wanted to make a film which would be entertaining enough to eat.

REMARK quoted in J.R. Colombo, *Wit and Wisdom of the Moviemakers* (1979).

Alan LADD

American actor (1913–64)

1 Hard, bitter and occasionally charming, he is after all a small boy's idea of a tough.

COMMENT by Raymond Chandler in *Raymond Chandler Speaking* (1962).

The LADY EVE

US 1941; screenwriter: Preston Sturges (from a story); cast: Charles Coburn (Colonel Harrington), Barbara Stanwyck (Jean Harrington).

2 *Colonel (to daughter Jean)*: Let us be crooked, but never common.

SOUNDTRACK. She is a cardsharper.

LADY IN THE DARK

US 1944; screenwriters: Frances Goodrich, Albert Hackett (from Moss Hart play); cast: Mischa Auer (Russell Paxton)

3 The minx in mink with a yen for men!

SLOGAN.

4 *Russell Paxton*: This is the end! The absolute end!

SOUNDTRACK.

The LADY VANISHES

UK 1938; screenwriters: Alma Reville, Sidney Gilliatt, Frank Launder (from a novel *The Wheel Spins* by Ethel Lina White); cast: Margaret Lockwood (Iris Henderson), Dame May Whitty (Miss Froy), Michael Redgrave (Gilbert), Basil Radford (Charters), Naunton Wayne (Caldicott), Paul Lukas (Dr Hartz).

5 *Iris (on her forthcoming marriage)*: I've no regrets. I've been everywhere and done everything. I've eaten caviar at Cannes, sausage rolls at the dogs. I've played baccarat at Biarritz, and darts with the rural dean. What is there left for me but marriage?

SOUNDTRACK.

1 *Iris (to man who has moved into her hotel room)*: You're the most contemptible person I've ever met in all my life.
Gilbert: Confidentially, I think you're a bit of a stick, too.

SOUNDTRACK.

2 *Iris (to cricket fanatics who show no interest in the missing Miss Froy)*: Well, I don't see how a thing like cricket can make you forget seeing people.
Charters: Oh, don't you? Well, if that's your attitude, obviously there's nothing more to be said.

SOUNDTRACK.

3 *Iris*: I don't think she's a nun at all. They don't wear high heels.

SOUNDTRACK.

4 *Gilbert (on why the British cricket fans deny seeing Miss Froy)*: Yes, just British diplomacy, Doctor. Never climb a fence if you can sit on it. An old foreign office proverb.

SOUNDTRACK.

5 *Hartz (to Gilbert)*: She will be removed from the hospital there and operated on. Unfortunately, the operation will not be successful. Oh, I should perhaps have explained. The operation will be performed by me.

SOUNDTRACK.

6 *Charters*: I mean, after all, people don't go about tying up nuns.

SOUNDTRACK.

Carl LAEMMLE

German-born producer (1867–1939)

7 Uncle Carl Laemmle
Has a very large family.

COMMENT attributed to Ogden Nash after it was revealed in 1936 that Laemmle had found jobs for more than seventy relatives at Universal Studios. At least, the couplet tells you how his name was pronounced.

Veronica LAKE

American actress (1919–73)

8 You could put all the talent I had in your left eye and still not suffer from impaired vision.

REMARK quoted in Leslie Halliwell, *The Filmgoer's Book of Quotes* (1978 edn).

Hedy LAMARR

Austrian-born American actress (1913–2000)

1 Ecstasy and Me.

TITLE of autobiography (1966).

2 Everywhere I find men pay homage to my beauty and show no interest in me. In a way my beauty was a curse.

QUOTED in *The Independent* (14 August 1999).

Constant LAMBERT

English composer (1905–51)

3 The cinema is undoubtedly the most important of the mechanical stimuli offered to the composer of today … Films have the emotional impact for the twentieth century that operas had for the nineteenth.

EXTRACTED from his book *Music Ho!* (1934).

Burt LANCASTER

American actor (1913–94)

4 Most people seem to think I'm the kind of guy who shaves with a blowtorch. Actually I'm, bookish and worrisome.

ATTRIBUTED remark.

5 Before he picks up an ashtray he discusses his motivation for an hour or two. You want to say, 'Oh, pick up the ashtray and shut up.'

COMMENT attributed to Jeanne Moreau.

Fritz LANG

Austrian-born director (1890–1976)

6 Don't forget the Western is not only the history of this country, it is what the Saga of the Nibelungen is for the European.

QUOTED in Peter Bogdanovich, *Fritz Lang in America* (1967).

Jessica LANGE

American actress (1949–)

7 She's like a delicate fawn, crossed with a Buick.

COMMENT by Jack Nicholson, in *Vanity Fair* (October 1984). The two had co-starred in *The Postman Always Rings Twice* (1981).

Anthony LAPAGLIA

Australian-born actor (1959–)

1 When your name ends in a vowel, you end up carrying a gun a lot.

QUOTED in *The Independent* (26 April 1997).

Jesse LASKY

American producer (1880–1958)

2 [on his desire to produce better films] I yearned to trespass on Quality Street.

QUOTED in *The New Yorker* (21 March 1994).

LAST ACTION HERO

US 1993; screenwriters: Zak Penn and others; cast: Arnold Schwarzenegger (Sgt Jack Slater).

3 *Slater*: This hero stuff has its limits.

SOUNDTRACK.

The LAST REMAKE OF BEAU GESTE

US 1977; screenwriters: Marty Feldman, Chris J. Allen; cast: Terry-Thomas (Governor), Ann-Margret (Flavia Geste).

4 *Terry-Thomas (as prison Governor to Flavia, who has slept with him to secure an escape)*: Delighted you came, my dear, and I'd like you to know that you made a happy man feel very old.

SOUNDTRACK.

LAST TANGO IN PARIS

Italy/France 1973; screenwriters: Bernardo Bertolucci, Franco Arcalli; cast: Marlon Brando (Paul), Maria Schneider (Jeanne).

5 *Paul (to Jeanne, as she leaves the apartment)*: *Quo vadis*, baby?

SOUNDTRACK.

6 Saddest movie I've ever seen – I cried all the way through. It's sad when you're 82.

COMMENT by Groucho Marx.

LAST YEAR AT MARIENBAD [L'ANNÉE DERNIÈRE À MARIENBAD]

France/Italy 1961; screenwriter: Alain Robbe-Grillet (from his novel/*ciné roman*); Giorgio Albertazzi (X/Stranger), Delphine Seyrig (A/Woman).

1 *X (narrating)*: *Et une fois de plus je m'avançais le long de ces même couloirs, marchant depuis des* jours, *depuis des* mois, *depuis des* années, *à votre rencontre* [And one more time, I advanced along these same hallways, walking for *days*, for *months*, for *years*, to meet you].

SOUNDTRACK. Towards the end of the film.

Charles LAUGHTON

English actor and director (1899–1962)

2 I have a face like the behind of an elephant.

ATTRIBUTED remark.

3 [on being told that he must not indicate incestuous interest in his role as Mr Moulton-Barrett in *The Barretts of Wimpole Street*] They can't censor the gleam in my eye.

ATTRIBUTED remark.

4 You can't direct a Laughton picture. The best you can hope for is to referee.

COMMENT by Alfred Hitchcock, quoted in Leslie Halliwell, *The Filmgoer's Book of Quotes* (1973).

5 With him acting was an act of childbirth. What he needed was not so much a director as a midwife.

COMMENT by Alexander Korda, quoted in Leslie Halliwell, *The Filmgoer's Book of Quotes* (1973). *Compare* Jean **RENOIR** 351:7.

LAURA

US 1944; screenwriters: Jay Dratler, Samuel Hoffenstein, Betty Reinhardt (from novel by Vera Caspary); cast: Clifton Webb (Waldo Lydecker), Dana Andrews (Mark McPherson).

6 *Lydecker (narrating)*: I shall never forget the weekend Laura died.

SOUNDTRACK.

7 *McPherson*: Nice little place you have here, Mr Lydecker.
Lydecker: It's lavish, but I call it home.

SOUNDTRACK.

8 *Lydecker*: In my case, self-absorption is completely justified.

SOUNDTRACK.

1 *Lydecker*: I'm not kind, I'm vicious. It's the secret of my charm.
SOUNDTRACK.

The LAVENDER HILL MOB

UK 1951; screenwriter: T.E.B. Clarke; cast: Alec Guinness (Henry Holland).

2 *Holland (narrating)*: Most men who long to be rich, know inwardly that they will never achieve their ambition, but I was in the unique position of having a fortune literally within my grasp, for it was my job to supervise the deliveries of bullion from the gold refinery to the bank.
SOUNDTRACK.

3 *Holland (declining promotion)*: I like the bullion office. It holds all I ever wished for.
SOUNDTRACK.

4 *Holland (on how much money he stole)*: Enough to keep me for one year in the style to which I was accustomed.
SOUNDTRACK.

5 Ealing studios never succeeded in killing me in spite of some quite good tries, the first of which was during the making of Lavender Hill … [He was told to run down a spiral staircase on the Eiffel Tower – but it broke off and led, as he said, to eternity] … No one had checked up on the staircase and no one apologized; that wasn't Ealing policy.
COMMENT by Alec Guinness in his book *My Name Escapes Me* (1996).

D.H. LAWRENCE

English novelist (1885–1930)

6 That triumph of the deaf and dumb, the cinematograph.
EXTRACTED from his book *Twilight in Italy*, Chap 1 (1916).

LAWRENCE OF ARABIA

UK 1962; screenwriters: Robert Bolt, Michael Wilson; cast: Peter O'Toole (T.E. Lawrence), Arthur Kennedy (Jackson Bentley), Harry Fowler (Corporal Potter), Claude Rains (Mr Dryden), Omar Sharif (Sherif Ali), Alec Guinness (Prince Feisal), I.S. Johar (Gasim), Jack Hawkins (General Allenby), Anthony Quinn (Auda Abu Tayi).

7 *Bentley (of Lawrence)*: He was a poet, a scholar and a mighty warrior … He was also the most shameless exhibitionist since Barnum and Bailey.
SOUNDTRACK.

1 *Lawrence (to Potter, on burning his fingers with matches)*: Of course it hurts. The trick ... is not *minding* that it hurts.

SOUNDTRACK.

2 *Lawrence*: Sherif Ali, so long as the Arabs fight tribe against tribe, so long will they be a little people, a silly people, greedy, barbarous, and cruel, as you are.

SOUNDTRACK.

3 *Lawrence (to Feisal, on where his loyalties lie)*: To England, and to other things.

SOUNDTRACK.

4 *Sherif (on crossing the waterless Nefud desert)*: If the camels die, we die. And in twenty days they will start to die.
Lawrence: There's no time to waste then, is there?

SOUNDTRACK.

5 *Lawrence (on being told that it is written that Gasim will die)*: Nothing is written.

SOUNDTRACK.

6 *Mr Dryden (to Lawrence)*: If we've told lies, you've told half-lies, and a man who tells lies, like me, merely hides the truth, but a man who tells half-lies has forgotten where he put it.

SOUNDTRACK.

7 *Allenby*: Not many people have a destiny, Lawrence. It's a terrible thing for a man to flunk it if he has.

SOUNDTRACK.

8 They only got two things right – the camels and the sand.

COMMENT by Lowell Thomas (who is portrayed in the film as 'Jackson Bentley'). Quoted in his obituary in *The Times* (29 August 1981).

(Sir) David LEAN

English editor and director (1908–91)

9 Even the smallest of his films had an epic quality which no other British director has ever quite been able to match.

COMMENT by David Puttnam, quoted in *The Independent* (20 April 1991).

C(aroline) A. LEJEUNE

English critic (1897–1973)

1 Sub-titles are the film. Everything of importance happens in them. Births, deaths, and marriages take place in them. Characters are fixed in them. Secrets are revealed in them … They are the end and the beginning of the whole matter.

EXTRACTED from 'The Sphere of the Sub-title', in *Manchester Guardian* (10 April 1926).

2 Today it is as foolish to argue that talking films cannot be successful as to declare that a man in London cannot possibly speak by telephone to a man in New York.

EXTRACTED from 'Talking Stars', in *The Observer* (4 November 1928).

3 [of *My Son My Son* (US, 1940)] My Son My Son, my sainted aunt!

ATTRIBUTED comment.

4 [of *Millions Like Us* (UK, 1943)] And millions don't.

ATTRIBUTED in *The C.A. Lejeune Film Reader*, ed. Anthony Lejeune (1991).

5 [of *I Was Framed* (US, 1942)] Yes, but was you hung?

EXTRACTED from *News Chronicle*. Quoted in *The Observer* (21 December 1997).

6 [of *Her Primitive Man* (US, 1944)] Cave.

ATTRIBUTED in *The Observer* (11 January 1998).

7 I always feel that Sonny Tufts
Is something rather large from Cruft's:
Which gives his work, in moderation,
A certain dogged fascination.

EXTRACTED from book *Cross My Heart* (1945), reviewing the appearance of Sonny Tufts (1911–70).

8 [of *No Leave No Love* (US, 1946)] No comment.

EXTRACTED from book *Chestnuts in Her Lap* (1947).

9 [of *Gilda* (US, 1946)] 'There was never a woman like Gilda' say the film's delighted owners. Blimey! there never was.

EXTRACTED from the same book.

10 [of *Ruthless* (US 1948)]
Beginning pictures at the end
Is, I'm afraid, a modern trend;
But I'd find *Ruthless* much more winning
If it could end at the beginning.

ATTRIBUTED remark.

1 [of *Anything Goes* (US, 1956)] Obviously.

ATTRIBUTED in *The Observer* (4 January 1998).

2 [of Charlton Heston's performance as a doctor in unidentified film (possibly *Bad for Each Other*, US 1954)] It makes me want to call out, Is there an apple in the house?

ATTRIBUTED in Nigel Rees, *The 'Quote … Unquote' Book of Love, Death and the Universe* (1980).

See also ***CITIZEN KANE*** 103:8; ***I AM A CAMERA*** 224:2.

V.I. LENIN

Russian revolutionary (1870–1924)

3 The cinema is the most important of all arts for us.

QUOTED in Roger Manvell, *Film* (1944).

The LEOPARD

Italy 1963; screenwriters: Luchino Visconti and others (from di Lampedusa novel); cast: Burt Lancaster (The Prince), Alain Delon (Tancredi).

4 Things will have to change in order that they can remain the same.

SUB-TITLE translation. The Prince's credo. Later on in the film, Tancredi also says: 'If we want things to stay as they are, things will have to change' (also sub-title translation).

Richard (Dick) LESTER

American director (1932–)

5 Film-making has become a kind of hysterical pregnancy.

REMARK, quoted in Leslie Halliwell, *The Filmgoer's Book of Quotes* (1973).

LETHAL WEAPON

US 1987; screenwriter: Shane Black; cast: Mel Gibson (Martin Riggs), Danny Glover (Roger Murtagh).

6 *Riggs (to drug dealers)*: That's a real badge. I'm a real cop. And this is a real firing gun.

SOUNDTRACK.

7 *Murtagh*: I'm too old for this.

SOUNDTRACK. Repeated as last line of film.

8 *Murtagh (to Riggs)*: I suppose we have to register *you* as a lethal weapon.

SOUNDTRACK.

1 *Murtagh (when Riggs is made his partner)*: God hates me. That's what it is.
Riggs: Hate him back. It works for me.

SOUNDTRACK.

2 *Riggs (to would-be suicide on top of building)*: Do you really want to jump? Do you want to? Well, then that's fine with me.

SOUNDTRACK. They jump off together.

3 *Riggs (to Murtagh, on suicide)*: Every single day, I wake up and I think of a reason not to do it. Every single day. And you know why I don't do it? This is going to make you laugh. You know why I don't do it? The job. Doing the job. Now, that's the reason.

SOUNDTRACK.

4 *Riggs (on mansion)*: I've seen this on *Lifestyles of the Rich and Shameless.*

SOUNDTRACK.

5 *Murtagh*: You ever met anybody you didn't kill?
Riggs: Well, I haven't killed you yet.
Murtagh: Well, don't do me no favours.

SOUNDTRACK.

6 *Riggs*: Let's do what one shepherd said to the other shepherd ... 'Let's get the flock out of here.'

SOUNDTRACK.

The LETTER

US 1940; screenwriter: Howard Koch (based on story by W. Somerset Maugham); cast: Bette Davis (Leslie Crosbie), Herbert Marshall (Robert Crosbie).

7 Yes, I killed him. And I'm glad, I tell you. Glad, glad, glad!

SLOGAN. Often inaccurately said to be actual dialogue from the film.

8 *Leslie (to Robert)*: With all my heart, I still love the man I killed.

SOUNDTRACK.

Oscar LEVANT

American pianist and performer (1906–72)

9 [in the early 1940s] Strip away the phoney tinsel off Hollywood and you'll find the real tinsel underneath.

EXTRACTED from his book *Memoirs of an Amnesiac* (1965).

Leonard Louis LEVINSON

American writer (1904–74)

1 Book – what they make a movie out of for television.

QUOTED in *Quotations for Our Times*, ed. Laurence J. Peter (1977).

Jerry LEWIS

American comedian and actor (1926–)

2 [on his compulsion to perform] When the light goes on in the refrigerator, I do twenty minutes.

ATTRIBUTED remark. As also to Debbie Reynolds in the form: 'I do twenty minutes every time the refrigerator door opens and the light comes on.' Something of a cliché hereabouts, obviously.

LICENCE TO KILL

UK 1989; screenwriters: Michael G. Wilson, Richard Maibaum; cast: Timothy Dalton (James Bond), Robert Davi (Franz Sanchez).

3 *Sanchez (on fate of American agent fed to sharks)*: He disagreed with something that ate him.

SOUNDTRACK.

Claudia LINNEAR

American singer

4 There are a lot of chicks who get laid by the director and still don't get the part.

ATTRIBUTED remark.

LITTLE CAESAR

US 1930; screenwriters: Francis Faragoh, Robert E. Lee (from novel by W.R. Burnett); cast: Edward G. Robinson (Rico), Stanley Fields (Sam Vettori), Tom Jackson (Sgt Flaherty).

5 *Vettori (giving Rico a nickname)*: Oh, Little Caesar, huh?

SOUNDTRACK.

6 *Rico (to Vettori, on killing the crime commissioner)*: You think I'm going to let a guy pull a gat on me.

SOUNDTRACK.

7 *Rico (to Vettori, on taking over his territory)*: You can dish it out, but you got so you can't take it no more.

SOUNDTRACK. An early appearance of the 'can dish out but can't take it in' expression.

1 *Rico (on phone to Flaherty)*: This is Rico speaking. Rico! R-I-C-O! Rico! Little Caesar, that's who! ... Listen, you crummy, flat-footed copper, I'll show you whether I've lost my nerve and my brains!

SOUNDTRACK.

2 *Rico (taunting police)*: You want me, you're going to have to come and get me!

SOUNDTRACK.

3 *Rico (dying)*: Mother of Mercy, is this the end of Rico?

SOUNDTRACK. Last line of film. Rico is a gangster (modelled on Al Capone). He meets his end on some church steps, hence the 'Mother of Mercy' cry.

The LITTLE FOXES

US 1941; screenwriter: Lillian Hellman (from her play); cast: Herbert Marshall (Horace Giddens).

4 *Horace Giddens*: Maybe it's easy for the dying to be honest ... I'll die my own way, and I'll do it without making the world any worse. I leave that to you.

SOUNDTRACK.

The LITTLE SHOP OF HORRORS

US 1960; screenwriter: Charles B. Griffith; cast: Mel Welles (Gravis Mushnik), Jonathan Haze (Seymour Krelboin), Jack Nicholson (Wilbur Force).

5 *Audrey Junior (the monster plant, hungry for meal)*: Feed me!

SOUNDTRACK. By the time of the 1986 re-make (based on the stage musical), this line had become: 'Seymour, feed me all night long!'

6 *Force (refusing anaesthetic from dentist)*: No Novocain – it dulls the senses.

SOUNDTRACK.

7 *Krelboin (to hungry plant, while bringing human corpse in a bag)*: Take it easy, Dracula, what do you think I'm carrying here, my dirty laundry?

SOUNDTRACK.

8 *Police sergeant*: My name is Fink. Sergeant Joe Fink. I'm a Fink.

SOUNDTRACK. Parodying *Dragnet* style.

9 *Krelboin*: You dirty rat plant, you messed up my whole life.

SOUNDTRACK.

The LIVES OF A BENGAL LANCER

US 1934; screenwriters: various (based on a novel by Francis Yeats-Brown); cast: Gary Cooper (Lieutenant McGregor), Franchot Tone (Lieutenant Forsythe), Sir Guy Standing (Colonel Stone), C. Aubrey Smith (Major Hamilton), Douglas Dumbrille (Mohammed Khan).

1 *McGregor (of Stone receiving his own son into the regiment)*: I can't imagine old ramrod ever having been that human.

SOUNDTRACK.

2 *Forsythe (to servant putting boots on him)*: You keep them shined and I'll keep them dirty.

SOUNDTRACK.

3 *McGregor (on Stone's coldness to his own son)*: What's a son to him compared to his blasted regiment?

SOUNDTRACK.

4 *Khan*: 'The little jackal barks, but the caravan passes.'

SOUNDTRACK. Quoting a proverb.

5 *Hamilton (to McGregor about Stone)*: Man, you are blind! Have you never thought how for generation after generation here, a handful of men have ordered the lives of three hundred million people? It's because he's here and a few more like him. Men of his breed have made a British India. Men who have put their jobs above everything ... When this breed of man dies out, that's the end. And it's a better breed of man than we'll ever make.

SOUNDTRACK.

6 *Khan (threatening torture)*: Well, gentlemen, we have ways to make men talk.

SOUNDTRACK. An early appearance of this line. *Compare* ***ODETTE*** 313:1.

Harold LLOYD

American comic and actor (1893–1971)

7 [on being asked his age when he was 77] I am just turning 40 and taking my time about it.

ATTRIBUTED remark, quoted in *The Times* (1970).

Ken LOACH

English director and screenwriter (1936–)

1 He's totally round the bend. You don't rehearse. Everything's a take.

COMMENT by actor Ricky Tomlinson.

The LONG GOOD FRIDAY

UK 1980; screenwriter: Barrie Keefe; cast: Bob Hoskins (Harold Shand).

2 *Harold (on dead colleague)*: Colin never hurt a fly. Well, only when it was necessary.

SOUNDTRACK.

The LONG HOT SUMMER

US 1958; screenwriters: Irving Ravetch, Harriet Frank Jr (from William Faulkner story); cast: Orson Welles (Will Varner), Angela Lansbury (Minnie Littlejohn).

3 The Long Hot Summer.

TITLE OF FILM. Based on 'The Hamlet', a story by William Faulkner published in 1928, which contained the chapter heading 'The Long Summer' (*sic*). This led to the cliché phrase that took hold in the 1960s, especially after a spin-off TV series was titled *The Long Hot Summer* (1965–66).

4 *Will*: Oh, I like life, Minnie. I like it so much I might just live forever.

SOUNDTRACK. Last line of film.

Anita LOOS

American writer and screenwriter (1893–1981)

5 [on being forced to return to Hollywood after the Wall Street Crash of 1929] Back to the mink-lined rut.

QUOTED by Stanley Reynolds in his obituary of Loos in *The Guardian* (20 August 1981).

6 Hollywood reflected, if it did not actually produce, the sexual climate of our land.

EXTRACTED from her book *Kiss Hollywood Good-by* (1974).

Sophia LOREN

Italian actress (1934–)

7 Everything you see I owe to spaghetti.

QUOTED in J.R. Colombo, *Wit and Wisdom of the Moviemakers* (1979).

8 Working with her was like being bombed by water melons.

COMMENT by Alan Ladd, quoted in Maria Leach, *The Ultimate Insult* (1996).

Joseph LOSEY

American director (1909–84)

1 Film is a dog: the head is commerce, the tail is art. And only rarely does the tail wag the dog.

ATTRIBUTED remark.

2 I feel very strongly that no film is worth much attention unless it has what I call a signature.

REMARK quoted in J.R. Colombo, *Wit and Wisdom of the Moviemakers* (1979).

LOST HORIZON

US 1937; screenwriter: Robert Riskin (from James Hilton novel); cast: Sam Jaffe (High Lama), Hugh Buckler (Lord Gainsford), Ronald Colman (Robert Conway).

3 *High Lama (on Shangri-La)*: A way of life based on one simple rule: Be kind.

SOUNDTRACK.

4 *Lord Gainsford (when asked whether he believes in Conway's Shangri-La)*: Yes, yes, I believe it. I believe it because I *want* to believe it. Gentlemen, I give you a toast. Here's my hope that Robert Conway will find his Shangri-La. Here's my hope that we all find our Shangri-La.

SOUNDTRACK. Last lines of film.

LOVE AND DEATH

US 1975; screenwriter/director: Woody Allen; cast: Woody Allen (Boris), Diane Keaton (Sonja), Olga Georges-Picot (Countess Alexandrovna).

5 *Countess Alexandrovna*: You are the greatest lover I have ever had.
Boris: Well, I practise a lot when I'm on my own.

SOUNDTRACK.

6 *Sonja*: Judgement of any system, or a priori relationship or phenomenon exists in any irrational, or metaphysical, or at least epistemological contradiction to an abstract empirical concept such as being, or to be, or to occur in the thing itself, or of the thing itself.
Boris: I've said that many times.

SOUNDTRACK.

7 *Boris*: You know, if, if it turns out that there is a God, I don't think that he's evil. I think that, that the worst you could say about him is that basically he's an underachiever.

SOUNDTRACK.

1 *Boris*: The, the key here, I think, is to, to not think of death as an end, but, but think of it more as a very effective way of, of cutting down on your expenses. Regarding love, huh, you know, uh, what can you say? It's, it's not the, the quantity of your sexual relations that count, it's the quality. On the other hand, if the quantity drops below once every eight months, I would definitely look into it. Well, that's about it from me, folks. Goodbye.

SOUNDTRACK. Last lines of film.

LOVE IS A MANY-SPLENDORED THING

US 1955; screenwriter: John Patrick (from Han Suyin novel); William Holden (Mark Elliott), Jennifer Jones (Han Suyin).

2 *Mark (to Han Suyin, in posthumously delivered note)*: We have not missed, you and I – we have not missed that many-splendored thing.

SOUNDTRACK. Han Suyin found the title phrase in 'The Kingdom of God' (1913) by the English poet, Francis Thompson (1859–1907): 'The angels keep their ancient places; / Turn but a stone and start a wing! / 'Tis ye, 'tis your estranged faces, / That miss the many-splendoured thing.'

LOVE STORY

US 1970; screenwriter: Erich Segal (from his novel); cast: Ryan O'Neal (Oliver Barrett IV), Ray Milland (Oliver Barrett III), Ali MacGraw (Jenny Cavilleri).

3 *Barrett IV*: What can you say about a twenty-five-year-old girl who died? That she was beautiful and brilliant? That she loved Mozart and Bach, The Beatles, and me?

SOUNDTRACK.

4 *Barrett IV (to Barrett III)*: Love means never having to say you're sorry.

SOUNDTRACK. Last line of film. Also used as a promotional tag for the film. Father tells son that he is sorry that his student wife (Jenny) has died; the son makes this response, quoting an earlier remark of Jenny's. In Segal's novelization of the story (where the line appears as the penultimate sentence), it is in the form 'Love means *not ever* having to say you're sorry.' *See also* ***WHAT'S UP, DOC?*** 445:8.

5 Happiness is a warm bed pan.

COMMENT on the film by Christopher Hudson, critic, quoted in *A Year of Stings and Squelches* (1985).

6 *Camille* with bullshit.

COMMENT by Alexander Walker, British film critic.

LOVE WITH THE PROPER STRANGER

US 1963; screenwriter: Arnold Schulman; cast: Steve McQueen (Rocky Papasano), Natalie Wood (Angie Rossini).

1 *Rocky (proposing to Angie by holding up a sign)*: Better wed than dead!

SOUNDTRACK.

Myrna LOY

American actress (1905–93)

2 They say movies should be more like life. I think life should be more like the movies.

ATTRIBUTED remark.

Ernst LUBITSCH

German-born American director (1892–1947)

3 I sometimes make pictures which are not up to my standard, but then it can only be said of a mediocrity that all his work is up to his standard.

QUOTED in Leslie Halliwell, *The Filmgoer's Book of Quotes* (1973).

4 He was the only director in Hollywood who had his own signature.

COMMENT by S.N. Behrman, quoted in Leslie Halliwell, *The Filmgoer's Book of Quotes* (1973).

5 [Lubitsch] could do more with a closed door than most of today's directors can do with an open fly.

COMMENT by Billy Wilder, quoted in *The Independent* (13 February 1999).

See also **SLOGANS** 384:1.

George LUCAS

American director and screenwriter (1944–)

6 Art is the retelling of certain themes in a new light, making them accessible to the public of the moment.

QUOTED in *The New York Times* (9 June 1988).

7 George, you can type this shit, but you sure can't say it.

COMMENT by Harrison Ford on Lucas's script for *Star Wars*, quoted in Peter Biskind, *Easy Riders, Raging Bulls* (1998).

Sidney LUMET

American director (1924–)

1 He's the only guy who could double park in front of a whore house. He's that fast.

COMMENT attributed to Paul Newman.

Auguste LUMIÈRE

French inventor (1862–1954)

2 *Mon frère, en une nuit, avait inventé le cinématographe* [My brother, in one night, had invented the cinema].

QUOTED in C.W. Ceram, *Archaeology of the Cinema* (1965). Louis Lumière (1864–1948) had a flash of inspiration that resulted in the '*Kinetoscope de projection*', patented in 1895.

3 Young man, you should be grateful, since, although my invention is not for sale, it would undoubtedly ruin you. It can be exploited for a certain time as a scientific curiosity, but, apart from that, it has no commercial future whatsoever.

QUOTED in J.R. Colombo, *Wit and Wisdom of the Moviemakers* (1979). In Jean-Luc Godard's *Le* ***MÉPRIS*** there is a sequence in a film studio screening room. On the wall is a slogan in Italian, attributed to *Louis* Lumière, meaning 'The cinema is an invention without any future.'

Louis-Jean LUMIÈRE

French inventor (1864–1948)

4 Talking films are a very interesting invention, but I do not believe that they will remain long in fashion. First of all, perfect synchronization between sound and image is absolutely impossible, and, secondly, cinema cannot, and must not, become theatre.

QUOTED in *Films sonores avant* (1928).

MACARTHUR

US 1977; screenwriters: Hal Barwood, Matthew Robbins; cast: Gregory Peck (Gen. Douglas MacArthur).

1 *MacArthur (speaking at West Point)*: But always in our minds ring the ominous words of Plato – 'Only the dead have seen the end of war.'

SOUNDTRACK.

2 *MacArthur*: The President of the United States ordered me to break through the Japanese lines and proceed from Corregidor to Australia for the purpose of organizing the American offensive against Japan – a primary object of which is the re-taking of the Philippines. I came through and I shall return.

SOUNDTRACK. A direct quotation of MacArthur's speech at Adelaide on 20 March 1942 – though he used the word 'relieving', not 're-taking'.

3 *MacArthur*: People of the Philippines, I have returned. By the grace of Almighty God, our forces stand again on Philippine soil. The hour of your redemption is here. Rally to me. Let the indomitable spirit of Bataan and Corregidor lead on. As the lines of battle roll forward, rise and strike. For your homes and hearths, strike! For future generations of your sons and daughters, strike! In the name of your sacred dead, strike! Let no heart be faint. Let every arm be steeled. The divine guidance of God points the way. Follow in His name to the Holy Grail of righteous victory.

SOUNDTRACK. On landing at Leyte, quoting most of the words MacArthur actually spoke and the way he spoke them on 20 October 1944.

4 *MacArthur (speaking at West Point)*: Today marks my final roll call with you. I want you to know that when I cross the river, my last conscious thoughts will be of the Corps, and the Corps, and the Corps. I bid you farewell.

SOUNDTRACK. Last words of film.

Mary McCARTHY

American novelist (1912–89)

1 The immense popularity of American movies abroad demonstrates that Europe is the unfinished negative of which America is the proof.

EXTRACTED from her book *On the Contrary*, 'America the Beautiful' (1936).

Ian McEWAN

English novelist and screenwriter (1948–)

2 [on a writer's life in Hollywood] It's an opportunity to fly first class, be treated like a celebrity, sit around the pool and be betrayed.

QUOTED in *The Observer*, 'Sayings of the Week' (22 August 1993).

(Sir) Compton MACKENZIE

English-born novelist and Scottish nationalist (1883–1972)

3 [on the film of his novel *Whisky Galore*, UK 1948] Well, I think it has become a kind of folk-tale … rather like Aladdin … because it goes on and on.

QUOTED from BBC radio interview (1966) by Murray Grigor, in *From Limelight to Satellite*, ed. Eddie Dick (1990).

Shirley MACLAINE

American actress (1934–)

4 The Oscar means one thing – an added million dollar gross for the picture. It's a big publicity contest. Oh, the voting is legitimate, but there's the sentimentality. One year when I was a candidate, when Elizabeth Taylor got a hole in her throat, I cancelled my plane.

ATTRIBUTED remark.

5 I believe that in previous lives I have been an elephant princess, a kidnapped maiden, a peg-legged pirate and a court jester beheaded by Louis XI.

QUOTED in *Sunday Today*, 'Quotes of the Week' (21 December 1986).

6 I've played so many hookers they don't pay me in the regular way any more. They leave it on the dresser.

QUOTED in *New Woman* (July 1989).

7 I must have been a hooker in some other life because I play prostitutes with such sympathy.

QUOTED in *The Independent* (10 November 1990).

Marshall McLUHAN

Canadian writer (1911–80)

1 There is a basic principle that distinguishes a hot medium like radio from a cool one like the telephone, or a hot medium like the movie from a cool one like TV … Hot media are … low in participation, and cool media are high in participation or completion by the audience.

EXTRACTED from his book *Understanding Media*, Chap. 2 (1964).

2 Movies as a non-verbal form of experience are like photographs: a form of statement without syntax.

ATTRIBUTED remark.

Steve McQUEEN

American actor (1930–80)

3 In my own mind, I'm not sure that acting is something for a grown man to be doing.

ATTRIBUTED remark.

The MAGNIFICENT AMBERSONS

US 1942; screenwriter/director: Orson Welles (from Booth Tarkington novel); cast: Orson Welles (Narrator).

4 *Narrator*: Something had happened, that thing which years ago had been the eagerest hope of many, many good citizens of the town. Now it came at last: George Amberson Minafer had got his comeuppance. He got it three times filled and running over.

SOUNDTRACK.

The MAGNIFICENT SEVEN

US 1960; screenwriters: William Roberts, Walter Newman, Walter Bernstein; cast: Steve McQueen (Vin), Yul Brynner (Chris), Horst Buchholz (Chico), Charles Bronson (O'Reilly), James Coburn (Britt), Eli Wallach (Calvera).

5 *Vin (to Chris)*: Never rode shotgun on a hearse before.

SOUNDTRACK.

6 *Chris (when Chico joins)*: Now we're seven.

SOUNDTRACK.

7 *Chico (congratulating Britt on shooting a bandit off his horse)*:
That was the greatest shot I've ever seen.
Britt: The worst. I was aiming at the horse.

SOUNDTRACK.

1 *Calvera (bandit leader, of villagers upon whom he preys)*: If God didn't want them sheared, he would not have made them sheep.

SOUNDTRACK.

2 *Calvera*: What I don't understand is why a man like you took the job in the first place. Why?
Chris: I wonder myself.
Calvera: No, come on, come on: tell me why.
Vin: Like a fellow I once knew in El Paso. One day he just took all his clothes off and jumped into a mess of cactus. I asked him the same question, *Why?*
Calvera: And?
Vin: He said it seemed to be a good idea at the time.

SOUNDTRACK. *Compare* **CATCHPHRASES** 94:4.

3 *O'Reilly (to farmer's son who said his father was a coward)*: Don't you ever say that again about your fathers because they are not cowards. You think I'm brave because I carry a gun? Well, your fathers are much braver because they carry responsibility – for you, your brothers, your sisters, and your mothers.

SOUNDTRACK.

4 *Chris*: The old man was right, only the farmers won. We lost. We'll always lose.

SOUNDTRACK. Last line of film.

The MAGNIFICENT YANKEE

US 1950; screenwriter: Emmet Lavery (from his play and Francis Biddle biography); cast: Louis Calhern (Oliver Wendell Holmes Jr).

5 *Holmes*: Do you know what I think when I see a pretty girl? ... Oh, to be eighty again!

SOUNDTRACK. Whether Holmes ever actually uttered this line in real life is not clear.

MAGNUM FORCE

US 1973; screenwriters: John Milius, Michael Cimino; cast: Clint Eastwood (Harry Callahan).

6 *Harry*: Read my lips.

SOUNDTRACK. When President Bush famously said 'Read my lips, no new taxes' in his speech accepting the Republican nomination at New Orleans on 18 August 1988, the hunt was on for the origins of the expression 'read my lips'. According to William Safire in an article in *The New York Times* Magazine

(September 1988), the phrase is rooted in 1970s rock music (despite there being a song with the title copyrighted by Joe Greene in 1957). The English actor/singer Tim Curry used the phrase as the title of an album of songs in 1978. Curry said he took it from an Italian-American recording engineer who used it to mean, 'Listen and listen very hard, because I want you to hear what I've got to say.' Several lyricists in the 1980s used the phrase for song titles. A football coach with the Chicago Bears became nicknamed Mike 'Read My Lips' Ditka. There has been a thoroughbred racehorse so named. Safire also cites a number of American politicians, also in the 1980s. In the film *Breathless* (1983), a scrap dealer says it to the Richard Gere character, encouraging him to believe that there is no money in the yard worth taking. However, despite these other instances, the use of the phrase in *Magnum Force* would appear to be much the earliest film citation.

1 *Harry*: A man's got to know his limitations.

SOUNDTRACK. Last line of film.

Norman MAILER

American novelist and journalist (1923–)

2 Each day a few more lies eat into the seed with which we are born, little institutional lies from the print of newspapers, the shock waves of television, and the sentimental cheats of the movie screen.

EXTRACTED from his book *Advertisement for Myself* (1959).

The MAJOR AND THE MINOR

US 1942; screenwriters: Billy Wilder, Charles Brackett; cast: Robert Benchley (Mr Osborne), Ginger Rogers (Susan Applegate).

3 *Osborne (offering drink to Applegate)*: No matter what the weather, I always say, 'Why don't you get out of that wet coat and into a dry Martini?'

SOUNDTRACK. This was a favourite line of Benchley's and may have actually originated with Benchley's press agent in the 1920s or with his friend Charles Butterworth. One account is that he uttered it on the set of – though not on screen during – *China Seas* (US 1935). In any case, Mae West also apparently picked up the line, as screenwriter, in *Every Day's a Holiday* (1937).

4 *Osborne (on his wife's joining a national defense program)*: My only regret is that I have but one wife to give to my country.

SOUNDTRACK. An allusion to American revolutionary Nathan Hale's famous remark before his execution by the British for spying (22 September 1776): 'I only regret that I have but one life to lose for my country.'

MAKE WAY FOR TOMORROW

US 1937; screenwriter: Viña Delmar (from a novel); cast: Victor Moore (Barkley 'Pa' Cooper).

1 *Barkley*: Two old-fashioneds, for two old-fashioned people.

SOUNDTRACK. An old-fashioned is a whiskey cocktail.

Dudley Field MALONE

American lawyer and actor

2 Hollywood is the place where inferior people have a way of making superior people feel inferior.

QUOTED in *A Treasury of Humorous Quotations*, eds. Prochnow & Prochnow (1969).

The MALTESE FALCON

US 1941; screenwriter/director: John Huston (from Dashiell Hammett novel); cast: Humphrey Bogart (Sam Spade), Sydney Greenstreet (Kasper Gutman), Mary Astor (Brigid O'Shaughnessy), Peter Lorre (Joel Cairo), Ward Bond (Detective Tom Polhaus), James Burke (Luke), Elisha Cook Jr (Wilmer).

3 *Spade (to Cairo)*: When you're slapped, you'll take it and like it.

SOUNDTRACK.

4 *Gutman (to Spade)*: Well, sir, here's to plain speaking and clear understanding.

SOUNDTRACK.

5 *Gutman (to Spade)*: I'll tell you right out, I'm a man who likes talking to a man who likes to talk.

SOUNDTRACK.

6 *Gutman (to Spade, on why he is handing over cash worth less than he had talked about earlier)*: But this is genuine coin of the realm. With a dollar of this you can buy ten dollars of talk.

SOUNDTRACK.

7 *Gutman (to Spade)*: By gad, sir, you are a character, that you are. There's never any telling what you'll say or do next, except that it's bound to be something astonishing.

SOUNDTRACK.

8 *Spade (replying to Polhaus's inquiry about the falcon, 'What is it?')*: The, uh, stuff that dreams are made of.
Polhaus: Huh?

SOUNDTRACK. Last lines of film.

MAME

US 1974; screenwriter: Paul Zindel (from musical by Jerry Herman and novel by Patrick Dennis); Beatrice Arthur (Vera Charles), Lucille Ball (Mame Dennis).

1 *Vera (waking in Mame's bathtub after drinking binge)*: Oh my God – someone's been sleeping in my dress!

SOUNDTRACK.

David MAMET

American playwright, screenwriter and director (1947–)

2 We Americans have always considered Hollywood, at best, a sinkhole of depraved venality. And, of course, it is. It is not a Protective Monastery of Aesthetic Truth.

EXTRACTED from book *Writing in Restaurants*, 'A Playwright in Hollywood' (1986).

3 The Film Industry is the American Monarchy: it is strict entailed succession and Horatio Alger in one. Except for the money manipulators and speculators, it is a society built on work, achievement and fealty to those in power.

EXTRACTED from the same book, 'Observations of a Backstage Wife'.

4 Life in the movie business is like the beginning of a new love affair: it's full of surprises and you are constantly getting fucked.

EXTRACTED from play *Speed the Plow*, Scene 1 (1988).

5 A good film script should be able to do completely without dialogue.

QUOTED in *The Independent* (11 November 1988).

6 Film is the least realistic of art forms.

INTERVIEWED in *The Guardian* (16 February 1989).

A MAN FOR ALL SEASONS

UK 1966; screenwriters; Constance Willis, Robert Bolt (from his play); cast: John Hurt (Thomas Rich), Paul Scofield (Sir Thomas More), Orson Welles (Cardinal Wolsey), Robert Shaw (Henry VIII), Wendy Hiller (Alice More), Corin Redgrave (William Roper), Nigel Davenport (Duke of Norfolk), Susannah York (Margaret More).

7 *More (to Rich, advising him to become a teacher)*: A man should go where he won't be tempted.

SOUNDTRACK.

8 *More (telling Rich who would know if he were a great teacher)*: You. Your pupils. Your friends. God. Not a bad public that.

SOUNDTRACK.

1 *More (to Duke of Norfolk, who has asked him to take the oath for the sake of fellowship)*: And when we die, and you are sent to Heaven for doing your conscience, and I am sent to Hell for not doing mine, will you come with me, for fellowship?

SOUNDTRACK.

2 *More*: Some men think the Earth is round, others think it flat. It is a matter capable of question. But if it is flat, will the king's word make it round, and if it is round, will the king's word flatten it?

SOUNDTRACK.

3 *More (to Rich, on learning that Rich has betrayed him in order to become attorney general for Wales)*: Why, Richard, it profits a man nothing to give his soul for the whole world – but for *Wales*?

SOUNDTRACK.

4 *More (to executioner)*: I forgive you right readily. Be not afraid of your office. You send me to God.

SOUNDTRACK.

The MAN WHO CAME TO DINNER

US 1941; screenwriter: Julius J. & Philip G. Epstein (from Kaufman & Hart play); cast: Monty Woolley (Sheridan Whiteside), Reginald Gardiner (Beverly Carlton); Jimmy Durante (Banjo); Mary Wickes (Nurse).

5 *Whiteside (to Nurse who has forbidden him to eat chocolates)*: I had an aunt who ate a box of chocolates every day of her life. She lived to be a hundred and two, and when she had been dead three days, she looked healthier than you do now.

SOUNDTRACK.

6 *Nurse*: If Florence Nightingale had ever nursed *you*, Mr Whiteside, she would have married Jack the Ripper instead of founding the Red Cross.

SOUNDTRACK. In fact, Nightingale had nothing to do with the founding of the Red Cross.

7 *Carlton*: Don't tell me how you are, Sherry. I want none of the tiresome details. I've very little time, and so the conversation will be entirely about me, and I shall love it. Shall I tell you how I glittered through the South Seas like a silver scimitar, or would you rather hear how I finished a three-act play with one hand and made love to a maharaja's daughter with the other?

SOUNDTRACK.

1 *Whiteside*: Gentlemen, will you all now leave quietly, or must I ask Miss Cutler to pass among you with a baseball bat?

SOUNDTRACK.

The MAN WHO SHOT LIBERTY VALANCE

US 1962; screenwriters: James Warner Bellah, Willis Goldbeck; cast: Carleton Young (Maxwell Scott), James Stewart (Ransom Stoddard).

2 *Scott (on not printing true story of a death)*: No, sir. This is the West, sir. When the legend becomes fact, print the legend.

SOUNDTRACK.

The MAN WHO WOULD BE KING

UK 1975; screenwriters: John Huston, Gladys Hill (from Kipling story); cast: Sean Connery (Danny Dravot), Christopher Plummer (Rudyard Kipling), Michael Caine (Peachy Carnehan), Saeed Jaffrey (Billy Fish).

3 *Danny (to Kipling)*: The less said about our professions, the better, for we have been most things in our times. We have been all over India. We know her cities and jungles, her jails and her palaces. And we have decided she isn't big enough for such as we.

SOUNDTRACK.

4 *Peachy (to Kipling)*: We're going away to another place where a man isn't crowded and can come into his own. We're not little men, so we're going away to be kings.

SOUNDTRACK.

5 *Danny (to Peachy, when told to stop singing)*: If a king can't sing, it ain't worth being king.

SOUNDTRACK.

6 *Peachy (when asked if he and Danny are gods)*: Not gods. Englishmen, which is the next best thing.

SOUNDTRACK.

7 *Danny*: Peachy, I'm heartily ashamed for getting you killed instead of going home rich like you deserved to, on account of me being so bleedin' high and bloody mighty. Can you forgive me?
Peachy: That I can and that I do, Danny.

SOUNDTRACK.

8 *Peachy (to Kipling)*: You knew, most worshipful brother – Daniel Dravot, Esquire? Well, he became the King of Kafiristan, with a crown on his head. And that's all there is to tell. I'll be on my way now, sir. I've got urgent business in the South. I have to meet a man at Marwar Junction.

SOUNDTRACK.

The MAN WITH THE GOLDEN GUN

UK 1974; screenwriters: Richard Maibaum, Tom Mankiewicz (after Ian Fleming novel); cast: Roger Moore (James Bond), Christopher Lee (Scaramanga), Britt Ekland (Mary Goodnight).

1 *Scaramanga (demonstrating solar-powered gun)*: You must admit, Mr Bond, that I am now undeniably the man with the golden gun.

SOUNDTRACK.

2 *Scaramanga (to Goodnight)*: I like a girl in a bikini – no concealed weapons.

SOUNDTRACK.

3 *Bond*: When I kill, it's on the specific orders of my government, and those I kill are themselves killers.

SOUNDTRACK. So that's all right then.

Henry MANCINI

American composer (1924–94)

4 God, it's an empty feeling watching a movie without any music!

ATTRIBUTED remark on album cover, *As You Remember Them* (1972).

MANHATTAN

US 1979; screenwriters: Woody Allen, Marshall Brickman; cast: Woody Allen (Isaac Davis), Diane Keaton (Mary Wilke); Tisa Farrow (Polly/Party Guest), Michael Murphy (Yale).

5 *Isaac (writing)*: 'Chapter One. He adored New York City. He idolized it all out of proportion.' No, make that, 'he romanticized it all out of proportion.' Better. 'To him, no matter what the season was, this was still a town that existed in black and white and pulsated to the great tunes of George Gershwin.' No, let me start this over … 'Chapter One. He was as tough and romantic as the city he loved. Behind his black-rimmed glasses was the coiled sexual power of a jungle cat … ' I love this! 'New York was his town and it always would be …'

SOUNDTRACK. Opening lines.

6 *Isaac (to Mary)*: I think people should mate for life – like pigeons or Catholics.

SOUNDTRACK.

1 *Isaac (to Mary)*: There must be something wrong with me because I've never had a relationship that lasted longer than the one between Hitler and Eva Braun.

SOUNDTRACK.

2 *Polly (party guest)*: I … uh, I finally had an orgasm and my doctor told me it was the wrong kind.

SOUNDTRACK. The identification of the party guest (named Polly in the script, though not in the credits) is not certain.

MANHATTAN MURDER MYSTERY

US 1993; screenwriters: Woody Allen, Marshall Brickman; cast: Woody Allen (Larry Lipton), Diane Keaton (Carol Lipton), Jerry Adler (Paul House), Lynn Cohen (Lillian House), Alan Alda (Ted), Anjelica Huston (Marcia Fox).

3 *Larry (to Carol)*: I forbid you. I forbid you to go. I'm forbidding! Is that what you do when I forbid you?

SOUNDTRACK.

4 *Larry*: I think it's a pretty fair assumption that if a person is dead they don't suddenly turn up in the New York City Transit System.

SOUNDTRACK.

5 *Hotel night clerk*: You are police?
Larry: Yes, I'm a detective. They lowered the height requirement.

SOUNDTRACK.

6 *Larry (when body drops through elevator roof)*: Claustrophobia and a dead body! This is a neurotic's jackpot!

SOUNDTRACK.

7 *Larry*: There's nothing wrong with you that a little Prozac and a polo mallet can't cure.

SOUNDTRACK.

8 *Larry (after shootings behind cinema screen)*: I'll never say that art doesn't imitate life again.

SOUNDTRACK.

9 *Larry*: I can't believe I was worried about you and Ted, I mean take away his fake tan, his capped teeth and his Cuban heels and what have you got?
Carol: You!

SOUNDTRACK.

Herman J. MANKIEWICZ

American screenwriter (1897–1953)

1 [cable to Ben Hecht from Hollywood in 1926] There are millions to be grabbed out here and your only competition is idiots. Don't let this get around.

QUOTED in *The New York Times* (8 January 1993).

2 That man [a fellow scriptwriter] is so bad he shouldn't be left alone in a room with a typewriter.

ATTRIBUTED remark.

3 Do you have any idea how bad the picture is? I'll tell you. Stay away from the neighbourhood where it's playing – don't even go near the street! It might rain – you could get caught in the downpour, and to keep dry you'd have to go inside the theatre.

ATTRIBUTED remark.

Joseph L. MANKIEWICZ

American screenwriter, producer and director (1909–93)

4 [while directing *Cleopatra*] I'm not [biting my fingernails]. I'm biting my knuckles. I finished the fingernails months ago.

QUOTED in Dick Sheppard, *Elizabeth* (1975).

See also Mel **BROOKS** 79:1.

Jayne MANSFIELD

American actress (1932–67)

5 [when asked by Robin Day in TV interview, 'Is it true you led a tiger down Sunset Boulevard by a pink ribbon?] Yes, I like pink.

QUOTED in *The Guardian* (23 December 1989).

Roger MANVELL

English writer (1909–87)

6 God made the fine arts but man made the film.

EXTRACTED from book *Film* (1944).

See also The ***BATTLESHIP POTEMKIN*** 51:10.

Sophie MARCEAU

French actress (1967–)

1 French films follow a basic formula: Husband sleeps with Jeanne because Bernadette cuckolded him by sleeping with Christophe, and in the end they all go off to a restaurant.

QUOTED in *The Observer*, 'Sayings of the Week' (26 March 1995).

Frances MARION

American screenwriter (1888–1973)

2 [on the Oscar] The statuette is a perfect symbol of the picture business – a powerful athletic body clutching a gleaming sword, with half of his head, the part that holds his brains, completely sliced off.

ATTRIBUTED remark from 1928.

The MARK OF ZORRO

US 1940; screenwriters: Garrett Fort and others; cast: Basil Rathbone (Esteban).

3 *Esteban*: Some men play with handkerchiefs, but I like to keep a rapier in my hand.

SOUNDTRACK.

MARNIE

US 1964; screenwriter: Jay Presson Allen (based on Winston Graham novel); cast: Sean Connery (Mark Rutland), Tippi Hedren (Marnie Edgar), Louise Latham (Bernice Edgar), Martin Gabel (Sidney Strutt), Diane Baker (Lil Mainwaring), Alan Napier (Mr Rutland).

4 *Sidney (of Marnie)*: Always pulling her skirt down over her knees as though they were a national treasure.

SOUNDTRACK.

5 *Mark (on his zoology paper, 'Arboreal Predators of the Brazilian Rain Forest')*: That paper deals with the instincts of predators. What you might call the criminal class of the animal world. Lady animals figure very largely as predators.

SOUNDTRACK.

6 *Marnie*: What about your tough childhood, Mr Rutland?
Mark: The old sad story, promising youth blighted, dragged down by money, position, *noblesse oblige*.

SOUNDTRACK.

1 *Mark (of his father)*: Dad goes by scent. If you smell anything like a horse, you're in.

SOUNDTRACK.

2 *Mr Rutland*: The best thing in the world for the inside of a man or a woman is the outside of a horse.

SOUNDTRACK. Quoting an American proverbial saying.

3 *Mark*: 'When Duty whispers low, *Thou Must*,
Then youth replies, *I can.*'
Lil: Ratfink! And you misquoted!

SOUNDTRACK. Not really. R.W. Emerson's 'Voluntaries, III' (1867) merely has '*The* youth replies …'

4 *Lil*: I always thought that a girl's best friend was her mother.

SOUNDTRACK.

5 *Marnie (to Mark, when asked to tell him about her disturbing dreams)*: You Freud – me Jane?

SOUNDTRACK.

6 *Marnie (to Mark)*: I don't want to go to jail. I'd rather stay with you.

SOUNDTRACK.

Gabriel Garciá MARQUEZ

Colombian novelist (1928–)

7 I can't think of any one film that improved on a good novel, but I can think of many good films that came from very bad novels.

INTERVIEWED in *Writers at Work* (6th series, 1984).

(Sir) Edward MARSH

English scholar and arts patron (1872–1953)

8 How I dislike Technicolor, which suffuses everything with stale mustard.

EXTRACTED from book *Ambrosia and Small Beer* (1964).

Dean MARTIN

American actor and singer (1917–95)

9 I'd hate to be a teetotaller. Imagine getting up in the morning and knowing that's as good as you're going to feel all day.

ATTRIBUTED remark.

MARTY

US 1955; screenwriter: Paddy Chayevsky (from his TV play); cast: Ernest Borgnine (Marty Piletti), Esther Minciotti (Mrs Piletti), Joe Mantell (Angie), Betsy Blair (Clara Snyder), Augusta Ciolli (Catherine).

1 *Marty (to Angie)*: Listen, Ange. I've been looking for a girl every Saturday night of my life. I'm thirty-four years old. I'm tired of looking, that's all.

SOUNDTRACK.

2 *Marty (to his mother, Mrs Pilletti)*: Sooner or later, there comes a point in a man's life when he's got to face some facts. And one fact I got to face is that whatever it is that women like, I ain't got it. I chased after enough women in my life. I went to enough dances. I got hurt enough. I don't want to get hurt no more.

SOUNDTRACK.

3 *Marty (to Angie)*: All I know is I had a good time last night. I'm going to have a good time tonight. If we have enough good times together, I'm going to get down on my knees. I'm going to beg that girl to marry me. If we make a party on New Year's, I got a date for that party. You don't like her? That's too bad!

SOUNDTRACK.

Chico MARX

American comedian (1886–1961)

4 [when his wife had caught him kissing a chorus girl] But I wasn't kissing her. I was whispering in her mouth.

QUOTED in Groucho Marx & Richard Anobile, *The Marx Brothers Scrapbook* (1974).

5 There are three things that my brother Chico is always on: a phone, a horse or a broad.

COMMENT by Groucho Marx, quoted in J.R. Colombo, *Wit and Wisdom of the Moviemakers* (1979).

Groucho MARX

American comedian (1890–1977)

6 We in the industry know that behind every successful screenwriter stands a woman. And behind her stands his wife.

ATTRIBUTED remark in 1977.

1 Hollywood brides keep the bouquets and throw away the grooms.

ATTRIBUTED remark.

2 Please accept my resignation. I don't care to belong to any club that will have me as a member.

ATTRIBUTED remark. Zeppo Marx recalled that this was about The Friars Club, a theatrical organization, for which his brother did not have much use. Hector Arce added that Groucho had some misgivings about the quality of the members – 'doubts verified a few years later when an infamous card-cheating scandal erupted there'. The wording varies, but the one here is taken from Arthur Sheekman's introduction to *The Groucho Letters* (1967). The actual letter unfortunately does not survive. In *Groucho and Me* (1959), he himself supplied the version: 'PLEASE ACCEPT MY RESIGNATION. I DON'T WANT TO BELONG TO ANY CLUB THAT WILL ACCEPT ME AS A MEMBER.' *Compare* ***ANNIE HALL*** 30:1.

3 The man was a major comedian, which is to say that he had the compassion of an icicle, the effrontery of a carnival shill, and the generosity of a pawnbroker.

COMMENT by S.J. Perelman, quoted in Maria Leach, *The Ultimate Insult* (1996).

MARY POPPINS

US 1964; music/lyrics: Richard M. & Robert B. Sherman; cast: Julie Andrews (Mary Poppins), Karen Dotrice (Jane Banks), Matthew Garber (Michael Banks).

4 *Jane/Michael*: Supercalifragilisticexpialidocious.

SOUNDTRACK. Repeating the word taught to them by Mary. The song containing the word was the subject of a copyright infringement suit brought in 1965 against the makers of the film by Life Music Co. and the writers of two earlier songs. 'Supercalafajalistickespialadojus' had been the title of an (unpublished) song in 1949. 'Supercalafajalistickespeealadojus; or, The super song' followed in 1951. The ruling went against the plaintiffs in view of earlier oral uses of the word sworn to in affidavits and of dissimilarity between the songs.

The MASK

US 1994; screenwriter: Mike Werb; cast: Jim Carrey (Stanley Ipkiss/The Mask), Richard Jeni (Charlie Schumacher), Amy Yasbeck (Peggy Brandt).

5 From Zero to Hero.

SLOGAN. Earlier there had been 'a hero from zero', a fairly meaningless rhyming phrase suggesting that a person has come from humble beginnings. It was used as the title of a document produced in 1988 by the British industrialist Tiny Rowlands in a prolonged war of words with Mohamed Al-Fayed. The Egyptian businessman had been able to gain control of the House of Fraser stores group (which includes Harrods) and thwarted Mr Rowlands's ambitions in that direction. The phrase was derived from an alleged tape recording of a conversation between Fayed (who was presumably talking about himself) and two Indian gurus said to have links with the Sultan of Brunei.

1 *Charlie (to Stanley)*: That girl will tear out your heart, put it in a blender and hit 'frappé'.

SOUNDTRACK.

2 *Peggy*: Most of them [the men in this town] think monogamy is some kind of wood.

SOUNDTRACK.

3 *The Mask*: 'Tell Tiny Tim I won't be coming home this Christmas.'

SOUNDTRACK. The Mask has a way of spouting movie lines, or lines which sound as if they are. Presumably this one comes from *A Christmas Carol* (US 1938). 'Well would you, punks?' is obvious (*see* ***DIRTY HARRY*** 136:5. How about: 'You were good, kid, real good, but as long as I'm around you'll always be second best, see?'; 'Hold me closer, Ed. It's getting dark'; 'Tell Annie, I'm the little yellow one'; 'Tell Scott I do give a damn'; 'You're incorrigible!'?

Marcello MASTROIANNI

Italian actor (1924–96)

4 *Quando ti chiamano Latin lover sei nei guai. Le donne a letto si aspettano da te una performance da Oscar* [When they call you a Latin lover you're in trouble. It means that, in bed, women will expect an Oscar performance from you].

ATTRIBUTED remark.

The MATCHMAKER

US 1958; screenwriter: John Michael Hayes (from Thornton Wilder play); cast: Shirley Booth (Dolly Levi).

5 *Dolly (to camera)*: Life's never quite interesting enough, somehow. You people who come to the movies know that.

SOUNDTRACK.

A MATTER OF LIFE AND DEATH

(also known as *Stairway to Heaven* in US) UK 1946; screenwriters/directors: Michael Powell, Emeric Pressburger; cast: David Niven (Squadron Leader Peter Carter), Roger Livesey (Dr Frank Reeves), Kim Hunter (June), Marius Goring (Conductor 71), Abraham Sofaer (Judge).

6 *Narration*: This is the story of two worlds, the one we know and another which exists only in the mind of a young airman whose life and imagination have been violently shaped by war. Any resemblance to another world, known or unknown, is purely coincidental.

SOUNDTRACK.

1 *Conductor 71 (having moved to earth from heaven – which is shown in black and white)*: One is starved for Technicolor up there.

SOUNDTRACK.

2 *Peter (on Plato, when discussing who will defend him at his heavenly trial)*: Didn't he quote Sophocles when somebody asked if he was still able to appreciate a woman? ... He said, 'I'm only too glad to be rid of all that. It's like escaping from bondage to a raving madman.'

SOUNDTRACK. Yes, Plato quoted Sophocles to this effect in *The Republic* (Bk. 1, l. 329b). It all depends on the translation from the Greek, of course. Another is: 'I have left it behind me and escaped from the madness and slavery of passion ... a release from slavery to all your many passions.' Peter Carter, an Oxford man before he joined the RAF, is quite a quoter. At the beginning of the film, when he is about to bale out of his plane, he quotes Walter Raleigh's 'scallop-shell' verse and also Andrew Marvell's 'Time's winged chariot'.

3 *Dr Reeves (in heaven, summing up his case to allow Peter to live and share his love with June on earth)*: Nothing is stronger than the law in the universe, but on earth nothing is stronger than love.

SOUNDTRACK.

4 *Judge (quoting Walter Scott)*: 'In peace, Love tunes the shepherd's reed; / In war, he mounts the warrior's steed; / In halls, in gay attire is seen; / In hamlets, dances on the green. / Love rules the court, the camp, the grove, / And men below, and saints above; / For love is heaven, and heaven is love.'

SOUNDTRACK. The passage comes from *The Lay of the Last Minstrel*, III (1805).

Walter MATTHAU

American actor (1920–2000)

5 My mother always said to me: 'You know, if you had had a decent father you could have been a lawyer.'

QUOTED in *The Observer*, 'Sayings of the Week' (4 September 1988).

Victor MATURE

American actor (1915–99)

6 [when told that he looked as though he had slept in his clothes] Don't be ridiculous. I pay someone to do that for me.

QUOTED by William Franklyn on BBC Radio *Quote ... Unquote* (20 July 1985).

1 [of the toothless animal employed in *Androcles and the Lion* (US 1952)] I don't want to be gummed to death.

QUOTED by Angela Carter in *The Guardian* (19 August 1988).

2 Actually I am a golfer. That is my real occupation. I never was an actor; ask anybody, particularly the critics.

ATTRIBUTED remark.

3 [on Mature's films] I never go to movies where the hero's bust is bigger than the heroine's.

COMMENT by Groucho Marx, quoted in Leslie Halliwell, *The Filmgoer's Book of Quotes* (1978 edn). Probably regarding Mature's appearance in *Samson and Delilah* (1949).

Louis B. MAYER

American producer (1885–1957)

4 Of course we shall have sex in pictures, but it will be normal, real, beautiful sex – the sex that is common to the people in the audience, to me and to you.

QUOTED in Bosley Crowther, *The Lion's Share* (1957).

5 What does [Upton] Sinclair know about anything – He's just a writer.

QUOTED in Philip French, *The Movie Moguls* (1969).

6 [to writers who complained of changes made to their work] The number one book of the ages was written by a committee, and it was called The Bible.

ATTRIBUTED by Arthur Freed, quoted in Leslie Halliwell, *The Filmgoer's Book of Quotes* (1973).

7 Throw the little old lady down the stairs! Throw the mother's good, home-made chicken soup in the mother's face! *Step* on the mother! *Kick* her! That is *art*, they say. Art!

QUOTED in Lillian Ross, *Picture*, 'Throw the Little Old Lady Down the Stairs!' (1952).

8 We are the only kind of company whose assets all walk out of the gate at night.

QUOTED in Leslie Halliwell, *The Filmgoer's Book of Quotes* (1973). As, 'The movie business is the only business in the world where the assets go home at night', this is attributed to Dorothy Parker in Steven Bach, *Final Cut* (1985).

9 Tsar of all the rushes.

COMMENT by B.P. Schulberg, American publicist, studio executive and producer (1892–1950), quoted in Norman Zierold, *The Hollywood Tycoons* (1969).

MEET ME IN ST LOUIS

US 1941; music/lyrics: Ralph Blane, Hugh Martin; cast: Judy Garland (Esther Smith).

1 *Esther (sings)*: Have yourself a merry little Christmas
Make the yuletide gay.
Next year all our troubles will be miles away.

SOUNDTRACK. Also sung ironically as background to an execution in *The Victors* (US 1963).

H.L. MENCKEN

American journalist and linguist (1880–1956)

2 Just outside pious Los Angeles is Hollywood, a colony of moving picture actors. Its morals are those of Port Said.

EXTRACTED from his book *Americana* (1922).

Le MÉPRIS

(also known as *Contempt*) France/Italy 1963; screenwriter: Jean-Luc Godard, adapted from Alberto Moravia's novel *A Ghost at Noon*, 1963; cast: Jack Palance (Jeremy Prokosh).

3 *Opening narration*: 'For what we see,' Bazin said, 'the cinema substitutes a world that conforms to our desires.' *Le Mépris* is the story of that world.

SUB-TITLE translation. *See also* André **BAZIN** 52:2.

4 *IL CINEMA E UN INVENZIONE SENZA AVVENIRE. LOUIS LUMIERE* [THE CINEMA IS AN INVENTION WITHOUT ANY FUTURE].

SLOGAN on wall of film studio projection suite. *See* Auguste **LUMIÈRE** 261:3.

5 *Prokosh (speaking English)*: When I hear the word culture, I bring out my chequebook.

SOUNDTRACK. Prokosh is a film producer.

Bette MIDLER

American actress and singer (1945–)

6 Underneath all this drag, I'm really a librarian, you know.

ATTRIBUTED remark.

7 I am a screen star, in the tradition of Shirley Temple, Liv Ullman and Miss Piggy.

QUOTED in *Time* Magazine (1979).

MIDNIGHT

US 1939; screenwriters: Charles Brackett, Billy Wilder (from a story); cast: Claudette Colbert (Eve Peabody).

1 *Eve*: The moment I saw you, I had an idea you had an idea.

SOUNDTRACK.

George MIKES

Hungarian-born writer (1912–87)

2 A little foreign blood is very advantageous, almost essential, to become a really great British film producer.

QUOTED in *The Treasury of Humorous Quotations*, eds. Esar & Bentley (1951 edn).

MILDRED PIERCE

US 1945; screenwriter: Ranald MacDougall (from James M. Cain novel); cast: Jack Carson (Wally Fay), Zachary Scott (Monte Beragon).

3 *Wally*: Oh brother! I'm so smart, it's a disease!

SOUNDTRACK.

4 *Monte*: In the spring a young man's fancy lightly turns to what he's been thinking about all winter.

SOUNDTRACK. *See also The* ***AWFUL TRUTH*** 41:2.

Lewis MILESTONE

American director (1895–1980)

5 [when asked to provide upbeat ending for *All Quiet on the Western Front*, in about 1929] I've got your happy ending. We'll let the Germans win the war.

ATTRIBUTED remark.

Darius MILHAUD

French composer (1892–1974)

6 For a long time the so-called symphonic composers were ostracized in film circles, and as a class [were] rather looked down upon by film producers ... Gradually the serious musicians managed to win their way into the studios by putting on false noses, that is by disguising their music in a style calculated to earn the approval of film producers and directors.

EXTRACTED from his book *Notes Without Music* (1952) (in translation).

Arthur MILLER

American playwright and screenwriter (1915–)

1 [when asked if he would attend his ex-wife Marilyn Monroe's funeral in 1962] Why should I go? She won't be there.

ATTRIBUTED remark. Miller enlarged on this in *The Sunday Telegraph* (11 October 1987): 'I found myself having to come about and force myself to encounter the fact that Marilyn had ended. I realized that I still, even then, expected to meet her once more, somewhere, sometime, and maybe talk sensibly about all the foolishness we had been through ... When a reporter called asking if I would be attending her funeral in California, the very idea of a burial was outlandish, and stunned as I was, I answered without thinking, "She won't be there." I could hear his astonishment, but I could only hang up.'

2 [*Variety* headline on his marriage to Marilyn Monroe in 1956] EGGHEAD WEDS HOURGLASS.

COMMENT quoted in Leslie Halliwell, *The Filmgoer's Book of Quotes* (1973).

Henry MILLER

American novelist (1891–1980)

3 The film is the freest of all media, you can do marvels with it. In fact I would welcome the day when the film would displace literature, when there'd be no more need to read. You remember faces in films, and gestures, as you never do when you read a book.

INTERVIEWED in *Writers at Work* (2nd series, 1963).

(Sir) John MILLS

English actor (1908–)

4 [on his part in *Tudor Rose* (1936)] I played the young Earl of Dudley and was beheaded in the third reel – not, in my opinion, a moment too soon.

EXTRACTED from his book *Up in the Clouds, Gentlemen Please* (1980).

Anthony MINGHELLA

English director (1954–)

5 [accepting Best Director Oscar for *The English Patient*] This goes to all the people whose shoulders I've been standing upon. Thanks to my family who have put up with me being away for so long. Thanks to my wife who has taught me the meaning of uxoriousness. This is a great day for the Isle of Wight.

SPEECH at Academy Awards ceremony (March 1997).

The MISFITS

US 1961; screenwriter: Arthur Miller; cast: Clark Gable (Gay Langland), Marilyn Monroe (Roslyn Taber).

1 *Roslyn*: How do you find your way back in the dark?
Gay: Just head for that big star straight on. The highway's under it. It'll take us right home.

SOUNDTRACK. Last lines of film (also Monroe's and Gable's last words spoken on screen).

MISSISSIPPI

US 1935; screenwriters: W.C. Fields and others; cast: W.C. Fields (Commodore Orlando Jackson).

2 *Jackson*: Women are like elephants to me. I like to look at them, but I wouldn't want to own one.

SOUNDTRACK.

MR AND MRS SMITH

US 1941; screenwriter: Norman Krasna; cast: Carole Lombard (Ann Smith), Robert Montgomery (David Smith).

3 *Ann Smith*: I've given you the best years of my life.

SOUNDTRACK. Early appearance of this cliché. *Compare* **CLICHÉS** 105:7.

MR BLANDINGS BUILDS HIS DREAM HOUSE

US 1948; screenwriters: Norman Panama, Melvin Frank; cast: Cary Grant (Jim Blandings), Louise Beavers (Gussie).

4 *Gussie*: 'If you ain't eating Wham, you ain't eating ham!'

SOUNDTRACK. Blandings is an advertising man in search of a slogan that eludes him until Gussie, his cook, inadvertently creates it in these immortal words.

MR DEEDS GOES TO TOWN

US 1936; screenwriter: Robert Riskin (from a story); cast: Gary Cooper (Longfellow Deeds), Margaret Seddon (Jane Faulkner), H.B. Warner (Judge Walker), Lionel Stander (Cornelius Cobb), Jean Arthur (Babe Bennett).

5 *Deeds (to Babe)*: People here [in New York] are funny. They work so hard at living they forget how to live. Last night, after I left you, I was walking along and – and looking at the tall buildings, and I got to thinking about what Thoreau said: 'They created a lot of grand palaces here, but they forgot to create the noblemen to put in them.' I'd rather have Mandrake Falls.

SOUNDTRACK.

1 *Faulkner*: Why, *everybody* in Mandrake Falls is pixilated – except us.
SOUNDTRACK.

2 *Deeds*: From what I can see, no matter what system of government we have, there'll always be leaders and always be followers. It's like the road out in front of my house, it's on a steep hill. Every day I watch the cars climbing up; some go lickety-split up that hill on high, some have to shift into second and some sputter and shake and slip back to the bottom again. Same cars, same gasoline, yet some make it and some don't. And I say the fellows who can make the hill on high should stop once in a while and help those who can't.
SOUNDTRACK. Once quoted verbatim by President Reagan in a speech (before 1986).

3 *Judge Walker*: Mr Deeds, there has been a great deal of damaging testimony against you. Your behavior, to say the least, has been most strange. But, in the opinion of the court, you are not only sane but you're the sanest man that ever walked into this courtroom.
SOUNDTRACK.

See also **CLICHÉS** 105:2.

MISTER ROBERTS

US 1955; screenwriters: Joshua Logan and others (from play by Thomas Heggen and Joshua Logan and novel by Thomas Heggen); cast: Jack Lemmon (Ensign Pulver), James Cagney (Captain Morton), Henry Fonda (Lieut. Doug Roberts), Ward Bond (CPO Dowdy), William Powell (Doc).

4 *Roberts (toasting Pulver)*: And to a great American, Frank Thurlowe Pulver, soldier, statesman, scientist –
Doc: Friend of the working girl.
SOUNDTRACK.

5 *Pulver (reading Roberts's letter to Doc and the crew)*: But I've discovered, Doc, that the unseen enemy of this war is the boredom that eventually becomes a faith and, therefore, a terrible sort of suicide – and I know now that the ones who refuse to surrender to it are the strongest of all.
SOUNDTRACK.

6 *Doc (reading Roberts's letter referring to the Order of the Palm bestowed on him by the ship's crew)*: I'd rather have it than the Congressional Medal of Honour.
SOUNDTRACK.

1 *Pulver (to Morton)*: Captain, it is I, Ensign Pulver, and I just threw your stinking palm tree overboard. Now, what's all this crud about no movie tonight?

SOUNDTRACK. Last line of film.

MR SMITH GOES TO WASHINGTON

US 1939; screenwriter: Sidney Buchman (from story by Lewis R. Foster); cast: James Stewart (Jefferson Smith), Claude Rains (Senator Joseph Paine), Thomas Mitchell (Diz Moore).

2 *Smith (to Paine)*: Dad always used to say the only causes worth fighting for were the lost causes.

SOUNDTRACK.

3 *Moore*: Every time I think of exercise, I have to lie right down till the feeling leaves me.

SOUNDTRACK.

4 *Smith*: I wouldn't give you two cents for all your fancy rules if, behind them, they didn't have a little bit of ordinary everyday human kindness – and a little looking out for the other fella, too.

SOUNDTRACK.

MRS MINIVER

US 1942; screenwriters: Arthur Wimperis and others (from Jan Struther novel); cast: Henry Wilcoxon (Vicar).

5 *Vicar (preaching in bombed church)*: This is the people's war. It is our war. We are the fighters. Fight it, then. Fight it with all that is in us, and may God defend the right.

SOUNDTRACK. Last words of film.

6 What wonderful propaganda for the Allied cause! What a wave of sympathy for the British and hatred for the Germans comes out of this film! Surely this isn't merely a work of art; it is also excellent propaganda.

COMMENT by Josef Goebbels, Nazi propaganda chief, quoted in R. Manvell & Heinrich Frankel, *Doctor Goebbels*: *His Life and Death* (1960).

Robert MITCHUM

American actor (1917–97)

7 It Sure Beats Working.

TITLE of biography (1975) by Mike Tomkies.

1 Movies bore me, especially my own.

QUOTED in Leslie Halliwell, *The Filmgoer's Book of Quotes* (1978 edn).

2 [recalling how he proposed to his wife, Dorothy] Marry me and you'll be farting through silk.

QUOTED in *Film Yearbook* (1985).

3 The only thing wrong with performing was that you couldn't phone it in.

QUOTED by Robert Robinson in *The Sunday Times* Magazine (11 May 1980).

4 I give hope to the hopeless. People look at me and say: 'If he can make it, I can be Queen of England.'

QUOTED in *The Observer*, 'Sayings of the Week' (28 October 1984).
In J.R. Colombo, *Wit and Wisdom of the Moviemakers* (1979), this had appeared as: 'You know something? What I represent to the public is hope. They look at me and they think: if that big slob can get somewhere, there's a chance for us.'

5 Paint eyeballs on my eyelids and I'll sleep through any picture.

ATTRIBUTED remark.

6 Nowadays Mitchum doesn't so much act as point his suit at people.

COMMENT by Russell Davies in *The Sunday Times* (18 September 1983), reviewing Mitchum's performance in the TV mini-series *The Winds of War*.

7 [to Mitchum] You're like a pay toilet, aren't you? You don't give a shit for nothing.

COMMENT by Howard Hughes, American producer and businessman (1905–76), quoted by Mitchum in *The Observer* (5 February 1989).

Tom MIX

American actor (1880–1940)

8 They say he rides like part of the horse but they don't say what part.

COMMENT by Robert Sherwood when a *Life* movie critic. Quoted in John Keats, *You Might as Well Live* (1970).

9 He was as elegant on a horse as Fred Astaire on the dance floor, and that's the elegantest there is.

COMMENT by Adela Rogers St Johns.

Wilson MIZNER

American playwright (1876–1933)

10 Hollywood is a sewer with service from the Ritz Carlton.

QUOTED in Leslie Halliwell, *The Filmgoer's Book of Quotes* (1973).

1 [on Hollywood, before 1933] A trip through a sewer in a glass-bottomed boat.

QUOTED in Alva Johnston, *The Legendary Mizners* (1953).

2 Once in Hollywood they almost made a great picture, but they caught it just in time.

ATTRIBUTED remark.

3 [to Jack Warner about the LA telephone directory] This might have been good for a picture – except it has too many characters in it.

QUOTED in Max Wilk, *The Wit and Wisdom of Hollywood* (1972).

4 Working for Warner Brothers is like fucking a porcupine; it's a hundred pricks against one.

QUOTED in David Niven, *Bring On the Empty Horses* (1975).

5 I've had several years in Hollywood and I still think the movie heroes are in the audience.

QUOTED in *The Treasury of Humorous Quotations*, eds. Esar & Bentley (1951 edn).

Hal MOHR

American cinematographer (1894–1974)

6 [when asked by Marlene Dietrich as they were working together on *Rancho Notorious* (1952) why she wasn't looking as good on film as when Mohr had shot her in *Destry Rides Again* thirteen years before] I am of course thirteen years older.

QUOTED in Leslie Halliwell, *The Filmgoer's Book of Quotes* (1973).
Also told as said by cinematographer Joe Ruttenberg to Greer Garson.
Compare Doris **DAY** 125:9

MOMMIE DEAREST

US 1981; screenwriters: Frank Yablans and others (from book by Christina Crawford); cast: Faye Dunaway (Joan Crawford), Mara Hobel (Christina Crawford, as a child).

7 *Joan (to maid)*: Helga, I'm not mad at you. I'm mad at the dirt!

SOUNDTRACK.

8 *Joan (cutting off Christina's hair)*: I'd rather you go bald to school than looking like a tramp!

SOUNDTRACK.

9 *Joan*: Tina! Bring me the axe!

SOUNDTRACK.

1 *Joan*: NO WIRE HANGERS!

SOUNDTRACK.

2 *Christina*: Yes, Mommie Dearest.
Joan: When I told you to call me that, I wanted you to mean it.

SOUNDTRACK.

3 *Joan (as widow, to directors of Pepsi Cola)*: Don't fuck with me, fellas. This ain't my first time at the rodeo.

SOUNDTRACK.

MONKEY BUSINESS

US 1931; screenwriters: S.J. Perelman, Will B. Johnstone, Arthur Sheekman; cast: Groucho, Chico, Harpo and Zeppo Marx (as stowaways), Ben Taggart (Captain Corcoran) Thelma Todd (Lucille).

4 *Groucho*: I want to register a complaint.
Captain Corcoran: Why, what's the matter?
Groucho: Matter enough. You know who sneaked into my room at three o'clock this morning?
Captain Corcoran: Who did that?
Groucho: Nobody, and that's my complaint.

SOUNDTRACK.

5 *Groucho (to Captain Corcoran)*: If you were a man you'd go in business for yourself. I know a fella started only last year with just a canoe. Now he's got more women than you could shake a stick at, if that's your idea of a good time.

SOUNDTRACK.

6 *Groucho (to Chico)*: Do you suppose I could buy back my introduction to you?

SOUNDTRACK.

7 *Lucille*: You're awfully shy for a lawyer.
Groucho: You bet I'm shy. I'm a shyster lawyer.

SOUNDTRACK.

8 *Groucho*: Oh, I realize it's a penny here and a penny there, but look at me: I worked myself up from nothing to a state of extreme poverty.

SOUNDTRACK.

9 *Groucho (when a woman says 'I don't like this innuendo')*: That's what I always say. Love flies out the door when money comes innuendo.

SOUNDTRACK.

1 *Groucho (to woman)*: How about you and I passing out on the veranda? Or would you rather pass out here?

SOUNDTRACK.

2 *Groucho (to Lucille)*: Come, Kapellmeister, let the violas throb! My regiment leaves at dawn.

SOUNDTRACK. Presumably this last phrase is a cliché of operetta, but no precise example has been traced. It was certainly the situation in many romantic tangles, even if the line itself was not actually spoken. However, the co-writer of the film, S.J. Perelman, is quoted in a magazine article (*Quest* Magazine, November, 1978) as saying the following about Groucho Marx: 'I saw him as a verbal clown with literary overtones. For instance, when he kissed Margaret Dumont, I'd have him say: "Goodbye, my little mountain flower. My regiment leaves at dawn." "What's this about a regiment?" he'd say. It's a parody of *The Merry Widow*, I'd say. And he'd worry over the intricacies of the line like a medieval schoolman. "How can an audience laugh at a joke about something they never even heard of?" he would complain.'

3 *Groucho (to Lucille)*: Oh, why can't we break away from all this, just you and I, and lodge with my fleas in the hills – I mean, flee to my lodge in the hills.

SOUNDTRACK.

4 *Woman*: I'm not happy with my husband. He should have married some little housewife.
Groucho: Madam, I resent that. Some of my best friends are a housewife.

SOUNDTRACK.

5 *Chico*: It's better to have lost a loft than never to have lost at all.

SOUNDTRACK.

Marilyn MONROE

American actress (1926–62)

6 I guess I *am* a fantasy.

QUOTED in Gloria Steinem, *Outrageous Acts and Everyday Rebellions* (1984).

7 Hollywood is a place where they'll pay you a thousand dollars for a kiss and fifty cents for your soul.

QUOTED in J.R. Colombo, *Wit and Wisdom of the Moviemakers* (1979). She went on: 'I know, because I turned down the first offer often enough and held out for the fifty cents.'

8 [when asked if all the haggling over money and contracts in the movie business ever got her down] I don't want to make money, I just want to be wonderful. I'll be smart – tomorrow.

ATTRIBUTED remark, quoted in J.R. Colombo, *Wit and Wisdom of the Moviemakers* (1979).

1 The camera just loves some people and it sure loves Marilyn. Look at Bogart. Funny little man you wouldn't notice in a crowd, but on camera ... ! Look at Gary Cooper. Wonderfully tall and good looking, yes, but can't act for toffee and never even tries. Doesn't ever change his expression by a hair's breadth, and yet when you see him on camera, everyone with him seems to be overacting. Just born with the magic. And so is Marilyn. However confused or difficult she is in real life, for the camera she can do no wrong.

COMMENT by Allan ('Whitey') Snyder, American make-up artist, quoted in Colin Clark, *The Prince, the Showgirl and Me*, diary entry for 19 July 1956 (1995). Snyder was Monroe's personal make-up artist. These views almost amounted to a cliché when they were expressed, but are nonetheless worth including in this book uttered by somebody.

2 There's a broad with her future behind her.

COMMENT by Constance Bennett, quoted in J.R. Colombo, *Wit and Wisdom of the Moviemakers* (1979).

3 [on having to make love to her on screen] It's like kissing Hitler.

COMMENT by Tony Curtis, quoted in Leslie Halliwell, *The Filmgoer's Book of Quotes* (1973).

4 Kissing Marilyn was like kissing Hitler – sure, I said that. It wasn't *that* bad. But you can see through that line: there was this woman, beautifully endowed, treating men like shit. Why did I have to take that?

COMMENT by Tony Curtis, interviewed in *Game* Magazine (September 1975).

5 A vacuum with nipples.

COMMENT attributed to Otto Preminger.

6 So we think of Marilyn who was every man's love affair with America, Marilyn Monroe who was blonde and beautiful and had a sweet little rinky-dink of a voice and all the cleanliness of all the clean American backyards.

COMMENT by Norman Mailer in *Marilyn* (1973).

7 It seems to me you lived your life
Like a candle in the wind.

COMMENT by Bernie Taupin in song 'Candle in the Wind (Goodbye Norma Jean)' (1973), music by Elton John. Monroe's original name was Norma Jean Mortenson/Baker. *H.L. Mencken's Dictionary of Quotations* (1942) gives 'Man's life is like a candle in the wind' as a 'Chinese proverb'.

1 She was good at being inarticulately abstracted for the same reason that midgets are good at being short.

COMMENT by Clive James in *Commentary*, 'Mailer's *Marilyn*' (October 1973).

2 She is a phenomenon of nature, like Niagara Falls or the Grand Canyon. You can't talk to it. It can't talk to you. All you can do is stand back and be awed by it.

COMMENT by Nunnally Johnson, quoted in Peter Harry Brown & Patte B. Barham, *Marilyn, the Last Take* (1990).

3 Copulation was, I'm sure, Marilyn's uncomplicated way of saying thank you.

COMMENT by Nunnally Johnson, quoted in Maria Leach, *The Ultimate Insult* (1996).

4 A professional amateur.

COMMENT attributed to Laurence Olivier.

5 The question is whether Marilyn is a person at all or one of the greatest Dupont products ever invented. She has breasts like granite and a brain like Swiss cheese, full of holes.

COMMENT by Billy Wilder, quoted in E. Goodman, *The Fifty-Year Decline and Fall of Hollywood* (1961).

6 I miss her. It was like going to the dentist, making a picture with her. It was hell at the time, but after it was all over, it was wonderful.

COMMENT by Billy Wilder, quoted in Earl Wilson, *The Show Business Nobody Knows* (1971). Compare 'Extracting a performance from her is like pulling teeth' cited in Leslie Halliwell, *The Filmgoer's Book of Quotes* (1978 edn).

7 [of Monroe's unpunctuality] My Aunt Minnie would always be punctual and never hold up production, but who would pay to see my Aunt Minnie?

COMMENT by Billy Wilder, quoted in *Hollywood Anecdotes*, eds. Boller & Davis (1988).

8 [being told that someone had worked with Monroe] Then you know the meaning of pure pain.

COMMENT by Billy Wilder, quoted in Colin Clark, *The Prince, the Showgirl and Me* (1995). Many years after working on *The Prince and the Showgirl*, Clark met Wilder at a Hollywood party. He growled this remark and stalked away. Clark adds: 'Yes – but of pure magic too.'

9 I have never met anyone as utterly mean as Marilyn Monroe. Nor as utterly fabulous on the screen, and that includes Garbo.

COMMENT by Billy Wilder.

See also Arthur **MILLER** 283:1.

Yves MONTAND

French actor and singer (1921–91)

1 We are not here out of curiosity, but for him. He was our youth. We adored him.

COMMENT by anonymous Parisienne at Montand's funeral, quoted in *The Observer*, 'Sayings of the Week' (17 November 1991).

MONTY PYTHON AND THE HOLY GRAIL

UK 1975; screenwriters: the Monty Python team; cast: ditto.

2 *Black Knight (after losing an arm in battle)*: 'Tis but a scratch.
King Arthur: A scratch? Your arm's off.
Black Knight: No, it isn't.

SOUNDTRACK.

3 *French sentry (to King Arthur)*: I fart in your general direction! Your mother was a hamster and your father smelt of elderberries.

SOUNDTRACK.

4 *Knight*: We are the Knights Who Say Ni!

SOUNDTRACK.

5 *King of Swamp Castle (at window)*: One day, lad, all this will be yours.
Prince Herbert: What, the curtains?

SOUNDTRACK.

MONTY PYTHON'S LIFE OF BRIAN

UK 1979; screenwriters: the Monty Python team; cast: ditto, plus Ken Colley (Jesus).

6 *Member of crowd (mishearing Christ's Sermon on the Mount)*: I think it was 'Blessed are the cheese-makers'.

SOUNDTRACK.

7 Always Look on the Bright Side of Life.

TITLE of song sung by a group of crucifixion victims.

MONTY PYTHON'S THE MEANING OF LIFE

UK 1983; screenwriters: the Monty Python team; cast: ditto.

8 *Graham Chapman (as surgeon, when mother asks him the sex of her new-born baby)*: I think it's a little early to start imposing roles on it, don't you?

SOUNDTRACK.

1 *John Cleese (as waiter, to mountainously obese customer)* And finally, monsieur, a wafer-thin mint. A tiny little thin one.
Terry Jones (as Mr Creosote): No, fuck off, I'm full.
John Cleese: It's only wafer-thin … just the one.

SOUNDTRACK. This precipitates his bodily explosion.

Dudley MOORE

English musician and actor (1935–)

2 The ability to enjoy your sex life is central. I don't give a shit about anything else. My obsession is total. What else is there to live for?

ATTRIBUTED remark.

Roger MOORE

English actor (1927–)

3 I used to work for a living, then I became an actor.

QUOTED in *The Independent* (1 July 1989).

4 I'm like fine wine, I get better with age.

QUOTED in *The Observer*, 'Sayings of the Week' (4 December 1994).

5 My acting range? Left eyebrow raised, right eyebrow raised.

ATTRIBUTED remark.

6 A woman recently asked, 'Are you Roger Moore?' I replied, 'Sometimes.'

QUOTED in *The Mail on Sunday* (25 August 1999).

Jeanne MOREAU

French actress (1928–)

7 Some people are addicts. If they don't act, they don't exist.

QUOTED in *The Observer*, 'Sayings of the Week' (19 November 1989).

8 Look, what is it with these black plastic macs? I never wore one. I wore Chanel.

REMARK quoted in the *Independent on Sunday*, 'Overheard' (21 April 1996).

9 [Jeanne Moreau] The distinguished Frenchman.

COMMENT by Stephen Dorrell, British National Heritage Secretary, at Cannes Film Festival (May 1995).

See also Burt **LANCASTER** 246:5.

Jan MORRIS

Welsh writer (1926–)

1 Hollywood, the Versailles of Los Angeles.

EXTRACTED from her book *Destinations* (1980).

(Sir) John MORTIMER

English playwright, novelist and screenwriter (1923–)

2 The writer, in the eyes of many film producers, still seems to occupy a position of importance somewhere between the wardrobe lady and the tea boy, with this difference: it's quite often difficult to replace the wardrobe lady.

EXTRACTED from his book *Clinging to the Wreckage* (1982).

The MUMMY

US 1932; screenwriter: John L. Balderston (from a story); cast: Boris Karloff (High Priest Imhotep); Bramwell Fletcher (Ralph Norton); Zita Johann (Helen Grosvenor/Princess).

3 'Oh! Amon-Ra – Oh! God of Gods! – Death is but the doorway to new life – We live today – we shall live again – In many forms shall we return – Oh, mighty one.'

SCREEN TITLE. It is supposedly quoting from 'The Scroll of Thoth'.

4 *Ralph (hysterically, of the mummy's whereabouts)*: He went for a little walk.

SOUNDTRACK.

5 *Helen*: Save me from that mummy! It's dead.

SOUNDTRACK. Unfortunately, it just won't lie down.

MURDER, INC See *The* **ENFORCER.**

MURDER MY SWEET See **FAREWELL MY LOVELY.**

MUTINY ON THE BOUNTY

US 1935; screenwriters: Talbot Jennings and others; cast: Charles Laughton (Bligh), Clark Gable (Fletcher Christian), Franchot Tone (Byam).

6 *Bligh (to Byam)*: A seaman's a seaman. A captain's a captain. And a shipman, Sir Joseph, is the lowest form of animal life in the British navy.

SOUNDTRACK.

1 *Christian (on Bligh)*: I've never known a better seaman, but as a man, he's a snake. He doesn't punish for discipline. He likes to see men crawl.

SOUNDTRACK.

2 *Christian (calling for mutiny)*: We'll be men again if we hang for it.

SOUNDTRACK.

3 *Christian (to Bligh)*: I'll take my chance against the law. You'll take yours against the sea.

SOUNDTRACK.

4 *Bligh (to Christian)*: Casting me adrift, not even five hundred miles from a port of call. You're sending me to my doom, eh? Well, you're wrong, Christian! I'll take this boat as she floats to England, if I must. I'll live to see you – all of you – hanging from the highest yard arm in the British fleet.

SOUNDTRACK. Famously impersonated by the English comedian Tony Hancock in the form: 'Mis–ter *Chris*–tian … I'll have you *hung* from the *high*–est *yard*–arm in the *Navy*.' Leslie Halliwell, *The Filmgoer's Book of Quotes* (1973) has 'cast adrift in an open boat' listed as a film cliché.

5 *Christian (to Byam)*: From now on, they'll spell mutiny with my name. I regret that, but not the taking of the ship.

SOUNDTRACK.

MY DARLING CLEMENTINE

US 1946; screenwriters: Samuel G. Engel, Winston Miller (from a book *Wyatt Earp, Frontier Marshal*, by Stuart N. Lake); cast: Walter Brennan (Old Man Clanton), Henry Fonda (Wyatt Earp), Linda Darnell (Chihuahua), Victor Mature (Doc John Holliday), Cathy Downs (Clementine Carter), Russell Simpson (John Simpson), J. Farrell MacDonald (Mac), Tim Holt (Virgil Earp).

6 *Chihuahua (to Clementine)*: I'm Chihuahua. I'm Doc Holliday's girl. Just wanted to make sure you were packing.

SOUNDTRACK.

7 *Simpson (at dedication of church)*: Now, I don't pretend to be no preacher, but I've read the good book from cover to cover and back again, and I've nary found a word agin dancin'. So we'll commence by havin' a dad-blasted good dance!

SOUNDTRACK.

8 *Holliday*: We're through talking, Marshal. My advice to you is start carrying your gun.
Earp: That's good advice.

SOUNDTRACK.

1 *Clanton (to Earp, after murdering Virgil Earp, his brother)*: We'll be waiting for you, Marshal, at the O.K. Corral.

SOUNDTRACK.

2 *Earp (to Clanton, after killing all his sons)*: I ain't gonna kill you. I hope you live a hundred years, feel just a little what my pa is going to feel. Now get out of town. Start wandering.

SOUNDTRACK.

MY FAIR LADY

US 1964; screenwriter: Alan J. Lerner (from his musical play based on Shaw's *Pygmalion*); cast: Audrey Hepburn (Eliza Doolittle), Rex Harrison (Henry Higgins).

3 *Eliza*: I'm a good girl, I am.

SOUNDTRACK.

4 *Eliza (at horse race)*: Come on, Dover, move your bloomin' arse!

SOUNDTRACK. The shock effect of 'not bloody likely' (*see* ***PYGMALION*** 343:7) was by now so mild that Eliza was given this line instead for the Ascot racing sequence.

5 *Eliza*: I sold flowers. I didn't sell myself. Now you've made a lady of me, I'm not fit to sell anything else.

SOUNDTRACK.

6 *Henry*: Eliza, where the devil are my slippers?

SOUNDTRACK. Last words of film. *Compare* ***PYGMALION*** 343:8.

MY LITTLE CHICKADEE

US 1939; screenwriters: Mae West, W.C. Fields; cast: W.C. Fields (Cuthbert J. Twillie), Mae West (Flower Belle Lee), Fuzzy Knight (Cousin Zeb), George Moran (Milton).

7 *Twillie (when Cousin Zeb asks, 'Is this a game of chance?')*: Not the way I play it.

SOUNDTRACK.

8 *Twillie*: Go back to the reservation and milk your elk.

SOUNDTRACK.

9 *Twillie (to Lee)*: Come up and see me some time.

SOUNDTRACK. As a catchphrase, Mae West's words from ***SHE DONE HIM WRONG*** 375:1 have been rearranged to make them easier to say. She herself took to saying them in the rearranged version.

1 *Twillie (to Lee)*: You chirped, my little wren?

SOUNDTRACK.

2 *Lee*: I generally avoid temptation, unless I can't resist it.

SOUNDTRACK.

3 *Milton*: Big Chief gottum new squaw?
Twillie: Yes, brand new. I haven't even unwrapped her yet.

SOUNDTRACK.

4 *Twillie (about to be strung up, and asked if he has a last request)*: Yes, I'd like to see Paris before I die. Philadelphia would do!

SOUNDTRACK. This reminds one of Fields's earlier suggestion of an epitaph for himself, usually remembered as: 'On the whole I'd rather be in Philadelphia.' In fact, what the comedian submitted to *Vanity Fair* Magazine in 1925 was: 'Here lies W.C. Fields. I would rather be living in Philadelphia.'

5 *Twillie*: Come up and see me sometime.
Lee: Yes, my little chickadee.

SOUNDTRACK. Last words of film. As she mounts the stairs, the words 'The End' appear across her posterior.

MY MAN GODFREY

US 1957; screenwriters: Morrie Ryskind and others; cast: David Niven (Godfrey Smith).

6 The butler did it! He made every lady in the house, oh, so very happy!

SLOGAN. This was a re-make of the 1936 film.

MYRA BRECKINRIDGE

US 1970; screenwriters: Mike Sarne, David Giler (from Gore Vidal novel); cast: Rex Reed (Myron), Raquel Welch (Myra), Mae West (Leticia Van Allen).

7 At last, the book that couldn't be written is now the motion picture that couldn't be made!

SLOGAN.

8 *Leticia*: *(to actor)*: How tall are you, son?
Actor: Ma-am, I'm six feet seven inches.
Leticia: Let's forget the six feet and talk about the seven inches.

SOUNDTRACK. Famously indelicate exchange, possibly inserted by West in Sarne's screenplay. It is a very old exchange: in Harriette Wilson's *Memoirs*, Chap. 2 (1825) (the book that supposedly gave rise to the Duke of Wellington's response, 'Publish and be damned!') a stranger says to her, 'A name is not important. I stand before you, an upright man of five feet nine inches.' Lord Alvanley then quips, also in French, 'The lady knows about your five feet, but she's not sure of your nine inches.'

1 *Leticia*: Is that a gun in your pocket or are you just pleased to see me?

SOUNDTRACK. Reviving another of her famous lines. *Compare* ***SHE DONE HIM WRONG*** 375:3.

2 *Myron*: It's a dangerous thing, ambition. Ruined Mickey Mouse's whole career.

SOUNDTRACK.

3 *Myron*: Where are my tits? Where are my tits?

SOUNDTRACK.

4 *Myra*: My purpose in coming to Hollywood is the destruction of the American male in all its particulars.

SOUNDTRACK.

The MYSTERY OF THE WAX MUSEUM

US 1933; screenwriters: Don Mullally, Carl Erickson (from a play Charles S. Belden); cast: Lionel Atwill (Ivan Igor).

5 *Ivan*: My dear, why are you so pitifully afraid? Immortality has been the dream, the inspiration of mankind through the ages. And I am going to give you immortality!

SOUNDTRACK.

6 *Ivan (as wax sculptor whose hands have been burned, to less talented apprentice)*: It is a cruel irony that you people without souls should have hands.

SOUNDTRACK.

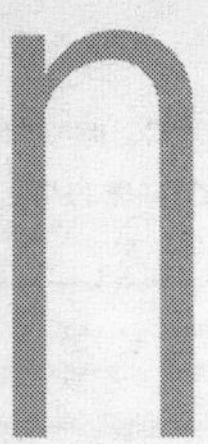

The NAKED CITY

US 1948; screenwriters: Malvin Wald, Albert Matz; producer/narrator: Mark Hellinger.

1 *Narrator*: This is the city as it is …

SOUNDTRACK. Opening words.

2 *Narrator*: There are eight million stories in the naked city. This has been one of them.

SOUNDTRACK. Last lines of film. Also used in the TV series (1958–63) with the same title.

George Jean NATHAN

American theatre critic (1882–1958)

3 Hollywood impresses me as being ten million dollars' worth of intricate and highly ingenious machinery functioning elaborately to put skin on baloney.

QUOTED in *A Treasury of Humorous Quotations*, eds. Prochnow & Prochnow (1969).

See also ***I AM A CAMERA*** 224:2.

The NAUGHTY NINETIES

US 1945; screenwriters: Edmund L. Hartmann and others; cast: Bud Abbott (Dexter), Lou Costello (Sebastian).

4 *Dexter*: You know, these days they give ballplayers very peculiar names. Take the St Louis team: Who's on first, What's on second, I Don't Know is on third …
Sebastian: That's what I want to find out. I want you to tell me the names of the fellows on the St Louis team.
Dexter: I'm telling you. Who's on first. What's on second. I Don't Know is on third …

SOUNDTRACK. From a classic routine 'Who's on first?', based on misunderstanding. *See also* ***PETE 'N' TILLIE*** 325:2.

NETWORK

US 1976; screenwriter: Paddy Chayevsky; cast: Peter Finch (Howard Beale).

1 *Howard*: I want you to get up right now and go to the window, open it and stick your head out and yell: 'I'm as mad as hell, and I'm not going to take this any more!'

SOUNDTRACK. A TV pundit-cum-evangelist exhorts his viewers to get mad with these words. Hence, this actual usage, reported in *New Society* (25 November 1982): 'Some years ago the irascible Howard Jarvis, author of California's Proposition 13 (the one that pegged property taxes), coined the immortal political slogan: I'm mad as Hell and I'm Not Taking Any More.' Well, no, he obviously didn't. In 1978, Jarvis (1902–86), the California social activist, merely adopted the slogan and came to be associated with it. As a result, 57 per cent voted to reduce their property taxes. Dire warnings about the effect on government if tax revenues were pegged were not borne out and Proposition 13 paved the way for Reaganomics three years later. Jarvis entitled a book *I'm Mad as Hell* but duly credited Chayevsky with the coinage of his slogan. He added: 'For me, the words "I'm mad as hell" are more than a national saying, more than the title of this book; they express exactly how I feel and exactly how I felt about the … countless other victims of exorbitant taxes.'

NEVER GIVE A SUCKER AN EVEN BREAK

US 1941; screenwriters: John T. Neville, Prescott Chaplin (from story by Otis Criblecoblis, i.e. W.C. Fields); cast: W.C. Fields (The Great Man).

2 *The Great Man*: Everything I like to do is either illegal, immoral or fattening.

SOUNDTRACK. Compare: 'All the things I really like to do are either illegal, immoral, or fattening' – Alexander Woollcott, *The Knock at the Stage Door* (1933) and Fields's own ***SIX OF A KIND*** 380:10.

3 *The Great Man*: I was in love with a beautiful blonde once, dear. She drove me to drink. 'Tis the one thing I'm indebted to her for.

SOUNDTRACK. Fields himself was a noted tippler, both on screen and off.

4 *The Great Man*: Somebody put too many olives in my martini last night.

SOUNDTRACK.

5 *The Great Man (with hangover, offered a bromo-seltzer)*: No. I couldn't stand the noise.

SOUNDTRACK.

6 *The Great Man*: Drown in a vat of liquor? Death, where is thy sting?

SOUNDTRACK.

7 *The Great Man*: This place was supposed to be a saloon, but the censor cut it out.

SOUNDTRACK.

NEVER SAY NEVER AGAIN

UK 1983; screenwriter: Lorenzo Semple Jr (from story by Ian Fleming and others); cast: Sean Connery (James Bond), Barbara Carrera (Fatima Blush).

1 Never Say Never Again.

TITLE OF FILM. This marked Sean Connery's return to the part of James Bond and was so called because he had evidently declared 'never again' after playing Bond in *Diamonds Are Forever* (UK 1971). The first title of a Bond film not to derive from an Ian Fleming story.

2 *Blush (splashing Bond while water skiing)*: How reckless of me. I've made you all wet.
Bond: Yes, but my martini is still dry.

SOUNDTRACK.

NEW MORALS FOR OLD

US 1932; screenwriter: Zelda Sears, Wanda Tuchock (from John Van Druten play); cast: Robert Young (Ralph Thomas), Myrna Loy (Myra).

3 *Ralph (to Myra)*: I want to walk barefoot through your hair.

SOUNDTRACK. This reappeared the following year in *Blonde Bombshell*, in which Franchot Tone said to Jean Harlow: 'Your hair is like a field of silver daisies. I should like to run barefoot through your hair.'

Paul NEWMAN

American actor (1925–)

4 [on marriage, in his case to the actress Joanne Woodward] Why fool around with hamburger when you have steak at home?

QUOTED in *Radio Times* (24 June 1971). In *The Observer* (11 March 1984), he was quoted as adding: 'That doesn't mean it's always tender.'

5 To work as hard as I've worked to accomplish anything and then have some yo-yo come up and say 'Take off those dark glasses and let's have a look at those blue eyes' is really discouraging.

QUOTED in *The Observer*, 'Sayings of the Week' (5 October 1986).

6 [after Oscar presentations] I'd been seven times and lost. I figured if I didn't go this time, I might win.

QUOTED in *Sunday Today*, 'Quotes of the Week' (5 April 1987).

7 Joanne [Woodward] gives great smoulder.

QUOTED in *The Observer*, 'Sayings of the Week' (23 December 1990).

1 Acting is a question of absorbing other people's personalities and adding some of your own experience.

ATTRIBUTED remark.

2 He has the attention span of a bolt of lightning.

COMMENT by Robert Redford, quoted in *The New York Times* (28 September 1986).

Haing S. NGOR

Cambodian doctor (1947–96)

3 I never took acting lessons, but for three years I had life or death training. I survived by pretending to be someone else.

QUOTED in *The Observer* (3 March 1996). Not a professional actor, Ngor won an Oscar for his role in *The Killing Fields*. But although he had escaped the death camps of the Khmer Rouge he was later murdered in Los Angeles.

NIAGARA

US 1953; screenwriters: Charles Brackett and others; cast: Marilyn Monroe (Rose Loomis), Joseph Cotten (George Loomis).

4 *Rose (to George, on where she is going)*: I'm meeting somebody, just anybody handy, as long as he's a man.

SOUNDTRACK.

Dudley NICHOLS

American screenwriter (1895–1960)

5 Every film is launched like a squid, in an obscuring cloud of spectacular publicity.

REMARK in the Introduction to Lewis Tacobe, *Art of the Movies* (untraced).

NIGHT AFTER NIGHT

US 1932; screenwriter: Vincent Laurence (from novel by Louis Bromfield) 'with additional dialogue' by Mae West; cast: Mae West (Mandie Triplett).

6 *Mandie (replying to cloakroom girl's exclamation, 'Goodness, what beautiful diamonds!)*: Goodness had nothing to do with it, dearie.

SOUNDTRACK. Hence the title of Mae West's autobiography *Goodness Had Nothing To Do With It* (1959).

7 *Mandie (when asked if she believes in love at first sight)*: I dunno, but it sure saves time.

SOUNDTRACK.

A NIGHT AT THE OPERA

US 1935; screenwriters: George S. Kaufman, Morrie Ryskind and others; cast: Groucho Marx (Otis B. Driftwood), Chico Marx (Fiorello), Margaret Dumont (Mrs Claypool).

1 *Otis (to Mrs Claypool)*: When I invite a woman to dinner, I expect her to look at my face. That's the price she has to pay.

SOUNDTRACK.

2 *Otis*: Every time I get romantic with you, you want to talk business. I don't know, there's something about me that brings out the business in every woman.

SOUNDTRACK.

3 *Otis (hammering out contract)*: 'The party of the first part shall be known in this contract as the party of the first part.' How do you like that? That's pretty neat, eh?
Fiorello: No, that's no good.

SOUNDTRACK.

4 *Otis (going through contract)*: 'If any of the parties participating in this contract is shown not to be in their right mind, the entire agreement is automatically nullified' … that's in every contract. That's what they call a sanity clause.
Fiorello: Ha-ha-ha! You can't fool me. There ain't no Sanity Clause!

SOUNDTRACK.

5 *Mrs Claypool (boarding liner)*: Are you sure you have everything, Otis?
Otis: I've never had any complaints yet!

SOUNDTRACK.

6 *Otis*: I want to be alone!

SOUNDTRACK.

7 *Otis (speaking at opening of opera season)*: Let joy be unconfined. Let there be dancing in the streets, drinking in the saloons and necking in the parlour.

SOUNDTRACK.

A NIGHT IN CASABLANCA

US 1946; screenwriters: Joseph Fields, Roland Kibbee; cast: Groucho Marx (Ronald Kornblow), Harpo Marx (Rusty), Chico Marx (Corbaccio), Lisette Verea (Beatrice), Dan Seymour (Prefect of police), Frederick Giermann (Kurt).

1 *Prefect of police*: What do you think you're doing, holding up the building?
Rusty: [*Nods and building falls down*].

SOUNDTRACK.

2 *Kornblow (to bearded man)*: I've seen five o'clock shadow, but this is ridiculous.

SOUNDTRACK.

3 *Kornblow (coughing)*: This is like living in Pittsburgh – if you can call that living.

SOUNDTRACK.

4 *Kurt*: He thinks that will protect him against me – the finest swordsman in Bavaria.

SOUNDTRACK.

5 *Beatrice*: I'm Beatrice Ryner. I stop at the hotel.
Kornblow: My name's Ronald Kornblow. I stop at nothing.

SOUNDTRACK.

6 *Kornblow*: Call me Montgomery.
Beatrice: Is that your name?
Kornblow: No, I'm just breaking it in for a friend.

SOUNDTRACK.

7 Up to the time that we contemplated making this picture, I had no idea that the city of Casablanca belonged exclusively to Warner Brothers … I just don't understand your attitude. Even if you plan on re-releasing your picture, I am sure that the average movie fan could learn in time to distinguish between Ingrid Bergman and Harpo. I don't know whether I could, but I would certainly like to try … What about 'Warner Brothers'? Do you own that, too? You probably have the right to use the name Warner, but what about Brothers? Professionally, we were brothers long before you were.

COMMENT in letter from Groucho Marx to Warner Brothers legal department, which had wanted to obstruct use of the name 'Casablanca' in the title on the grounds that Warners had released *Casablanca* five years before. After this and another of Groucho's missives, their opposition evaporated. Included in *The Groucho Letters* (1967).

NIGHT MAIL

UK 1935; screenwriter: W.H. Auden.

1 *Narrator*: This is the Night Mail crossing the Border
Bringing the cheque and the postal order,
Letters for the rich, letters for the poor,
The shop at the corner, the girl next door.

SOUNDTRACK. Commentary for Post Office Film Unit documentary about mail carried on a train. 'We were experimenting,' Auden said, 'to see whether poetry could be used in films, and I think we showed it could.' The first draft contained lines that Harry Watt, the director, felt 'could not be matched with adequate images on the screen – lines such as "Uplands heaped like slaughtered horses" … Watt observed: "No picture we put on the screen could be as strong as that"' (source: Humphrey Carpenter, *W.H. Auden*, 1981). Nevertheless, the cut line has not been forgotten and is still quoted.

The NIGHT OF THE HUNTER

US 1955; screenwriter: James Agee (from a novel by Davis Grubb); cast: Robert Mitchum (Preacher Harry Powell), Lilian Gish (Rachel Cooper).

2 *Powell (giving his sermon based on the words tattooed on his hands)*: Would you like me to tell you the little story of right hand, left hand? The story of good and evil? H-A-T-E. It was with this left hand that old brother Cain struck the blow that laid his brother low. L-O-V-E. You see these fingers, dear hearts? These fingers has veins that run straight to the soul of man – the right hand, friends, the hand of love.

SOUNDTRACK.

3 *Rachel Cooper (on children)*: They abide and they endure.

SOUNDTRACK.

NIGHT TRAIN TO MUNICH

UK 1940; screenwriters: Frank Launder, Sidney Gilliat (from a novel *Report on a Fugitive* by Gordon Wellesley); Rex Harrison (Gus Bennett), Paul Henreid (Karl Marsen).

4 *Bennett*: Captain Marsen was only obeying orders.

SOUNDTRACK. An early appearance of the cliché excuse often given to Germans. The Charter of the International Military Tribunal at Nuremberg (1945–46) specifically excluded the traditional German defence of 'superior orders'. But the plea was, nevertheless, much advanced. This approach was summed up in the catchphrase 'I was only obeying orders', often used grotesquely in parody. Kenneth Mars as a mad, Nazi-fixated playwright in *The Producers* (US, 1967) says, 'I only followed orders!'

Not that everyone seemed aware of the parodying. From *The New York Times*

(6 July 1983): 'Herbert Bechtold, a German-born officer in the [US] counter-intelligence who became [the "handler" of Klaus Barbie, the Nazi war criminal] was asked if he questioned the morality of hiring a man like Barbie by the United States. "I am not in a position to pass judgement on that," Mr Bechtold replied, "I was just following orders".'

NINOTCHKA

US 1939; screenwriters: Charles Brackett, Billy Wilder, Walter Reisch; cast: Greta Garbo (Ninotchka), Felix Bressart (Buljanoff), Alexander Granach (Kopalski), Melvyn Douglas (Count Leon Dalga).

1 Don't pronounce it – see it!

SLOGAN. *Compare* **SLOGANS** 382:12.

2 Garbo laughs!

SLOGAN. Coined by Howard Dietz.

3 *Kopalski*: If we had known, we would have greeted you with flowers. *Ninotchka*: Don't make an issue of my womanhood.

SOUNDTRACK.

4 *Ninotchka*: The last mass trials were a great success. There are going to be fewer but better Russians.

SOUNDTRACK.

5 *Leon*: Ninotchka, it's midnight. One half of Paris is making love to the other half.

SOUNDTRACK.

6 *Buljanoff*: No, no, Ninotchka. Don't ask for it. There is an old Turkish proverb that says, if something smells bad, why put your nose in it? *Ninotchka*: And there is an old Russian saying, the cat who has cream on his whiskers had better find good excuses.

SOUNDTRACK.

7 *Ninotchka*: Go to bed, little father. We want to be alone.

SOUNDTRACK.

David NIVEN

English actor (1909–83)

8 I have a face that is a cross between two pounds of halibut and an explosion in an old-clothes closet. If it isn't mobile, it's dead.

QUOTED in J.R. Colombo, *Wit and Wisdom of the Moviemakers* (1979).

1 [advice on film-making] Just remember that when the cameraman or the technicians bitch up, they will always say there's a hair in the gate.

QUOTED in J.K. Galbraith, *A Life in Our Times* (1981). Recalling his participation in a documentary film, Galbraith writes: 'A "hair in the gate" means that, on post-operative inspection, the camera lens – or something else – shows some defect. A retake is required. Briefing me on what I could expect in my new career, David Niven had warned ...'

2 [on streaker at Oscar ceremony] Just think, the only laugh that man will probably ever get is for stripping and showing off his shortcomings.

QUOTED in F.L. Worth, *Complete Unabridged Super Trivia Encyclopedia* (1979). Just as Niven was about to introduce Elizabeth Taylor at the Academy Awards ceremony on 2 April 1974, a streaker appeared. Henry Mancini and the orchestra played 'Sunny Side Up' as the streaker was led off by security guards. The streaker was Robert Opal, who later reappeared in the news when he was found murdered in his San Francisco sex shop.

NO WAY TO TREAT A LADY

US 1967; screenwriter: John Gay (from William Goldman novel); cast: Lee Remick (Kate Palmer), Michael Dunn (Mr Kupperman), George Segal (Morris Brummel).

3 *Mr Kupperman (midget claiming to be murderer who was a much taller man)*: You see how I fooled them? I'm a master of disguise.

SOUNDTRACK.

4 *Kate*: And I said, 'You don't love me. You don't love me – you only love my body.'

SOUNDTRACK. An earlyish appearance of the cliché complaint. A little earlier, in *Harlow* (US 1965), Carroll Baker had said to Angela Lansbury: 'Oh, Mama, all they want is my body.'

NONE BUT THE LONELY HEART

US 1944; screenwriter: Clifford Odets (from Richard Llewellyn novel); cast: Cary Grant (Ernie Mott).

5 *Ernie*: Money talks, they say. All it ever said to me was 'goodbye'.

SOUNDTRACK.

Peggy NOONAN

American speechwriter (1950–)

6 We are all actors now ... Everyone in America now explains a moment in their lives by saying, 'It was like a scene out of ...'

EXTRACTED from book *What I Saw at the Revolution* (1990).

NORTH BY NORTHWEST

US 1959; screenwriter: Ernest Lehman; cast: Cary Grant (Roger Thornhill), Jessie Royce Landis (Clara Thornhill), Eva Marie Saint (Eve Kendall), Malcolm Atterbury (Man in field).

1 North by Northwest.

TITLE OF FILM. A typical Alfred Hitchcock tease. Possibly alluding to 'I am mad north-north-west. When the wind is southerly, I know a hawk from a handsaw' (Shakespeare, *Hamlet*, II.ii.374). After all, Cary Grant has to feign madness just as Hamlet does. More likely it is an allusion to a slogan of Northwest Airlines (glimpsed on display in the airport sequence).

2 *Clara Thornhill (to spies in lift)*: You gentlemen aren't really trying to kill my son, are you?

SOUNDTRACK.

3 *Eve (to Roger)*: It's going to be a long night … and I don't particularly like the book I started.

SOUNDTRACK.

4 *Man in field*: That's funny … That plane's dustin' crops where there ain't no crops.

SOUNDTRACK.

NOTHING SACRED

US 1937; screenwriter: Ben Hecht; cast: Charles Winninger (Dr Enoch Downer), Fredric March (Wally Cook), Walter Connolly (Editor).

5 New York, skyscraper champion of the world, where suckers and know-it-alls peddle gold bricks to each other and where truth, crushed to earth, rises again more phony than a glass eye.

SCREEN TITLE.

6 *Dr Downer (to Wally Cook)*: I'll tell you briefly what I think of newspapermen. The hand of God, reaching down into the mire, couldn't elevate one of them to the depths of degradation.

SOUNDTRACK.

NOTORIOUS

US 1946; screenwriter: Ben Hecht; cast: Cary Grant (Bruce Devlin), Ingrid Bergman (Alicia Huberman), Ivan Triesault (Eric Mathis).

7 *Alicia*: Someone is coming. Alex, he's seen us.
Bruce: Wait a minute. I'm going to kiss you.
Alicia: No, he'll only think that we …
Bruce: It's what I want him to think.

SOUNDTRACK.

1 *Alicia*: Say it again, it keeps me awake.
Bruce: I love you.

SOUNDTRACK.

2 *Eric Mathis*: Alex, will you come in, please? I wish to talk to you.

SOUNDTRACK. Last line of film.

La NOTTE

Italy/France 1960; screenwriters: Michelangelo Antonioni (director) and others; cast: Monica Vitti (Valentina Gherardini).

3 *Valentina*: Each time I have tried to communicate with someone, love has disappeared.

SCREEN TITLE in translation. Near the end.

NOTTING HILL

UK 1999; screenwriter: Richard Curtis; cast: Julia Roberts (Anna Scott), Hugh Grant (William Thacker).

4 Can the most famous film star in the world fall for the man in the street?

SLOGAN.

5 *Anna (as film star, to William)*: Rita Hayworth used to say – 'They go to bed with Gilda – they wake up with me.' Do you feel that?

SOUNDTRACK. *See* Rita **HAYWORTH** 209:2.

6 *Anna (to William)*: I'm also just a girl standing in front of a boy. Asking him to love her.

SOUNDTRACK.

NOW VOYAGER

US 1942; screenwriter: Casey Robinson (from novel by Olive Higgins Prouty); cast: Bette Davis (Charlotte Vale), Paul Henreid (Jerry Durrance), Gladys Cooper (Mrs Vale).

7 *Mrs Vale (mother)*: And what do you intend to do with your life?
Charlotte: Get a cat and a parrot and live alone in single blessedness.

SOUNDTRACK.

8 *Charlotte (reading Walt Whitman poem)*: 'The untold want by life and land ne'er granted / Now voyager sail thou forth to seek and find ...'

SOUNDTRACK. Hence, the title.

1 *Jerry (to Charlotte)*: Shall we just have a cigarette on it?

SOUNDTRACK. Preceding the most famous cigarette moment in screen history – he lights cigarettes for both of them.

2 *Charlotte*: Oh, Jerry, don't let's ask for the moon – we have the stars.

SOUNDTRACK. Last line of film.

Sven NYKVIST

Swedish cinematographer (1922–)

3 Today we make everything so complicated. The lighting, the camera, the acting. It has taken me thirty years to arrive at simplicity.

QUOTED in *The Observer*, 'Sayings of the Week' (11 April 1993).

O BROTHER, WHERE ART THOU?

US 2000; screenwriters: Ethan Coen, Joel Coen (director) (after Homer's *Odyssey*).

1 O Brother, Where Art Thou?

TITLE OF FILM. Alludes to the film-within-a-film of Preston Sturges's *Sullivan's Travels* (US 1941). In that, the comedy director wishes to produce a serious film to be called 'O Brother, Where Art Thou?'

2 O Muse!
Sing in me, and through me tell the story
Of that man skilled in all the ways of contending,
A wanderer, harried for years on end.

SCREEN TITLE. At start of film. A translation of the start of Bk 1 of *The Odyssey*.

The ODD COUPLE

US 1968; screenwriter: Neil Simon (from his play); cast: Walter Matthau (Oscar Madison), Jack Lemmon (Felix Unger).

3 *Oscar (to Felix)*: You can't spend the rest of your life crying. It annoys people in the movies.

SOUNDTRACK.

4 *Oscar*: I cannot stand little notes on my pillow. 'We are all out of corn-flakes, F.U.' It took me three hours to figure out 'F.U.' was Felix Ungar. It's not your fault, Felix; it's a rotten combination, that's all.

SOUNDTRACK.

5 *Felix*: It's not spaghetti, it's linguini.
Oscar (after throwing linguini at the wall): Now it's garbage.

SOUNDTRACK.

6 *Oscar (to fellow poker players)*: Boys, let's watch the cigarette butts, shall we? This is my house, not a pigsty.

SOUNDTRACK. Last line of film.

ODETTE

UK 1950; screenwriter: Warren Chetham Strode; cast: Anna Neagle (Odette Hallowes), Frederick Wendhausen (Colonel).

1 *Colonel (German interrogator, to Odette, while stoking fire with poker)*: We have ways and means of making you talk ... I told you, we have ways and means to make a woman talk.

SOUNDTRACK. A possible first appearance of this future cliché.

OH, MR PORTER!

UK 1937; screenwriters: Marriott Edgar and others; cast: Will Hay (William Porter); Moore Marriott (Jeremiah Harbottle); Sebastian Smith (Mr Trimbletow), Agnes Lauchlan (Mrs Trimbletow).

2 *Mrs Trimbletow (managing director's wife, to William Porter, who is wheel-tapping a train)*: You may think me a little stupid, but why do they tap them?
William Porter: Well, you see, it's like this, madam. If I tap the wheel with this hammer and the wheel goes clang, then I know the wheel's there, you see.
Mr Trimbletow (managing director): But suppose the wheel doesn't go clang?
William Porter: Well, then I know the train's gone!

SOUNDTRACK.

3 *Harbottle (to William Porter, slinging up shutter of railway ticket office)*: Next train's gone!

SOUNDTRACK. The origin of this famous line occurs, almost certainly, in the caption to an anonymous *Punch* cartoon (20 May 1871) – '*Gent*: I say, Porter, when does the next train start? *Irish Porter*: The next train! Sure, the nixt train has gone tin minutes ago.'

Maureen O'HARA

Irish-born actress (1920–)

4 She looked as though butter wouldn't melt in her mouth. Or anywhere else.

COMMENT by Elsa Lanchester, English actress (1902–86), quoted in *News Summaries* (30 January 1950).

OLD ACQUAINTANCE

US 1943; screenwriter: John Van Druten (from his play), Lenore Coffee; cast: Bette Davis (Kitty Marlowe).

5 *Kitty*: There comes a time in every woman's life when the only thing that helps is a glass of champagne.

SOUNDTRACK.

The OLD DARK HOUSE

US 1932; screenwriters: Benn W. Levy, R.C. Sherriff (from J.B. Priestley novel *Benighted*); cast: Ernest Thesiger (Horace Femm).

1 *Horace*: Have some gin, it's my only weakness.

SOUNDTRACK. *Compare The* ***BRIDE OF FRANKENSTEIN*** 72:4.

Gary OLDMAN

English actor and director (1958–)

2 I made *Nil by Mouth* for Britain; I said f--- the rest of the world, f--- America. I'm not watering down the accents.

QUOTED in *The Observer*, 'Soundbites' (7 September 1997).

OLIVER!

UK 1968; screenwriter: Vernon Harris (from Lionel Bart musical of Dickens novel); cast: Mark Lester (Oliver Twist), Oliver Reed (Bill Sikes), Ron Moody (Fagin).

3 *Oliver*: Please, sir. I want some more.

SOUNDTRACK. First line of film.

4 *Sikes (threatening Fagin)*: Have you ever heard the sound a chicken makes when they're wringing off its neck?

SOUNDTRACK.

Laurence OLIVIER (Lord Olivier)

English actor (1907–89)

5 They criticize me: 'Why's he doing such muck?' To pay for three children in school, for my family and their future.

QUOTED in the *Daily Mail* (28 March 1979).

6 [on his attitude to longueurs in film-making] Acting I do for free. They pay me to wait.

QUOTED in Martin Jarvis, *Acting Strangely* (1999).

7 [to Dustin Hoffman during filming of *Marathon Man* (in about 1975) – Hoffman having stayed up for three nights in order to portray a sleepless character] Dear boy, you look absolutely awful. Why don't you try acting? It's so much easier.

ATTRIBUTED in *The Times* (17 May 1982).

8 Mr President and governors of the Academy, committee members, Fellows, my very noble and approved good masters, my friends, my fellow students … in the great wealth, the great firmament of your nation's generosities, this particular choice may perhaps be found by future generations as a trifle eccentric but the mere fact of it, the prodigal, pure, human kindness of it must be seen as a beautiful star in that firmament which shines upon me at this moment, dazzling me a little, but filling me with warmth and the extra-ordinary elation, the euphoria that happens to so many of us at the first breath of the majestic glow of the new tomorrow. From the top of this moment, in the solace, in the kindly emotion that is charging my soul and my heart at this moment, I thank you for this great gift which lends me such a very splendid part in this glorious occasion. Thank you.

SPEECH on receiving a special Oscar at the Academy Awards in 1979. His acceptance speech had some of the audience weeping into their tuxedos, the rest wondering whether perhaps he would have done better to leave his scriptwriting to Shakespeare, or someone like that.

ON HER MAJESTY'S SECRET SERVICE

UK 1969; screenwriters: Richard Maibaum, Simon Raven (after Ian Fleming novel); cast: George Lazenby (James Bond), Diana Rigg (Tracy Draco), Angela Scoular (Ruby), Desmond Llewellyn (Q), Sir Hilary Bray (George Baker).

1 *Bond*: This never happened to the other fellow.

SOUNDTRACK. Having lost Tracy in the opening sequence. An in-joke referring to Sean Connery, Lazenby's predecessor in the role of Bond.

2 *Sir Hilary Bray*: 'The World Is Not Enough.'

SOUNDTRACK. At the College of Heralds, Bray is showing the Bond family coat of arms on which the Latin motto is '*Orbis non sufficie*'. The English phrase became the title of a much later film in the series (UK 1999). Only the English is given in Fleming's novel but it would appear that he had done his research. '*Non sufficit orbis*' is the motto of the Bond family and, in this form, would appear to be a quotation from Juvenal's *Satires*, No. 10, line 168, where the satirist is illustrating the folly of military glory. The once great Hannibal is reduced to living in exile and finally committing suicide at the arrival of Roman troops at his desert hideaway: 'Whilst one globe seemed too small for the youthful Alexander [*unus pellaeo iuveni non sufficit orbis*], yet a small coffin was enough to contain him when he died of a fever at Babylon.' *The World Is Not Enough* was also used as the title of a 1948 translation of *Argile et cendres* by the novelist Zoë Oldenbourg.

3 *Ruby (on seeing Bond's endowments for the first time, as he takes off his kilt)*: It's true!

SOUNDTRACK. Though perhaps she is just remarking on the truth of the suggestion that Scotsman wear nothing under their kilts!

ON THE WATERFRONT

US 1954; screenwriter: Budd Schulberg (from his novel); cast: Marlon Brando (Terry), Rod Steiger (Charley).

1 *Terry (blaming his lost career as a boxer on his brother Charley's betrayal)*: I coulda had class! I coulda been a contender! I coulda been somebody – instead of a bum, which is what I am! Let's face it. It was you, Charley!

SOUNDTRACK.

2 *Terry*: So what happens? He gets the title shot outdoors in the ball park – and whadda I get? A one-way ticket to Palookaville.

SOUNDTRACK. Continuation of scene. Although, as so often, the *Oxford English Dictionary* (2nd edition, 1989) has 'orig. unknown' for the American word 'palooka', it does at least define it. Firstly, it means an inferior or average boxer, and secondly, a stupid or mediocre person. The coinage is generally credited, however, to an ex-baseball player and sports writer, Jack Conway (d. 1928), who put the word in its original sense into the pages of *Variety* in the 1920s. It was then popularized by the name 'Joe Palooka', the title of a syndicated comic strip in the 1930s. This concerned an unsophisticated and oafish prizefighter who was nevertheless a world champion and not a loser. In *It Happened One Night* (US 1934), Clark Gable pretends to call the editor who has just fired him, 'You gashouse palooka!' By extension, 'Palookaville' would be the kind of town inhabited by palookas, therefore the equivalent of ignominy and oblivion. Hence the title *Palookaville* chosen for yet another 'incompetents plan a heist' movie (US, 1997).

ONCE UPON A TIME IN THE WEST [C'ERA UNA VOLTA IL WEST]

Italy 1968; screenwriters: Sergio Leone (director), Sergio Donati; cast: Jason Robards (Cheyenne), Claudia Cardinale (Jill McBain), Charles Bronson (Harmonica).

3 Once Upon a Time in the West.

TITLE OF FILM. The original Italian is actually, 'Once upon a time *there was* the West.'

4 *Cheyenne (to Jill, about Harmonica)*: People like that have something inside, something to do with death.

SOUNDTRACK. *Compare* **ASSAULT ON PRECINCT 13** 37:4.

ONE-EYED JACKS

US 1961; screenwriters: Guy Trosper, Calder Willingham (from a novel *The Authentic Death of Hendry Jones* by Charles Neider); cast: Karl Malden (Dad Longworth), Marlon Brando (Rio).

5 *Dad Longworth (to Rio)*: You've been trying for ten years to get yourself hung in this town, and I think you're gonna make it.

SOUNDTRACK.

1 *Rio (to Dad Longworth)*: You're a real one-eyed jack in this town.

SOUNDTRACK.

ONE FLEW OVER THE CUCKOO'S NEST

US 1975; screenwriters: Lawrence Hauben, Bo Goldman (based on Ken Kesey novel); cast: Jack Nicholson (R.P. MacMurphy).

2 *MacMurphy (on electric shock treatment)*: They was giving me ten thousand watts a day, you know, and I'm hot to trot. Next woman takes me on's going to light up like a pinball machine, and playoff in silver dollars.

SOUNDTRACK.

3 *MacMurphy*: I must be crazy to be in a looney bin like this.

SOUNDTRACK.

ONE MILLION YEARS BC

UK 1966; screenwriter: Michael Carreras; cast: Raquel Welch (Loana); John Richardson (Tumak).

4 The characters and incidents portrayed and the names used herein are fictitious and any similarity to the names, character or history of any person is entirely accidental and unintentional.

SCREEN TITLE. Standard disclaimer, applied here to film where the characters are all cave persons and the dialogue mostly consists of grunts.

5 *Loana*: Tumak!

SOUNDTRACK. The only decipherable word she says in the film.

ORPHÉE

France 1949; screenwriter/director: Jean Cocteau.

6 *Radio code message*: *L'oiseau chante avec ses doigts* [the bird sings with its fingers].

SOUNDTRACK. The inspiration behind this is given in M.R.D. Foot's *SOE: The Special Operations Executive 1940–1946* (1984). Talking about BBC broadcasts of coded messages to the French Resistance: 'F section's first wireless operator in France, Georges Bégué, started up a variant in the autumn of 1941. After the news bulletins in French, personal messages were sometimes broadcast; on Bégué's system, these became a daily event. Mixed in with genuine fragments of family reporting and inquiries came coded messages, which gradually grew odder and odder: such as *Aesculape n'aime pas le mouton.* From this stream of apparent gibberish, an agent could pick out the one phrase that meant an impending drop to him or her, and could set out to mobilize transport and labour for the night to come. The resonant tone and impenetrable sense of these arcane sentences was wonderfully picked up by Jean Cocteau … in the opening minutes of *Orphée.*'

Albert William Thomas OSBORN

English Salvation Army General

1 Hollywood is a combination of Heaven, Hell and a lunatic asylum.

QUOTED in *News Review* (28 November 1946).

OUT OF AFRICA

US 1985; screenwriter: Kurt Luedtke (from Isak Dinesen/Karen Blixen book); cast: Meryl Streep (Karen).

2 *Karen (narrating)*: I had a farm in Africa …

SOUNDTRACK. Curiously memorable and much imitated, presumably because of Streep's curious (though no doubt impeccable) Danish accent.

The OUTLAW

US 1946; screenwriter: Jules Furthman; cast: Jane Russell (Rio), Jack Beutel (Billy the Kid).

3 Mean! Moody! Magnificent!

SLOGAN. The most notorious of all film promotional campaigns is the one for this Howard Hughes production. To various pictures of the skimpily clad new star (one version had her reclining with a long whip), Hughes attached a smouldering succession of slogans:

4 The two great reasons for Jane Russell's rise to stardom.

SLOGAN. The two great reasons were skilfully supported by the Hughes-designed cantilever bra.

5 How'd you like to tussle with Russell?

SLOGAN.

6 The girl with the summer-hot lips … and the winter-cold heart.

SLOGAN.

7 Tall … terrific … and trouble!

SLOGAN.

8 Who wouldn't fight for a woman like this?

SLOGAN.

9 *Rio*: Let me go!
Billy the Kid: Hold still, lady, or you won't have much dress left.

SOUNDTRACK.

10 *Rio (climbing into bed to nurse the wounded Billy the Kid)*: You can bring a minister in the morning if it'll make you feel better about it.

SOUNDTRACK.

The OUTLAW JOSEY WALES

US 1976; screenwriters: Phil Kaufman, Sonia Chernus; cast: John Vernon (Fletcher), Frank Schofield (Senator Lane).

1 *Fletcher*: There's another old saying, Senator. Don't piss down my back and tell me it's raining.

SOUNDTRACK.

OUTRAGEOUS

Canada 1977; screenwriter/director: Richard Benner; cast: Craig Russell (Robin).

2 *Robin (arriving in New York to make his club debut as a drag artiste)*: Isn't anybody straight anymore?

SOUNDTRACK.

3 *Robin*: Canada is a country so square that even the female impersonators are women.

SOUNDTRACK.

The OWL AND THE PUSSYCAT

US 1970; screenwriter: Buck Henry (from a play); cast: Barbara Streisand (Doris), George Segal (Felix).

4 *Doris (to Felix)*: I always feel so selfish sleeping alone in a double bed, when there are people in China sleeping on the ground.

SOUNDTRACK.

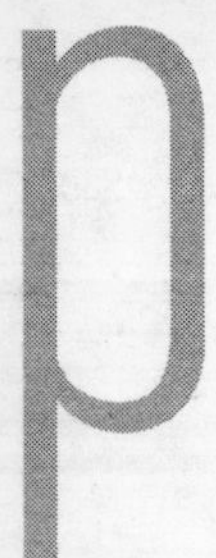

Al PACINO

American actor (1940–)

1 He gets to do a lot of takes. That's what I think stardom means.

COMMENT by Lindsay Duncan (about making of *City Hall*), quoted in the *Independent on Sunday*, 'Overheard' (5 February 1995).

Camille PAGLIA

American writer (1947–)

2 Hollywood: America's Greatest Achievement.

TITLE of article (with Stewart Brand) in *The Utne Reader* (1994).

The PAINTED DESERT

US 1930; screenwriters: Howard Higgins, Tom Buckingham; cast: Clark Gable (Rance Brett).

3 *Rance Brett*: Water? Do I need it. I've had to shoot my horse.

SOUNDTRACK. Gable's first spoken words on screen.

The PALM BEACH STORY

US 1942; screenwriter/director: Preston Sturges; cast: Rudy Vallee (Hackensacker), Robert Dudley (Weenie King).

4 *Hackensacker*: That's one of the tragedies of this life, that the men most in need of beating up are always enormous.

SOUNDTRACK.

5 *Weenie*: Anyway, I'd be too old for you. Cold are the hands of time that creep along relentlessly, destroying slowly but without pity that which yesterday was young. Alone, our memories resist this disintegration and grow more lovely with the passing years. That's hard to say with false teeth.

SOUNDTRACK.

Gwyneth PALTROW

American actress (1973–)

1 Fortunately, I was raised in such a way that I know that family and friends and dogs and flowers and walks are what's important about life, not movies and fame.

QUOTED in *The Observer*, 'Soundbites' (8 September 1996).

2 She's very young and lives in a rarefied air that's very thin. It's like she's not getting enough oxygen.

COMMENT by Sharon Stone, quoted in *The Observer* (12 September 1999).

PAPILLON

US 1973; screenwriters: Dalton Trumbo, Lorenzo Semple Jr (from Henri Charrière autobiography); cast: Steve McQueen (Papillon), Dustin Hoffman (Dega).

3 *Papillon (putting money in a tube prior to hiding it)*: We're really something aren't we? The only animals in the world that shove things up their ass for survival.

SOUNDTRACK.

4 *Dega (on not blaming Papillon for giving in to torture)*: Blame is for God and small children.

SOUNDTRACK.

5 *Papillon (to Dega)*: Me they can kill. You they own.

SOUNDTRACK.

6 *Papillon (having escaped)*: Hey, you bastards! I'm still here.

SOUNDTRACK.

The PARADINE CASE

US 1947; screenwriters: David O. Selznick and others (from Robert Hichens novel); cast: Louis Jourdan (André Latour), Gregory Peck (Anthony Keane), Valli (Anna Paradine/Maddalena).

7 *Latour (to lawyer Keane about his client)*: I will tell you about Mrs Paradine. She's bad, bad to the bone. If there was an evil woman, she is one.

SOUNDTRACK.

Dorothy PARKER

American critic and humorist (1893–1967)

1 Oh come, my love, and join with me
The oldest infant industry.
Come seek the bourne of palm and pearl
The lovely land of Boy-Meets-Girl.
Come grace this lotus-laden shore,
This Isle of Do-What's-Done-Before.
Come, curb the new, and watch the old win,
Out where the streets are paved with Goldwyn.

EXTRACTED from poem, 'The Passionate Screenwriter to His Love' (1937).

2 Hollywood money isn't money. It's congealed snow, melts in your hand, and there you are.

QUOTED in Malcolm Cowley, *Writers at Work*, 1st Series (1958). Quoted by John Keats in *You Might As Well Live* (1970) as: 'Sure, you make money writing on the coast … but that money is like so much compressed snow. It goes so fast it melts in your hand.'

3 [on Hollywood] Oh, it's all right. You make a little money and get caught up on your debts. We're up to 1912 now.

QUOTED in Max Wilk, *The Wit and Wisdom of Hollywood* (1972).

4 The only 'ism' Hollywood believes in is plagiarism.

QUOTED in *The Treasury of Humorous Quotations*, eds. Esar & Bentley (1951 edn).

5 I don't believe the films have anything to do with writing except in a crossword puzzle sort of way. Writing a script is drawing together a lot of ends which can be worked into a moving picture.

ATTRIBUTED in *The Sayings of Dorothy Parker*, ed. S.T. Brownlow (1992).

6 [to Sam Goldwyn who had asked, 'Do you really say all those things which the papers report that you say?'] Do you?

ATTRIBUTED remark.

7 [to an actor with a large nose and no chin to speak of, who told her of his hopes in Hollywood] Oh, they've been *searching* for a new Cary Grant.

ATTRIBUTED in *The Sayings of Dorothy Parker*, ed. S.T. Brownlow (1992).

PASSAGE TO MARSEILLES

US 1943; screenwriters: Casey Robinson, Jack Moffitt (from a story by Charles Nordhoff and James Hall); cast: Sydney Greenstreet (Major Duval).

1 *Major Duval*: The British will fight to the very last drop of French blood.

SOUNDTRACK. This echoes an actual propaganda line. From Anthony Rhodes, *Propaganda: The Art of Persuasion in World War II* (1976): 'Already in the "phony war" of 1939–40 the [German] Propaganda Ministry was organizing broadcasts to France, sowing discord between the Western Allies. The French were told that the British had sent only six divisions, and that the eighty French divisions would have to bear the brunt of the fighting. The British, as usual, would fight "to the last Frenchman".'

Charles PATHÉ

French producer (1863–1957)

2 [to his directors] Will you gentlemen never learn, that in the cinema an actor must be photographed so that his feet touch the bottom of the screen and his head the top.

QUOTED in Alexander Walker, *Stardom* (1970).

PATTON

US 1970; screenwriters: Franklin J. Schaffner, Edmund H. North; cast: George C. Scott (George S. Patton).

3 *Patton*: I want you to remember that no bastard ever won a war by dying for his country. He won it by making the other poor dumb bastard die for his country.

SOUNDTRACK.

Sean PENN

American actor (1960–)

4 The difference between being a director and being an actor is the difference between being the carpenter banging the nails into the wood, and being the piece of wood the nails are being banged into.

INTERVIEWED in *The Guardian* (28 November 1991).

Walker PERCY

American novelist (1916–90)

5 The fact is I am quite happy in a movie, even a bad movie. Other people, so I have read, treasure memorable moments in their lives: the time one climbed the Parthenon at sunrise, the summer night one met a lonely girl in Central Park and achieved with her a sweet and natural relationship, as they say in the books. I too once met a girl in Central Park, but it is not much to remember. What I remember is the time John Wayne killed three men with a carbine as he was falling to the dusty street in *Stagecoach*, and the time the kitten found Orson Welles in the doorway in *The Third Man*.

EXTRACTED from his novel *The Moviegoer*, Chap 1 (1961).

S.J. PERELMAN

American writer and screenwriter (1904–79)

1 'Oh, son, I wish you hadn't become a scenario writer!' she sniffed. 'Aw, now, Moms,' I comforted her, 'it's no worse than playing the piano in a call house.'

EXTRACTED from article 'Strictly from Hunger' – which later became the title of his second book (1937). Quoted in Leslie Halliwell, *The Filmgoer's Book of Quotes* (1978 edn) as: 'Movie scriptwriting is no worse than playing piano in a call house.'

2 The violet hush of twilight was descending over Los Angeles as my hostess, Violet Hush, and I left its suburbs and headed towards Hollywood. In the distance a glow of huge piles of burning motion-picture scripts lit up the sky. The crisp tang of frying writers and directors whetted my appetite. How good it was to be alive, I thought, inhaling deep lung-fulls of carbon monoxide.

EXTRACTED from the same article.

3 A fine mist hovered over the City of the Walking Dead as we swung up over the Cahuenga Pass … Hirschfield leaned out and stared pensively at the myriad twinkling lights of Los Angeles … 'I'd rather be embalmed here than any place I know,' he said slowly.

EXTRACTED from his book *Westward Ha!* (1948).

4 The mere mention of Hollywood induces a condition in me like break-bone fever. It was a hideous and untenable place when I dwelt there, populated with few exceptions by Yahoos, and now that it has become the chief citadel of television, it's unspeakable.

INTERVIEWED in *Paris Review* (1964).

5 Hollywood – the city of dreadful day.

QUOTED in Joe Adamson, *Groucho, Harpo, Chico and Sometimes Zeppo* (1973).

6 [Hollywood] A dreary industrial town controlled by hoodlums of enormous wealth.

REMARK quoted at his death.

PETE 'N' TILLIE

US 1972; screenwriter: Julius J. Epstein (from Peter de Vries novella); cast: Carol Burnett (Tillie Schlaine), Walter Matthau (Pete Seltzer).

1 *Pete (on a quotation thief)*: He's a cultural Robin Hood. He steals from the witty and gives to the dull.

SOUNDTRACK.

2 *Pete (to Tillie)*: The Abbott and Costello 'Who's on First' routine is literature. It ranks with the Songs of Solomon, the sonnets of Shakespeare, and the speeches of Spiro Agnew.

SOUNDTRACK. *See The* ***NAUGHTY NINETIES*** 300:4.

Le PETIT SOLDAT

France 1960; screenwriter/director: Jean-Luc Godard; cast: Michel Subor (Bruno Forestier).

3 *Bruno*: *La photographie, c'est la vérité. Le cinéma: la vérité vingt-quatre fois par seconde* [Photography is truth. And cinema is truth twenty-four times a second].

SOUNDTRACK.

The PETRIFIED FOREST

US 1936; screenwriters: Charles Kenyon, Delmer Daves (from Robert E. Sherwood play); cast: Humphrey Bogart (Duke Mantee), Leslie Howard (Alan Squier), Joe Sawyer (Jackie).

4 *Squier*: Let there be killing. All this evening I've had a feeling of destiny closing in.

SOUNDTRACK.

5 *Squier*: Living, I'm worth nothing to her. But dead, I can buy her the tallest cathedrals, golden vineyards, and dancing in the streets. One well-directed bullet will accomplish all that.

SOUNDTRACK.

6 *Jackie*: Now, just behave yourself and nobody'll get hurt. This is Duke Mantee, the world-famous killer, and he's hungry.

SOUNDTRACK.

Michelle PFEIFFER

American actress (1957–)

1 I look like a duck. It's the way my mouth sort of curls up, or my nose tilts up. I should have played 'Howard the Duck.'

ATTRIBUTED remark.

2 Just three years ago, Richard Gere bought Julia Roberts for … what was it, $3,000? Now James Caan snaps up Sarah Jessica Parker for $65,000, Uma Thurman went for $40,000 to Robert de Niro, and Demi Moore was sold to Robert Redford for $1 million. I'd say that was real progress.

SPEECH quoted in the *Daily Mail* (2 August 1993). Pfeiffer was referring respectively to the stars of *Pretty Woman, Honeymoon In Vegas, Mad Dog and Glory* and *Indecent Proposal.*

The PHILADELPHIA STORY

US 1940; screenwriters: Donald Ogden Stewart, Waldo Salt (from Philip Barry play); cast: Katharine Hepburn (Tracy Lord), Margaret Lord (Mary Nash), Henry Daniell (Sidney Kidd), John Halliday (Seth Lord), James Stewart (Macauley Connor).

3 *Mary Nash (to daughter)*: Don't say 'stinks', darling. If absolutely necessary, 'smells' – but only if absolutely necessary.

SOUNDTRACK.

4 *Macauley Connor*: There's a magnificence in you, Tracy … A magnificence that comes out of your eyes and your voice and the way you stand there and the way you walk. You're lit from within, Tracy. You've got fires banked down in you, hearth fires and holocausts.

SOUNDTRACK.

5 *Tracy Lord*: Why, was I so unattractive, so distant, so forbidding or something?
Macauley Connor: You were extremely attractive, and as for distant and forbidding, on the contrary. But you were also a little the worse, or better, for wine, and there are rules about that.

SOUNDTRACK. Tracy thinks she misbehaved with Macauley but he tells her she was simply a little drunk.

Julia PHILLIPS

American producer (1944– 2002)

6 She had known the title for years; she would call it *You'll Never*

Eat Lunch in This Town Again. As in: You'll never eat shit in this town again ... Prophetic, no doubt. That's okay, I'm always on a diet.

EXTRACTED from her book *You'll Never Eat Lunch in This Town Again* (1991). Referring to herself in a memoir that describes Phillips's decline as a producer in Hollywood. With her former husband Michael she had produced some notable films including *The Sting, Taxi Driver* and *Close Encounters of the Third Kind*. In the book she sought to expose the moguls of tinsel-town and seemed to describe all the men she had to deal with as pricks.

1 Hollywood is a place that attracts people with massive holes in their souls.

REMARK quoted in *The Times* (3 April 1991).

The PIANO

New Zealand 1993; screenwriter/director: Jane Campion; cast: Holly Hunter (Ada McGrath).

2 *Ada*: 'There is a silence where hath been no sound,
There is a silence where no sound may be,
In the cold grave, under the deep, deep sea.'

SOUNDTRACK. Last words of film, they are 'spoken' by the dumb heroine who has just consigned her piano to the bottom of the sea and who has also come near to death herself by being dragged down with it. She is quoting lines from the sonnet 'Silence' by the English poet, Thomas Hood (1799–1845).

Mary PICKFORD

Canadian-born American actress (1893–1979)

3 Adding sound to movies would be like putting lipstick on the Venus de Milo.

ATTRIBUTED remark in about 1925, recalled at her death.

4 It took longer to make one of Mary's contracts than it did one of Mary's pictures.

COMMENT attributed to Sam Goldwyn.

PICNIC

US 1955; screenwriter: Daniel Taradash (from William Inge play); cast: William Holden (Hal Carter)

5 *Hal*: I gotta get somewhere in this world. I just gotta.

SOUNDTRACK.

PICNIC AT HANGING ROCK

Australia 1975; screenwriter: Cliff Green (from Joan Lindsay novel); cast: Anne Lambert (Miranda).

1 *Introductory voice*: 'What we see and what we seem,
Are but a dream, a dream within a dream.'

SOUNDTRACK. Though unattributed, this is a quotation from Edgar Allen Poe: 'All that we see or seem / Is but a dream within a dream' – 'A Dream Within a Dream' 1849. *See also The* **FOG** 164:7.

2 *Miranda*: Everything begins and ends at exactly the right time and place.

SOUNDTRACK. As in the original novel, Chap. 10.

The PICTURE OF DORIAN GRAY

US 1945; screenwriter/director: Albert Lewin (from Oscar Wilde novel); cast: Hurd Hatfield (Dorian Gray); George Sanders (Sir Henry).

3 *Sir Henry*: If I could get back my youth, I'd do anything in the world – except get up early, take exercise or be respectable.

SOUNDTRACK.

4 *Sir Henry*: I apologize for the intelligence of my remarks, Sir Thomas, I had forgotten that you were a Member of Parliament.

SOUNDTRACK.

5 *Dorian*: If only the picture could change and I could be always what I am now. For that, I would give anything. Yes, there's nothing in the whole world I wouldn't give. I'd give my soul for that.

SOUNDTRACK.

PIERROT LE FOU

France/Italy 1968; screenwriter/director: Jean-Luc Godard; cast: Sam Fuller (himself).

6 *Fuller*: The film is like a battleground … love … hate … action … violence … death … in one word: emotions.

SOUNDTRACK. Spoken by Fuller (American writer and director, 1912–97) in a cameo appearance as a visiting film director who makes his pronouncement at a party. It has been wrongly attributed to Nicholas Ray.

PILLOW TALK

US 1959; screenwriters: Stanley Shapiro, Maurice Richlin; cast: Doris Day (Jan Morrow), Rock Hudson (Brad Allen), Thelma Ritter (Alma).

1 *Brad*: Don't take your bedroom problems out on me.
Jan: There's nothing in my bedroom that bothers me.

SOUNDTRACK.

2 *Alma*: If there's anything worse than a woman living alone, it's a woman saying she likes it.

SOUNDTRACK.

PIMPERNEL SMITH

UK 1941; screenwriters: Roland Pertwee and others; cast: Leslie Howard (Pimpernel Smith).

3 *Smith*: I'll be back … we'll all be back.

SOUNDTRACK. Last words of film. Smith is a professor of archaeology who goes into war-torn Europe to rescue refugees. *Compare The* ***TERMINATOR*** 409:2.

The PINK PANTHER STRIKES AGAIN

UK 1976; screenwriters: Frank Waldman, Blake Edwards (director); cast: Peter Sellers (Inspector Clouseau), Herbert Lom (Dreyfus), Vanda Godsell (Mrs Leverlilly), André Maranne (François), Graham Stark (Hotel clerk).

4 *Clouseau (to Dreyfus)*: You have a massive beump upon the head.

SOUNDTRACK.

5 *François*: Do you know what kind of a bomb it was?
Clouseau: The exploding kind.

SOUNDTRACK.

6 *Mrs Leverlilly (after Clouseau accidentally demolishes a piano)*: You've ruined that piano!
Clouseau: What is the price of one piano compared to the terrible crime that has been committed here?
Mrs. Leverlilly: But that's a priceless Steinway!
Clouseau: Not any more!

SOUNDTRACK.

7 *Clouseau*: Tell me, do you have a rheum?
Hotel clerk: I do not know what a rheum is.

SOUNDTRACK.

8 *Clouseau*: Does your dog bite?
Hotel clerk: No.
Clouseau (bending down to pet the dog): Nice doggie.
(Dogs barks and bites him). I thought you said your dog did not bite!
Hotel clerk: That is not my dog.

SOUNDTRACK.

PINOCCHIO

US 1940; screenwriters: Ted Sears and others (from Carlo Collodi story); music/lyrics: Leigh Harline, Ned Washington, Paul J. Smith; cast: Cliff Edwards (voice of Jiminy Cricket); Evelyn Venable (voice of The Blue Fairy), Dickie Jones (voice of Pinocchio), Walter Catlett (voice of J. Worthington Foulfellow).

1 *Jiminy Cricket*: When you wish upon a star,
Your dreams come true …

SOUNDTRACK. Song 'When You Wish Upon a Star', sung over opening titles.

2 *The Blue Fairy (to Pinocchio)*: Always let your conscience be your guide.

SOUNDTRACK.

3 *Jiminy Cricket (to Pinocchio)*: And any time you need me, you know, just whistle.

SOUNDTRACK.

4 *J. Worthington Foulfellow*: Hi diddle dee dee,
An actor's life for me.

SOUNDTRACK. Song 'An Actor's Life for Me'.

5 *Jiminy Cricket (when Pinocchio joins the marionettes)*: Well, I guess he won't need me anymore. What does an actor want with a conscience, anyway?

SOUNDTRACK.

6 *The Blue Fairy (to Pinocchio, on why his nose is growing)*: A lie keeps growing and growing, until it's as plain as the nose on your face.

SOUNDTRACK.

The PIRATE

US 1948; music/lyrics: Cole Porter; cast: Judy Garland (Manuela), Gene Kelly (Serafin).

7 *Manuela, Serafin & Co. (sing)*: Be a clown, be a clown,
All the world loves a clown.

SOUNDTRACK. Song, 'Be a Clown'.

PLATOON

US 1986; screenwriter/director: Oliver Stone; cast: Charlie Sheen (Chris).

8 *Chris*: I think looking back, we did not fight the enemy, we fought ourselves. And the enemy was in us …

SOUNDTRACK.

PLAY IT AGAIN SAM

US 1972; screenwriter: Woody Allen (from his play); cast: Woody Allen (Allan Felix), Susan Anspach (Nancy Felix).

1 Play It Again Sam.

TITLE OF FILM. *See* ***CASABLANCA*** 90:1.

2 *Allan (on sunbathing)*: I don't tan – I stroke!

SOUNDTRACK.

3 *Nancy (as departing wife)*: My lawyer will call your lawyer.
Allan: I don't have a lawyer.

SOUNDTRACK.

PLEASE DON'T EAT THE DAISIES

US 1960; screenwriter: Isobel Lennart (from Jean Kerr novel); cast: David Niven (Lawrence Mackay).

4 *Mackay*: This poor failure gives poor failures a bad name.

SOUNDTRACK. An earlyish outing for the 'gives –– a bad name' critical format.

Roman POLANSKI

Polish-born screenwriter and director (1933–)

5 I like to be frightened when I see a film. Not to upset people would be an obscenity.

QUOTED in *The Observer*, 'Sayings of the Week' (30 January 1972).

POLICE ACADEMY

US 1984; screenwriter: Neal Israel and others; cast: Ted Ross (Captain Reed), Steve Guttenberg (Carey Mahoney).

6 *Captain Reed (to Mahoney)*: The academy is taking all kinds today. Anybody can get in. Even you.

SOUNDTRACK.

Carlo PONTI

Italian producer (1913–)

7 *Se un film ha successo, è un affare: se non ha successo, è arte* [If a film is successful, it is commercial; if it isn't, it's art].

ATTRIBUTED remark.

POPPY

US 1936; screenwriters: Waldemar Young, Virginia Van Upp (from a play by Dorothy Donnelly); cast: W.C. Fields (Prof. Eustace McGargle), Rochelle Hudson (Poppy).

1 *McGargle*: I'm like Robin Hood. I steal from the rich and give to the poor – us poor.

SOUNDTRACK.

2 *McGargle (advice to daughter, Poppy)*: Let me give you one word of fatherly advice. Never give a sucker an even break.

SOUNDTRACK. This saying has been attributed to various people but has largely become associated with Fields. He is believed to have ad-libbed it in the stage musical *Poppy* (1923) and certainly spoke it in the film version. The words are not uttered, however, in the film called *Never Give a Sucker an Even Break* (1941).

The POSEIDON ADVENTURE

US 1972; screenwriters: Stirling Silliphant, Wendell Mayes (from Paul Gallico novel); cast: Shelley Winters (Belle Rosen), Red Buttons (James Martin), Leslie Nielsen (Captain), William Holden (Scott).

3 Hell, upside down.

SLOGAN.

4 *Captain (sighting tidal wave)*: Oh, my God!

SOUNDTRACK.

5 *Belle*: You see, Mr Scott, in the water, I'm a very skinny lady.

SOUNDTRACK.

POTEMKIN *See The* ***BATTLESHIP POTEMKIN.***

Hortense POWDERMAKER

American anthropologist (1896–1970)

6 Hollywood itself is not an exact geographical area, although there is such a postal district. It has commonly been described as a state of mind, and it exists wherever people connected with the movies live and work.

EXTRACTED from her book *Hollywood, the Dream Factory: An Anthropologist Looks at the Movie-Makers* (1950).

7 In Hollywood, primitive magical thinking exists side by side with the most advanced technology.

EXTRACTED from the same book.

1 South Sea natives who have been exposed to American movies classify them into two types, 'kiss-kiss' and 'bang-bang'.

EXTRACTED from the same book. *Compare* Pauline **KAEL** 236:1.

Michael POWELL

English screenwriter, producer and director (1905–90)

2 [on metropolitan criticism of his rural film *Gone to Earth* (1950)] What do they know of England, who only the West End know?

ATTRIBUTED remark. From a poem by Rudyard Kipling, entitled 'The English Flag': 'And what should they know of England who only England know?'.

Tyrone POWER

American actor (1913–58)

3 [when his Fox contract expired] I've done an awful lot of stuff that's a monument to public patience.

QUOTED in David Shipman, *The Great Movie Stars*, Vol. 1 (1970).

Otto PREMINGER

Austrian-born American director (1906–86)

4 I always think that sex is so much healthier than violence.

QUOTED in *The Observer* (1967).

5 I hear Otto Preminger's on holiday. In Auschwitz.

COMMENT by Billy Wilder, attributed in *Films Illustrated* (January 1980).

PRETTY WOMAN

US 1990; screenwriter: J.F. Lawton; cast: Richard Gere (Edward Lewis), Julia Roberts (Vivian Ward), Elinor Donahue (Bridget), Hector Elizondo (Hotel manager), Abdul Salaam El Razzac (Happy Man).

6 *Vivian (to Edward, when he tells her she can't charge to give directions)*: I can do anything I want to, baby. I ain't lost.

SOUNDTRACK.

7 *Vivian (to Edward, when asked her name)*: What do you want it to be?

SOUNDTRACK.

8 *Vivian (to Edward)*: Well, this hotel is not the kind of establishment that rents rooms by the hour.

SOUNDTRACK.

1 *Edward (to onlookers, about Vivian)*: First time in an elevator.
SOUNDTRACK.

2 *Female hotel guest (to her husband looking at Vivian)*: Close your mouth, dear.
SOUNDTRACK.

3 *Vivian (to Edward)*: Listen, I ... I appreciate this whole seduction scene you got going, but let me give you a tip: I'm a sure thing.
SOUNDTRACK.

4 *Vivian (of Edward)*: He's not really my uncle.
Bridget (in fashion store): They never are, dear.
SOUNDTRACK. The film also contains an entertaining disquisition between Vivian and the Hotel manager on whether she is really Edward's 'niece'. Purporting to be uncles/nieces is a venerable activity – not least in the world of film-makers. According to the *Independent*'s obituary of English film producer Nat Cohen (11 February 1988), 'He was much loved – not least by the young ladies usually introduced as "Have you met my niece?"' From BBC radio *Round the Horne* (26 March 1967): [A butler announces] 'Lord Grisley Makeshift and his niece – *he says* – Mrs Costello Funf.' Clearly, this is a well-established piece of usage. In James Thurber's story 'Something to Say' (1927), there is this: 'Elliot Vereker ... arrived about noon on 4th July ... accompanied by a lady in black velvet whom he introduced as "my niece, Olga Nethersole". She was, it turned out, neither his niece nor Olga Nethersole.' In the film *Road to Utopia* (US 1945), an elderly Bing Crosby introduces his two 'nieces' to an equally aged Bob Hope.

5 *Vivian (to Edward, on how her fairy tale ends)*: She rescues him right back.
SOUNDTRACK.

6 *Happy Man*: Welcome to Hollywood! What's your dream? Everybody comes here. This is Hollywood, land of dreams. Some dreams come true, some don't, but keep on dreamin'. This is Hollywood. Always time to dream, so keep on dreamin'.
SOUNDTRACK. Last spoken lines of film.

Vincent PRICE

American actor (1911–93)

7 Someone called actors 'sculptors in snow'. Very apt. In the end, it's all nothing.
QUOTED in the *Sunday Express* (1964).

PRIMARY COLORS

US 1998; screenwriter: Elaine May (from novel by Anonymous); cast: John Travolta (Governor Jack Stanton), Kathy Bates (Libby Holden).

1 *Libby (to Jack, refusing to smear an opponent)*: So, here's the deal: if you move on Freddie Picker who, I think we all agree, is a flawed but decent man, I move on you. Yes, I will destroy this village in order to save it.

SOUNDTRACK. Alluding to the remark, 'To save the town, it became necessary to destroy it,' made by an unnamed American major on the town of Ben Tre, Vietnam, during the Tet offensive, according to an AP dispatch headed 'Major Describes Move' in *The New York Times* (8 February 1968). A token of the futility of American activities in Vietnam. In 1970, there was a 'psychedelic biker comedy' movie with the title *Gas-s-s-s! Or It Became Necessary to Destroy the World in Order to Save It.*

The PRIME OF MISS JEAN BRODIE

UK 1969; screenwriter: Jay Presson Allen (from Muriel Spark novel); cast: Maggie Smith (Jean Brodie), Pamela Franklin (Sandy).

2 *Jean (to pupils)*: I am dedicated to you in my prime. My summer in Italy has convinced me that I am, truly, in my prime.

SOUNDTRACK.

3 *Jean*: I believe I am past my prime. I had reckoned on my prime lasting till I was at least fifty.

SOUNDTRACK.

4 *Sandy (to Jean)*: I didn't betray you. I simply put a stop to you.

SOUNDTRACK.

5 *Jean*: Little girls, I am in the business of putting old heads on young shoulders and all my pupils are the crème de la crème. Give me a girl at an impressionable age, and she is mine for life.

SOUNDTRACK. Last line of film, reprising what has been said earlier. This speech brings together and slightly modifies two separate passages from the novel.

The PRISONER OF ZENDA

US 1937; screenwriters: John L. Balderston and others (from dramatization of Anthony Hope novel); cast: Ronald Colman (Rudolf Rassendyl/Rudolph V), Madeleine Carroll (Princess Flavia), Douglas Fairbanks Jr (Rupert of Hentzau), Mary Astor (Antoinette de Mauban).

6 *Rupert (to Antoinette)*: Somebody once called fidelity a fading woman's greatest weapon and a charming woman's greatest hypocrisy.

SOUNDTRACK. Antoinette is a prince's mistress and Rupert is attempting to seduce her.

1 *Rudolf (when revealed as impostor, to Flavia)*: I love you ... In all else I've been an impostor, but not in that.

SOUNDTRACK.

2 *Rudolf (to Flavia)*: There's a world outside. Our world. And a throne for you. A woman's throne in my heart.

SOUNDTRACK.

PRIVATE BENJAMIN

US 1980; screenwriters: Nancy Meyers and others; cast: Goldie Hawn (Judy Benjamin)

3 *Judy (on army uniforms)*: Excuse me, sir. Is green the only colour these come in?

SOUNDTRACK.

4 *Judy (after orgasm with French lover)*: Now I know what I've been faking all these years.

SOUNDTRACK.

The PRIVATE LIFE OF DON JUAN

US 1934; screenwriters: Lajos Biro, Frederick Lonsdale (from play by Henri Bataille); cast: Douglas Fairbanks (Don Juan).

5 *Don Juan*: Marriage is like a beleaguered city. Those who are out want to get in; those who are in want to get out.

SOUNDTRACK.

The PRIVATE LIFE OF HENRY VIII

UK 1933; screenwriters: Lajos Biro, Arthur Wimperis; cast: Charles Laughton (Henry VIII).

6 *Henry (plunging his fingers inside a bird)*: There's no delicacy nowadays. No consideration for others. Refinement's a thing of the past *(throws carcass over shoulder)*. Manners are dead! *(belches)*.

SOUNDTRACK. The published screenplay (1934), declares: 'This is the first complete script of a British film to be published in book form.'

7 *Henry*: Marry, *marry*, MARRY! Am I the king or a breeding bull?

SOUNDTRACK.

8 *Henry (with a deep sigh, entering the bedchamber where Anne of Cleves awaits him)*: The things I've done for England!

SOUNDTRACK. Popularly misquoted as 'the things I *do* for England'

1 I won't be showing any more films in which men write with feathers.

COMMENT on this film attributed to a Missouri cinema owner in Peter Hay, *Movie Anecdotes* (1990). Has also been ascribed to Broadway producers Max Gordon and Lee Shubert on costume drama in the theatre.

PRIVATE'S PROGRESS

UK 1956; screenwriters: Frank Harvey, John Boulting (from Alan Hackney novel); cast: Terry-Thomas (Major Hitchcock).

2 *Major Hitchcock (of two privates spending an age on a painting job)*: You're an absolute shower!

SOUNDTRACK.

PRIZZI'S HONOR

US 1985; screenwriter: Richard Condon (from his novel), Janet Roach; cast: Anjelica Huston (Maerose Prizzi), Jack Nicholson (Charley Partanna), Kathleen Turner (Irene Walker).

3 *Maerose (to Charley)*: Come on Charley. You wanna do it? Let's do it right here on the Oriental. With all the lights on.

SOUNDTRACK.

4 *Charley (on Irene)*: Do I ice her? Do I marry her? Which one a dese?

SOUNDTRACK.

The PRODUCERS

US 1967; screenwriter/director: Mel Brooks; cast: Zero Mostel (Max Bialystock), Gene Wilder (Leo Bloom), Kenneth Mars (Frank Liebkind), Bill Macy (Jury Foreman), Christopher Hewett (Roger de Bris), Dick Shawn (Lorenzo St Dubois/LSD).

5 *Max (out of window, to owner of large white limo)*: That's it, baby! When you got it, flaunt it! Flaunt it!

SOUNDTRACK. Later in film he says, 'Flaunt it, baby, flaunt it!' and 'Take it when you can get it. Flaunt it! Flaunt it!' These utterances popularized the expression.

6 *Leo (to Max)*: Under the right circumstances, a producer could make more money with a flop than he could with a hit.

SOUNDTRACK. The idea upon which the plot of the movie turns.

7 *Max*: How can a producer make more money with a flop than he could with a hit?
Leo: It's simply a matter of creative accounting. Let's assume just for the moment that you are a dishonest man.
Max: Assume away.
Leo: It's very easy, you simply raise more money than you need.

SOUNDTRACK.

1 *Max*: Bloom, do me a favour. Move a few decimal points around. You can do it. You're an accountant. You're in a noble profession. The word count is part of your title.

SOUNDTRACK.

2 *Max*: You miserable, cowardly, wretched little caterpillar! Don't you ever want to become a butterfly? Don't you want to spread your wings and flap your way to glory?

SOUNDTRACK.

3 *Max*: Leo, he who hesitates is poor.

SOUNDTRACK.

4 *Leo (after Max throws water in his face to calm him down)*: I'm wet! I'm wet! I'm hysterical and I'm wet!

SOUNDTRACK.

5 *Leo*: I want everything I've ever seen in the movies!

SOUNDTRACK.

6 *Leo*: This won't run a week!
Max: A week? Are you kidding? This play has got to close on page four.

SOUNDTRACK.

7 *Frank (a Nazi-fixated playwright)*: I am not responsible! I only followed orders!

SOUNDTRACK. *Compare* ***NIGHT TRAIN TO MUNICH*** 306:4.

8 *Frank (of Hitler)*: Hitler, there was a painter! He could paint an entire apartment in one afternoon. Two coats!

SOUNDTRACK.

9 *Frank*: Let me tell you this, and you are hearing this straight from the horse, Hitler was better looking than Churchill, he was a better dresser than Churchill, he had more hair, he told funnier jokes and he could dance the pants off of Churchill.

SOUNDTRACK.

10 *Max*: That's exactly why we want to produce this play: to show the world the true Hitler, the Hitler you loved, the Hitler you knew, the Hitler with a song in his heart.

SOUNDTRACK.

1 *Max (of Roger de Bris)*: He stinks! He's perhaps the worst director that ever lived. He's the only director whose plays close on the first day of rehearsal.

SOUNDTRACK.

2 *Leo (to Max, on first seeing de Bris)*: Max. He's wearing a dress!

SOUNDTRACK.

3 *De Bris (on the play)*: Do you know, I never realized that the Third Reich meant Germany? I mean, it's drenched with historical goodies like that.

SOUNDTRACK.

4 *De Bris*: And that whole third act has to go. They're losing the war. It's too depressing.

SOUNDTRACK.

5 *De Bris (to auditioners for role of Hitler)*: Will the dancing Hitlers please wait in the wings? We are only seeing singing Hitlers.

SOUNDTRACK.

6 *LSD (as Hitler in play to actress playing Eva Braun)*: Hey, man, I *liebe* you. I *liebe* you, baby. Now, leave me alone.

SOUNDTRACK.

7 Springtime for Hitler and Germany,
Deutschland is happy and gay.
We're marching to a faster pace,
Look out, here comes the Master Race!

SOUNDTRACK. Song in musical *Springtime for Hitler.*

8 Don't be stupid, be a smarty
Come and join the Nazi party.

SOUNDTRACK. From the same song. Lines dubbed by Mel Brooks himself.

9 *Frank (refusing to keep quiet during his play)*: You are the audience. I am the author. I outrank you.

SOUNDTRACK.

10 *Max*: How could this happen? I was so careful. I picked the wrong play, the wrong director, the wrong cast. Where did I go right?

SOUNDTRACK.

1 *Leo (on Max's suggestion that the actors be shot to close the play)*: Have you lost your mind? How can you kill the actors? … Actors are not animals. They're human beings.
Max: They are? Have you ever eaten with one?

SOUNDTRACK.

2 *Leo (at trial, on why he likes Max)*: No one ever called me Leo before.

SOUNDTRACK.

3 *Jury foreman*: We find the defendants incredibly guilty.

SOUNDTRACK.

PRODUCTION CODE

(A Code to Govern the Making of Motion and Talking Pictures by the Motion Picture Producers of America, Inc., 31 March 1930 – also known as the Hays Code)

4 1. No picture shall be produced which will lower the moral standards of those who see it. Hence the sympathy of the audience should never be thrown to the side of crime, wrongdoing, evil or sin. 2. Correct standards of life, subject only to the requirements of drama and entertainment, shall be presented. 3. Law, natural or human, shall not be ridiculed, nor shall sympathy be created for its violation.

General Principles (1).

5 The technique of murder must be presented in a way that will not inspire imitation.

Particular Applications. 1. Murder.

6 The sanctity of the institution of marriage and the home shall be upheld. Pictures shall not infer [*sic*] that low forms of sex relationship are the accepted or common thing … Adultery, sometimes necessary plot material, must not be explicitly treated, or justified, or presented attractively.

Particular Applications. 2. Sex.

7 Obscenity in word, gesture, reference, song, joke or by suggestion … is forbidden.

Particular Applications. 4. Obscenity.

8 Complete nudity is never permitted. This includes nudity in fact or in silhouette, or any lecherous or licentious notice thereof by other characters in the picture.

Particular Applications. 6. Costume.

1 [on the establishment of the 'Hays Office' in 1922 to monitor the Hollywood film industry] Will Hays is my shepherd, I shall not want, He maketh me to lie down in clean postures.

COMMENT by Gene Fowler, American screenwriter (1890–1960), quoted in Clive Marsh & Gaye Ortiz (eds), *Explorations in Theology and Film* (1997).

PSYCHO

US 1960; screenwriter: Joseph Stefano; cast: Anthony Perkins (Norman Bates), Simon Oakland (Dr Richmond), Virginia Gregg (voice of Mother).

2 Don't give away the ending. It's the only one we have.

SLOGAN.

3 *Norman*: Mother – what's the phrase? – isn't quite herself today.

SOUNDTRACK.

4 *Norman*: A boy's best friend is his mother.

SOUNDTRACK. The obviously proverbial expression is little recorded before this. 'Tell him I said a boy's best friend is his mother' is in Judson Phillips, *The Fourteenth Trump* (1942), where he is 'quoting an old song'. Indeed. The saying seems to have been set in concrete – if not in treacle – by an American songwriter called Henry Miller (not that one) in 1883. The music was by the prolific Joseph P. Skelly, who was also a plumber. Their song with the expression as the title contains the chorus: 'Then cherish her with care, / And smooth her sil'vry hair, / When gone you will never get another. / And wherever we may turn, / This lesson we shall learn, / A boy's best friend is his Mother.'

5 *Dr Richmond (of Norman)*: He tried to *be* his mother – and now he is.

SOUNDTRACK.

6 *'Mother'*: They'll see and they'll know and they'll say, why, she wouldn't even harm a fly.

SOUNDTRACK.

PUBLIC ENEMY

US 1931; screenwriters: Kubec Glasmon and others; cast: James Cagney (Tom Powers), Mae Clarke (Kitty).

7 *Tom (to Kitty, just before squashing a grapefruit in her face)*: I wish you was a wishing well, so I could tie a bucket to you and sink you.

SOUNDTRACK.

PULP FICTION

US 1994; screenwriter/director: Quentin Tarantino; cast: John Travolta (Vincent Vega), Samuel L. Jackson (Jules Winnfield), Uma Thurman (Mia Wallace), Ving Rhames (Marsellus Wallace).

1 *Vincent*: And you know what they call a … a … a Quarter Pounder with Cheese in Paris?
Jules: They don't call it a Quarter Pounder with Cheese?
Vincent: No man, they got the metric system. They wouldn't know what the fuck a Quarter Pounder is.
Jules: Then what do they call it?
Vincent: They call it a 'Royale' with cheese.
Jules: A 'Royale' with cheese! …What do they call a Big Mac?
Vincent: A Big Mac's a Big Mac, but they call it 'le Big-Mac'.
Jules: 'Le Big-Mac'! Ha ha ha ha! What do they call a Whopper?
Vincent: I dunno, I didn't go into Burger King.

SOUNDTRACK.

2 *Vincent*: I'm gonna take a piss.
Mia: That's a little bit more information than I needed, Vince, but go right ahead.

SOUNDTRACK.

3 *Marsellus (about to take revenge on man who has raped him)*: I'm gonna git Medieval on your ass.

SOUNDTRACK.

David PUTTNAM (Lord Puttnam)

English producer and studio executive (1941–)

4 Leaving Los Angeles is like giving up heroin.

QUOTED in *Radio Times* (21–27 October 1978).

5 Making films solely for entertainment is like making soup with only one ingredient.

QUOTED in *The Independent* (29 April 1989).

6 I'm hopelessly stranded somewhere in mid-Atlantic. But I would trade the Americans' generosity and affection for British snottiness and cynicism any day.

QUOTED in *The Independent* (31 May 1997).

1 The thing I dread is getting on a bit and walking up and down Wardour Street, trying to collar people and saying, 'I'm sure I've got one more film left in me.'

QUOTED in *The Independent* (5 July 1997).

PYGMALION

UK 1938; screenwriters: Bernard Shaw (after his play) and others; cast: Leslie Howard (Henry Higgins), Wendy Hiller (Eliza Doolittle), David Tree (Freddy Eynsford-Hill).

2 *Higgins (to Eliza)*: Yes, you squashed cabbage leaf, you disgrace to the noble architecture of these columns, you incarnate insult to the English language, I could pass you off as the Queen of Sheba.

SOUNDTRACK.

3 *Eliza*: I washed my face and hands afore I come, I did.

SOUNDTRACK.

4 *Higgins*: The rain in Spain stays mainly in the plains.

SOUNDTRACK. (Note it is *plains*). An elocution exercise said to have been invented by the director, Anthony Asquith, and approved by Shaw (though this and the next do not appear in Shaw's published scenes for the film script).

5 *Higgins*: In Hampshire, Hereford and Hertford,
Hurricanes hardly ever happen.

SOUNDTRACK. Elocution exercise said to have been introduced for the film and approved by Shaw.

6 *Freddie (to Eliza)*: The new slang, you do it ever so well!

SOUNDTRACK. In the play, it is 'new small talk'.

7 *Eliza*: I must go now. Goodbye, Mrs Higgins …
Freddy: Excuse me, Miss Doolittle, would you be walking across the Park because if so … ?
Eliza: Walk! Not bloody likely. I am going in a taxi.

SOUNDTRACK. First time the word 'bloody' had been heard in the cinema.

8 *Higgins*: Where the devil are my slippers, Eliza?

SOUNDTRACK. Last words of film, not in Shaw's original text at this point nor in his screenplay. He disapproved of anything that even hinted at a romantic interest between Higgins and Eliza.

See also ***MY FAIR LADY***.

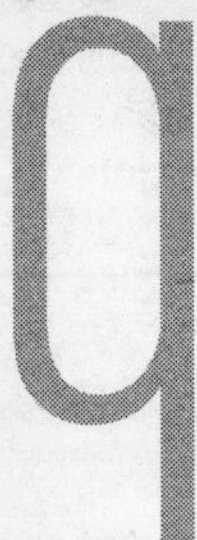

QUEEN CHRISTINA

US 1933: screenwriters: Salka Viertel and others; cast: Greta Garbo (Queen Christina), John Gilbert (Antonio).

1 *Antonio*: It's all a question of climate. You cannot serenade a woman in a snowstorm. All the graces in the art of love – elaborate approaches that will make the game of love amusing – can only be practised in those countries that quiver in the heat of the sun.

SOUNDTRACK.

2 *Christina*: I have been memorizing this room. In the future, in my memory, I shall live a great deal in this room.

SOUNDTRACK. The room is where she and Antonio have made love.

Horacio QUIROGA

Uruguayan short story writer (1878–1938)

3 It is easy to understand that, for me, cinema was the beginning of a new era which marked my nights, one after the other, as I left the theatre, dizzy and pale after leaving my heart on the screen … on that screen that for forty-five minutes was impregnated by Brownie Vernon's charm.

EXTRACTED from his book *Anaconda*, 'Miss Dorothy Phillips, My Wife' (1921). Translated from the original Spanish.

QUO VADIS

US 1951; screenwriters: John Lee Mahin, S.N. Behrman, Sonya Levien (after Henryk Sienkiewicz novel); cast: Leo Genn (Petronius), Peter Ustinov (Nero), Robert Taylor (Marcus Vinicius), Patricia Laffan (Poppaea), Finlay Currie (Peter).

4 In making this film, MGM feel privileged to add something of permanent value to the cultural treasure house of mankind …

SLOGAN.

5 Ancient Rome is going to the dogs, Robert Taylor is going to the lions, and Peter Ustinov is going crazy!

SLOGAN.

1 *Narrator*: This is the Appian Way. The most famous road that leads to Rome, as all roads lead to Rome.

SOUNDTRACK.

2 *Petronius*: Why don't you come down to Sicily for the weekend, Marcus? And bring the children.

APOCRYPHAL LINE.

3 *Nero*: What pulsating purity there is in fire! And my new Rome shall spring from the loins of fire!

SOUNDTRACK.

4 *Poppaea (to Marcus Vinicius)*: It is foolish to kill those you hate, because, once dead, they are beyond pain.

SOUNDTRACK.

5 *Nero (dying words)*: Is this the end of Nero?

SOUNDTRACK. *Compare* ***LITTLE CAESAR*** 255:3.

6 *Peter (asking 'Whither goest thou?' to Christ)*: *Quo vadis?*

SOUNDTRACK.

7 *Peter (facing crucifixion)*: To die as our Lord died is more than I deserve.

SOUNDTRACK.

8 I grew a beard for Nero, in *Quo Vadis*, but Metro-Goldwyn-Mayer thought it didn't look real, so I had to wear a false one.

COMMENT attributed to Peter Ustinov.

RADIO DAYS

US 1986; screenwriter/director: Woody Allen; cast: Woody Allen (Narrator), Julie Kavner (Mother), Seth Green (Little Joe), Dianne Wiest (Aunt Bea).

1 *Mother*: Pay more attention to your school work and less to the radio.
Little Joe: You always listen to the radio.
Mother: It's different. Our lives are ruined already. You still have a chance to grow up and be somebody.

SOUNDTRACK.

2 *Mother (to Bea)*: I like to daydream, but I have my two feet firmly planted on my husband.

SOUNDTRACK.

3 *Narrator*: I never forgot that New Year's Eve, when Aunt Bea awakened me to watch 1944 come in. And I've never forgotten any of those people, or any of the voices we used to hear on the radio. Although the truth is, with the passing of each New Year's Eve, those voices do seem to grow dimmer and dimmer.

SOUNDTRACK. Last lines of film.

RAGING BULL

US 1980; screenwriters: Paul Schrader, Mardik Martin; cast: Robert de Niro (Jake LaMotta), Joe Pesci (Joey).

4 *La Motta (to himself in nightclub dressing room)*:
I know I'm no Olivier
But if he fought Sugar Ray
He would say
That the thing ain't the ring
It's the play.
So give me a stage
Where this bull here can rage
And though I can fight
I'd much rather hear myself recite
That's entertainment!

SOUNDTRACK.

1 *LaMotta (to nightclub audience)*: It's a thrill to be standing before you wonderful people tonight – well, in fact, it's a thrill to be standing.

SOUNDTRACK.

2 *Joey (to LaMotta, about throwing a fight)*: Gave me the old good news/bad news routine. The good news is you're gonna get the shot at the title. The bad news is they want you to do the old flip-flop for 'em.

SOUNDTRACK.

3 *LaMotta (to mirror, before nightclub appearance)*: Go get 'em, champ … I'm the boss, I'm the boss, I'm the boss, I'm the boss … boss, boss, boss, boss, boss, boss.

SOUNDTRACK. Last words of film.

Claude RAINS

British-born actor (1889–1967)

4 [during the filming of Shaw's *Caesar and Cleopatra* in the early 1940s, becoming exasperated by the author's frequent interruptions] If you're not very careful, Mr Shaw, I shall play this part as you want it.

QUOTED by Kenneth Williams on BBC Radio *Quote...Unquote* (19 February 1979).

RAMBO: FIRST BLOOD PART TWO

US 1985; screenwriters: Sylvester Stallone, James Cameron; cast: Sylvester Stallone (John Rambo), Richard Crenna (Major Trautman).

5 *Rambo (to Trautman, his former commander)*: Sir, do we get to win this time?

Trautman: This time it's up to you.

SOUNDTRACK. Rambo is a hunk bringing home American prisoners left behind in the Vietnam War. The terms 'Ramboesque', 'Rambo-like' and 'Ramboism' were rapidly adopted for mindless, forceful heroics. President Reagan quoted the line 'Do we get to win this time?' in a speech (undated) in all seriousness, but did have the grace to credit it for once rather than pass it off as one of his own.

6 *Rambo*: To survive a war, you've got to become a war.

SOUNDTRACK.

7 Rambo isn't violent. I see Rambo as a philanthropist.

COMMENT by Sylvester Stallone, quoted in *Today* (27 May 1988).

Nicholas RAY

American director (1911–79)

1 [on the movies] The biggest, most expensive electric-train set anyone could be given.

ATTRIBUTED in Penelope Houston, *Contemporary Cinema* (1963). *Compare* Orson **WELLES** 443:2.

The RAZOR'S EDGE

US 1946; screenwriter: Lamarr Trotti (from W. Somerset Maugham novel); cast: Clifton Webb (Elliott Templeton).

2 *Elliott*: The enjoyment of art is the only remaining ecstasy that's neither immoral nor illegal.

SOUNDTRACK.

3 *Elliott*: If I live to be a hundred, I shall never understand how any young man can come to Paris without evening clothes.

SOUNDTRACK.

REACH FOR THE SKY

UK 1956; screenwriter/director: Lewis Gilbert (from Paul Brickhill book); cast: Kenneth More (Douglas Bader), Michael Warre (Harry Day).

4 *Harry Day (as supervising officer, to Bader)*: You know my views of some regulations. They're written for the obedience of fools and the guidance of wise men.

SOUNDTRACK. Bader indicates in his reply that this is something Day is always saying, but it is not clear where it comes from. Day was an actual person, and in Brickhill's biography of Bader, Day makes the observation when Bader's squadron is in training for the team aerobatics display in the annual Hendon air show. Day was acting squadron commander. Compare what is attributed to General Douglas MacArthur: 'Rules are mostly made to be broken and are too often for the lazy to hide behind' – quoted in William A. Ganoe, *MacArthur Close-Up* (1962).

Ronald REAGAN

American actor and Republican President (1911–)

5 Learn your lines, don't bump into the furniture – and in kissing scenes, keep your mouth closed.

QUOTED in *Time* Magazine (16 June 1986). *Compare* Spencer **TRACY** 428:5.

6 To grasp and hold a vision, that is the very essence of successful leadership – not only on the movie set where I learned it, but everywhere.

ATTRIBUTED remark, in *The Wilson Quarterly* (Winter 1994).

1 I have a strange feeling that he will wake up one day and ask, 'What movie am I in?'

COMMENT by Sheilah Graham in *The Times* (22 August 1981).

2 What's really worrying about Reagan is that he always seems to be waiting for someone to say 'CUT' and has no idea how they've decided the script should end.

COMMENT by Katharine Whitehorn in *The Observer* (4 December 1982).

3 California's power to cloud men's minds must never be forgot. Under its spell we submitted for eight years to the governance of Ronald Reagan, who had trouble distinguishing history from old movie plots.

COMMENT by Russell Baker in *The New York Times* (1 August 1995).

See also **STAR WARS** 397:1, 397:3; Jack L. **WARNER** 439:5.

REBECCA

US 1940; screenwriters: Robert E. Sherwood, Joan Harrison (from Daphne du Maurier novel); cast: Joan Fontaine (Mrs de Winter).

4 *Mrs de Winter (narrating)*: Last night, I dreamt I went to Manderley again. It seemed to me I stood by the iron gate leading to the drive, and for a while I could not enter, for the way was barred to me. Then like all dreamers, I was possessed of a sudden with supernatural powers and passed like a spirit through the barrier before me … And finally, there was Manderley – Manderley – secretive and silent. Time could not mar the perfect symmetry of those walls. Moonlight can play odd tricks upon the fancy and suddenly it seemed to me that light came from the windows. And then a cloud came upon the moon, and hovered an instant like a dark hand before a face.

SOUNDTRACK. Opening of the film, an edited version of the first short chapter in the novel.

RED DUST

US 1932; screenwriter: John Mahin (from play by Wilson Collison); cast: Jean Harlow (Vantine), Clark Gable (Dennis Carson).

5 He treated her rough – and she loved it!

SLOGAN.

6 *Vantine (on the climate making sleep difficult)*: Guess I'm not used to sleeping nights anyway.

SOUNDTRACK.

1 *Vantine (to Dennis)*: So long, it's been nice having you.

SOUNDTRACK.

RED RIVER

US 1948; screenwriters: Borden Chase (from his novel), Charles Schnee; cast: John Wayne (Tom Dunson); Montgomery Clift (Matthew Garth).

2 *Dunson (to Garth)*: Take 'em to Missouri, Matt.

SOUNDTRACK.

The RED SHOES

UK 1948; screenwriters/directors: Michael Powell, Emeric Pressburger; cast: Moira Shearer (Victoria Page).

3 *Victoria (dying after her red shoes have made her unable to stop dancing)*: Take off the red shoes.

SOUNDTRACK. Last line of film.

Robert REDFORD

American actor and director (1937–)

4 I often feel I'll opt out of this rat-race and buy another hunk of Utah.

ATTRIBUTED remark.

5 Robert Redford's the very best kisser I ever met.

COMMENT by Meryl Streep.

Vanessa REDGRAVE

English actress (1937–)

6 I give myself to my parts as to a lover.

ATTRIBUTED remark.

7 I choose all my roles very carefully so that when my career is finished I will have covered all our recent history of oppression.

ATTRIBUTED remark.

Rex REED

American journalist and critic (1938–)

8 Cannes [Film Festival] is where you lie on the beach and stare at the stars – or vice versa.

QUOTED in *Playboy* Magazine (in about 1980).

1 In Hollywood, if you don't have happiness you send out for it.

QUOTED in J.R. Colombo, *Wit and Wisdom of the Moviemakers* (1979).

Christopher REEVE

American actor (1952–)

2 The thought that keeps going through your mind is, 'This can't be my life. There's been a mistake.'

QUOTED in *The Observer*, 'Soundbites' (25 August 1996). This was after he had been paralysed in a riding accident.

REFLECTIONS IN A GOLDEN EYE

US 1967; screenwriters: Chapman Mortimer, Gladys Hill (from Carson McCullers novella); cast: Elizabeth Taylor (Leonora Penderton), Brian Keith (Morris Langdon).

3 *Leonora (to Morris, about his wife)*: She cut off her nipples with garden shears. You call that normal?

SOUNDTRACK.

The REMAINS OF THE DAY

UK/US 1993; screenwriter: Ruth Prawer Jhabvala (from Kazuo Ishiguro novel); cast: Anthony Hopkins (Stevens), Christopher Reeve (Lewis).

4 *Stevens (to Lewis who has asked his opinion of the political situation)*: I'm sorry, sir, I was too busy serving to listen to the speeches.

SOUNDTRACK.

Jean RENOIR

French director (1894–1979)

5 [on leaving Hollywood] Goodbye Mr Zanuck. It certainly has been a pleasure working for 16th Century Fox.

ATTRIBUTED remark.

6 [on the shape of the CinemaScope screen] Our contemporaries see things horizontally; the previous generation saw things vertically.

QUOTED in Penelope Houston, *Contemporary Cinema* (1963).

7 A film director is not a creator, but a midwife. His business is to deliver the actor of a child that he did not know he had inside him.

EXTRACTED from his book *My Life and My Films* (1974).

8 Renoir has a lot of talent, but he isn't one of us.

COMMENT by Darryl F. Zanuck.

RESERVOIR DOGS

US 1991; screenwriter/director: Quentin Tarantino; cast: Steve Buscemi (Mr Pink)

1 Reservoir Dogs.

TITLE OF FILM. One theory is that it derives from Tarantino's inability to pronounce the title of the French film *Au Revoir les Enfants* when working as a clerk in a video store …

2 Let's go to work.

SLOGAN. Created for the UK advertising campaign and then exported to other territories when the film was relaunched. The UK version became the new standard international campaign, replacing the earlier flopped campaign (information: Christopher Fowler, the Creative Partnership).

3 *Mr Pink (in restaurant)*: I don't tip.

SOUNDTRACK.

4 *Mr Pink (objecting to his alias)*: Why can't we pick our own colours?

SOUNDTRACK.

See also Quentin **TARANTINO** 405:4.

The RETURN OF SHERLOCK HOLMES

US 1929; screenwriter/director: Basil Dean (after Conan Doyle novel); cast: Clive Brook (Sherlock Holmes); H. Reeves-Smith (Watson).

5 *Watson*: Amazing, Holmes!
Holmes: Elementary, my dear Watson, elementary.

SOUNDTRACK. Final lines of dialogue in the first Holmes film with sound. Helped popularize but did not coin the catchphrase that otherwise does not appear in Conan Doyle's stories.

Burt REYNOLDS

American actor (1936–)

6 Actors marrying actors play a dangerous game. They're always fighting over the mirror.

QUOTED in *Sunday Today*, 'Quotes of the Week' (24 May 1987).

7 I haven't had a hit film since Joan Collins was a virgin.

QUOTED in *The Observer*, 'Sayings of the Week' (27 March 1988).

8 I've shaved off my moustache and people say I look a whole two days younger.

QUOTED in *The Independent* (10 July 1993).

Debbie REYNOLDS

American actress (1932–)

1 [as Academy Awards presenter, using teleprompter] Now to the teleprompter: 'The precious gift of laughter film comedy provides ... ' Who wrote this drivel?

REMARK at Academy Awards ceremony (March 1997).

See also Jerry **LEWIS** 254:2.

RICHARD III

UK 1955; screenwriter: Laurence Olivier (director), Alan Dent (from Shakespeare's play, with additions); cast: Laurence Olivier (Richard).

2 *Richard*: Why, I can smile; and murder while I smile;
And wet my cheeks with artificial tears
And frame my face to all occasions!

SOUNDTRACK. These lines come not from Shakespeare's *Richard III* but from his *Henry VI, Part 3* and are bolted on to 'Now is the winter of our discontent' along with other material to make it a more substantial soliloquy. The lines were also incorporated in Ian McKellen's film of *Richard III* (UK 1995), for which the first was used as a promotional slogan on posters, in the form, 'I can smile ... and murder while I smile.'

3 *Richard*: Off with his head – so much for Buckingham.

SOUNDTRACK. In his 1700 edition of Shakespeare's *Richard III*, Colly Cibber added the four last words after 'off with his head'. It proved a popular and lasting emendation. However, when Shakespeare uses the original phrase, Richard of Gloucester is speaking about Hastings. This was one of the many Cibber and Garrick interpolations included in Olivier's film.

4 *Richard*: Conscience avaunt, Richard's himself again:
Hark! the shrill trumpet sounds, to horse, away,
My soul's in arms, and eager for the fray.

SOUNDTRACK. Another of Cibber's interpolations adopted by Olivier.

Tony RICHARDSON

English director (1928–91)

5 [on Britain] People in this country haven't got the cinema in their blood – the real creative talent has been drained off into theatre.

QUOTED in the *Monthly Film Bulletin* (April 1993).

Leni RIEFENSTAHL

German documentary director (1902–)

1 I filmed the truth as it was then. Nothing more.

REMARK quoted in J.R. Colombo, *Wit and Wisdom of the Moviemakers* (1979).

The RIVER

India 1951; screenwriters: Jean Renoir, Rumer Godden (from her novel).

2 The river runs, the round world spins,
Dawn and lamplight, midnight, noon.
Sun follows day, night stars and moon.
The day ends, the world begins.

SOUNDTRACK.

ROAD TO MOROCCO

US 1942; music/lyrics: Jimmy van Heusen, Johnny Burke; cast: Bob Hope (Turkey Jackson), Bing Crosby (Jeff Peters).

3 *Turkey (on seeing desert)*: This must be the place where they empty all the old hourglasses.

SOUNDTRACK.

4 Like Webster's Dictionary
We're Morocco bound.

SOUNDTRACK. Song, 'Road to Morocco'.

5 *Camel (addressing camera)*: This is the screwiest picture I was ever in.

SOUNDTRACK.

Julia ROBERTS

American actress (1967–)

6 I hate love scenes in which the woman's naked and the man's wearing a three-piece suit. I mean, fair's fair.

QUOTED in *The Independent* (28 December 1991).

7 I've never discussed this before, but as a child I used to bite my toenails off instead of clipping them. I was very limber.

QUOTED in *The Observer* (30 May 1999).

8 I live a privileged life – hugely privileged. I'm rich. I'm happy. I have a great job. It would be absurd to pretend that it's anything different. I'm like a pig in shit.

QUOTED in *The Observer* (13 June 1999).

ROBIN HOOD: PRINCE OF THIEVES

US 1991; screenwriters: Pen Densham, John Watson; cast: Alan Rickman (Sheriff of Nottingham), Morgan Freeman (Azeem), Kevin Costner (Robin Hood), Nick Brible (Little John), Mary Elizabeth Mastrantonio (Maid Marian).

1 *Sheriff*: Cancel the kitchen scraps for lepers and orphans. No more merciful beheadings. And call off Christmas.

SOUNDTRACK.

2 *Maid Marian (to Robin)*: Men speak conveniently of love when it serves their purpose. And when it doesn't, 'tis a burden to them. Robin of the Hood, prince of thieves – is he capable of love?

SOUNDTRACK.

ROBOCOP

US 1987; screenwriters: Edward Neumeier, Michael Miner; cast: Peter Weller (Robocop), Nancy Allen (Anne Lewis).

3 *Robocop (to thief)*: Thank you for your cooperation.

SOUNDTRACK.

4 *Robocop (to Lewis)*: I have to go. Somewhere there is a crime happening.

SOUNDTRACK.

The ROCKY HORROR PICTURE SHOW

UK 1975; screenwriter: Richard O'Brien (based on his musical), Jim Sharman (director); cast: Charles Gray (Criminologist), Tim Curry (Frank N. Furter), Barry Bostwick (Brad Majors), Susan Sarandon (Janet Weiss), Meat Loaf (Eddie), Peter Hinwood (Rocky).

5 *Criminologist*: I would like, if I may, to take you on a strange journey … It was a night out they [Brad and Janet] were going to remember for a very long time.

SOUNDTRACK.

6 *Frank (to Brad and Janet after having them stripped)*: And what charming underclothes you both have.

SOUNDTRACK.

7 *Frank (having just killed Eddie)*: He had a certain naive charm, but no muscle.

SOUNDTRACK.

8 *Frank (to Janet and Rocky when finding them in bed together)*: Excellent. Under the circumstances, formal dress is to be optional.

SOUNDTRACK.

Pascal ROGARD

French producer

1 French films are the cinema of creation. American films are products of marketing.

QUOTED in *The Observer*, 'Sayings of the Week' (28 November 1993).

Will ROGERS

American actor and humorist (1879–1935)

2 There is only one thing that can kill the Movies, and that is education.

EXTRACTED from *The Autobiography of Will Rogers*, Chap. 6 (1949).

3 I am sorry somebody referred to Movies as an art ... For since then everybody connected with them stopped doing something to make them better and they commenced getting worse.

QUOTED in Donald Day, *Will Rogers: A Biography*, Chap. 21 (1962).

4 The movies are the only business where you can go out front and applaud yourself.

QUOTED in Leslie Halliwell, *The Filmgoer's Book of Quotes* (1973).

The ROMAN SPRING OF MRS STONE

US 1961: screenwriters: Gavin Lambert, Jan Read (from Tennessee Williams novel); cast: Vivien Leigh (Karen Stone), Lotte Lenya (Contessa Gonzales).

5 *Karen Stone (to Contessa Gonzales)*: People who are very beautiful make their own laws.

SOUNDTRACK.

La RONDE

France 1950; screenwriters: Jacques Natanson, Max Ophüls (director) (after Arthur Schnitzler's *Reigen*); cast: Anton Walbrook (Destiny, Master of Ceremonies).

6 *Master of Ceremonies*: La Ronde? ... And me, what am I in this little story? ... The author? ... The master of ceremonies? ... A passer-by? ... Let us say I am one of you. I am the incarnation of your desire ... your desire to know everything.

SOUNDTRACK.

ROOM AT THE TOP

UK 1958; screenwriter: Neil Paterson (from novel by John Braine); cast: Laurence Harvey (Joe Lampton), Simone Signoret (Alice Aisgill), Heather Sears (Susan Brown), Ambrosine Phillpotts (Mrs Brown).

1 A savage story of lust and ambition.

SLOGAN.

2 *Joe (to Alice)*: Let me tell you, I am working class … working class and proud of it.

SOUNDTRACK.

3 *Joe (to Alice)*: You know what Joe wants. It's what all the Joes want.

SOUNDTRACK.

4 *Mrs Brown*: We've decided on a white wedding, in spite of all the circumstances.

SOUNDTRACK.

5 *Susan*: Joe, wasn't it absolutely the most wonderful wedding? Now we *really* belong to each other, till death us do part. Darling, you're crying. I believe you really are sentimental, after all.

SOUNDTRACK. Last lines of film.

6 Certainly, *Room at the Top* was the first British film in which a man and woman went to bed without one of them having one foot on the floor.

COMMENT by Laurence Harvey, interviewed in *Premiere* (UK 1970).

Mickey ROONEY

American actor (1920–)

7 Had I been brighter, had the gods been kinder, had the dice been hotter, this could have been a one-sentence story: Once upon a time Mickey Rooney lived happily ever after.

EXTRACTED from *I.E. An Autobiography*, Chap. 1 (1965). The blurb to a British edition (possibly using material from an earlier draft) inserts the words 'had the ladies been gentler, had the Scotch been weaker' after 'Had I been brighter'.

8 His favourite exercise is climbing tall people.

COMMENT by Phyllis Diller.

9 Tennessee Williams once told me that he considered Rooney the best actor in the history of the movies.

COMMENT reported by Gore Vidal.

ROPE

US 1948; screenwriters: Arthur Laurents, Hume Cronym, Ben Hecht (from Patrick Hamilton play); cast: John Dall (Shaw Brandon), James Stewart (Rupert Cadell), Farley Granger (Philip).

1 *Brandon (after murder)*: A lovely evening! Pity we couldn't have done it with the curtains open, in bright sunlight.
SOUNDTRACK.

2 *Brandon (to Philip)*: An immaculate murder. We've killed for the sake of danger and for the sake of killing.
SOUNDTRACK.

3 *Brandon*: Nobody commits a murder just for the experiment of committing it. Nobody except us.
SOUNDTRACK.

4 *Philip*: How did you feel?
Brandon: When?
Philip: During it.
Brandon: I felt tremendously exhilarated.
SOUNDTRACK.

5 *Philip*: Brandon, you don't think the party is a mistake, do you? …
Brandon (to Philip): The party … it's the signature of the artist.
SOUNDTRACK.

6 *Brandon*: Being weak is a mistake.
Philip: Because it's being human?
Brandon: Because it's being ordinary.
SOUNDTRACK.

7 *Cadell*: Murder is – or should be – an art … and as such, the privilege of committing it should be reserved for those few who are really superior individuals?
Brandon: And the victims – inferior beings whose lives are unimportant anyway!
Cadell: Obviously!
SOUNDTRACK.

8 *Brandon*: Good and evil, right and wrong, were invented for the ordinary, average man, the inferior man, because he needs them.
SOUNDTRACK.

9 *Cadell (to Brandon and Philip)*: There must have been something deep inside you from the very start that would let you do this thing …

By what right did you dare decide that that boy in there was inferior and therefore could be killed?

SOUNDTRACK.

Bernard ROSE

English director and screenwriter

1 A film is only truly called British if it's dull.

QUOTED in *The Observer*, 'Sayings of the Week' (4 June 1987).

ROSEMARY'S BABY

US 1968; screenwriter/director: Roman Polanski (from Ira Levin novel); cast: Mia Farrow (Rosemary Woodhouse).

2 Pray for Rosemary's Baby.

SLOGAN.

3 *Rosemary (as she is raped by the Devil in her sleep)*: This isn't a dream, this is really happening.

SOUNDTRACK.

Talbot ROTHWELL

English screenwriter (1916–74)

4 [explaining his writing method for the *Carry On* films] I try very hard, first of all, to write a story which if it was made as a straight film would stand up – in other words, it has all the dramatic clichés … Having got all that, I then say, now, instead of having (shall we say) Jack Hawkins playing the British Ambassador, [we'll have] Sid James playing the British Ambassador. And then it all starts to become funny.

INTERVIEWED by Nigel Rees on BBC Radio *Movie-Go-Round* (16 March 1969).

See also ***CARRY ON CAMPING***; ***CARRY ON CLEO***.

Richard ROWLAND

American studio executive (?1881–1947)

5 The lunatics have taken over the asylum.

QUOTED in Terry Ramsaye, *A Million and One Nights* (1926). Attributed remark when the United Artists film company was established in 1919 by Charles Chaplin, Mary Pickford, Douglas Fairbanks and D.W. Griffith, to exploit their own talent. Rowland was one of their erstwhile employers at Metro. Also attributed to

Laurence Stallings, American writer (1894–1968) in the form 'Hollywood – a place where the inmates are in charge of the asylum' in Laurence J. Peter, *Quotations for Our Time* (1977). Also attributed to Robert Lord, American writer and producer (1900–76), who also supposedly said it in 1919.

ROXIE HART

US 1942; screenwriter: Nunnally Johnson (from a play *Chicago* by Maurine Watkins).

1 Dedication: To all the beautiful women in the world who have shot their husbands full of holes out of pique.

SCREEN TITLE.

The RULING CLASS

UK 1972; screenwriter: Peter Barnes (from his play); cast: Peter O'Toole (Jack).

2 *Jack (on how he knows he is God)*: When I pray to him, I find I'm talking to myself.

SOUNDTRACK.

Ken RUSSELL

English director (1927–)

3 I know my films upset people. I *want* to upset people.

ATTRIBUTED remark.

4 Mr Ken Russell, the film director who now specializes in vulgar travesties of the lives of dead composers.

COMMENT by Nicholas de Jongh in *The Guardian*, quoted in Leslie Halliwell, *The Filmgoer's Book of Quotes* (1978 edn).

Meg RYAN

American actress (1962–)

5 [on not stripping for camera] Words can be sexy and eyes can be sexy. I don't think you need to see naked bodies writhing around all the time.

QUOTED in *The Independent* (2 December 1995).

SABRINA

(also known as *Sabrina Fair* in the UK) US 1954; screenwriters: Billy Wilder, Samuel Taylor (from his play *Sabrina Fair*), Ernest Lehman.

1 Sabrina.

TITLE OF FILM. Why was the film given the more allusive title in the UK? This could have been because the distributors thought that British cinema-goers would relish an allusion to the poetic name for the river Severn, as applied to the nymph in Milton's masque *Comus*. On the other hand, might the distributors have been sending them a message that the film had nothing at all to do with Sabrina, a busty (41-18-36) model, who featured on TV shows with Arthur Askey, the comedian, in the 1950s? Alas, this second theory does not fit, as Norma Sykes (her real name) did not start appearing until 1956 and, in fact, actually took her stage name from the title of the film. So, it must have been the allusion to Milton after all.

Mort SAHL

American satirist (1926–)

2 [during a viewing of the lengthy film *Exodus* (US, 1960)] Let my people go!

QUOTED on his record album 'The New Frontier' (1961). Another version is that Sahl, invited by the director, Otto Preminger, to a preview, stood up after three hours and said, 'Otto – let my people go.'

Adela Rogers ST JOHNS

American screenwriter and journalist (1894–1988)

3 The motion picture is the people's art.

EXTRACTED from her book *Love, Laughter and Tears* (1978).

Harry SALTZMAN

American producer (1915–94)

4 [when Ken Russell said he would like to make a film on Tchaikovsky] You can't do Tchaikovsky ... Dimitri Tiomkin's gonna do that, *and he's already writing the music.*

REMARK quoted in John Baxter, *An Appalling Talent* (1973).

SAMSON AND DELILAH

US 1949; screenwriters: Jesse L. Lasky Jr, Fredric M. Frank; cast: Victor Mature (Samson), Hedy Lamarr (Delilah), Henry Wilcoxon (Ahtur), Angela Lansbury (Semadar), George Sanders (The Saran of Gaza), Olive Deering (Miriam), Russell Tamblyn (Saul).

1 *Samson's mother (to him on his rejection of Miriam)*: Oh, Samson, Samson, you're blind.

SOUNDTRACK.

2 *Delilah (handing him spear to kill lion as Philistines approach)*: Here – kill him before they get here.
Samson (refusing spear): I won't need that. He's a *young* lion.

SOUNDTRACK.

3 *Samson (to Ahtur, who has answered his riddle by conniving with Samson's wife, Semadar)*: If you had not ploughed with my heifer, you would not have answered my riddle.

SOUNDTRACK. A direct quote from Judges 14:18.

4 *The Saran (Philistine leader, to Ahtur)*: Like all soldiers, when you fail by the sword, you ask for more swords.

SOUNDTRACK.

5 *The Saran*: Delilah, what a dimpled dragon you can be, flashing fire and smoke.

SOUNDTRACK.

6 *Samson (to Delilah, who is trying to lure him into the hands of his Philistine enemies)*: The oldest trick in the world – a silk trap baited with a woman.

SOUNDTRACK.

7 *Samson (to Delilah)*: You daughter of hell!

SOUNDTRACK.

8 *Delilah (to Samson)*: Your power is in your hair. What a beautiful power it is. Look how it curls around my finger, black as a raven's wing, as wild as a storm.

SOUNDTRACK.

9 *Lecherous Philistine*: If you still have the same shears, Delilah, my hair's rather long.

SOUNDTRACK.

1 *The Saran*: No man alive could resist you, Delilah, but only a fool would trust you.

SOUNDTRACK.

2 *Miriam*: His strength will never die, Saul. Men will tell his story for a thousand years.

SOUNDTRACK. Last line of film.

George SANDERS

English actor (1906–72)

3 Dear World, I am leaving because I am bored. I feel I have lived long enough. I am leaving you with your worries in this sweet cesspool. Good luck.

ATTRIBUTED remark, in suicide note.

4 [of her former husband] We were both in love with George Sanders.

COMMENT by Zsa Zsa Gabor, quoted in J.R. Colombo, *Wit and Wisdom of the Moviemakers* (1979).

Susan SARANDON

American actress (1946–)

5 Do you really have to be the ice queen intellectual or the slut whore? Isn't there some way to be both?

QUOTED in *The Observer*, 'Sayings of the Week' (14 July 1991).

Victor SAVILLE

English director (1897–1979)

6 She [Jessie Matthews] had a heart. It photographed.

QUOTED in her obituary in *The Guardian* (21 August 1981). Saville directed Matthews in *Evergreen* (1934) and other films.

SCARFACE

US 1983; screenwriter: Oliver Stone; cast: Al Pacino (Tony Montana), Steven Bauer (Manny Ray), Michelle Pfeiffer (Elvira).

7 *Tony (wielding massive machine gun)*: Say hello to my little friend!

SOUNDTRACK.

James SCHAMUS

American screenwriter and producer

1 The budget *is* the aesthetic.

QUOTED in *The Observer*, 'Sayings of the Week' (6 October 1991).

Jerry SCHATZBERG

American director (1927–)

2 One is never an ex-photographer; it's like being an ex-alcoholic.

QUOTED in *The Observer*, 'Sayings of the Week' (1 July 1990).

SCHINDLER'S LIST

US 1993; screenwriter: Steve Zaillian (from Thomas Keneally novel); cast: Ben Kingsley (Itzhak Stern), Liam Neeson (Oskar Schindler).

3 *Stern (to Schindler, on engraving in gold ring)*: It's Hebrew, from the Talmud. It says, 'Whoever saves one life saves the world entire.'

SOUNDTRACK. The quotation was also used as a slogan to promote the film.

4 *Schindler (on not saving more lives)*: I could have got one more person, but I didn't.

SOUNDTRACK.

Arnold SCHOENBERG

Austrian-born American composer (1874–1951)

5 [A young man] had been assigned to write some music for an airplane sequence and was not sure how he should go about it. He posed the problem to Schoenberg, who thought for a moment and then said, 'Airplane music? Just like music for big bees, but louder.'

QUOTED in Oscar Levant, *A Smattering of Ignorance* (1940).

Arnold SCHWARZENEGGER

Austrian-born American body-builder and actor (1947–)

6 There are some girls who are turned on by my body and some others who are turned off. But for the majority I just use it as a conversation piece. Like someone walking a cheetah down Forty-Second Street would have a natural conversation piece.

REMARK quoted in Barbara Rowes, *The Book of Quotes* (1979).

7 [on his body] A condom full of walnuts.

COMMENT attributed to Clive James.

George C. SCOTT

American actor (1927–99)

1 It's just a meat parade in front of an international television audience – degrading to have actors in competition with each other.

QUOTED in the *Evening Standard* (London) (9 February 1971). Scott had just declined to accept his Best Actor award for *Patton* at the Oscars.

2 Actors are the world's oldest, underprivileged minority – looked upon as nothing but buffoons, one step above thieves and charlatans. These award ceremonies simply compound the image for me.

QUOTED in *Time* Magazine (22 March 1971).

3 I mean, don't you think it's a pretty spooky way to earn a living?

QUOTED in J.R. Colombo, *Wit and Wisdom of the Moviemakers* (1979).

4 The essence of art should be life and change – and that can't be where films are concerned. The film freezes your art for forever. No matter how much better you become, there is no way to improve the performance you've done for the camera. It's locked. And there's a certain sad death in that.

QUOTED in the above book.

5 After a while the pleasure stops but the self-contempt stays.

QUOTED in the above book.

6 I really wanted [an Oscar for *Anatomy of a Murder*]. I became anxious and I didn't like that in myself. I said: 'I'm never going to allow myself to be put in that position again, of wanting something just for what it is.' Once I got the nomination [for *Patton*] I made it perfectly clear should I win, I would not accept it. I didn't do what Marlon did. I didn't wait until I won the fucking thing and tell them to jam it up their ass – which I think is rude.

INTERVIEWED in *Playboy* (December 1980).

7 With that long fleshy nose, penetrating stare, chilly smile and gravelly voice, he had the menacing presence of an unexploded bomb.

COMMENT by Philip French in *The Observer* (26 September 1999).

See also Bette **DAVIS** 125:3.

SCREEN TITLES

Including captions, credits, inter-titles, opening titles, sub-titles, title cards and translation sub-titles. *See also* under individual films.

1 By William Shakespeare with additional dialogue by Sam Taylor.

Writing credit caption for *The Taming of the Shrew* (US 1929). Sometimes erroneously quoted as 'with additional dialogue by William Shakespeare'. Taylor was the director.

2 Came the Dawn.

Said by C.A. Lejeune to have been one of the screen title captions illustrated by Alfred Hitchcock in his early days in the cinema. This is confirmed in François Truffaut, *Hitchcock* (English version, 1968) in which Hitchcock refers to it as 'narrative title'. He also mentions the common: 'The next morning …'. Quoted as 'Comes the Dawn' in Stuart Berg Flexner, *Listening to America* (1982).

3 Harness my zebras.

Jacqueline Logan playing Mary Magdalene 'said' this in Cecil B. DeMille's *King of Kings* (1925). Quoted in Stuart Berg Flexner, *Listening to America* (1982).

4 Heart spoke to heart in the hush of the evening.

Said by C.A. Lejeune to have been one of the sub-titles drawn by Alfred Hitchcock in his early days in the cinema.

5 If annoyed when here please tell the management.

Standard cinema announcement caption.

6 In darkest Africa.

Documentary title. Quoted in Stuart Berg Flexner, *Listening to America* (1982).

7 Kiss me, my fool.

A Fool There Was (US 1914). Theda Bara 'spoke' the inter-title (scattering rose petals over the body of a dead lover) and this was taken up as a fad expression. Quoted in Stuart Berg Flexner, *Listening to America* (1982). The film was based on a play (1906) and novel (1909) by Porter Emerson Browne, following a poem 'The Vampire' (1897) by Rudyard Kipling written to accompany a painting by Philip Burne-Jones. The poem includes the lines: 'A fool there was and he made his prayer / (Even as you and I!) / To a rag and a bone and hank of hair / (We called her the woman who did not care) / But the fool he called her his lady fair – / (Even as you and I!)' Alexander Walker in *The Celluloid Sacrifice* (1966) notes how the phrase 'became a camp password to the romantic flippancy of the young at the turn of the 1920s.'

8 Ladies and gentlemen may safely visit this theatre as no offensive films are ever shown here.

Standard cinema announcement caption.

9 Ladies we like your hats but please remove them.

Standard cinema awareness caption. Quoted in Stuart Berg Flexner, *Listening to America* (1982).

1 Meanwhile back at the ranch.

Quoted in Stuart Berg Flexner, *Listening to America* (1982). Perhaps also used in US radio horse operas.

2 One moment while the operator changes reels.

Standard cinema announcement caption. Quoted in Stuart Berg Flexner, *Listening to America* (1982).

3 Please read the titles to yourself. Loud reading annoys your neighbours.

Standard silent cinema announcement caption.

4 To be continued next week.

Standard cinema announcement caption at end of serials. Quoted in Stuart Berg Flexner, *Listening to America* (1982).

5 We aim to present the pinnacle of motion picture perfection.

Standard cinema announcement caption.

6 You would not spit on the floor at home. Do not do it here.

Standard cinema announcement caption. Quoted in Stuart Berg Flexner, *Listening to America* (1982).

Peter SELLERS

English actor (1925–80)

7 There used to be a me behind the mask, but I had it surgically removed.

ATTRIBUTED remark.

8 The only way to make a film with him is to let him direct, write and produce it as well as star in it.

COMMENT by Charles Feldman, quoted in Leslie Halliwell, *The Filmgoer's Book of Quotes* (1973).

David O. SELZNICK

American producer (1902–65)

9 [of his stars during the filming of *The Garden of Allah*] If they will only do their job … that is all that they are being overpaid for.

QUOTED in Maria Riva, *Marlene Dietrich* (1992).

10 I have no middle name … I had an uncle, whom I greatly disliked, who was also named David Selznick, so in order to avoid the growing confusion between the two of us, I decided to take a middle initial and went through the alphabet to find one that seemed to give me the best punctuation and decided on 'O'.

QUOTED in Rudy Behlmer, *Memo from David O. Selznick* (1973).

Mack SENNETT

Canadian-born producer (1880–1960)

1 The only thing he claims to have invented is the pie in the face, and he insists, 'Anyone who tells you he has discovered something new is a fool, or a liar or both.'

QUOTED in James Agee, *Agee on Film* (1958).

2 [defining a joke] An idea going in one direction meets an idea going in the opposite direction.

ATTRIBUTED remark, quoted in *The 'Quote … Unquote' Newsletter* (July 1994).

3 [summing up his comedy technique] It's got to *move*!

QUOTED in Leslie Halliwell, *The Filmgoer's Book of Quotes* (1973).

SERGEANT YORK

US 1941; screenwriters: Abem Finkel and others; cast: Gary Cooper (Sergeant Alvin C. York).

4 *York*: Folks back home used to say I could shoot a rifle before I was weaned. They was exaggerating some.

SOUNDTRACK.

Rod SERLING

American playwright and screenwriter (1924–75)

5 Every writer is a frustrated actor who recites his lines in the hidden auditorium of his skull.

REMARK quoted in *Vogue* (1 April 1957).

The SEVEN PER CENT SOLUTION

US 1977; screenwriter: Nicholas Meyer (from his novel); cast: Nicol Williamson (Sherlock Holmes), Alan Arkin (Sigmund Freud).

6 *Holmes*: I never guess. It is an appalling habit destructive to the logical faculty.

SOUNDTRACK.

7 *Holmes (to Freud)*: Elementary, my dear Freud.

SOUNDTRACK.

The SEVEN YEAR ITCH

US 1955; screenwriters: George Axelrod (from his play), Billy Wilder; cast: Tom Ewell (Richard Sherman), Marilyn Monroe (The Girl); Marguerite Chapman (Miss Morris).

1 The Seven Year Itch.

TITLE. Axelrod's play (1952) started the popularization of this term for the urge to be unfaithful to a spouse after a certain period of matrimony. *The Oxford English Dictionary* (2nd edition, 1989) provides various examples of this phrase going back from the mid-20th to the mid-19th century, but without the specific matrimonial context. For example, the 'seven-year itch' describes a rash from poison ivy that was believed to recur every year for a seven-year period. Then one has to recall that since biblical days seven-year periods (of lean or fat) have had especial significance, and there has also been the Army saying, 'Cheer up – the first seven years are the worst!'

'Itch' had long been used for the sexual urge and, as Axelrod commented on BBC Radio *Quote ... Unquote* (15 June 1979): 'There was a phrase which referred to a somewhat unpleasant disease but nobody had used it in a sexual [he meant 'matrimonial'] context before. I do believe I invented it in that sense.'

Oddly, there is no mention in reference books of 'itch' being used in connection with venereal diseases. Nonetheless, the following remark occurs in Robert Lewis Taylor, *W.C. Fields: His Follies and Fortunes* (published as early as 1950): 'Bill exchanged women every seven years, as some people get rid of the itch.'

2 *The Girl*: My fan's caught in the door.

SOUNDTRACK. In fact she is referring to an electric fan whose lead is shut in the door.

3 *Miss Morris (Richard's secretary, in fantasy sequence)*: I am in love with you, that's what's the matter with me ... deeply, madly, desperately, all consumingly.

SOUNDTRACK.

4 *Richard (to The Girl, in fantasy sequence)*: Now I am going to take you in my arms and kiss you very quickly and very hard ... *(suddenly realizing what he has said:)* This is terrible ... I am terribly sorry. Nothing like this ever happened to me before in all my life.
The Girl: Honest? It happens to me all the time.

SOUNDTRACK.

5 *The Girl (standing over subway grating)*: It sort of cools the ankles, doesn't it?

SOUNDTRACK.

The SEVENTH SEAL

Sweden 1956; screenwriter/director: Ingmar Bergman; cast: Max von Sydow (The Knight, Antonius Block); Bengt Ekerot (Death), Gunnar Björnstrand (The Squire, Jöns); Nils Poppe (Jof), Åke Fridell (The Smith, Plog), Bibi Andersson (Mia), Inga Landgre (The Knight's Wife, Karin).

1 The Seventh Seal.

TITLE OF FILM. From Revelation 8:1: 'And when he had opened the seventh seal, there was silence in heaven about the space of half an hour.' In the film, Karin reads this passage from the Bible.

2 *Block*: Who are you?
Death: I am Death.

SUB-TITLE translation.

3 *Block (facing death)*: Wait a moment.
Death: That's what they all say. I grant no reprieves.

SUB-TITLE translation.

4 *Jof (to Plog, who is plotting to kill the actor who ran away with his wife)*: The actor! Now I understand. There are too many of them, so even if he hasn't done anything in particular you ought to kill him merely because he's an actor.

SUB-TITLE translation.

5 *Death*: Don't you ever stop asking questions?
Block: No, I'll never stop.

SUB-TITLE translation.

6 *Jof (to his wife, Mia)*: I see them, Mia! I see them! Over there against the dark stormy sky. They are all there. The smith and Lisa and the knight and Raval and Jöns and Skat. And Death, the severe master, invites them to dance.

SUB-TITLE translation.

The SEVENTH VOYAGE OF SINBAD

US 1958; screenwriter: Kenneth Kolb; cast: Kerwin Matthews (Captain Sinbad), Torin Thatcher (Sokurah the Magician), Richard Eyer (Baronni).

7 *Sokurah the Magician (summoning genie)*: From the land beyond beyond, from the world past hope and fear, I bid you, genie, now appear.

SOUNDTRACK.

8 *Sinbad (when his crew kill a roc chick)*: Hungry men don't ask – they take.

SOUNDTRACK.

1 *Sinbad*: Well done, Baronni. I know you will be as good a sailor as you are a genie.
Baronni: I shall try, Captain. I shall try.

SOUNDTRACK. Last lines of film.

sex, lies, and videotape

US 1989; screenwriter/director: Steven Soderbergh; cast: Andie McDowell (Ann Millaney), James Spader (Graham Dalton).

2 sex, lies, and videotape.

TITLE OF FILM – that has appealed hugely to headline writers and others. From the *Sunday Telegraph* (29 March 1992): 'FURY AT "SEX, LIES AND STEREOTYPES": GAY PROTESTERS THREATEN TO DISRUPT OSCARS CEREMONY OVER NEW MOVIE'; title of TV programme about men prosecuted for having gay sex in privacy of own home (5 July 1998): *Sex, Guys and Videotape*; headline from *The Independent* (30 May 1998): 'Sex, lies and Louise Woodward's lawyer'; headline from *The Independent* (17 July 1998): 'Sickies, lies, videos and tapes' [about private eyes]; headline from *The Independent* (12 September 1998): 'Sex, lies and a cover-up: the case against William Jefferson Clinton'.

3 *Graham*: I think men get more and more in love with the person they're [fucking] and women get more and more attracted to the person they love.
Ann: That's beautiful.

SOUNDTRACK.

SHADOW OF A DOUBT

US 1943; screenwriters: Thornton Wilder, Sally Benson, Alma Reville; cast: Joseph Cotten (Uncle Charlie Oakley), Teresa Wright (Young Charlie Newton), Edwin Stanley (Mr Green).

4 *Uncle Charlie*: The cities are full of women, middle-aged widows, husbands dead, husbands who've spent their lives making fortunes and then they die and leave their money to their wives. Their silly wives. And what do the wives do, these useless women? You see them in the hotels, the best hotels, every day by the thousands, drinking the money, eating the money, losing the money at bridge, playing all day and all night, smelling of money … Horrible, faded, fat, greedy women …

SOUNDTRACK.

5 *Uncle Charlie (to Young Charlie)*: We're old friends. More than that. We're like twins. You said so yourself.

SOUNDTRACK.

SHADOWLANDS

UK 1993: screenwriter: William Nicholson (from his TV and stage play); cast: Anthony Hopkins (C.S. Lewis).

1 *Lewis*: Shadows ... It's one of my stories. We live in the shadowlands. The sun is always shining, somewhere else, round a bend in the road, over the brow of a hill.

SOUNDTRACK. What 'Shadowlands' refers to is not completely clear. The term first occurs in *The Last Battle* (1956), last of Lewis's 'Narnia' books. In the play/film, it seems to imply that where we are in this world is the shadowy place and that death is where the light is (and thus a preferable place to be). From the play (Act 1): 'For believe me, this world that seems to us so substantial, is no more than the shadowlands. Real life has not begun yet.'

SHAKESPEARE IN LOVE

US/UK 1998; screenwriters: Marc Norman, Tom Stoppard; cast: Joseph Fiennes (Will), Geoffrey Rush (Henslowe), Simon Day (First Boatman).

2 *Boatman (to Will, as they cross the Thames)*: I had that Christopher Marlowe in my boat once.

SOUNDTRACK.

3 *Will*: We are lost.
Henslowe: It will turn out well.
Will: How will it?
Henslowe: I don't know, it's a mystery,

SOUNDTRACK. On how the inexplicable occurs in the creation of the theatrical experience. 'It's a mystery' passes from character to character like a relay baton – most movingly, when Mark Williams, as Wabash the tailor-turned-player who acts the Prologue in *Romeo and Juliet*, overcomes his stutter to voice that play's opening lines.

4 I was covered in ink. Shakespeare must have been. Jesus! You have to resharpen your quill after a page of writing. Shakespeare must've gone through so many geese.

COMMENT by Joseph Fiennes, quoted in *The Independent* (30 January 1999).

SHAMPOO

US 1975; screenwriters: Robert Towne, Warren Beatty; cast: Warren Beatty (George Roundy), Julie Christie (Jackie Shawn).

5 *George (to Jackie)*: Want me to do your hair?

SOUNDTRACK.

SHANE

US 1953; screenwriters: A.B. Guthrie Jr, Jack Sher (from Jack Schaefer novel); cast: Alan Ladd (Shane), Brandon de Wilde (Joey Starrett), Van Heflin (Joe Starrett), Jean Arthur (Marian Starrett).

1 *Joey (on catching sight of Shane)*: Someone's coming, Pa.
Joe: Well, let him come.

SOUNDTRACK. Opening lines of film.

2 *Shane (introducing himself to Joe)*: Call me Shane.

SOUNDTRACK.

3 *Marian (to Shane and Joe, on going to face Ryker's men)*: This isn't worth a life, anybody's life. What are you fighting for? This shack, this little piece of ground, and nothing but work, work, work? I'm sick of it. I'm sick of trouble.

SOUNDTRACK.

4 *Shane (to Joey)*: A man has to be what he is, Joey. Can't break the mould. I tried it and it didn't work for me.

SOUNDTRACK.

5 *Joe*: I couldn't do what I gotta do if ... Joey, there's no living with a killing. There's no going back from it. Right or wrong, it's a brand, a brand that sticks. There's no going back.

SOUNDTRACK.

6 *Marian*: Shane did what he had to do.

SOUNDTRACK. Apocryphally 'A man's gotta do what man's gotta do' is spoken in this film. But no. Nor in the book. The preceding three lines are the nearest the film gets.

7 *Joey (as Shane rides off)*: Pa's got things for you to do, and Mother wants you. I know she does. Shane. Shane. Come back. 'Bye, Shane.

SOUNDTRACK. Last words of film.

SHANGHAI EXPRESS

US 1932; screenwriter: Jules Furthman; cast: Marlene Dietrich (Lily), Clive Brook (Capt. Donald Harvey).

8 *Lily (to Harvey)*: I changed my name .... No, it took more than one man to change my name to Shanghai Lily.

SOUNDTRACK. When asked if her name change is due to marriage.

Bernard SHAW

Irish playwright and critic (1856–1950)

1 [telegraphed version of the outcome of a conversation with Sam Goldwyn] The trouble, Mr Goldwyn, is that you are only interested in art and I am only interested in money.

QUOTED in Alva Johnson, *The Great Goldwyn* (1937). It has been said that this witticism was, in fact, the creation of Howard Dietz but that Shaw approved it.

2 [on the proposed presentation to him of an Academy Award] An insult! It's perfect nonsense. My position as a playwright is known throughout the world. To offer me an award of this sort is an insult ...

ATTRIBUTED remark, quoted by Stuart Berg Flexner in *Listening to America* (1982). Shaw was offered an award for Best Screenplay for his scenario of *Pygmalion* (1938).

3 *Alfred Hitchcock*: One look at you, Mr Shaw, and I know there's famine in the land.
Shaw: One look at you, Mr Hitchcock, and I know who caused it.

ATTRIBUTED exchange, quoted in Blanche Patch, *Thirty Years With GBS* (1951).

SHE DONE HIM WRONG

US 1933; screenwriter: Mae West (based on her play *Diamond Lil*, 1928); cast: Mae West (Lady Lou), Cary Grant (Capt. Cummings).

4 *Lady Lou*: When women go wrong, men go right after them.

SOUNDTRACK.

5 *Bystander (of Lady Lou)*: One of the finest women who ever walked the streets.

SOUNDTRACK.

6 *Lady Lou*: I wasn't always rich. No, there was a time I didn't know where my next husband was coming from.

SOUNDTRACK.

7 *Lady Lou*: Warm, dark and handsome.

SOUNDTRACK. A comment to the character Serge who has just kissed her on the hand. Obviously playing upon the established phrase 'tall, dark and handsome'. This description of a romantic hero's attributes (as likely to be found especially in women's fiction) had surfaced by 1906. Flexner, *I Hear America Talking* (1976) puts it in the late 1920s as a Hollywood term referring to Rudolph Valentino (though, in fact, he was not particularly tall). Sophie Tucker recorded a song called 'He's Tall, Dark and Handsome' (by Tobias & Sherman) in 1928. Cesar Romero played the lead in the 1941 film *Tall, Dark and Handsome*. However, in a piece called 'Loverboy of the Bourgeoisie' (collected in 1965), Tom Wolfe writes: 'It was Cary Grant that Mae

West was talking about when she launched the phrase "tall, dark and handsome" in *She Done Him Wrong* (1933).' This appears to be an inaccurate assumption.

1 *Lady Lou (to Cummings)*: You know I always did like a man in a uniform. And that one fits you grand. Why don't you come up some time and see me? I'm home every evening.

SOUNDTRACK. Cummings (a coy undercover policeman) declines the offer. As a catchphrase, the words have been rearranged into 'Come up and see me some time' to make them easier to say. And that is how W.C. Fields says them *to* Mae West in ***MY LITTLE CHICKADEE*** (1939). She herself also took to mouthing them in the easier-to-say form.

2 *Lady Lou*: The wolf at my door? Why, I remember when he came right into my room and had pups!

SOUNDTRACK.

3 *Lady Lou*: Is that a gun in your pocket or are you just glad to see me?

APOCRYPHAL. John P. Fennell, *Film Quotes* (1989) has this as said to 'Charles Osgood' in this film. But neither the line nor this name is to be found in the film. The line is quoted without naming a play or film in Joseph Weintraub, *Peel Me a Grape* (1975). Sometimes remembered as 'pistol' and also in connection with her play *Catherine Was Great* (1944) in the form: 'Lieutenant, is that your sword, or are you just glad to see me?' Leslie Halliwell in *The Filmgoer's Book of Quotes* (1978 edn, has this last as West's reaction in a Broadway costume play, when the romantic lead got his sword tangled in his braid so that it stuck up at an unfortunate angle. *Compare* ***MYRA BRECKINRIDGE*** 299:1.

SHE WORE A YELLOW RIBBON

US 1949; screenwriters: Frank S. Nugent, Laurence Stallings; cast: John Wayne (Capt. Nathan Brittles), Ben Johnson (Sergeant Tyree).

4 *Brittles*: Don't apologize. It's a sign of weakness.

SOUNDTRACK. Stock saying.

5 *Tyree*: Well, that ain't my department.

SOUNDTRACK. Stock disclaimer.

6 *Brittles*: The Army is always the same. The sun and the moon change, but the Army knows no seasons.

SOUNDTRACK.

Norma SHEARER

Canadian actress (1900–83)

7 A face unclouded by thought.

COMMENT by Lillian Hellman.

Charlie SHEEN

American actor (1965–)

1 Acting made the most sense because, Lord knows, you don't need much of an education to be an actor.

QUOTED in *The Observer*, 'Sayings of the Week' (5 January 1992).

Sam SHEPARD

American playwright and actor (1943–)

2 In this business we make movies, American movies. Leave the films to the French.

EXTRACTED from play *True West,* Act 2, Scene 5 (1980).

Cybill SHEPHERD

American actress (1950–)

3 A no-talent dame with nice boobs and a toothpaste smile and all the star quality of a dead hamster.

COMMENT by anonymous critic, quoted in Peter Biskind, *Easy Riders, Raging Bulls* (1998).

Louis SHERWIN

American screenwriter

4 [on leaving Hollywood, in about 1920] They know only one word of more than one syllable here, and that is *fillum*.

ATTRIBUTED remark, quoted in *H.L. Mencken's Dictionary of Quotations* (1942).

Brooke SHIELDS

American actress (1965–)

5 Smoking kills. If you're killed, you've lost a very important part of your life.

QUOTED in *The Observer*, 'Sayings of the Week' (5 April 1998).

6 The Russians love Brooke Shields because her eyebrows remind them of Leonid Brezhnev.

COMMENT by Robin Williams, quoted in Maria Leach, *The Ultimate Insult* (1996).

The SHINING

US 1980; screenwriters: Stanley Kubrick, Diane Johnson (from Stephen King novel); cast: Jack Nicholson (Jack Torrance), Shelley Duvall (Wendy Torrance).

1 *Jack*: Wendy, darling, light of my life. I'm not gonna hurt ya ... I'm just gonna bash your brains in.

SOUNDTRACK.

2 *Jack*: Here's Johnny!

SOUNDTRACK. A psychopath chops through a door with an axe and cries this when attempting to catch his wife. Originally, said with a drawn-out, rising inflection on the first word, this was Ed McMahon's introduction to Johnny Carson on NBC TV's *Tonight* show in the US (from 1961 until the early 1990s).

A SHOT IN THE DARK

US 1964; screenwriters: Blake Edwards, William Peter Blatty; cast: Elke Sommer (Maria Gambrelli), Peter Sellers (Inspector Clouseau).

3 *Maria (a maid, to Clouseau who has fallen into a fountain)*:
You should get out of these clothes immediately. You'll catch your death of pneumonia, you will.
Clouseau: Yes, I probably will. It's all part of life's rich pageant, you know.

SOUNDTRACK.

Don SIEGEL

American director (1912–91)

4 I once told Godard that he had something I wanted – freedom. He said: 'You have something I want – money.'

ATTRIBUTED remark.

5 Most of my pictures, I'm sorry to say, are about nothing. Because I'm a whore. I work for money. It's the American way.

ATTRIBUTED remark.

Simone SIGNORET

French actress (1921–85)

6 Age is not a friend of women, it is the enemy, but it can be a good ally of an actor.

QUOTED in *The Observer*, 'Sayings of the Week' (23 June 1985).

The SILENCE OF THE LAMBS

US 1991; screenwriter: Ted Tally (from Thomas Harris novel); cast: Anthony Hopkins (Dr Hannibal Lecter), Jodie Foster (Clarice Starling).

1 *Hannibal*: A census taker once tried to test me. I ate his liver with some fava beans and a nice chianti.

SOUNDTRACK.

2 *Hannibal (to Clarice, on phone)*: Have the lambs stopped screaming?

SOUNDTRACK. Referring to the female victims of a serial killer she has been pursuing.

3 *Hannibal (to Clarice, on phone)*: I do wish we could chat longer but I'm having an old friend for dinner.

SOUNDTRACK.

SILENT MOVIE

US 1976; screenwriters: Mel Brooks (director) and others; cast: Mel Brooks (Mel Funn), Marcel Marceau (as himself).

4 *Marceau (when asked to appear in Funn's silent movie)*: *Non!*

SOUNDTRACK. The only spoken line in the entire film – appropriately by a mime artist.

SILK STOCKINGS

US 1957; screenwriters: Leonard Gershe, Leonard Spigelgass (after stage musical and after screenplay **NINOTCHKA**); music/lyrics: Cole Porter; cast: Cyd Charisse (Ninotchka), Fred Astaire (Steve Canfield), George Tobias (Commisar Markovich), Janis Paige (Peggy Dainton).

5 *Markovich*: I want to look somebody up. Does this office have a copy of *Who's Still Who*?

SOUNDTRACK.

6 Paris Loves Lovers.

SOUNDTRACK. Title of song.

7 *Peggy Dainton*: Today to get the public to attend a picture show,
It's not enough to advertise a famous star they know …
You've got to have glorious Technicolor,
Breathtaking Cinemascope and
Stereophonic sound.

SOUNDTRACK. Song, 'Stereophonic Sound'.

8 *Ninotchka (to Steve)*: Where is the little comrade's room?

SOUNDTRACK.

1 *Ninotchka*: I have made a discovery: Champagne is more fun to drink than goat's milk.

SOUNDTRACK.

Joel SILVER

American producer (1939–)

2 I don't make art. I buy it.

QUOTED in *Vanity Fair* (August 1990).

SILVER STREAK

US 1976; screenwriter: Colin Higgins; cast: Jill Clayburgh (Hilly Burns), Gene Wilder (George Caldwell).

3 *Hilly (as secretary)*: I can't even read my own writing. I don't do shorthand and I can't type.
George: How do you keep your job?
Hilly: I give good phone.

SOUNDTRACK.

Neil SIMON

American playwright and screenwriter (1927–)

4 It was a cute picture. They used the basic story of *Wuthering Heights* and worked in surf-riders.

EXTRACTED from play *Last of the Red Hot Lovers* (1970).

SINGIN' IN THE RAIN

US 1952; screenwriters: Adolph Green, Betty Comden; cast: Gene Kelly (Don Lockwood), Jean Hagen (Lina Lamont), Donald O'Connor (Cosmo Brown), Debbie Reynolds (Kathy Selden), Millard Mitchell (R.F. Simpson).

5 *Lockwood (beginning to relate his life story)*: I've had one motto which I've always lived by: Dignity … always dignity. This was instilled in me by Mom and Dad from the very beginning.

SOUNDTRACK.

6 *Lockwood*: Well, we movie stars get the glory. I guess we have to take the little heartaches that go with it. People think we lead lives of glamour and romance, but we're really lonely – terribly lonely.

SOUNDTRACK.

7 *Lamont*: What's wrong with the way I talk? Am I dumb or something?

SOUNDTRACK. This becomes her stock phrase.

1 *Brown*: Now look at me, I got no glory, I got no fame, I got no big mansions, I got no money, but I've got – what have I got?

SOUNDTRACK.

2 *R.F. Simpson (studio chief)*: The Warner Brothers are making a whole talking picture with this gadget. *The Jazz Singer.* They'll lose their shirts.

SOUNDTRACK.

3 Make 'Em Laugh.

TITLE OF SONG. Written by Nacio Herb Brown and Arthur Freed (who earlier jointly wrote the song that inspired the picture and its title).

4 *Lockwood (on Lamont)*: I'd rather kiss a tarantula.

SOUNDTRACK.

5 *Brown (on loss of job)*: At last I can start suffering and write that symphony.

SOUNDTRACK.

6 *Lamont*: Why, I make more money than … than Calvin Coolidge put together.

SOUNDTRACK.

7 *Lamont*: People? I ain't people. I am a … 'a shimmering, glowing star in the cinema firmament.' It says so – right here.

SOUNDTRACK.

8 *Lamont*: If we bring a little joy into your humdrum lives, it makes us feel as though our hard work ain't been in vain for nothin'.

SOUNDTRACK.

SIROCCO

US 1951; screenwriters: A.I. Bezzerides, Hans Jacoby (from the novel Coup de Grâce by Joseph Kessel); cast: Humphrey Bogart (Harry Smith), Marta Toren (Violette).

9 *Violette (of Harry)*: How can a man so ugly be so handsome?

SOUNDTRACK.

SIX OF A KIND

US 1934; screenwriters: Walter de Leon, Harry Ruskin; cast: W.C. Fields (Sheriff Hoxley).

10 *Hoxley*: According to you, everything I like to do is either illegal, immoral or fattening.

SOUNDTRACK. *Compare* ***NEVER GIVE A SUCKER AN EVEN BREAK*** 301:2.

SLEEPER

US 1973; screenwriters: Woody Allen, Marshall Brickman; cast: Woody Allen (Miles Monroe), Diane Keaton (Luna Schlosser).

1 *Miles*: My brain is my second favourite organ.

SOUNDTRACK.

2 *Luna*: It's hard to believe that you haven't had sex for two hundred years.
Miles: Two hundred and four if you count my marriage.

SOUNDTRACK.

SLEEPING BEAUTY

US 1959; screenwriters: not credited; voices: Mary Costa (Briar Rose/Sleeping Beauty), Bill Shirley (Prince Phillip).

3 *Briar Rose/Sleeping Beauty*: They say if you dream a thing more than once, it's sure to come true.

SOUNDTRACK.

4 *Prince Philip*: Father, you're living in the past. This is the fourteenth century.

SOUNDTRACK.

SLOGANS

Used as promotional strap-lines or tag lines on posters and in advertisements for films. *See also* under individual films.

5 All talking! All singing! All dancing!

Broadway Melody (US 1929). When sound came to the movies, this very first Hollywood musical – from MGM – was promoted with posters bearing the slogan (and variations on it):

The New Wonder of the Screen!
ALL TALKING
ALL SINGING
ALL DANCING
Dramatic Sensation

Oddly enough, in that same year, two rival studios both hit on the same selling pitch. Alice White in *Broadway Babes* (using Warners' Vitaphone system) was '100% TALKING, SINGING, DANCING'. And Radio's *Rio Rita* (with Bebe Daniels) was billed as 'ZIEGFELD'S FABULOUS ALL-TALKING, ALL-SINGING SUPER SCREEN SPECTACLE'. It was natural that the studios should wish to promote the most obvious aspect of the new sound cinema, but it is curious that they should all have made use of much the same phrase.

1 Are you ready for Freddy?

Nightmare on Elm Street – Part 4 (1989) – referring to Freddy Krueger, a gruesome character in the film.

2 *The Birds* is coming!

The Birds (US 1963).

3 The body count continues.

Friday the 13th Part II (US 1981).

4 Boy! Do we need it now!

That's Entertainment (US 1974).

5 *The Boys in the Band* is *not* a musical.

The Boys in the Band (US 1970).

6 Brings the world to the world.

Gaumont-British cinema newsreel; UK, from the 1930s.

7 Can you survive *The Texas Chain Saw Massacre* ... It happened!

The Texas Chain Saw Massacre (US 1974).

8 Cast of thousands.

Now only used jokingly and ironically, this type of film promotion line *may* have made its first appearance in connection with the 1927 version of *Ben Hur*, where the boast was 'Cast of 125,000!' It was still being used with apparent seriousness in a trailer for DeMille's *Samson and Delilah* (US 1949).

9 A completely new experience between men and women!

The Men (US 1950). It was about paraplegic war veterans.

10 *The Curse of Frankenstein* will haunt you forever (Please try not to faint).

The Curse of Frankenstein (UK 1957).

11 Don't call me babe.

Barb Wire (US 1996) – from a line spoken in the picture by Pamela Anderson as a no-nonsense agent.

12 Don't pronounce it – See it!

See ***NINOTCHKA*** 307:1; also *Phffft!* (US 1954).

13 The eyes and ears of the world.

Paramount News (cinema newsreel) 1927–57.

14 Fridays will never be the same again.

Friday the 13th (US 1980).

1 Gable's back and Garson's got him.

Adventure (US 1945), Gable's first postwar film. Coined by Howard Dietz. The slogan riled Gable because it subordinated him to a woman. '[So] screamed the billboards all over the world. Clark was being re-launched by M-G-M in a dreary pot boiler with, as co-star, someone not among his favourite leading ladies' – David Niven, *Bring On the Empty Horses*, 'The King' (1975).

2 Greater than *Ivanhoe*.

Julius Caesar (US 1953).

3 He's back – and he's angry!

Unattached. This strap-line was being alluded to in the UK by 1996. 'He's back' on its own was used variously for *Halloween 4: The Return of Michael Myers* (1988), *Robocop 2* (1990) and *Robocop 3* (1993). Could the full version have been used for any of these? Or could it be a reference to Arnold Schwarzenegger's famous line in *The* ***TERMINATOR*** 409:2, or to ***RAMBO: FIRST BLOOD PART TWO***, or to any of the *Nightmare on Elm Street* or *Halloween* sequels?

4 If there was an 11th Commandment, they would have broken that too.

The Postman Always Rings Twice (US, 1981 – the re-make).

5 In space, no one can hear you scream!

Alien (US 1979). Critic Sue Heal said of *Alien 3*, 'In space no one can hear you yawn.'

6 It crawls! It creeps! It eats you alive! Run – don't walk from *The Blob*.

The Blob (US 1958).

7 It speaks for itself.

British Movietone News (cinema newsreel) (UK 1930s).

8 Just when you thought it was safe to go back in the water …

Jaws 2 (US, 1978).

9 Let's Go to a Movie.

1940s campaign.

10 Life isn't like the movies. Life is harder.

Cinema Paradiso (Italy/France 1990).

11 A lion in your lap.

Bwana Devil, shot in 'Natural Vision'. Quoted in Penelope Houston, *Contemporary Cinema* (1963).

12 Love means never having to say you're ugly.

The Abominable Dr Phibes (UK, 1971).

1 The Lubitsch touch that means so much.

Various films directed by Ernst Lubitsch, from about 1925. Or, 'It's the Lubitsch touch that means so much.'

2 The man of a thousand faces.

Sobriquet of Lon Chaney (1883–1930), the American film actor and master of macabre make-up. A 1957 biopic with the title *The Man of a Thousand Faces* starred James Cagney.

3 More stars than there are in heaven.

MGM studios in Hollywood, and created by Howard Dietz (1896–1983), the writer and film executive, in the 1920s/30s. The slogan appears on a poster for *Broadway Melody* (1929), the very first film musical.

4 The motion picture with something to offend everyone.

The Loved One (US 1965).

5 The movies are Better than Ever.

Movietime, US campaign in the 1950s to counter the threat of television. May have been coined by Howard Dietz when he was vice-president of the Council of Motion Picture Organizations.

6 Never let the truth get in the way of a good story.

The Paper (US 1994).

7 The picture of the century.

Robbery Under Arms (Australia 1907).

8 Selznick Pictures Make Happy Hours.

Selznick Select Pictures – coined by Lewis J. Selznick (father of David O.).

9 The spice of variety.

Pathetone Weekly (newsreel), 1930s?

10 There is no escape from something you cannot see.

The Entity (US 1981).

11 This time … it's personal.

Jaws: *The Revenge* (1987) and, as 'This time, it's personal', *Die Hard*: *With a Vengeance* (1995).

12 A thousand thrills … and Hayley Mills.

In Search of the Castaways (UK 1961).

13 To you these will be the most incredible things to appear on the screen. To the Maitresse it's a job.

Maîtresse (France 1976). (Also 'She will open your eyes'). The film was about a dominatrix.

1 When he pours, he reigns.

Cocktail (US 1989).

2 When the going gets tough, the tough get going.

The Jewel of the Nile (US, 1985). Using an already established popular saying.

Wesley SNIPES

American actor (1962–)

3 In films you don't have actors, but personalities.

QUOTED in *The Observer*, 'Sayings of the Week' (17 October 1993).

SNOW WHITE AND THE SEVEN DWARFS

US 1937; screenwriters: Ted Sears and others (from Brothers Grimm tale *Sneewittchen*); music/lyrics: Frank Churchill, Larry Morey; voices of: Lucille La Verne (Wicked Queen), Billy Gilbert (Sneezy), Pinto Colvig (Grumpy), Adriana Caselotti (Snow White).

4 'Each day the vain Queen consulted her Magic Mirror, "Magic Mirror on the Wall, / Who is the fairest one of all?" … and as long as the Mirror answered, "You are the fairest one of all", Snow White was safe from the Queen's cruel jealousy.'

SCREEN TITLE at opening. Often remembered as 'Mirror, mirror, on the wall … ?' You might think that this famous line – in these words – existed before the Disney cartoon, but apparently not. The original German is: '*Spieglein, spieglein an der Wand, / wer is die schönste im ganzen Land*? [Little mirror, little mirror on the wall, / who is the fairest [woman] in all the land?].' In an 1823 translation from the German, we find rather this: 'Tell me, glass, tell me true! / Of all the ladies in the land, / Who is the fairest? Tell me who?'

5 With a Smile and a Song.

TITLE of song, sung by Snow White.

6 Whistle While You Work.

TITLE of song, sung by Snow White.

7 Heigh ho, heigh ho,
It's off to work we go.

SONG, 'Heigh-Ho', sung by the Seven Dwarfs.

8 *Seven Dwarfs (finding a clean house and suspecting a monster in it)*: Jiminy Crickets!

SOUNDTRACK.

9 *Wicked Queen (as she transforms herself)*: Mummy dust to make me old. To shroud my clothes, the black of night. To age my voice, an old hag's cackle. To whiten my hair, a scream of fright. A blast of wind to fan my hate. A thunderbolt to mix it well. And now begin thy magic spell.

SOUNDTRACK.

1 Some Day My Prince Will Come.

TITLE of song, sung by Snow White.

2 *Grumpy (leaving for work)*: Now, I'm warning you. Don't let nobody or nothing in the house.
Snow White: Why, Grumpy! You do care!

SOUNDTRACK.

3 *Grumpy (on learning that the Wicked Queen is holding Snow White)*: The Queen'll kill her! We've got to save her!

SOUNDTRACK.

4 *Wicked Queen*: This is no ordinary apple. It's a magic wishing apple ... One bite and all your dreams will come true.
Snow White: Really?
Wicked Queen: Yes, girlie. Now, make a wish and take a bite.

SOUNDTRACK.

5 *Snow White (making her wish)*: ... And he'll carry me away to his castle where we'll live happily ever after.

SOUNDTRACK.

SOAK THE RICH

US 1935; screenwriters: Ben Hecht, Charles MacArthur; cast: George Watts (Rockwell).

6 *Rockwell*: Communism is the growing pains of the young.

SOUNDTRACK.

Steven SODERBERGH

American director and screenwriter (1963–)

7 [on winning the Palme d'Or at Cannes for *sex, lies, and videotape*] It's all down hill from here.

ATTRIBUTED remark in 1989.

8 Some of the worst films of all time have been made by people who think too much.

INTERVIEWED in *The Guardian* (7 September 1989).

SODOM AND GOMORRAH

US/France/Italy 1962; screenwriters: Hugo Butler, Giorgio Prosperi; cast: Anouk Aimée (the Queen), Stewart Granger (Lot), Pier Angeli (Ilda).

1 *Lot*: The Sodomite cavalry are notoriously unreliable!

SOUNDTRACK.

2 *Lot (arriving at an oasis)*: Where there's water, there's danger also.

SOUNDTRACK.

3 *Ilda*: Where I come from, nothing is evil. Everything that gives pleasure is good.
Lot: Where do you come from?
Ilda: There. Not far. Just ahead. Sodom and Gomorrah.

SOUNDTRACK.

4 *The Queen (to Lot, after he has killed a man)*: In the name of righteousness and your God, you have abandoned yourself to the lust for blood. You are a true Sodomite, Lot. Welcome.

SOUNDTRACK.

The SOLID GOLD CADILLAC

US 1956; screenwriter: Abe Burrows (based on a play by George S. Kaufman and Howard Teichmann); cast: Judy Holliday (Laura Partridge), Paul Douglas (Edward L. McKeever).

5 *Laura (a part-time actress)*: Do you like Shakespeare?
Edward: Well, I've read a lot of it.
Laura: Well, take my advice, don't play it. It's so tiring. They never let you sit down unless you're a king.

SOUNDTRACK. Compare what Josephine Hull, the American actress (1884–1957) had earlier advised: 'Shakespeare is so tiring. You never get a chance to sit down unless you're a king' – quoted in *Time* Magazine (16 November 1953).

SOME LIKE IT HOT

US 1959; screenwriters: Billy Wilder, I.A.L. Diamond; cast: Tony Curtis (Joe/Josephine), Marilyn Monroe (Sugar Kane), Jack Lemmon (Jerry/Daphne), Joe E. Brown (Osgood E. Fielding III), Joan Shawlee (Sweet Sue).

6 *Jerry (on seeing Sugar, to Joe)*: Look at that! Look how she moves! It's just like Jell-O on springs ... I tell you, it's a whole different sex.

SOUNDTRACK.

7 *Sugar (on her love life)*: I always get the fuzzy end of the lollipop.

SOUNDTRACK.

1 *Joe/Josephine*: Just keep telling yourself you're a girl.
Jerry/Daphne: I'm a girl … I'm a girl … I'm a girl …

SOUNDTRACK.

2 *Sugar (to Joe)*: I have this thing about saxophone players, especially tenor sax … I don't know what it is, but they just curdle me. All they have to do is play eight bars of 'Come to Me, My Melancholy Baby' and my spine turns to custard. I get goose pimply all over and I come to 'em.

SOUNDTRACK.

3 *Sugar (on the millionaires she hopes to find in Florida)*: They get those weak eyes from reading – you know, those long tiny little columns in the *Wall Street Journal.*

SOUNDTRACK.

4 *Joe (pretending to be millionaire)*: With all the unrest in the world, I don't think anybody should have a yacht that sleeps more than twelve.

SOUNDTRACK.

5 *Joe*: Syncopators? Does that mean you play that very fast music … er … jazz?
Sugar: Yeah … real hot!
Joe: Oh, well, I guess some like it hot. I personally prefer classical music.

SOUNDTRACK. Perhaps explaining the title, perhaps not. *Some Like It Hot* was also used as the title of a 1939 Bob Hope film.

6 *Sweet Sue*: Well, that's it for tonight, folks. This is Sweet Sue, saying good night, reminding all you daddies out there that every girl in my band is a virtuoso – and I intend to keep it that way.

SOUNDTRACK.

7 *Sugar*: Water polo? Isn't it terribly dangerous?
Joe: I'll say. I had two ponies drowned under me.

SOUNDTRACK.

8 *Joe*: I think you're on the right track.
Sugar: I must be. Your glasses are beginning to steam up.

SOUNDTRACK.

9 *Joe*: But you're not a girl. You're a guy. And why would a guy want to marry a guy?
Jerry: Security.

SOUNDTRACK.

1 *Joe*: Just keep telling yourself you're a boy. You're a boy.
Jerry: I'm a boy!
Joe: That's a boy.

SOUNDTRACK.

2 *Jerry*: Osgood, I'm going to level with you. We can't get married at all … *(removing wig)* I'm a man.
Osgood: Well, nobody's perfect.

SOUNDTRACK. Last lines of film. 'Daphne' (Lemmon, in drag) confesses that he is not a woman and is thus unable to marry the wealthy Osgood.

SON OF ALI BABA

US 1952; screenwriter: Gerald Drayson Adams; cast: Tony Curtis (Kashma Baba).

3 *Kashma Baba*: Yonda lies da palace of my foddah da sheikh [Yonder lies the palace of my father the sheikh].

SOUNDTRACK. Curtis's Brooklyn accent survives well in this Arabian Nights tale. This is the true origin of the legendary line usually and mistakenly placed in *The* ***BLACK SHIELD OF FALWORTH***.

SON OF MONTE CRISTO

US 1940; screenwriter: George Bruce; cast: George Sanders (Gurko Lanen), Louis Hayward (Count of Monte Cristo).

4 *Count of Monte Cristo*: Don't worry. My father was the best swordsman in France!

SOUNDTRACK (unverified). In *Punch* (4 November 1970), the line was said to have been spoken in this film by Douglas Fairbanks Jr. Unfortunately, he does not actually appear in it, though perhaps he may have delivered it in another?

SONG WITHOUT END

US 1960; screenwriter: Oscar Millard; cast: Dirk Bogarde (Lizst).

5 *Lizst*: Hiya Chopin, this is my great friend George Sand. She's a great friend of Beethoven.

APOCRYPHAL LINE – though according to Dirk Bogarde, *Snakes and Ladders* (1978), he had originally been required to speak something like it. When George Cukor took over direction of the film, Bogarde 'did manage to clear up quite a number of "Hi! Lizst … meet my friend, Schubert, he's a pal of Chopin's."'

Susan SONTAG

American writer and critic (1933–)

1 Cinema is a kind of pan-art. It can use, incorporate, engulf virtually any other art: the novel, poetry, theater, painting, sculpture, dance, music, architecture. Unlike opera, which is a (virtually) frozen art form, the cinema is and has been a fruitfully conservative medium of ideas and styles of emotions.

EXTRACTED from 'A Note on Novels and Films' (1961), collected in *Against Interpretation* (1966).

2 In good films, there is always a directness that entirely frees us from the itch to interpret.

EXTRACTED from 'Against Interpretation' in *The Evergreen Review* (December 1964), collected in *Against Interpretation* (1966).

3 [on the late 1960s and early 70s] It was at this specific moment in the 100-year history of cinema that going to movies became a passion among university students and other young people. You fell in love not just with actors but with cinema itself.

EXTRACTED from 'The Decay of Cinema' in *The New York Times* Magazine (25 February 1996).

4 [the essential movie experience lies in the desire] To be kidnapped by the movie ... overwhelmed by the physical presence of the image.

EXTRACTED from the same article.

Terry SOUTHERN

American novelist and screenwriter (1924–95)

5 She says, 'Listen, who do I have to fuck to get *off* this picture?'

EXTRACTED from novel *Blue Movie* (1970). *Compare* **ANONYMOUS** 33:5.

SPARTACUS

US 1960; screenwriter: Dalton Trumbo (from novel by Howard Fast); cast: Kirk Douglas (Spartacus), Peter Ustinov (Batiatus), Tony Curtis (Antoninus), Laurence Olivier (Marcus Crassus), Charles Laughton (Gracchus).

6 *Crassus (to Antoninus)*: Do you eat oysters? ... Do you eat snails? ... Do you consider the eating of oysters to be moral and the eating of snails to be immoral? ... It is all a matter of taste ... And taste is not the same as appetite and therefore is not a question of morals ... My taste includes both snails and oysters.

SOUNDTRACK. Only in the 1991 restored version. It was deleted from the original because of the homo-erotic undertones.

1 *Gracchus*: Corpulence makes a man reasonable, pleasant and phlegmatic. Have you noticed that the nastiest of talents are invariably thin?

SOUNDTRACK.

2 *Rebel slaves hiding the identity of the real Spartacus*: I'm Spartacus! ... I'm Spartacus! ... I'm Spartacus!

SOUNDTRACK.

(Sir) Stephen SPENDER

English poet (1909–95)

3 I have been ... taken by surprise several times at my poetry readings ... A man asked, "How many movies have been made of your poems?" Alas, there've been none, none at all.

INTERVIEWED in *Writers at Work* (6th series, 1984).

Sam SPIEGEL

Polish-born producer (1901–85)

4 You make a star, you sometimes make a monster.

REMARK quoted in Leslie Halliwell, *The Filmgoer's Book of Quotes* (1973).

Steven SPIELBERG

American director (1947–)

5 The most expensive habit in the world is celluloid, not heroin, and I need a fix every few years.

INTERVIEWED in *Time* Magazine (16 April 1979).

6 If a person can tell me the idea [of a film] in twenty-five words or less, it's going to make a pretty good movie. I like ideas, especially movie ideas, that you can hold in your hand.

QUOTED in Justin Wyatt, *High Concept* (1994).

7 [on making *E.T.*] Oh torture. Torture. My pubic hairs went grey.

ATTRIBUTED remark.

8 The people who say these things about me are the ones who drink my Evian water with me and call themselves my friends.

QUOTED in *The Observer*, 'Sayings of the Week' (19 December 1993).

1 [Steven] Spielberg, the most popular, is bright and articulate, but his idea of intellection is to skip an hour's TV.

COMMENT by Martin Amis, English novelist and screenwriter (1949–)., *The Moronic Inferno*, 'Brian De Palma' (1986).

2 I am a stickler for smells, having been cursed with a wretchedly sensitive nose, yet I cannot remember Steve smelling of anything. He never sweated either. It was as if he was pure and innocent both inside and out.

COMMENT by Sarah Miles, quoted in *The Observer*, 'Soundbites' (8 September 1996).

SPLENDOR IN THE GRASS

US 1961; screenwriter: William Inge; cast: Natalie Wood (Wilma Dean Loomis), Audrey Christie (Mrs Loomis, Wilma's mother), Warren Beatty (Bud Stanford).

3 *Mrs Loomis*: Your father never laid a hand on me until we were married and then I just gave in because a wife has to. A woman doesn't enjoy those things the way a man does. She just lets her husband come near her in order to have children.

SOUNDTRACK.

4 *Wilma*: Though nothing can bring back the hour
Of splendour in the grass, of glory in the flower;
We will grieve not, rather find
Strength in what remains behind.

SOUNDTRACK. Wilma twice speaks these lines – first in class when she is made to read them aloud and suddenly understands their relevance to her present position. She realises for the first time that her relationship with Bud is over and that the ideals of youth have to give way in time to something else. She also recites them as the last lines in the film. They are from William Wordsworth's 'Ode, Intimations of Immortality from Recollections of Early Childhood', St. 10 (1807).

STAGE DOOR

US 1937; screenwriters: Morrie Ryskind, Anthony Veiller (based on Edna Ferber/George S. Kaufman play); cast: Katharine Hepburn (Terry).

5 *Terry (in play within the film)*: The calla lilies are in bloom again. Such a strange flower, suitable to any occasion. I carried them on my wedding day, and now I place them here in memory of something that has died.

SOUNDTRACK. These lines were taken from a 1933 Broadway play called *The Lake* in which Hepburn had starred. It had been a flop. From here on in they became an essential part of all Hepburn impressions.

STAGECOACH

US 1939; screenwriter: Dudley Nichols (from story 'Stage to Lordsburg' by Ernest Haycox); cast: Berton Churchill (Henry Gatewood).

1 *Gatewood*: And remember this, what's good for the banks is good for the country.

SOUNDTRACK. One wonders what influence this line had, if any, upon Charles E. Wilson, American Republican politician (1890–1961), who is forever quoted as having said: 'What's good for General Motors is good for the country.' President Eisenhower wished to appoint Wilson as Secretary for Defense. At hearings of the Senate Committee on Armed Services in January 1953, the former President of General Motors was asked about any possible conflict of interest, as he had accepted several million dollars' worth of General Motors shares. When he was asked whether he would be able to make a decision against the interests of General Motors and his stock, what Wilson in fact replied was not the above, but: 'Yes, sir, I could. I cannot conceive of one because for years I thought what was good for our country was good for General Motors, and vice versa. The difference did not exist.' Wilson was finally persuaded to get rid of his stock, but he never quite lived down his (misquoted) remarks.

STALAG 17

US 1953; screenwriters: Billy Wilder, Edwin Blum (from a play by Donald Bevan and Edmund Trzinski); cast: Gil Stratton Jr (Cookie), Robert Strauss ('Animal' Stosh), Otto Preminger (Oberst Von Scherbach), William Holden (Sefton), Robinson Stone (Joey), Don Taylor (Dunbar), Peter Graves (Price).

2 *Cookie (voice over)*: I don't know about you, but it always makes me sore when I see those war pictures. All about flying leather-necks and submarine patrols and frogmen and guerrillas in the Philippines. What gets me is that there never was a movie about POWs – about prisoners of war.

SOUNDTRACK. Opening lines of film. Not really true as there had already been *The Wooden Horse* (UK 1950).

3 *Von Scherbach (to prisoners)*: Nasty weather we are having, eh? And I so much hoped we could give you a white Christmas, just like the ones you used to know. Aren't those the words that clever little man wrote, you know, the one who stole his name from our capital, that something-or-other Berlin?

SOUNDTRACK.

4 *Von Scherbach (to prisoners)*: Nobody has ever escaped from Stalag 17. Not alive, anyway.

SOUNDTRACK.

5 *Stosh (to shell-shocked Joey)*: Hey, you don't want to be no stinking lawyer with a stinking briefcase in a stinking office, do ya, Joey? Nah.

Next time we write to your folks, you know what we're gonna say? You're gonna say that you don't want to be no lawyer. You want to be a musician, play maybe, huh, the flute?

SOUNDTRACK.

1 *Sefton (to Geneva Convention delegate who asks who beat him)*: Nobody beat me. We were playing pinochle. It's a rough game.

SOUNDTRACK.

2 *Mail carrier to prisoners*: Always remember, just because the Krauts are dumb that doesn't mean they're stupid.

SOUNDTRACK.

3 *Price (cornered as spy)*: I don't like you. I never did and never will. *Sefton*: A lot of people say that, and the first thing you know is they're getting married.

SOUNDTRACK.

4 *Sefton (to prisoners, as he enters escape hatch to rescue Dunbar)*: Just one more word. If I ever run into any of you bums on the street corner, just let's pretend we never met before.

SOUNDTRACK.

5 *Stosh (to prisoners, on why Sefton rescued Dunbar)*: Maybe he just wanted to steal our wire cutters. Did ya ever think of that?

SOUNDTRACK. Last line of film.

Josef STALIN

Soviet leader (1879–1953)

6 The cinema in the hands of the Soviet power represents a great and priceless force.

QUOTED in Roger Manvell, *Film* (1944).

Sylvester STALLONE

American actor (1946–)

7 [as spokesman for The Gift of Literacy Society] I am keenly aware of the printed word to all that I do [*sic*].

QUOTED in *Sunday Today*, 'Quotes of the Week' (3 May 1987).

8 The biggest misconception about me is that I am a very negative person, antisocial and uneducated.

QUOTED in *The Observer*, 'Sayings of the Week' (19 June 1988).

1 I'm a sensitive writer, actor and director. Talking business disgusts me. If you want to do business, call my disgusting personal manager.

QUOTED in *The Guinness Book of Movie Facts & Feats* (ed. Patrick Robertson)(1993 edn).

2 His career is more mysterious than cot death.

COMMENT attributed to Rex Reed and quoted by Stallone as an example of the criticism he has had to put up with.

3 [on a role model] Sylvester Stallone was very influential – I thought he was the bee's knees.

COMMENT by Quentin Tarantino, interviewed at British Film Institute, quoted in the *Independent on Sunday*, 'Overheard' (5 February 1995).

See also ***RAMBO: FIRST BLOOD PART TWO*** 347:7.

A STAR IS BORN

US 1937; screenwriter: Dorothy Parker and others; cast: Janet Gaynor (Esther Blodgett/Vicki Lester).

4 *Vicki Lester (commemorating her now dead husband)*:
Hello, everybody. This is Mrs Norman Maine.

SOUNDTRACK. Last line. This was delivered exactly the same by Judy Garland in the 1954 re-make.

STAR NIGHT AT THE COCOANUT GROVE

US 1935 (musical short); cast: Leo Carrillo (as himself).

5 *Leo Carrillo*: Hollywood, Hollywood …
Fabulous Hollywood …
Celluloid Babylon,
Glorious, glamorous …
City delirious,
Frivolous, serious …
Bold and ambitious,
And vicious and glamorous.
Drama – a city-full,
Tragic and pitiful …
Bunk, junk, and genius
Amazingly blended …
Tawdry, tremendous,
Absurd, stupendous;

Shoddy and cheap,
And astonishingly splendid …
HOLLYWOOD!

SOUNDTRACK. The poem has been credited to Don Blanding. Coupled with the popularization of the idea of Babylon as a city of decadence given by D.W. Griffith in his film *Intolerance* (1916), this probably led to the association between Hollywood and the biblical city. Kenneth Anger quoted the poem in his book of movie scandals, *Hollywood Babylon* in 1975.

STAR TREK: THE MOTION PICTURE

US 1979; screenwriters: Harold Livingston, Gene Roddenberry; cast: William Shatner (Capt. James T. Kirk).

1 It's life, Captain, but not as we know it.

APOCRYPHAL LINE. As far as can be ascertained, the catchphrase 'It's life, Jim, but not as we know it', was never said in any of the original TV episodes of *Star Trek*, nor in any of the several feature films that belatedly spun off from them. This is Mr Spock's line from the song 'Star Trekkin'' by The Firm – a No. 1 hit record in the UK (June 1987) – in which impersonators of the main *Star Trek* characters simply intone would-be lines from the show to music. Other lines from this song include: 'There's Klingons on the Starboard Bow' and 'It's worse than that, he's dead, Jim.'

The catchphrase had a certain vogue in the UK in the early 1990s. A 1995 poster advertisement in London stated 'It's direct insurance, but not as we know it, Jim'. A headline from *The Independent* (19 April 1996) had: 'It's the weekend, Jim, but not as we know it.'

A belief still persists that something like it *was* said in one of the TV episodes but, if so, this remains to be found. Nowlan & Nowlan, *Film Quotations* (1994) confidently assert that in *Star Trek*: *The Motion Picture* (1979), Spock says to Kirk, 'It's life, Captain, but not life as we know it.' However, given that the Nowlans refer to '*Dr* Spock' it is hardly surprising to find that, in fact, the line is not actually uttered in the film. This is not the least of the apocryphal lines they happily include in their book.

2 *Captain Kirk (ordering a new course for the* Enterprise*)*: Out there. That-a-way!

SOUNDTRACK. Last line of film.

STAR TREK V: THE FINAL FRONTIER

US 1989; screenwriter: David Loughery.

3 *Narrator*: To boldly go where no one has gone before.

SOUNDTRACK. Introductory matter, retaining the split infinitive of the original TV series but replacing 'where no man has gone before' in accordance with current political correctness.

STAR WARS

US 1977; screenwriter/director: George Lucas; cast: Mark Hamill (Luke Skywalker), Alec Guinness (Obi-Wan 'Ben' Kenobi).

1 Star Wars.

TITLE OF FILM. This title was borrowed when President Ronald Reagan first propounded his 'Star Wars' proposal as part of a campaign to win support for his defence budget and arms-control project (23 March 1983). The proposal, more properly known by its initials SDI (for Strategic Defense Initiative), was to extend the nuclear battleground into space. The President did not use the term 'Star Wars', but it was inevitably applied by the media, given his own fondness for adapting lines from the movies.

2 A long time ago in a galaxy far, far away …

SCREEN TITLE. Not spoken. Opening line.

3 Episode IV. A NEW HOPE. It is a period of civil war. Rebel spaceships, striking from a hidden base, have won their first victory against the evil Galactic Empire.

SCREEN TITLE. Not spoken. Continuation of opening sequence, scrolling. This was apparently the origin of President Reagan's phrase 'evil empire' for the Soviet Union: ' In your discussions of the nuclear freeze proposals, I urge you to beware the temptation of pride – the temptation blithely to declare yourselves above it all and label both sides equally at fault, to ignore the facts of history and the aggressive impulses of an evil empire' – speech to the national Association of Evangelicals at Orlando, Florida (8 March 1983). *Compare The* ***EMPIRE STRIKES BACK*** 152:1.

4 *Obi-Wan (to Luke)*: Vader was seduced by the dark side of The Force … The Force is what gives the Jedi its power. It's an energy field created by all living things. It surrounds us, it penetrates us, it binds the galaxy together.

SOUNDTRACK.

5 *Obi-Wan (to Luke)*: The Force will be with you – always.

SOUNDTRACK.

6 *General*: Man your ships – and may the Force be with you.

SOUNDTRACK. And at other times by various characters.

7 I like Darth Vader, he's the best, he's the boy. He's the baddest man on the planet, isn't he?

COMMENT by Noel Gallagher, pop singer, quoted in *The Observer*, (23 March 1997).

STATE OF THE UNION

US 1948; screenwriters: Anthony Veiller, Myles Connolly (from Robert Harling play); cast: Spencer Tracy (Grant Matthews).

1 *Grant Matthews*: Don't you shut me off, I'm paying for this broadcast.

SOUNDTRACK. Famously quoted by Ronald Reagan. Just prior to a broadcast debate at Nashua, New Hampshire, during the presidential primary there in 1980, Reagan turned the tables on George Bush (then also a challenger) by insisting that the other Republican candidates be allowed to participate. Reagan won the dispute over who should speak in the debate by declaring 'Don't you cut me off, I am paying for this microphone, Mr Green!' Never mind that the moderator's name was actually 'Breen'. The borrowing was pointed out by Christopher J. Matthews writing in *The Washington Post* (6 May 1984).

STEEL MAGNOLIAS

US 1989; screenwriter: Robert Harling; cast: Olympia Dukakis (Clairee Belcher).

2 *Clairee*: As somebody always said, if you can't say anything nice about anybody, come sit by me.

SOUNDTRACK. The 'somebody' was, in fact, Alice Roosevelt Longworth, American political hostess (1884–1980) and daughter of President Theodore Roosevelt. 'If you haven't got anything nice to say about anyone, come and sit by me' was embroidered on a cushion at Longworth's Washington, DC, home. She had a reputation for barbed wit, but many of her lines were not entirely original.

Rod STEIGER

American actor (1925–)

3 If I've survived McCarthy, a quadruple heart by-pass and depression, I think I deserve to be called a survivor.

QUOTED in *The Independent* (20 May 1989).

Gertrude STEIN

American poet (1874–1946)

4 [when asked after a visit to Hollywood what it was like out there] There is no 'There' – there.

QUOTED in David Niven, *Bring on the Empty Horses* (1975).

STELLA DALLAS

US 1937; screenwriters: Sarah Y. Mason, Victor Heerman (from dramatization of Olive Higgins Prouty novel); cast: Barbara Stanwyck (Stella Dallas), Anne Shirley (Laurel Dallas).

5 *Stella*: All my life I just about died to go to the real places and get in with the right crowd.

SOUNDTRACK.

1 *Police officer (to crowd at townhouse where Laurel is getting married)*: All right, folks, you've seen enough. Move along, please. Come on, clear the sidewalk.

SOUNDTRACK. Last line of film. In the crowd is Laurel's mother, Stella Dallas, whose sacrifice has made the marriage possible. She has just asked the police officer, 'Oh, please let me see her face when he kisses her.'

Jennifer STONE

American writer (1933–)

2 Movies have mirrored our moods and myths since the century began. They have taken on some of the work of religion.

EXTRACTED from her book *Mind Over Media*, 'Epilogue' (1988).

Oliver STONE

American director and screenwriter (1946–)

3 One of the joys of going to the movies was that it was trashy, and we should never lose that.

REMARK quoted in the *International Herald Tribune* (15 February 1988).

4 Media spits out surface; art or a film is penetrative, seeks to go beyond the skin of events to shape, form and dramatize.

REMARK quoted in *Time Out* (January 1995).

Sharon STONE

American actress (1957–)

5 If you have a vagina *and* an attitude in this town, then that's a lethal combination.

QUOTED in *Empire* (June 1992).

6 I think men believe what they see in the movies – that I am going to throw my head back and have an orgasm in two minutes. I have never done that. It is implausible.

QUOTED in *The Independent* (11 January 1997).

STORMY WEATHER

US 1943; screenwriters: Frederick Jackson, Ted Koehler; cast: Fats Waller, Cab Calloway (as themselves).

7 *Waller*: One never knows, do one?

SOUNDTRACK.

1 *Calloway*: Everybody dance!
SOUNDTRACK.

Igor STRAVINSKY

Russian composer (1882–1971)

2 Film music should have the same relationship to the film drama that somebody's piano-playing in my living-room has on the book I'm reading.
QUOTED in *The Music Digest* (September 1946).

3 The only way to avoid Hollywood is to live there.
ATTRIBUTED remark.

The STRAWBERRY BLONDE

US 1941; screenwriters: Julius J. & Philip G. Epstein (from a play *One Sunday Afternoon* by James Hagan); cast: James Cagney (Biff Grimes).

4 *Biff (on his wife)*: When I want to kiss my wife, I'll kiss her anytime, anyplace, anywhere. That's the kind of hairpin I am.
SOUNDTRACK. Last line. *Compare* ***HIS GIRL FRIDAY*** 215:2.

A STREETCAR NAMED DESIRE

US 1951; screenwriter: Tennessee Williams (from his play); cast: Marlon Brando (Stanley Kowalski), Vivien Leigh (Blanche Dubois).

5 *Stanley*: Hey, mind if I make myself comfortable? ... The unrefined type, heh?
SOUNDTRACK.

6 *Blanche*: Whoever you are, I have always depended on the kindness of strangers.
SOUNDTRACK.

Barbra STREISAND

American singer and actress (1942–)

7 I don't care what you say about me. Just be sure to spell my name wrong.
QUOTED in *Time* Magazine (10 April 1964).

8 I am a nice person. I care about my driver having lunch, you know ...
QUOTED in *The Sunday Times*, 'Words of the Week' (1 April 1984).

1 To know her is not necessarily to love her.

COMMENT by Rex Reed.

2 [to Streisand on set of *Hello Dolly*] I have more talent in my smallest fart than you have in your entire body.

COMMENT attributed to Walter Matthau.

See also ***FUNNY GIRL*** 174:4; ***WHAT'S UP, DOC?*** 445:9.

Hunt STROMBERG

American producer (1894–1968)

3 [on taking over *White Shadows in the South Seas* (1928)] Boys, I've got a great idea. Let's fill the whole screen with tits!

QUOTED in Philip French, *The Movie Moguls* (1969).

SUDDEN IMPACT

US 1983; screenwriter: Joseph C. Stinson; cast: Clint Eastwood (Harry Callahan).

4 *Harry Callahan (as cop brandishing a .44 Magnum, to gunman he is holding at bay)*: Go ahead, make my day!

SOUNDTRACK. At the end of the film he says (to another villain, similarly armed), 'Come on, make my day'. In neither case does he add 'punk', as is sometimes supposed (from *The Independent*, 14 July 1993: 'When Clint Eastwood said "Go ahead, punk, make my day" ...') – this may come from confusion with ***DIRTY HARRY*** 136:5. The line became a popular laconicism – in March 1985, President Ronald Reagan told the American Business Conference: 'I have my veto pen drawn and ready for any tax increase that Congress might even think of sending up. And I have only one thing to say to the tax increasers. Go ahead – make my day.' The phrase may have been eased into Reagan's speech by having appeared in a parody of the *New York Post* put together by other journalists, many of them anti-Reagan, in the autumn of 1984. Reagan was shown starting a nuclear war by throwing down this dare to the Kremlin (source: *Time* Magazine, 25 March 1985).

SUNSET BOULEVARD

US 1950; screenwriters: Charles Brackett, Billy Wilder, D.M. Marshman Jr; cast: Gloria Swanson (Norma Desmond), William Holden (Joe Gillis), Fred Clark (Sheldrake), Cecil B. DeMille (himself), Erich von Stroheim (Max von Meyerling).

5 *Joe (narrating)*: Yes, this is Sunset Boulevard, Los Angeles, California. It's about five o'clock in the morning. That's the homicide squad – complete with detectives and newspapermen. A murder has been reported from one of those great big houses in the ten thousand block ...

SOUNDTRACK. Opening lines of film.

1 *Joe (narrating, of his dead self)*: Poor dope. He always wanted a pool. Well, in the end, he got himself a pool – only the price turned out to be a little high.

SOUNDTRACK. His body is floating in Norma's pool.

2 *Joe*: You'd have turned down *Gone With the Wind* …
Sheldrake: … That was me. I said, who wants to see a Civil War picture?

SOUNDTRACK. Joe, a less than successful Hollywood scriptwriter, is pitching an idea to Sheldrake, a producer. *Compare* ***IN A LONELY PLACE*** 226:3.

3 *Joe*: Wait a minute, haven't I seen you before? I know your face … You're Norma Desmond! Used to be in silent pictures. Used to be big.
Norma: I *am* big. It's the pictures that got small.

SOUNDTRACK.

4 *Norma (on silent film stars)*: We didn't need dialogue. We had faces.

SOUNDTRACK.

5 *Norma*: There was a time in this business when they had the eyes of the whole wide world. But that wasn't good enough for them. Oh, no! They had to have the ears of the world, too. So they opened their big mouths, and out came talk, talk, talk!

SOUNDTRACK.

6 *Joe (narrating, on Norma)*: Poor devil. Still waving proudly to a parade which had long since passed her by.

SOUNDTRACK.

7 *Norma (to Joe)*: Great stars have great pride.

SOUNDTRACK.

8 *Joe (narrating)*: Audiences don't know somebody sits down and writes a picture. They think the actors make it up as they go along.

SOUNDTRACK.

9 *Max von Meyerling (butler, about Norma)*: Madam is the greatest star of them all.

SOUNDTRACK.

10 *Norma (on Joe leaving her)*: No one ever leaves a star. That's what makes one a star.

SOUNDTRACK.

11 *Norma*: This is my life. It always will be. There's nothing else. Just us, the cameras and those wonderful people out there in the dark. All right, Mr DeMille, I'm ready for my close-up.

SOUNDTRACK. Last line of film. Norma has been trying to stage a come-back with Cecil B. DeMille (played by himself). Finally, she fools herself that movie cameras are waiting for her return, whereas in fact they are newsreel cameras that have come to her house following her murder of Joe. The musical (1993) made after the movie, with book by Christopher Hampton and music by Andrew Lloyd Webber, has rather the spoken line, 'And now, Mr DeMille, I'm ready for my close-up.'

The SUNSHINE BOYS

US 1975; screenwriter: Neil Simon (from his play); cast: Walter Matthau (Willy Clark), Richard Benjamin (Ben Clark).

1 *Willy (to Ben, passing on his vaudeville experience)*: Words with a K are funny.

SOUNDTRACK.

SUPERMAN

UK 1978; screenwriters: Mario Puzo and others (from the comic strip); cast: Christopher Reeve (Clark Kent/Superman), Margot Kidder (Lois Lane).

2 You'll believe a man can fly.

SLOGAN.

3 *Announcer*: Faster than a speeding bullet! *(ricochet)* More powerful than a locomotive! *(locomotive roar)* Able to leap tall buildings at a single bound! *(rushing wind)* Look! Up in the sky!
Voice 1: It's a bird!
Voice 2: It's a plane!
Voice 3: It's Superman!
Announcer: Yes, it's Superman – a strange visitor from another planet, who came to earth with powers and abilities far beyond those of mortal men. Superman! – who can change the course of mighty rivers, bend steel in his bare hands, and who – disguised as Clark Kent, mild-mannered reporter for a great metropolitan newspaper – fights a never-ending battle for truth, justice and the American way.

SOUNDTRACK. Reproducing the original American radio introduction of the 1940s.

4 *Superman (to Lois)*: I never drink when I fly.

SOUNDTRACK.

Gloria SWANSON

American actress (1897–1983)

1 [telegram to Adolph Zukor, on her marriage to a French Marquis in 1926] AM ARRIVING WITH THE MARQUIS TOMORROW STOP PLEASE ARRANGE OVATION.

QUOTED in Alexander Walker, *Stardom* (1970).

2 In those days the public wanted us to live like kings and queens. So we did – and why not? We were in love with life. We were making more money than we ever dreamed existed and there was no reason to believe that it would ever stop.

QUOTED by De Witt Bodeen in *Films in Review* (April 1965).

3 I have gone through a long apprenticeship. I have gone through enough of being nobody. I have decided that when I am a star I will be every inch and every moment the star. Everyone from the studio gateman to the highest executive will know it.

QUOTED in Alexander Walker, *The Celluloid Sacrifice* (1966). *Compare* ***SUNSET BOULEVARD*** 402:7.

TAKE THE MONEY AND RUN

US 1969; screenwriters: Woody Allen (director), Mickey Rose; cast: Woody Allen (Virgil Starkwell).

1 *Virgil*: I think crime pays. The hours are good, you travel a lot.

SOUNDTRACK.

2 *Virgil*: The psychiatrist asked me if I thought sex was dirty and I said, 'It is if you're doing it right.'

SOUNDTRACK

A TALE OF TWO CITIES

US 1935; screenwriters: W.P. Lipscomb, S.N. Behrman (from Charles Dickens novel); cast: Ronald Colman (Sydney Carton).

3 *Carton (in narration, as he goes to execution)*: It's a far, far better thing I do than I have ever done. It's a far, far better rest I go to than I have ever known.

SOUNDTRACK. Last words of film. At the end of the novel (Bk 3, Chap. 15), these are not represented as Carton's 'last words' as he ascends the scaffold to be guillotined. He does not actually speak them. They are prefaced with: 'If he had given any utterance to his [last thoughts], and they were prophetic, they would have been these ...'

One editor refers to this as, 'A complicated excursus into the pluperfect subjunctive.' In most dramatizations, however, Carton has actually *said* the lines – as did Sir John Martin-Harvey in the play, *The Only Way* (1898) by F. Wills. This pattern has been followed in subsequent film re-makes.

Quentin TARANTINO

American director, screenwriter and actor (1963–)

4 We're gonna sell you this seat, but you're only going to use the edge of it.

QUOTED in advertising for his *Reservoir Dogs* (1992).

5 Violence in real life is terrible; violence in the movies can be cool. It's just another colour to work with.

QUOTED in *The Observer*, 'Sayings of the Week' (16 October 1994).

1 I don't think you can go too far with violence if what you're doing is right for the movie. What's too far?

QUOTED in *Time Out* (September 1994).

2 To be elitist about the film industry is a cancer, and that is what Europe is suffering from now.

REMARK from the same interview.

3 I get a kick out of violence in movies. The worst thing about movies is, no matter how far you can go, when it comes to violence you are wearing a pair of handcuffs that novelists … don't wear.

QUOTED in introduction to *Reservoir Dogs* (screenplay, 1995).

4 I steal from every single movie ever made. I love it – if my work has anything it's that I'm taking this from this and that from that and mixing them together. If people don't like that, then tough titty, don't go and see it, all right? I steal from everything. Great artists steal, they don't do homages.

QUOTED in Jami Bernard *Quentin Tarantino: The Man and His Movies* (1995).

See also **PULP FICTION**; **RESERVOIR DOGS**.

TARZAN THE APE MAN

US 1932; screenwriters: Cyril Hume, Ivor Novello; cast: Johnny Weissmuller (Tarzan), Maureen O'Sullivan (Jane).

5 *Tarzan*: Tarzan – Jane.

SOUNDTRACK. At one point the ape man whisks Jane away to his tree-top abode and indulges in some elementary conversation with her. Thumping his chest, he says, 'Tarzan!'; pointing at her, he says, 'Jane!' So, in fact, he does not say the catchphrase commonly associated with him, though Weissmuller did use the words in an interview for *Photoplay Magazine* (June 1932) – 'I didn't have to act in "Tarzan, the Ape Man" – just said, "Me Tarzan, you Jane"' – so it is not surprising the misquotation arose. In the original novel, *Tarzan of the Apes* (1914) by Edgar Rice Burroughs, the line does not occur, not least because, in the jungle, Tarzan and Jane are able to communicate only by writing notes to each other.

A TASTE OF HONEY

UK 1961; screenwriter: Shelagh Delaney (from her play); cast: Rita Tushingham (Jo).

6 *Jo*: I'm not just talented. I'm geniused.

SOUNDTRACK.

See also Shelagh **DELANEY** 130:6.

TAXI!

US 1931; screenwriters: Kubec Glasmon, John Bright (from a play *The Blind Spot* by Kenyon Nicholson); cast: James Cagney (Matt Nolan).

1 *Matt*: Come out and take it, you dirty yellow-bellied rat, or I'll give it to you through the door.

SOUNDTRACK. *Compare* ***BLONDE CRAZY*** 64:3.

TAXI DRIVER

US 1976; screenwriter: Paul Schrader; cast: Robert De Niro (Travis Bickle).

2 *Travis (to himself in the mirror)*: You talkin' to me?

SOUNDTRACK.

A.J.P. TAYLOR

English historian (1906–90)

3 I now formulate a general rule: 'The best films are those no one has heard of.' I name two for a start: *Closely Observed Trains* and *The Lady with the Little Dog*, the latter of which could take the place of *Battleship Potemkin*, which was always very boring.

REMARK in *London Review of Books* (18 November–1 December 1982).

(Dame) Elizabeth TAYLOR

British-born actress (1932–)

4 If someone was stupid enough to offer me a million dollars to make a picture – I was certainly not dumb enough to turn it down.

QUOTED in David Niven, *The Moon's a Balloon* (1975).

5 Some of my best leading men have been horses and dogs.

ATTRIBUTED remark.

6 I'm still trying to find the real Elizabeth Taylor and make her stand up.

QUOTED in *The Observer*, 'Sayings of the Week' (11 March 1984).

7 I, along with the critics, have never taken myself very seriously.

QUOTED in *The Independent* (20 March 1993).

8 [recuperating from brain surgery] I've still got a lot of living left to do. It's not over. The Fat Lady has not sung.

QUOTED in *The Observer* (23 March 1997).

1 [accepting BAFTA Lifetime Achievement Fellowship] I have never really thought of myself as an actor, I haven't tried, really, to act for God knows how many years. I don't think of myself as an actor and I didn't think any of you did. This award makes me want to act again.

SPEECH in London (11 April 1999).

2 Just how garish her commonplace accent, squeakily shrill voice, and the childish petulance with which she delivers her lines are, my pen is neither scratchy nor leaky enough to convey.

COMMENT by John Simon on her 'Kate' in *The Taming of the Shrew* (US 1967).

3 There are three things I never saw Elizabeth Taylor do – tell a lie, be unkind to anyone and be on time.

COMMENT by Mike Nichols, German-born American actor and director (1931–), quoted in *Sunday Today*, 'Quotes of the Week' (12 April 1987).

4 Elizabeth is a wonderful movie actor: she has a deal with the film lab – she gets better in the bath over night.

COMMENT by Mike Nichols, interviewed in *Vanity Fair* (June 1994).

5 Elizabeth Taylor is a pre-feminist woman. This is the source of her continuing greatness and relevance. She wields the sexual power that feminism cannot explain and has tried to destroy. Through stars like Taylor, we sense the world-disordering impact of legendary women like Delilah, Salome, and Helen of Troy.

COMMENT by Camille Paglia in *Penthouse* (US) (March 1992).

See also Earl **WILSON** 450:5.

Shirley TEMPLE

American child actress and diplomat (1928–)

6 I stopped believing in Santa Claus when I was six. Mother took me to see him in a department store and he asked for my autograph.

ATTRIBUTED remark. There is a version in *The Guinness Book of Movie Facts & Feats* (ed. Patrick Robertson)(1993 edn).

7 During this depression, when the spirit of the people is lower than at any other time, it is a splendid thing that for just fifteen cents an American can go to a movie and look at the smiling face of a baby and forget his troubles.

COMMENT by President F.D. Roosevelt in 1935, quoted in J.R. Colombo, *Wit and Wisdom of the Moviemakers* (1979).

1 Shirley Temple acts and dances with immense vigour and assurance, but some of her popularity seems to rest on a coquetry quite as mature as [Claudette] Colbert's and an oddly precocious body as voluptuous in grey flannel trousers as Miss Dietrich's.

COMMENT by Graham Greene, reviewing *Captain January* in *The Spectator* (7 August 1936). Greene's subsequent comments in *Night and Day* (28 October 1937) famously formed the basis of a libel action that Temple won. The statement of claim held that Greene had accused Twentieth-Century Fox of 'procuring' Miss Temple, 'a depraved and degraded child' [she was then nine years old], 'to play the leading part in the said film for which she had accordingly become well-fitted by virtue of her sexual precocity.'

The TERMINATOR

US 1984; screenwriters: Gale Anne Hurd, James Cameron; cast: Arnold Schwarzenegger (The Terminator).

2 *The Terminator*: I'll be back!

SOUNDTRACK. He said it only once in the film, but it still became a catchphrase. *Compare* ***PIMPERNEL SMITH*** 329:3.

TERMINATOR 2: JUDGMENT DAY

US 1991; screenwriters: James Cameron, William Wisher; cast: Arnold Schwarzenegger (Terminator T-800).

3 He said 'I'll be back!' ... and he meant it!

SLOGAN.

4 It's nothing personal.

SLOGAN.

5 *Terminator T-800*: *Hasta la vista*, baby.

SOUNDTRACK. The Spanish for 'goodbye', 'au revoir', 'until we meet again' was given a distinctive twist by Schwarzenegger in the film.

Le TESTAMENT D'ORPHÉE

France 1959; screenwriter/director: Jean Cocteau; cast: Maria Casarès (Princess), Jean Cocteau (Himself, the Poet).

6 *Princess*: What do you understand 'film' to mean?
Poet: A film is a petrifying source of thought. A film resuscitates dead actions. A film permits one to give the appearance of reality to the irreal.

SUB-TITLE translation.

THELMA AND LOUISE

US 1991; screenwriter: Callie Khouri; cast: Geena Davis (Thelma Dickinson)

1 Someone said get a life … so they did.

SLOGAN.

2 *Thelma (to policeman whom she is about to lock in trunk of car)*: You be sweet to them, especially your wife. I had a husband that wasn't sweet to me and look how I turned out.

SOUNDTRACK.

THEY SHOOT HORSES, DON'T THEY?

US 1969; screenwriters: James Poe, Robert E. Thompson (from Horace McCoy novel); cast: Gig Young (Rocky).

3 *Rocky*: There can only be one winner, folks, but isn't that the American way?

SOUNDTRACK.

4 *Rocky*: Yowsir, yowsir, yowsir! Here they are again – these wonderful, wonderful kids, still struggling, still hoping as the clock of fate ticks away. The dance of destiny continues. The marathon goes on and on and on. How long can they last? Let's hear it. C'mon, let's hear it. Let's hear it.

SOUNDTRACK. Last lines of film. Portraying a dance marathon contest of the Depression years, this film appropriately highlighted the cry 'yowsir, yowsir' (meaning 'yes, sir, yes, sir'), originated in the 1930s by the orchestra leader and entertainer, Ben Bernie.

The THIEF OF BAGHDAD

UK 1940; screenwriters: Miles Malleson, Lajos Biro; cast: Conrad Veidt (Jaffar), Rex Ingram (Genie), Sabu (Abu the Thief).

5 *Genie (to Abu)*: You're a clever little man, little master of the universe, but mortals are weak and frail.

SOUNDTRACK.

6 *Jaffar*: Chain them to opposite walls. In the morning they die the death of a thousand cuts.

SOUNDTRACK.

The THING

US 1951; screenwriter: Charles Lederer; cast: Douglas Spencer (Ned 'Scotty' Scott).

7 *Scott*: I bring you warning – to every one of you listening to my voice, tell the world. Tell this to everybody, wherever they are: watch the skies, everywhere, keep looking. Keep watching the skies!

SOUNDTRACK. The phrase 'Watch the skies' was later used to promote ***CLOSE ENCOUNTERS OF THE THIRD KIND***, and was indeed the original title of that film.

THINGS TO COME

UK 1936; screenwriters: Lajos Biro, H.G. Wells (from his book *The Shape of Things to Come*); cast: Cedric Hardwicke (Theotocopulos), Raymond Massey (John Oswald/Cabal), Edward Chapman (Pippa/Raymond Passworthy).

1 *Theotocopulos*: An end to progress! Make an end to progress now! Let this be the last day of the scientific age.

SOUNDTRACK.

2 *John*: It is this, or that – all the universe, or nothing. Which shall it be, Passworthy? Which shall it be?

SOUNDTRACK. Last line of film.

The THIRD MAN

UK 1949; screenwriters: Graham Greene, Carol Reed; cast: Orson Welles (Harry Lime), Joseph Cotten (Holly Martins), Trevor Howard (Major Calloway), Alida Valli (Anna Schmidt).

3 *Narration (spoken by Carol Reed)*: I never knew the old Vienna, before the war, with its Strauss music, its glamour and easy charm. I really got to know it in the period of the black market. We'd run anything if people wanted it enough and had the money to pay.

SOUNDTRACK.

4 *Calloway (to Holly)*: Death's at the bottom of everything, Martins. Leave death to the professionals.

SOUNDTRACK.

5 *Harry (to Holly)*: What can I do, old man? I'm dead, aren't I?

SOUNDTRACK.

6 *Harry (to Holly, while both are at the top of a fairground wheel)*: Look down there. Tell me, would you really feel any pity if one of those dots stopped moving forever? If I offered you twenty thousand pounds for every dot that stopped, would you really, old man, tell me to keep my money or would you calculate how many dots you could afford to spare? Free of income tax, old man, free of income tax. It's the only way to save money nowadays.

SOUNDTRACK.

1 *Harry (comparing himself to governments)*: They have their five-year plans and so have I.

SOUNDTRACK.

2 *Harry (to Holly)*: The dead are happier dead. They don't miss much here, poor devils.

SOUNDTRACK.

3 *Harry (to Holly)*: When you make up your mind, send me a message – I'll meet you any place, any time …

SOUNDTRACK.

4 *Harry (to Holly)*: You know what the fellow said – in Italy, for thirty years under the Borgias, they had warfare, terror, murder and bloodshed, but they produced Michelangelo, Leonardo da Vinci and the Renaissance. In Switzerland, they had brotherly love; they had five hundred years of democracy and peace – and what did that produce? The cuckoo clock.

SOUNDTRACK. Lines added by Welles. Indeed, it appears only as a footnote in the published script of the film. In a letter, dated 13 October 1977, Greene confirmed to me that it *had* been written by Welles during shooting: 'What happened was that during the shooting of *The Third Man* it was found necessary for the timing to insert another sentence and the speech you mention was put in by Orson Welles.' In a John Player Lecture, London (1970), Greene said: 'He [Welles] wrote … the best line in the film. He wrote the piece about the cuckoo clock.'

Whether the idea was original to Welles is another matter. After all, he introduces the speech with, 'You know what the fellow said …' Welles apparently later suggested that the lines came originally from 'an old Hungarian play'. Anthony Powell in his *Journals 1982–1986* (1995 – entry for 21 December 1986) points out that the painter Whistler 'initially made joke about the Swiss having invented the Cuckoo Clock as chief fame in their cultural achievements. This I corroborated (*Whistler's Ten O'Clock*, 1885), so joke just over century old.'

Indeed, in Mr Whistler's 'Ten O'Clock' (1888), which is the text of a lecture he gave on art in 1885, Whistler spoke of: 'The Swiss in their mountains … What more worthy people! … yet, the perverse and scornful [goddess, Art] will none of it, and the sons of patriots are left with the clock that turns the mill, and the sudden cuckoo, with difficulty restrained in its box! For this was Tell a hero! For this did Gessler die!'

In *This Is Orson Welles* (1993), Welles is quoted as saying: 'When the picture came out, the Swiss very nicely pointed out to me that they've never made any cuckoo clocks – they all come from the Schwarzwald in Bavaria!' Actually the Schwarzwald [Black Forest] is in Baden-Württemberg.

5 *Holly (on being told to be sensible about Anna)*: Haven't got a sensible name, Calloway.

SOUNDTRACK. Last line of film.

The THIRTY-NINE STEPS

UK 1935; screenwriters: Charles Bennett, Alma Reville, Ian Hay (from John Buchan novel): cast: Robert Donat (Richard Hannay), Lucie Mannheim (Annabella/ 'Miss Smith'), Frank Cellier (Sheriff Watson), Madeleine Carroll (Pamela), Wylie Watson (Mr Memory).

1 *'Miss Smith'*: I'd like to come home with you.
Hannay: It's your funeral.

SOUNDTRACK. And so it is – she is knifed when she gets there.

2 *Hannay (of 'Miss Smith')*: Beautiful, mysterious woman pursued by gunmen. Sounds like a spy story.

SOUNDTRACK.

3 *'Miss Smith' (to Hannay)*: Have you ever heard of the Thirty-Nine Steps?
Hannay: No, what's that – a pub?

SOUNDTRACK.

4 *'Miss Smith'*: He can look like a hundred people, but one thing he cannot disguise – this: half of his little finger is missing – so if ever you should meet with no top joint there, be very careful about that.

SOUNDTRACK.

5 *Sheriff Watson*: Well, it's a lesson to us all, Mr Hannay – not to mix with doubtful company on the Sabbath.

SOUNDTRACK.

6 *Hannay (to Pamela)*: There are twenty million women in this island and I've got to be chained to you.

SOUNDTRACK.

7 *Hannay*: I've got it! I've got it! Of course, there is nobody that's missing. All the information's inside Memory's head.

SOUNDTRACK.

8 *Mr Memory (on stage at the Palladium)*: The Thirty-Nine Steps is an organization of spies, collecting information on behalf of the foreign office of --.

SOUNDTRACK. At this point he is shot. *Compare* **CLICHÉS** 106:2.

9 *Mr Memory (dying words)*: Thank you, sir. Thank you. I'm glad it's off my mind at last.

SOUNDTRACK. Last line of film.

THIS IS SPINAL TAP

US 1984; screenwriters: Christopher Guest, Michael McKean, Harry Shearer, Rob Reiner; cast: Rob Reiner (Marty DeBergi), Michael McKean (David St Hubbins), Christopher Guest (Nigel Tufnel), Ed Begley Jr (John 'Stumpy' Pepys), Bruno Kirby (Tommy Picchedda), Fran Drescher (Bobbi Flekman), Tony Hendra (Ian Faith), Harry Shearer (Derek Smalls), Fred Willard (Lieut. Bob Hopkstratten).

1 *Marty (introducing his film)*: The, if you will, 'rockumentary' that you are about to see …

SOUNDTRACK.

2 *David (of rock drummer, 'Stumpy' Pepys)*: He died in a bizarre gardening accident.

SOUNDTRACK.

3 *Tommy (to Marti, of Frank Sinatra)*: When you've loved and lost, the way Frank has, then you, uh, you know what life's about.

SOUNDTRACK.

4 *Bobbi (to Ian, about the* Smell the Glove *album cover)*: You put a greased, naked, woman on all fours, with a dog collar around her neck, and a leash, and a man's arm extended out up to here, holding on to the leash and pushing a black glove in her face to sniff it. You don't find that offensive?

SOUNDTRACK.

5 *David*: It's such a fine line between stupid and …
Derek: … and clever.

SOUNDTRACK.

6 *Ian (on whether Spinal Tap's appeal is waning, with their audiences down to 10% of what they once were)*: Oh, no, no, no, no, no, no, no, no, no, not at all. I just think that their appeal is becoming more selective.

SOUNDTRACK.

7 *David (complaining about stage scenery)*: I think that the problem may have been that there was a Stonehenge monument on the stage that was in danger of being crushed by a dwarf. That tended to understate the hugeness of the object.

SOUNDTRACK.

8 *Lieut. Bob (welcoming group to perform at military installation)*: We are such fans of your music, and all of your records. I'm not speaking of yours personally, but the whole genre of the rock and roll.

SOUNDTRACK.

1 *David (to Marti about Nigel's quitting the group)*: I'm sure I'd feel much worse if I wasn't under such heavy sedation.

SOUNDTRACK.

Emma THOMPSON

English actress and screenwriter (1959–)

2 [on her then husband Kenneth Branagh and herself] Ken's this kind of plumber figure and I'm this hulking great bluestocking.

QUOTED in *The Independent* (23 May 1992).

3 [on receiving Oscar for Best Actress] I am very, very gobsmacked.

QUOTED in *The Independent* (3 April 1993).

4 Before I came, I went to visit Jane Austen's grave to pay my respects – and tell her about the grosses. I don't know how she would react to an evening like this, but I do hope she knows how big she is in Uruguay.

SPEECH accepting Oscar for screenplay of *Sense and Sensibility* (March 1996).

Virgil THOMSON

American composer (1896–1989)

5 [I] realize where the fault in our Hollywood musical credo lies. It lies in the simple truth that it is not possible to write real music about an unreal emotion.

QUOTED in *New York Herald-Tribune* (10 April 1949).

A THOUSAND CLOWNS

US 1965; screenwriter: Herb Gardner (from his play): cast: Jason Robards (Murray Burns), Martin Balsam (Arnold Burns).

6 *Murray*: I want him to know the sneaky, subtle, important reason he was born a human – and not a chair.

SOUNDTRACK.

The THREE LITTLE PIGS

US 1933; music/lyrics: Frank Churchill/Vance Colvig.

7 Who's Afraid of the Big Bad Wolf?

TITLE of song.

THUNDERBALL

UK 1965; screenwriters: Richard Maibaum, John Hopkins (after Ian Fleming novel); cast: Sean Connery (James Bond), Lois Maxwell (Miss Moneypenny), Claudine Auger (Domino), Desmond Llewellyn (Q), Luciana Paluzzi (Fiona Volpe), Philip Locke (Varga).

1 *Bond (to Miss Moneypenny, on his womanizing)*: There's never been a man more misunderstood.

SOUNDTRACK.

2 *Domino*: What sharp little eyes you've got.
Bond: Wait till you get to my teeth.

SOUNDTRACK.

3 *Bond (sending minor criminal back to his bosses)*: Tell them, the little fish I throw back into the sea.

SOUNDTRACK.

4 *Q*: Try to be a little less than your usual frivolous self, 007.

SOUNDTRACK.

5 *Bond (to shark he has escaped)*: Now you can tell about the one that got away.

SOUNDTRACK.

6 *Bond (to Fiona)*: My dear girl, don't flatter yourself. What I did this evening was for king and country. You don't think it gave me any pleasure, do you?

SOUNDTRACK.

7 *Bond (to nightclubbers, referring to Fiona who has just been shot on the dance floor and whom he deposits in a chair)*: Mind if my friend sits this one out? She's just dead.

SOUNDTRACK.

8 *Bond (to Domino, after underwater love-making)*: I hope we didn't frighten the fish.

SOUNDTRACK.

9 *Bond (after harpooning Varga)*: I think he got the point.

SOUNDTRACK.

TILLIE AND GUS

US 1933; screenwriter: Walter de Leon, Francis Martin; cast: W.C. Fields (Augustus Q. Winterbottom).

1 *Winterbottom (asked if he likes children)*: I do – if they are properly cooked.

SOUNDTRACK.

Dimitri TIOMKIN

Russian-born American composer (1899–1979)

2 [accepting Academy Award for his score for *The High and the Mighty* (1955)] I would like to thank Beethoven, Brahms, Wagner, Strauss, Rimsky-Korsakov …

ATTRIBUTED remark, quoted in Ned Shapiro, *An Encyclopedia of Quotations About Music* (1978).

TITANIC

US 1997; screenwriter/director: James Cameron; cast: Kate Winslet (Rose).

3 *Maid (looking at new painting)*: What's the artist's name?
Rose: Something Picasso.

SOUNDTRACK.

4 *Rose*: Do you know of Dr Freud … ? His ideas about the male preoccupation with size might be of particular interest to you.

SOUNDTRACK.

5 [when *Titanic* won the first of many awards] Does this prove once and for all that size does matter?

COMMENT by James Cameron, quoted in *The Observer* (25 January 1998).

TITLES OF FILMS

See also under individual titles.

6 An Angel at My Table (New Zealand/Australia 1990).

The film is based on the autobiographies of the New Zealand poet Janet Frame. This is taken from the title of Vol. 2 (1984), where the source is given in an epigraph as from Raine Maria Rilke's '*Vergers*': '*Reste tranquille, si soudain / L'ange à ta table se décide; / Efface doucement les quelques rides / Que fait la nappe sous ton pain*.'

7 At Play in the Fields of the Lord (US 1992).

Taken from the title of the novel by Peter Matthiessen (1965).

1 Bellman and True (UK 1988).

Based on a novel by Desmond Lowden, *Bellman and True* (1975), which is about a 'bellman' in the criminal sense: that is, a man who disables alarm systems so that robberies can take place. However, the phrase 'Bellman and True' comes from the list of hounds in John Woodcock Graves's song 'D'ye ken John Peel' (1832): 'Yes, I ken John Peel, and Ruby too, / Ranter and Ringwood, Bellman and True, / From a find to a check, from a check to a view, / From a view to a death in the morning.'

2 Blonde Bombshell (US 1933).

This was the British title of *Bombshell* – perhaps to indicate that it was not a war film but about a character played by Jean Harlow. Hence, the much later journalistic cliché used to describe *any* (however vaguely) blonde woman, but especially if a dynamic personality – usually a film star, show business figure or model. In June 1975, Margo Macdonald complained of being described by the *Daily Mirror* as 'the blonde bombshell MP' who 'hits the House of Commons today'.

3 The Discreet Charm of the Bourgeoisie [*Le charme discret de la bourgeoisie/El discreto encanto de la burgesía*] (France/Spain/Italy 1972).

Coined by the director Luis Buñuel.

4 Do Not Fold Spindle or Mutilate (US 1971).

In the US, when punched cards and computer cards began to accompany bills and statements in the 1950s, this immortal phrase (or bossy injunction) was printed on them (though did people really know what 'spindle' meant?). By the 1960s, the words were seen as a token of a machine age that was taking over, and a slogan of the student revolution was: 'I am a human being – do not fold, spindle or mutilate me.' A graffito (quoted 1974) read: 'I am a masochist – please spindle, fold or mutilate'. By the 1980s, the cards were no longer necessary and the phrase died with it. *Bartlett's Familiar Quotations* originally dated the introduction of the words to the 1930s, but has now plumped for the 1950s. But if the dating is somewhat of a mystery, there is confusion, too, over the actual wording. Janet Lewis says she learnt the words as 'Do not fold, roll or spindle' on 'punch card cheques' and 'as the chorus to a rather dirty song at my Quaker college [Swarthmore] between 1946 and graduation in June 1950. A high proportion of the men were studying under the GI Bill of Rights. Their monthly cheques were an important event, so the words found their way into a song … I can only remember one feeble example of the innumerable verses':When you're out with your girl friend, / And you've been trying to sell her, / When she asks to see it / Don't forget to tell her: / *Chorus* / Do not fold, roll or spindle, / Mutilate or damage; / When you want to cash it / Endorse it on the back.

5 Do the Right Thing (US 1989)

About black people in a Brooklyn slum. From *Harper's Index* (January 1990): 'Number of times the phrase "do the right thing" has been used in Congress since Spike Lee's film was released last June: 67. Number of times the phrase was used in reference to congressional pay rise: 16. Number of times it was used in reference to racial issues: 1.'

1 Eat the Peach (Ireland 1986).

Alluding to the line 'Do I dare to eat a peach?' from T.S. Eliot, 'The Love Song of J. Alfred Prufrock' (1917).

2 Eyes Wide Shut (US 1999).

Basil Copper wrote to *The Observer* (19 September 1999): 'I have a close friend who appears in the film and over many weeks on the shoot he came to know [Stanley Kubrick, the director]. He told me that the director often repeated to friends and colleagues an aphorism of his own coinage: "Governments, politicians and generals are leading the world with their eyes wide shut."'

3 Favourites of the Moon [*Les Favoris de la Lune*] (France 1984).

This was a quirky piece about Parisian crooks, petty and otherwise, whose activities overlapped in one way or another, but the English title hardly seemed relevant to the subject. Not surprisingly, as it was a translation back into English. As a caption acknowledged, the original French title was a translation of the original Shakespearean phrase 'minions of the moon'. In *Henry IV, Part 1*, I.ii.25-, Falstaff says to Prince Hal: 'Let not us that are squires of the night's body be called thieves of the day's beauty: let us be Diana's foresters, gentlemen of the shade, minions of the moon.' ('minions of the moon' = night-time robbers)

4 The Four Hundred Blows [*Les Quatre Cents Coups*] (France 1959).

François Truffaut's first major film took its title from the French slang expression *faire les quatre cents coups* (meaning, 'to paint the town red' or 'to be up to all sorts of tricks').

5 Fun in a Chinese Laundry (US 1900).

This was the title of a Thomas A. Edison short. Later used by Joseph Von Sternberg as the title of his memoirs (1966).

6 The Good, the Bad and the Ugly [*Il Buono, il Brutto, il Cattivo*] (Italy 1966).

Title of the 'spaghetti Western' co-written and directed by Sergio Leone. Examples of how the phrase has passed into popular use range from Colonel Oliver North, giving evidence to the Washington hearings on the Irangate scandal in the summer of 1987: 'I came here to tell you the truth – the good, the bad, and the ugly'; to two headlines, both from *The Independent* (16 September 1996): 'The Good ... the Bad ... and the Ugly: The Premiership's Leading Scorers'; 'The Good, the Bad and the Spoilt: How Children React'.

7 The Great Train Robbery (US 1903).

Title of an eleven-minute silent film that is sometimes considered to be the first 'real' movie, as well as the first movie Western. In 1963, when £2.5 million was stolen from a British mail train, the event rapidly acquired the sobriquet of 'The Great Train Robbery'. This event, in turn, was celebrated in a film entitled (simply) *Robbery* (UK 1967).

1 Hallelujah, I'm a Bum (US 1933).

From the title of a song (1928) by Harry Kirby McClintock. For the film, a new song with the title was written by Lorenz Hart (music by Richard Rodgers), which, in fact, only included the line 'Hallelujah, I'm a bum again!' Even so, a separate version had to be made for the sensitive British censor, who also insisted on the film being re-titled *Hallelujah, I'm a Tramp* for British audiences.

2 A Hard Day's Night (UK 1964).

Chosen towards the end of filming when Ringo Starr used the phrase to describe a 'heavy' night out (according to Ray Coleman, *John Lennon*, 1984). Hunter Davies, *The Beatles* (1968) noted, however: 'Ringo Starr came out with the phrase, though John [Lennon] had used it earlier in a poem.' The phrase was also used for the title song.

3 How the West Was Won (US 1962).

Could this be an origin? – in *San Antonio* (US 1945), cowboy Errol Flynn gets into a stagecoach and sits next to dance-hall entertainer Alexis Smith. She asks, 'Is it a Western custom to push yourself in where you're not wanted?' He replies: 'Yes, ma'am, that's the way the West was won.'

4 I Cover the Waterfront (US 1933).

Film about a newspaper reporter exposing corruption, based on a book (1932) by Max Miller, a 'waterfront reporter' on the *San Diego Sun*. Hence 'cover' is in the journalistic sense. The song with this title (by John W. Green and Ed Heyman), sung notably by Billie Holiday, is unconnected with the film and sounds as if it might be about laying paving stones or some other activity. It was so successful, however, that it was later added to the soundtrack. Since the film, 'to cover the waterfront' has meant 'to cover all aspects of a topic' or merely 'to experience something'.

5 I Went Down (UK/Ireland/Spain 1997).

Quirky film about small-time Irish crooks. A caption identifies the title as taken from the opening words of Plato, *The Republic*: 'I went down to the Piraeus yesterday with Glaucon, the son of Ariston', but the film makes plain that it is also intended as a multiple pun on the prison, sexual and other uses of the term.

6 I've Heard the Mermaids Singing (Canada 1987).

Alluding to the line 'I have heard the mermaids singing, each to each. / I do not think that they will sing to me' from T.S. Eliot, 'The Love Song of J. Alfred Prufrock' (1917).

7 If It's Tuesday This Must Be Belgium (US 1969).

Film about a group of American tourists rushing around Europe. It popularized a format phrase that people could use when they were in the midst of some hectic activity, whilst also reflecting on the confused state of many tourists superficially 'doing' the sights without really knowing where they are. A *Guardian* headline (7 April 1989) on a brief visit to London by Mikhail Gorbachev: 'If It's Thursday, Then It Must Be Thatcherland'.

1 Let's Kill All the Lawyers (US 1992).

Line taken from Shakespeare, *Henry VI, Part 2*, IV.ii.73 (1590–91): 'The first thing we do, let's kill all the lawyers' (spoken by Dick the Butcher, one of Jack Cade's rebels).

2 Life Is Beautiful [*La vita è bella*] (Italy 1998).

Proverbial saying? *Compare* ***CABARET*** 82:1.

3 Like Water for Chocolate [*Como agua para chocolate*] (Mexico 1991).

Referring to the temper of the heroine – kept just below boiling point as in the making of chocolate. The title of Laura Esquival's novel, on which the film was based, is *Like Water for Hot Chocolate*.

4 Love and Pain and the Whole Damn Thing (US 1972).

Directed by Alan J. Pakula and scripted by Alvin Sargent, this appears to have inspired *Love, Pain and the Whole Damn Thing*, the English title of a short story collection (1989) by the German writer and film director, Doris Dorie.

5 Mean Streets (US 1973).

The title is taken from Raymond Chandler's description of the heroic qualities a detective should have: 'Down these mean streets a man must go who is not himself mean; who is neither tarnished nor afraid' – 'The Simple Art of Murder' (in the *Atlantic Monthly*, December 1944, reprinted in *Pearls Are a Nuisance*, 1950). However, the phrase 'mean streets' was not original. In 1894, Arthur Morrison had written *Tales of Mean Streets* about impoverished life in the East End of London. The usage was well established by 1922 when the *Weekly Dispatch* was using the phrase casually: 'For him there is glamor in the mean streets of dockland.'

6 Morgan – A Suitable Case for Treatment (UK 1966).

David Mercer's original 1962 TV play was simply entitled *A Suitable Case for Treatment*.

7 Naked As Nature Intended (UK 1961).

Title of the most famous British nudist film.

8 Naughty But Nice (US 1939).

Eric Partridge in his slang dictionary glossed this phrase as 'a reference to copulation since about 1900 ex a song that Minnie Schult sang and popularized in the USA, 1890s'. There have been various other songs with the title subsequently – not least by Johnny Mercer and Harry Warren in *The Belle of New York* (US 1952). Compare, 'It's Foolish But It's Fun' (Gus Kahn/Robert Stolz) sung by Deanna Durbin in *Spring Parade* (US 1940).

9 Never On Sunday [*Pote tin Kyriaki*] (Greece 1959).

The title refers to the fact that the main character, a prostitute (played by Melina Mercouri), rests on the sabbath.

1 The Ploughman's Lunch (UK 1983).

The theme of this film, scripted by Ian McEwan, was the way that history (especially recent history) tends to get re-written. The title, unexplained, must have puzzled many, including those who were familiar with the term for a meal of bread, cheese and pickle. The point was that, though redolent of olden days, the term was introduced as a marketing ploy by the English Country Cheese Council in the late 1960s. B.H. Axler's *The Cheese Handbook* (1970) has a preface by Sir Richard Trehane, Chairman of the English Country Cheese Council & Milk Marketing Board. He writes: 'English cheese and beer have for centuries formed a perfect combination enjoyed as the Ploughman's Lunch.' Another source credits Trehane with introducing the term as a marketing tool. It is clear, however, that the concept and the name had long existed. In Lockhart's *Memoirs of the Life of Sir Walter Scott* (1837), there is this: 'The surprised poet swung forth to join them, with an extemporised sandwich, that looked like a ploughman's luncheon, in his hand.'

2 Poor Little Rich Girl (US 1917).

This gave Noël Coward the title of his song for *Charlot's Revue of 1926* rather than the other way round. The Mary Pickford film of 1917 was re-made in 1936.

3 Prick Up Your Ears.

This title for a Joe Orton film script that was never made was suggested by his lover (and eventual murderer) Kenneth Halliwell. It was, however, used by John Lahr for his biography of Orton (1978) and, at last, by Alan Bennett for a film about Orton and Halliwell (UK 1987).

4 Rebel Without a Cause (US 1955).

According to the *Oxford Dictionary of Modern Quotations* (1991), this was originally the title of a book (sub-titled 'The hypnoanalysis of a criminal psychopath') published by the American psychologist R.M. Lindner in 1944. In the *Oxford Dictionary of Quotations* (1992) Lindner is described as a 'novelist'. The screenplay credit, however, is given to Stewart Stern 'from an original story by the director, Nicholas Ray'. Even so, *The Motion Picture Guide* (1990) gives the provenance of the script as 'based on an adaptation by Irving Shulman of a story line by Ray inspired by the story *The Blind Run* by Dr Robert M. Lindner.'

The film's study of adolescent misbehaviour had little to do with what one would now think of as psychopathic, but it helped popularize the phrase 'rebel without a cause' to describe a certain type of alienated youth of the period. It was the film that projected its star, James Dean, to the status of chief 1950s rebel, a position confirmed when he met his premature end soon after.

5 The Sea Shall Not Have Them (UK 1954).

John Harris's original book (1953) has a note explaining it as 'the motto of Air-Sea Rescue High-Speed Launch Flotillas'. In other words, this was the motto of Coastal Command's ASR Service during the Second World War. The title gave rise to the following anecdote: passing a Leicester Square movie poster that proclaimed 'Michael Redgrave and Dirk Bogarde in *The Sea Shall Not Have Them*', Noël Coward remarked, 'I don't see why not: everyone else has.' Quoted by Sheridan Morley in the *Independent on Sunday* Magazine (12 November 1995).

1 Straw Dogs (US 1971).

The source novel was *The Siege of Trencher's Farm* by Gordon M. Williams. The screenplay by David Z. Goodman and the director, Sam Peckinpah, apparently derived the title from the Chinese philosopher Lao-Tzu: 'Heaven and Earth have no pity; they regard all things as straw dogs.' No reference was made to the title or its possible relevance in the film.

2 Sunday Bloody Sunday (UK 1971).

Since the 19th century there has been the exclamation 'Sunday, *bloody* Sunday!' to reflect frustration at the inactivity and boredom traditionally associated with the Sabbath. This was presumably the cue for the title of Penelope Gilliatt's screenplay. The term 'bloody Sunday', in the literal sense, had been applied to a number of occasions. On 13 November 1887, two men died during a baton charge on a prohibited socialist demonstration in Trafalgar Square, London. On 22 January 1905, hundreds of unarmed peasants were mown down when they marched to petition the Tsar in St Petersburg. In Irish history, there was a Bloody Sunday on 21 November 1920 when, among other incidents, 14 undercover British intelligence agents in Dublin were shot by Sinn Féin. Then, the year following the film's release, the name 'Bloody Sunday' was applied to Sunday 30 January 1972 when British troops killed 13 Catholics after a protest rally in Londonderry, Northern Ireland. In 1983, the Irish group U2 had a song with the title 'Sunday Bloody Sunday'; in 1973, the UK/US group Black Sabbath had released an album with the title *Sabbath Bloody Sabbath.*

3 Sweet Smell of Success (US 1957).

An apparently original coinage by Ernest Lehman (who shares the screenwriting credit with Clifford Odets). It was evidently the title of a short story by Lehman.

4 That Obscure Object of Desire [*Cet obscur objet du désir*] (France/Spain 1977).

Apparently a coinage of the director, Luis Buñuel, as the novel by Pierre Louys upon which the film is based is called *La Femme et le Pantin* [guy/puppet]. The story is about a man whose infatuation with a girl is unrequited.

5 That Was Then ... This Is Now (US 1985).

Based on a novel by S.E. Hinton (1971), this film may have encouraged any number of variations on this phrase. A number of songs and albums have been called something like 'That Was Then, [But] This Is Now', including those by ABC (1983), The Monkees (1986) and Ten City (1994). More recently, in 1996, Orchestral Manoeuvres in the Dark had a number with the title simply 'That Was Then'.

6 The Three Faces of Eve (US 1957).

Based on a book about 'multiple personality', by two MDs, this film launched a journalistic format phrase 'the -- faces of --'. (In Fritz Spiegl's splenetic *Keep Taking the Tabloids*, 1983, he concludes wrongly that the film title was *The Four Faces of Eve* on the basis of a newspaper headline, 'THE FOUR FACES OF STEVE'.) When BBC2 TV started transmissions in 1964 each evening's viewing had its own theme – education, entertainment, minorities – and this scheduling was billed as 'The Seven Faces of the Week' (and was soon abandoned, as it was ratings death). Walter Terry in the *Daily Mail* (19 June 1964) listed the 'ten faces of Harold [Wilson]' – 'Little Englander Harold, Capitalist Harold, Russian Harold …', etc.

1 *Tirez sur le Pianiste* [Shoot the Piano-Player] (France 1960).

Ultimately this probably alludes to the sign 'Please don't shoot the pianist; he is doing his best' that Oscar Wilde reported having seen in a bar or dancing saloon in the Rocky Mountains ('Leadville' from *Impressions of America*, published 1906). Later came the title of pianist/singer Elton John's 1972 record album, 'Don't Shoot Me, I'm Only the Piano-Player'.

2 Truly, Madly, Deeply (UK 1990).

Compare The ***SEVEN YEAR ITCH*** 369:3.

3 *Vaghe stelle dell'Orsa* [Of a Thousand Delights/Sandra] (Italy 1964).

Luchino Visconti's film takes its original Italian title from lines in '*Le Ricordanze*', a poem by Giacomo Leopardi: '*Vaghe stelle dell'Orsa io non credea / Tornare ancora per uso a contemplarvi / Sul paterno giardino scintillanti, / E ragionar con voi dalle finistre / Di questo albergo ove abitai fanciullo / E delle gioie mie vidi la fine* [O you bright stars of the Bear … I did not think that I should come once more, as was my custom, to gaze upon you glittering above my father's garden, or converse with you from the windows of this house, where as a boy I lived, and saw the end of happiness].'

4 Where Were You When the Lights Went Out? (US 1968).

This film was inspired by the great New York blackout of 1965 when the electricity supply failed and, it was popularly believed, the birth rate shot up nine months later. The phrase echoes a nonsense rhyme (of probable American origin) – 'Where was Moses when the light went out? / Down in the cellar eating sauerkraut.'

5 Women On the Verge of a Nervous Breakdown [*Mujeres al borde de un ataque de nervios*] (Spain 1988).

Apparently a coinage of the screenwriter/director, Pedro Almodóvar.

TO BE OR NOT TO BE

US 1942; screenwriter: Edwin Justis Mayer (from story by Ernst Lubitsch (director) and Melchior Lengyel); cast: Jack Benny (Joseph Tura), Sig Rumann (Colonel Ehrhardt).

6 *Ehrhardt (to Tura whom he does not recognize)*: Oh yes, I saw him once. What he [Tura, the actor] did to Shakespeare, we are doing now to Poland.

SOUNDTRACK.

7 *Tura (disguised as Ehrhardt)*: So, they call me Concentration Camp Ehrhardt?!

SOUNDTRACK.

TO CATCH A THIEF

US 1955; screenwriter: John Michael Hayes (from a novel by David Dodge); cast: Cary Grant (John Robie, 'The Cat'), Grace Kelly (Frances Stevens), Brigitte Auber (Danielle Foussard), John Williams (H.H. Hughson), Jessie Royce Landis (Mrs Stevens).

1 *John (to Hughson, insurance investigator)*: For what it's worth, I only stole from people who wouldn't go hungry.

SOUNDTRACK.

2 *John (to Hughson)*: You don't have to spend every day of your life proving your honesty – but I do.

SOUNDTRACK.

3 *Mrs Stevens*: And so to bed, where I can cuddle up to my jewellery.

SOUNDTRACK.

4 *Danielle (to John, of Frances)*: What has she got more of than me – except money?

SOUNDTRACK.

5 *Frances (to John, about his attentions to Danielle)*: Are you sure you were talking about water-skis? From where I sat, it looked as though you were conjugating some irregular verbs.

SOUNDTRACK.

6 *John (to Frances)*: Not only did I enjoy that kiss last night, I was awed by the efficiency behind it.

SOUNDTRACK.

7 *Frances*: Palaces are for royalty. We're just common people with a bank account.

SOUNDTRACK. Subsequently, of course, Grace Kelly became minor royalty herself, as Princess Grace of Monaco.

8 *Frances (to John, offering chicken at picnic)*: You want a leg or a breast?
John: You make the choice.

SOUNDTRACK. In the subsequent *The Horse Soldiers* (US 1959), Constance Towers leans over John Wayne with a platter of delicacies and asks, 'Now what is your preference, the leg or the breast?' *Compare* ***HEAVENS ABOVE*** 209:4.

9 *Frances*: If you really want to see fireworks, it's better with the lights off. I have a feeling that tonight you're going to see one of the Riviera's most fascinating sights … I was talking about the fireworks.

SOUNDTRACK.

1 *Frances (catching sight of John's villa)*: So this is where you live. Oh, Mother will love it up here.

SOUNDTRACK. Last line of film.

TO HAVE AND HAVE NOT

US 1944; screenwriters: Jules Furthman, William Faulkner (from Ernest Hemingway novel); cast: Lauren Bacall (Slim), Humphrey Bogart (Steve), Hoagy Carmichael (Cricket).

2 *Slim*: Anybody got a match?

SOUNDTRACK. Bacall's screen debut line.

3 *Slim (to Bogart before kissing him for the first time)*: You know, Steve, you're not very hard to figure. Only at times. Sometimes I know exactly what you're going to say – most of the time. The other times … The other times you're just a stinker.

SOUNDTRACK.

4 *Slim (on kissing Steve the second time)*: It's even better when you help.

SOUNDTRACK.

5 *Slim*: You know, you don't have to act with me, Steve. You don't have to say anything, and you don't have to do anything. Not a thing. Oh, maybe just whistle. You know how to whistle, don't you, Steve? You just put your lips together and blow.

SOUNDTRACK.

6 *Slim*: I'm hard to get, Steve. All you have to do is ask me.

SOUNDTRACK.

7 *Steve (to piano-player)*: But don't make it sad, Cricket. I don't feel that way.

SOUNDTRACK.

8 *Cricket*: Hey, Slim. Are you still happy?
Slim: What do you think?

SOUNDTRACK. Last lines of film.

TOM JONES

UK 1963; screenwriter: John Osborne (from Henry Fielding novel): cast: Albert Finney (Tom Jones), Susannah York (Sophie Western), David Warner (Blifil), Diane Cilento (Molly Seagrim), Micheál MacLiammóir (Narrator), Hugh Griffith (Squire Western), Joan Greenwood (Lady Bellaston), George Devine (Squire Allworthy).

1 Tom Jones. Of whom the opinion of all was that he was born to be hanged.

SCREEN TITLE.

2 *Blifil (putting down the illegitimate Tom)*: I had the good fortune to know who my parents were. Consequently I am grieved by their loss.

SOUNDTRACK.

3 *Narrator*: Tom had always thought that any woman was better than none, while Molly never felt that one man was quite as good as two.

SOUNDTRACK.

4 *Narrator*: We are all as God made us, and many of us much worse.

SOUNDTRACK.

5 *Tom (to Lady Bellaston)*: If you take my heart by surprise, the rest of my body has the right to follow.

SOUNDTRACK.

6 *Narrator*: In London, love and scandal are considered the best sweeteners of tea.

SOUNDTRACK.

7 *Squire Western (consenting to Tom and Sophie's marriage)*: Tom, thou art as hearty a cock as any in the kingdom. Go on after your mistress.

SOUNDTRACK.

8 *Squire Western (to Allworthy)*: I'll bet thee a thousand pounds to a crown we have a boy tomorrow nine months.

SOUNDTRACK.

9 *Narrator*: Happy the man and happy he alone,
He who can call today his own,
He who secure within can say:
Tomorrow do thy worst!
For I have lived today.

SOUNDTRACK. Last lines of film.

TOMORROW NEVER DIES

US 1997; screenwriter: Bruce Feirstein; cast: Pierce Brosnan (James Bond), Jonathan Pryce (Carver).

10 Tomorrow Never Dies …

TITLE OF FILM. After ***NEVER SAY NEVER AGAIN*** 302:1, this was the first Bond film title not to be taken from an Ian Fleming story nor to have any other Fleming association (*Goldeneye* was the name of Fleming's house in Jamaica). Whether the title has any meaning is, of course, another matter: the villain of the piece is a media mogul and *Tomorrow* is on the masthead of one of his publications. The plot hinges on the mogul's creation of wars and other news events so that his paper can get scoops on them. Presumably, the title also alludes lightly to the proverb 'Tomorrow never comes' (a warning against procrastination).

1 *Carver*: Hold the presses!

SOUNDTRACK.

2 *Carver*: Let the mayhem begin!

SOUNDTRACK.

3 *Carver*: William Randolph Hearst ... who told his photographers, 'You provide the pictures, I'll provide the war.' I've just taken it one step further.

SOUNDTRACK. *Compare* ***CITIZEN KANE*** 102:6.

TOY STORY

US 1995; screenwriters: Joss Whedon and others; cast: Tim Allen (voice of Buzz Lightyear).

4 *Buzz (the astronaut figure)*: To infinity and beyond.

SOUNDTRACK. Also in *Toy Story 2* (2000). Note how in the Preface to his (unrelated) book *To Infinity and Beyond: A Cultural History of the Infinite* (1987), Eli Maor states: 'I took the title *To Infinity and Beyond*, from a telescope manual that listed among the many virtues of the instrument the following: "The range of focus of your telescope is from fifteen feet to infinity and beyond".'

Spencer TRACY

American actor (1900–67)

5 [advice to actors] Just know your lines and don't bump into the furniture.

ATTRIBUTED remark, quoted in *Bartlett's Familiar Quotations* (15th edn, 1980), but ascribed to Noël Coward in the 1992 edition. In Leslie Halliwell, *The Filmgoer's Book of Quotes* (1973), Alfred Lunt is credited with the line: 'The secret of my success? I speak in a loud clear voice and try not to bump into the furniture.' *See also* Ronald **REAGAN** 348:5. Coward seems to be the originator, and Dick Richards in *The Wit of Noël Coward* (1968) has it that he said it during the run of his play *Nude With Violin* (1956–57). *The Sayings of Noel Coward*, ed. Philip Hoare (1997) has this from a 'speech to the Gallery First-Nighter's Club, 1962': 'Speak clearly, don't bump into people, and if you must have motivation think of your pay packet on Friday.'

6 [defending his demands for equal billing with Katharine Hepburn] This is a movie, not a lifeboat.

ATTRIBUTED remark.

1 [explaining what he looked for in a script] Days off.

ATTRIBUTED remark.

2 Spence is the best we have, because you don't see the mechanism working.

COMMENT attributed to Humphrey Bogart.

3 [visiting the set of the 1941 remake of *Dr Jekyll and Mr Hyde* with Tracy in the title roles] Which is he playing now?

COMMENT by W. Somerset Maugham, English novelist and playwright (1874–1965), quoted in Leslie Halliwell, *The Filmgoer's Book of Quotes* (1978 edn). The point of this story is that Tracy did not use any shock make-up, other than a pair of false teeth, to show the transformation from Dr Jekyll to Mr Hyde. The effect was rather subtle – obviously for Maugham. Discussed in John Sutherland, *Can Jane Eyre Be Happy?* (1997).

TRAINSPOTTING

UK 1996; screenwriter: John Hodge (from Irvine Welsh novel); cast: Ewan McGregor (Mark Renton).

4 *Renton (voice over)*: Choose life. Choose a job. Choose a career. Choose a family. Choose a fucking big television, choose washing machines, cars, compact disc players and electrical tin openers … Choose your future. Choose life. But why would I want to do a thing like that? I chose not to choose life: I chose something else. And the reasons? There are no reasons. Who needs reasons when you've got heroin?

SOUNDTRACK. The opening speech of the film, based loosely on a passage that occurs later on in the Welsh novel. Renton is an unrepentant drug abuser.

5 *Renton (as estate agent in London)*: There was no such thing as society and, even if there was, I most certainly had nothing to do with it. For the first time in my adult life, I was almost content.

SOUNDTRACK.

TREASURE ISLAND

UK 1950; screenwriter: Lawrence Edward Watkin (after R.L. Stevenson novel); cast: Robert Newton (Long John Silver).

6 *Silver*: Ha-harr, Jim, lad!

SOUNDTRACK. Stock phrase. Nowadays used to indicate how any piratical old sea dog would talk. The English comedian Tony Hancock may actually have attempted the impersonation of Newton on stage, but the phrase tended to be trotted out in his BBC radio and TV shows in the 1950s in emulation of *bad* impressionism.

The TREASURE OF THE SIERRA MADRE

US 1948; screenwriter/director: John Huston (from B. Traven novel); cast: Humphrey Bogart (Fred C. Dobbs), Alfonso Bedoya (Gold Hat).

1 *Gold Hat (to Dobbs)*: Badges? We ain't got no badges! We don't need no badges! I don't have to show you any stinking badges!

SOUNDTRACK. *Compare* ***BLAZING SADDLES*** 63:6.

John TREVELYAN

English censor (1904–85)

2 We are paid to have dirty minds.

QUOTED in *The Observer*, 'Sayings of the Week' (15 November 1959). Trevelyan was secretary of the British Board of Film Censors 1958–70.

TROUBLE ALONG THE WAY

US 1953; screenwriters: Melville Shavelson, Jack Rose; cast; John Wayne (Steve Williams).

3 *Steve*: Winning isn't everything. It's the only thing.

SOUNDTRACK. Various versions of this oft-repeated statement exist. Vince Lombardi, coach and general manager of the Green Bay Packers team from 1959 onwards, claimed *not* to have said it in this form but, rather, 'Winning is not everything – but making the effort to win is' (interview 1962). The first version of Lombardi's remarks to appear in print was in the form, 'Winning is not the most important thing, it's everything.' One Bill Veeck is reported to have said something similar. Henry 'Red' Sanders, a football coach at Vanderbilt University, *does* seem to have said it, however, in about 1948, and was so quoted in *Sports Illustrated* (26 December 1955). John Wayne, playing a football coach, said it in this film.

TROUBLE IN PARADISE

US 1932; screenwriters: Grover Jones, Samson Raphaelson; cast: Herbert Marshall (Gaston Monescu), Kay Francis (Mariette Colet).

4 *Gaston*: I want you to take five dozen roses – deep red roses – and I want you to put them in a basket and send them to Madame Colet … Charge it to Madame Colet.

SOUNDTRACK. *Compare* ***A DAY AT THE RACES*** 126:3.

The TROUBLE WITH HARRY

US 1955; screenwriter: John Michael Hayes (from Jack Trevor Story novel); Mildred Natwick (Miss Gravely), Edmund Gwenn (Capt. Albert Wiles).

5 *Miss Gravely (to Wiles who is dragging a corpse)*: What seems to be the trouble, Captain?

SOUNDTRACK. 'One of the best lines is when old Edmund Gwenn is dragging the body along for the first time and a woman comes up to him on the hill and says, "What seems to be the trouble, Captain?" To me that's terribly funny; that's the spirit of the whole story' – Alfred Hitchcock, quoted in François Truffaut, *Hitchcock* (English version, 1968).

Fernando TRUEBA

Spanish critic and director (1955–)

1 *La vida es un película mal montada* [Life is a badly edited film].

ATTRIBUTED remark.

François TRUFFAUT

French screenwriter, director and critic (1932–84)

2 A film is a boat which is always on the point of sinking – it always tends to break up as you go along and drag you under with it.

INTERVIEWED in Peter Graham, *The New Wave* (1968).

3 To make a film is to improve on life, arrange it to suit oneself, it is to prolong the games of childhood, to construct something that is at once a new toy and a vase in which one can arrange, as if they were a bouquet of flowers, the ideas one feels at the moment or in a permanent way.

REMARK in *Esquire* (1970).

4 I have a great tendency to talk about myself, and a very great revulsion against doing so directly.

INTERVIEWED in *Le Monde* (1971).

5 I loved the cinema passionately enough not to remain a spectator.

QUOTED in Don Allen, *Finally Truffaut* (1985 edn).

6 A film director's total work is a diary kept over a lifetime.

QUOTED in Don Allen, *Finally Truffaut* (1985 edn).

7 I renew myself at the fountain of the past.

ATTRIBUTED remark.

The TRUMAN SHOW

US 1998; screenwriter: Andrew Niccol; cast: Jim Carrey (Truman).

8 *Truman (routine greeting to neighbours)*: Good morning! … and in case I don't see ya: good afternoon, good evening and goodnight!

SOUNDTRACK.

Kathleen TURNER

American actress (1954–)

1 Being a sex symbol has to do with an attitude, not looks. Most men think it's looks, most women know otherwise.

QUOTED in *The Observer*, 'Sayings of the Week' (28 April 1986).

2 [on being described as a sex symbol] The older I get, the less I mind.

QUOTED in *The Observer*, 'Sayings of the Week' (2 May 1993).

TWENTIETH CENTURY

US 1934; screenwriter: Charles MacArthur, Ben Hecht (from play *Napoleon of Broadway* by Charles Bruce Millholland); cast: John Barrymore (Oscar Jaffe).

3 *Oscar*: Get out! From now on, I close the iron door on you!

SOUNDTRACK.

TWO-FACED WOMAN

US 1941; screenwriters: S.N. Behrman and others (from a play by Ludwig Fulda); cast: Greta Garbo (Katherine Borg), Melvyn Douglas (Larry Blake).

4 *Katherine (to Larry)*: I like older men. They are so grateful.

SOUNDTRACK. Compare Benjamin Franklin's *Reasons for Preferring an Elderly Mistress* (1745): '8th and lastly. They are so grateful!'

2001: A SPACE ODYSSEY

UK 1968; screenwriters: Stanley Kubrick (director), Arthur C. Clarke (from his story 'The Sentinel'); cast: Keir Dullea (Dave Bowman).

5 *Bowman (to errant computer)*: Open the pod-bay doors, Hal!

SOUNDTRACK.

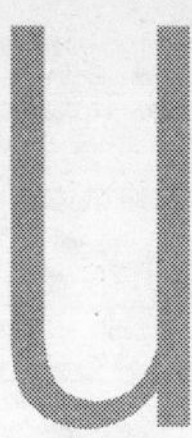

John UPDIKE

American novelist (1932–)

1 [on the film of his novel *The Witches of Eastwick*] The less it resembled my book, the better I felt.

REMARK in letter to his agent (10 July 1987).

(Sir) Peter USTINOV

English playwright, actor and director (1921–)

2 Thanks to the movies, gunfire has always sounded unreal to me, even when being fired at.

EXTRACTED from his book *Dear Me* (1977).

See also ***QUO VADIS*** 345:8.

Jack VALENTI

American executive and Presidential aide (1921–)

1 I think politicians and movie actors and movie executives are similar in more ways than they're different. There is an egocentric quality about both; there is a very sensitive awareness of the public attitude, because you live or die on public favour or disfavour. There is the desire for publicity and for acclaim, because, again, that's part of your life ... And in a strange and bizarre way, when movie actors come to Washington, they're absolutely fascinated by the politicians. And when the politicians go to Hollywood, they're absolutely fascinated by the movie stars. It's a kind of reciprocity of affection by people who both recognize in a sense they're in the same racket.

INTERVIEWED on National Public Radio (13 December 1974). Valenti had been special assistant to President Lyndon Johnson as well as being himself President of the Motion Picture Association of America.

Rudolph VALENTINO

Italian-born actor (1895–1926)

2 Here was a young man who was living daily the dreams of millions of other young men. Here was one who was catnip to women. Here was one who had wealth and fame. And here was one who was very unhappy.

COMMENT by H.L. Mencken in 'Appendix from Moronia', *Prejudices*, 6th Series (1927).

3 He had the acting talents of the average wardrobe.

COMMENT by Clyde Jeavons & Jeremy Pascall, *A Pictorial History of Sex in the Movies* (1975).

See also Bette **DAVIS** 124:2.

The VAMPIRE BAT

US 1931; screenwriter: Edward Lowe; cast: Lionel Atwill (Dr Otto von Niemann).

1 *Otto*: Mad? Is one who has solved the secret of life to be considered mad? Life! Created in the laboratory! … Think of it! I have lifted the veil! I have created life!

SOUNDTRACK. An early appearance of the mad scientist's remark. *Compare* **CLICHÉS** 109:2.

Agnès VARDA

Belgian-born director (1926–)

2 In my films I always wanted to make people see deeply. I don't want to show things, but to give people the desire to see.

QUOTED in J.R. Colombo, *Wit and Wisdom of the Moviemakers* (1979).

Ralph VAUGHAN WILLIAMS

English composer (1872–1958)

3 I believe that film music is capable of becoming, and to a certain extent already is, a fine art.

REMARK in *The Royal College of Music* Magazine (1944).

4 I believe that the film contains potentialities for the combination of all the arts such as Wagner never dreamt of. I would therefore urge those distinguished musicians who have entered into the world of the cinema … to realize their responsibility in helping to take the film out of the realm of hackwork and make it a subject worthy of a real composer.

EXTRACTED from book *Composing for the Films* (1945).

Queen VICTORIA

British sovereign (1819–1901)

5 At twelve went down to below the terrace, near the ballroom, and we were all photographed by Downey by the new cinematograph process, which makes moving pictures by winding off a reel of films. We were walking up and down.

REMARK in her journal for 3 October 1896. Curiously, this is the earliest citation for 'moving pictures' in *The Oxford English Dictionary* (2nd edn, 1989). On 23 November 1896, Victoria recorded: 'After tea went to the Red drawing-room, where so-called "animated pictures" were shown off, including the groups taken in September at Balmoral. It is a very wonderful process, representing people, their movements and actions, as if they were alive.'

Gore VIDAL

American writer and screenwriter (1925–)

1 So Beckett stammers into silence, and the rest is cinema.

INTERVIEWED in *Writers at Work* (5th series, 1981).

2 All Americans born between 1890 and 1945 wanted to be movie stars.

EXTRACTED from his book *Pink Triangle and Yellow Star* (1982).

3 When Ronald Reagan's career in show business came to an end, he was hired to impersonate, first a California Governor and then an American President.

EXTRACTED from article 'Armageddon' in *The Observer* (15 November 1987).

4 We fight wars which we lose, then we make films showing how we won them and the films make more money than the wars lost.

INTERVIEWED in *Weekend Guardian* (4–5 November 1989).

5 [propounding Vidal's Law] Good directors often make bad films, bad directors always make bad films.

QUOTED by Philip French in *The Observer* (2 May 1999).

6 As I now move graciously, I hope, towards the door marked Exit, it occurs to me that the only thing I ever liked to do was go to the movies. Naturally, Sex and Art always took precedence over the cinema. Unfortunately, neither ever proved to be as dependable as the filtering of present light through that moving strip of celluloid which projects past images and voices on to a screen.

ATTRIBUTED remark.

The VIRGINIAN

US 1929; screenwriters: Edward E. Paramore Jnr, Howard Estabrook (from Owen Wister novel); cast: Gary Cooper (The Virginian), Walter Huston (Trampas).

7 *The Virginian*: Yup!

SOUNDTRACK. Cooper's first and frequently to be repeated line on screen. In time, Cooper made certain that 'Yup' and 'Nope' were deleted from his scripts, lest he lapse into self-parody.

8 *The Virginian (standing up to Trampas who has called him a 'son of a bitch')*: If you want to call me that, smile.

SOUNDTRACK. The film was based on Wister's play and original novel (1902) where the line is, 'When you call me that, *smile*!'

The VIRGINIAN

US 1946; screenwriters: Frances Goodrich, Albert Hackett (remake of above); cast: Joel McCrea (The Virginian), Brian Donleavy (Trampas).

1 *Trampas (to The Virginian)*: I'm giving you till sundown to get out of town.

SOUNDTRACK. *Compare* **CLICHÉS** 105:5.

Joseph VON STERNBERG

Austrian-born American director (1894–1969)

2 [on Hollywood] You can seduce a man's wife there, attack his daughter and wipe your hands on his canary, but if you don't like his movie, you're dead.

ATTRIBUTED remark, quoted in Nigel Rees, *Quote ... Unquote* (1978).

Eric VON STROHEIM

Austrian-born American actor and director (1885–1957)

3 The man who cut my picture [*Greed*] had nothing on his mind but a hat.

QUOTED in Kevin Brownlow & John Kobal, *Hollywood: The Pioneers*, Chap. 22 (1979).

4 The man you love to hate.

SLOGAN referring to von Stroheim when he appeared in the 1918 propaganda film *The Heart of Humanity*. However, Harry Reichenbach, the American publicity expert (1882–1931) wrote in *Phantom Fame* (1932) that he had once come up with this: '*Foolish Wives* by and with ERIC VON STROHEIM – THE MAN YOU WILL LOVE TO HATE!' This film came out in 1921.

WALL STREET

US 1987; screenwriters: Stanley Weiser, Oliver Stone (director); cast: Michael Douglas (Gordon Gekko).

1 *Gekko*: Lunch? You gotta be kidding. Lunch is for wimps.

SOUNDTRACK.

2 *Gekko*: If you need a friend, get a dog.

SOUNDTRACK.

3 *Gekko (to stockholders)*: Greed, for lack of a better word, is good. Greed is right. Greed works. Greed clarifies, cuts through, and captures the essence of the evolutionary spirit. Greed, in all of its forms. Greed … will save the … USA!

SOUNDTRACK. Clearly based on what the American financier Ivan Boesky (1937–) said as part of a commencement address when receiving an honorary degree at the University of California at Berkeley (18 May 1986): 'Greed is all right … Greed is healthy. You can be greedy and still feel good about yourself.' He also said, 'Seek wealth, it's good.' In December 1987, Boesky was sentenced to three years imprisonment for insider dealing on the New York Stock Exchange. *Bartlett's Familiar Quotations* (1992 edn) has Boesky's words as, rather: 'Greed is good! Greed is right! Greed works! Greed will save the USA!'

Raoul WALSH

American director (1887–1980)

4 I'm going to get out of here faster than I left my first wife.

QUOTED in *The Independent* (12 January 1989), supposedly as a line he included in the scripts of his movies without relevance to plot. Walsh's ex-wife had taken to attending all his films to make sure he was still working and that her alimony payments were secure; the line was for her benefit.

See also Jack L. **WARNER** 439:8.

Andy WARHOL

American artist, painter and director (1928–87)

5 If you want to know all about Andy Warhol, just look at the surface of my paintings and films and me, there I am. There's nothing behind it!

QUOTED by Gretchen Berg, in 'Andy: My True Story' in *LA Free Press* (17 March 1967).

1 People sometimes say that the way things happen in the movies is unreal, but actually it's the way things happen in life that's unreal. The movies make emotions look so strong and real, whereas when things really do happen to you, it's like watching television – you don't feel anything.

EXTRACTED from book *From A to B and Back Again*, Chap. 6 (1975).

2 I like making movies because it's easier than painting paintings.

ATTRIBUTED remark.

Harry M. WARNER

Polish-born American producer (1881–1958)

3 Who the hell wants to hear actors talk?

ATTRIBUTED remark in 1927, quoted in J.R. Colombo, *Wit and Wisdom of the Moviemakers* (1979).

4 [of a troublesome producer, possibly Adolph Zukor] Never let the bastard back in here – unless we need him!

ATTRIBUTED remark, quoted in J.R. Colombo, *Wit and Wisdom of the Moviemakers* (1979).

Jack L. WARNER

Polish-born American producer (1892–1978)

5 [on hearing that Ronald Reagan was running for Governor of California] No, *no! Jimmy Stewart* for governor – Reagan for his best friend.

QUOTED in Max Wilk, *The Wit and Wisdom of Hollywood* (1972).

6 [on subjects for movies] Anything but Beethoven. Nobody wants to see a movie about a blind composer.

QUOTED in J. Lawrence, *Actor* (1975).

7 Films are fantasy and fantasy needs music.

QUOTED in *The New York Times* (28 March 1976).

8 To Raoul Walsh a tender love scene is burning down a whorehouse.

QUOTED in *Hollywood Anecdotes*, eds. Boller & Davis (1988).

9 [on writers] Schmucks with Underwoods.

ATTRIBUTED remark.

See also ***GONE WITH THE WIND*** 195:4.

Evelyn WAUGH

English novelist (1903–66)

1 What is it about being on a boat that makes everyone behave like a film star?

EXTRACTED from his novel *Brideshead Revisited*, Bk 3 Chap. 1 (1945). Julia says it to Charles, who has just sent her some roses.

The WAY TO THE STARS

UK 1945; screenwriters: Anatole de Grunwald, Terence Rattigan (from his play *Flare Path*); cast: John Mills (Peter Penrose).

2 The Way to the Stars.

TITLE OF FILM. This presumably alludes to the RAF motto '*Per ardua ad astra* [through striving/struggle to the stars]', first proposed in 1912. However, the words '*Macte nova virtute, puer, sic itur ad astra*' from Virgil's *Aeneid* (Bk 9, l. 641) are often translated as: 'Go to it with fresh courage, young man; this is the way to the stars' – the words of Ascanius, son of Aeneas, before battle.

3 *Peter (reading)*: 'Do not despair
For Johnny-head-in-air;
He sleeps as sound
As Johnny underground.

Fetch out no shroud
For Johnny-in-the-cloud;
And keep your tears
For him in after years.'

SOUNDTRACK. Lines recited to the wife of a recently deceased RAF pilot (Michael Redgrave), who is taken to be their fictive author. They were found among his possessions (and in his handwriting), but are in fact the poem 'For Johnny' (1942) by John Pudney. The film was called *For Johnny* in the United States, and the poem has some claim to be the best-known of the Second World War.

John WAYNE

American actor (1907–79)

4 [advice on acting] Talk low, talk slow, and don't say much.

ATTRIBUTED remark, in *Bartlett's Familiar Quotations* (15th edn, 1980).

5 If they played my favourite tune everyone would have to stand up.

QUOTED on BBC Radio *Quote … Unquote* (14 August 1980).

1 Nobody should come to the movies unless he believes in heroes.

QUOTED in Charles John Kieskalt, *The Official John Wayne Reference Book* (1985).

2 I've spent my whole career playing myself.

QUOTED in Barry Norman, *The Film Greats* (1985).

3 I'm just an ordinary goddamn American and I talk for all the ordinary goddamn Americans, the butchers and bakers and plumbers. I know these people; I know what they think.

QUOTED in the same book.

4 John Wayne has an endless face and he can go on forever.

COMMENT by Louis B. Mayer, quoted in J.R. Colombo, *Wit and Wisdom of the Moviemakers* (1979).

WAYNE'S WORLD

US 1992; screenwriters: Mike Myers and others; cast: Mike Myers (Wayne Campbell), Dana Carvey (Garth Algar), Alice Cooper (himself).

5 *Wayne/Garth*: *Wayne's World! Wayne's World!* Party on! Excellent!

SOUNDTRACK. Introducing their TV show with stock phrases.

6 *Wayne*: Garth, marriage is punishment for shoplifting, in some countries.

SOUNDTRACK.

7 *Wayne/Garth*: Not!

SOUNDTRACK. Stock phrase.

8 *Wayne/Garth*: No way?!/Way!

SOUNDTRACK. Stock phrase.

9 *Wayne/Garth (to Alice Cooper)*: We're not worthy, we're not worthy!

SOUNDTRACK. This, like some of the other catchphrases, had had an earlier outing in *Bill and Ted's Excellent Adventure* (US 1988) and *Bill and Ted's Bogus Journey* (US 1991).

WAYNE'S WORLD 2

US 1993; screenwriters: Mike Myers and others; cast: Michael Nickles (Jim Morrison).

10 *Jim Morrison*: If you book them, they will come.

SOUNDTRACK. The ghost of rock star Jim Morrison inspires the teenage heroes of the film to put on a rock concert called 'Waynestock'. When Morrison is asked whether big-name groups will actually show up, this is his reply. *Compare* ***FIELD OF DREAMS*** 159:3.

Sigourney WEAVER

American actress (1949–)

1 All the scripts I get sent still have Meryl Streep's fingerprints on them.

QUOTED in *Sunday Today*, 'Quotes of the Week' (26 April 1987).

2 I want to be the Margaret Rutherford of my generation.

QUOTED in *The Observer*, 'Sayings of the Week' (23 April 1995).

The WEDDING SINGER

US 1998; screenwriter: Tim Herlihy; cast: Adam Sandler (Robbie), Sally Pierce (Grandma Molly).

3 *Molly (very old woman)*: When I got married I wasn't a virgin. I already had intercourse with eight men.
Robbie: Yeah, that's actually something I don't want to know about.
Molly: That was a lot back then. That would be like two hundred today.

SOUNDTRACK.

Raquel WELCH

American actress (1940–)

4 Being a sex symbol was rather like being a convict.

QUOTED in *The Observer*, 'Sayings of the Week' (25 February 1979).

5 I can't say the mini made me an actor, but it sure made me a star.

QUOTED in *Sunday Today*, 'Quotes of the Week' (3 May 1987).

6 Today anarchy reigns in Hollywood. The town is run by power brokers with a Wall Street mentality and little to offer artistically.

QUOTED in *The Independent* (22 October 1994).

Fay WELDON

English novelist (1933–)

7 Reading about sex in yesterday's novels is like watching people smoke in old films.

REMARK in *The Guardian* (1 December 1989).

Colin WELLAND

English actor and screenwriter (1934–)

1 I'd like to finish with a word of warning. You may have started something. The British are coming.

SPEECH accepting an Oscar for his ***CHARIOTS OF FIRE*** screenplay (30 March 1982).

Orson WELLES

American director, writer and actor (1915–85)

2 [on learning how to use a Hollywood studio] This is the biggest electric train [set] any boy ever had!

QUOTED in Leo Rosten, *Hollywood* (1941). Frank Brady in *Citizen Welles* (1989) suggests that this remark was made just prior to the filming of *Citizen Kane* at RKO studios in about 1939. Compare Nicholas **RAY** 348:1.

3 A film is never really good unless the camera is an eye in the head of a poet.

QUOTED in '*Un ruban de rêves* [a ribbon of dreams]'in *L'Express* (5 June 1958). Translation.

4 The cinema has no boundaries. It's a ribbon of dream.

QUOTED by Kenneth Tynan in *Show* (October/November 1961) – referring to the article in the previous entry.

5 A typewriter needs only paper; a camera uses film, requires subsidiary equipment by the truckload and several hundreds of technicians. That is always the central fact about the film-maker as opposed to any other artist: he can never afford his own tools.

REMARK in letter to the *New Statesman* (1958).

6 I began at the top and I've been working my way down ever since.

QUOTED in J.R. Colombo, *Wit and Wisdom of the Moviemakers* (1979).

7 I'm just in love with making movies. Not very fond of movies – I don't go to them much. I think it's very harmful for movie-makers to see movies, because you either imitate them or worry about not imitating them.

INTERVIEWED on BBC TV *Arena* and quoted in *The Listener* (17 October 1985).

8 The trouble with a movie these days is that it's old before it's released – it's no accident that it comes in a can.

ATTRIBUTED remark.

9 A poet needs a pen, a painter a brush, and a film-maker an army.

QUOTED in Steven Bach, *Final Cut* (1985).

1 It's like meeting God without dying.

COMMENT attributed to Dorothy Parker.

See also ***CITIZEN KANE***; John **FORD** 167:1.

H.G. WELLS

English novelist and writer (1866–1946)

2 I think the cinema is the very greatest art, with the possibilities of becoming the greatest art form that has ever existed.

REMARK on 23 November 1935, attributed by C.A. Lejeune in *The Observer* (in 1938).

WENT THE DAY WELL?

UK 1942 (re-titled *48 Hours* in the US); screenwriters: Angus McPhail, John Dighton, Diana Morgan (from story by Graham Greene).

3 Went the day well?
We died and never knew.
But, well or ill,
Freedom, we died for you.

SCREEN TITLE. Based on a story by Graham Greene entitled 'The Lieutenant Died Last', the film tells of a typical English village managing to repel Nazi invaders. The anonymously presented epigraph thus presumably refers to the villagers who die defending 'Bramley End'. At the time the film was released, some thought the epigraph was a version of a Greek epitaph. Penelope Houston in her 1992 British Film Institute monograph on the film describes it as a quotation from an anonymous poem that appeared in an anthology of tributes to people killed in the war, to which Michael Balcon, head of Ealing Studios, contributed a memoir of the dead director Pen Tennyson. In fact, it is based on 'Went the day well? we died and never knew; / But well or ill, England we died for you', from lines entitled 'On Some who died early in the Day of Battle' in 'Four Epitaphs' by J.M. Edmonds, English poet and academic (1875–1958), published in *The Times* (6 February 1918). It is said that the words were based on a suggestion given to Edmonds by Sir Arthur Quiller-Couch, who in turn got them from a Romanian folk song (*Notes and Queries*, Vol. 100).

Mae WEST

American actress and screenwriter (1893–1980)

4 It wasn't what I did, but how I did it. It wasn't what I said, but how I said it; and how I looked when I did it and said it. I had evolved into a symbol and didn't know it.

EXTRACTED from her book *Goodness Had Nothing To Do With It*, Chap. 4 (1959).

1 The bite of existence did not cut into one in Hollywood ... Life elsewhere was real and slippery and struggled in the arms like a big fish dying in the air.

EXTRACTED from the same book, Chap. 13.

2 I ... always found it a good policy to slip a few items into a script that the censors would cut out. It gave them a sense of accomplishing their job and they were less likely to cut out the things I really wanted to keep in.

EXTRACTED from the same book, Chap. 15.

3 Hollywood was like a mouse being followed by a cat called television.

EXTRACTED from the same book, Chap. 20.

4 I'm the girl that works at Paramount all day and Fox all night.

ATTRIBUTED remark.

5 [of West in her films] A plumber's idea of Cleopatra.

COMMENT by W.C. Fields, quoted in Louise Brooks, *Lulu in Hollywood*, 'The Other Face of W.C. Fields' (1982).

6 [on his co-star in her film debut, *Night After Night*] In this picture, Mae West stole everything but the cameras.

COMMENT by George Raft, American actor (1895–1980), in his autobiography (untraced) according to Mae West in hers. Also quoted in Leslie Halliwell, *The Filmgoer's Book of Quotes* (1973).

WHAT'S UP, DOC?

US 1972; screenwriters: Buck Henry and others; cast: Barbra Streisand (Judy Maxwell), Ryan O'Neal (Howard Bannister).

7 What's Up, Doc?

TITLE OF FILM. *See* **CATCHPHRASES** 95:4.

8 *Judy*: Love means never having to say you're sorry.
Howard: That's the dumbest thing I ever heard!

SOUNDTRACK. O'Neal is here sinking the line he launched in ***LOVE STORY*** 259:2.

9 [on Barbra Streisand in this film] She's playing herself – and it's awfully soon for that.

COMMENT by Pauline Kael in *Deeper Into Movies*, 'Collaboration and Resistance' (1973).

WHEN HARRY MET SALLY

US 1989; screenwriter: Nora Ephron; cast: Meg Ryan (Sally), Estelle Reiner (Woman in restaurant).

1 *Woman in restaurant (when asked by a waiter what she would like to order, Sally having just faked an orgasm)*: I'll have what she's having.

SOUNDTRACK.

2 It struck me that the movies had spent more than half a century saying 'They lived happily ever after' and the following quarter-century warning that they'll be lucky to make it through the weekend. Possibly now we are entering a third era in which the movies will be sounding a note of cautious optimism: You know it just might work.

COMMENT by Nora Ephron on her screenplay.

WHITE CARGO

US 1942; screenwriter: Leon Gordon (from his play, based on the novel *Hell's Playground* by Vera Simonton); cast: Hedy Lamarr (Tondelayo).

3 *Tondelayo*: I am Tondelayo.

SOUNDTRACK.

WHITE HEAT

US 1949; screenwriters: Ivan Goff, Ben Roberts (from story by Virginia Kellogg); James Cagney (Cody Jarrett), Margaret Wycherly (Ma).

4 *Cody*: Made it Ma, [to the] top of the world!

SOUNDTRACK. Last words of character, shooting it out with police from the top of an oil tank. Earlier Ma had said to him: 'Now go out there and show 'em who's boss, son ... Remember, top of the world.'

WHITE SHADOWS IN THE SOUTH SEAS

US 1928; screenwriters: John Colton, Jack Cunningham; cast: Raquel Torres (Fayaway).

5 *Fayaway*: Hello!

SOUNDTRACK. This was the first film with sound made by MGM (and thus the first to feature the roar of Leo the lion, the MGM symbol). The only word of dialogue in the entire picture was this.

See also Hunt **STROMBERG** 401:3.

Katharine WHITEHORN

English journalist (1928–)

1 I wouldn't say when you've seen one Western you've seen the lot; but when you've seen the lot you get the feeling you've seen one.

EXTRACTED from article in book *Sunday Best* (1976) 'Decoding the West'

WHO FRAMED ROGER RABBIT

US 1988; screenwriters: Jeffrey Price, Peter S. Seaman; voice of Kathleen Turner (Jessica).

2 *Jessica*: I'm not bad. I'm just drawn that way.

SOUNDTRACK. Jessica is, of course, a cartoon character – and probably the sexiest there has ever been.

WHO'S AFRAID OF VIRGINIA WOOLF?

US 1966; screenwriter: Ernest Lehman (from Edward Albee play); cast: Elizabeth Taylor (Martha), Richard Burton (George), Sandy Dennis (Honey), George Segal (Nick).

3 *Martha*: What a dump. Hey, what's that from? 'What a dump!'

SOUNDTRACK. Opening line. As in the stage play, this opening game concerns the question as to which Bette Davis film this line comes from. For the answer, *see* ***BEYOND THE FOREST*** 58:6. As with so much of the film, the screenplay sticks closely to the stage original.

4 *Martha*: Look, sweetheart, I can drink you under any goddamn table you want so don't worry about me.
George: I gave you the prize years ago, Martha. There isn't an abomination award going that you haven't won.
Martha: I swear, if you existed, I'd divorce you.

SOUNDTRACK.

5 *George (directing Honey to the bathroom)*: Martha, will you show her where we keep the, er, euphemism?

SOUNDTRACK.

6 *George (to Nick, on sparring with his wife)*: Martha and I are merely exercising, that's all. We're merely walking what's left of our wits. Don't pay any attention.

SOUNDTRACK.

7 *Nick*: It's just that I don't like to become involved in other people's affairs.
George: Oh, you'll get over that. Small college and all. Musical beds is the faculty sport around here.

SOUNDTRACK.

1 *George*: Now that we're through with Humiliate the Host – we're through with that one for this round anyway, and we don't want to play Hump the Hostess yet, not yet – so I know what we do: how about a little round of Get the Guests? How about that? How about a little game of Get the Guests.

SOUNDTRACK.

2 Twenty-seven words, all bad.

COMMENT attributed to Edward Albee on Ernest Lehman's contribution to the screenplay – 27 words, four of which were 'Screenplay by Ernest Lehman'. Lehman did, however, produce the movie.

See also The ***THREE LITTLE PIGS*** 415:7.

Richard WIDMARK

American actor (1914–)

3 It is clear that murder is one of the kindest things he is capable of.

COMMENT by James Agee.

Elie WIESEL

Romanian-born American writer and educator (1928–)

4 One written sentence is worth 800 hours of film.

QUOTED in J.R. Colombo, *Wit and Wisdom of the Moviemakers* (1979).

The WILD ONE

US 1953; screenwriter: John Paxton; cast: Marlon Brando (Johnny).

5 *Johnny (asked by woman in bar what he is rebelling against)*: What've you got?

SOUNDTRACK.

Billy WILDER

American director and screenwriter (1906–)

6 [to lighting cameraman, John Seitz, while working on *Sunset Boulevard*] Johnny, it's the usual slashed-wrist shot ... Keep it out of focus. I want to win the foreign picture award.

QUOTED in *Hollywood Anecdotes*, eds. Boller & Davis (1988).

7 [of television] It used to be that we in films were the lowest form of art. Now we have something to look down on.

QUOTED in Axel Madsen, *Billy Wilder* (1968).

1 What they [critics] call dirty in our pictures, they call lusty in foreign films.

QUOTED in same book.

2 [to actor Cliff Osmond when filming *Irma La Douce*] You have Van Gogh's ear for music.

QUOTED in Leslie Halliwell, *The Filmgoer's Book of Quotes* (1973).

3 Hindsight is always twenty-twenty.

QUOTED in J.R. Colombo, *Wit and Wisdom of the Moviemakers* (1979).

4 An actor entering through the door, you've got nothing. But if he enters through the window, you've got a situation.

ATTRIBUTED remark.

5 The first nine commandments for a director are 'Thou shalt not bore.' The tenth is 'Thou shalt have the right of the final cut.'

ATTRIBUTED remark.

6 [on *Nouvelle Vague*] You watch, the New Wave will discover the slow dissolve in ten years or so.

ATTRIBUTED remark.

7 [at age 87] I'm very uncomfortable living in a world where the Pope is 25 years younger than I am.

QUOTED in *The Independent* (17 July 1993).

8 Any director who doesn't believe in miracles isn't a realist.

QUOTED by Don Black on BBC Radio *Quote ... Unquote* (19 April 1999).

9 No man ever said to his wife, 'Let's go and see this picture, the director brought it in under budget.'

QUOTED in *The Observer* (30 January 2000).

10 He's not a director, he's a dictator.

COMMENT attributed to Marilyn Monroe at the time of *Some Like It Hot* (1959).

See also Otto **PREMINGER** 333:5.

Thornton WILDER

American playwright and novelist (1897–1975)

11 We'll trot down to the movies and see how girls with wax faces live.

EXTRACTED from play *The Skin of Our Teeth*, Act 3 (1942).

Michael WILDING

English actor (1912–79)

1 You can pick out actors by the glazed look that comes into their eyes when the conversation wanders away from themselves.

ATTRIBUTED remark. *Compare* Marlon **BRANDO** 68:6.

Esther WILLIAMS

American swimmer and actress (1923–)

2 Wet, she was a star – dry she ain't.

COMMENT by Joe Pasternak, Hungarian-born producer (1901–91), quoted (except for the last three words) in Leslie Halliwell, *The Filmgoer's Book of Quotes* (1973). This is rendered in *The Faber Book of Movie Verse*, eds. French & Wlaschin (1993), as 'I used to keep her in the water 99% of the time. Wet she was a star.'

Robin WILLIAMS

American comic and actor (1951–)

3 Cocaine is God's way of saying you're making too much money.

QUOTED in *Screen International* (15 December 1990).

Bruce WILLIS

American actor (1955–)

4 Balding is God's way of showing you are only human … he takes the hair off your head and sticks it in your ears.

QUOTED in *The Observer* (3 March 1996).

Earl WILSON

American journalist (1907–87)

5 The way things are going I'd be more interested in seeing Cleopatra play the life of Elizabeth Taylor.

QUOTED in *Radio Times* (November 1962).

Woodrow WILSON

American Democratic President (1856–1924)

6 [on *The Birth of a Nation* – the first ever film to be shown in the White House, 18 February 1915] It is like writing history with lightning. And my only regret is that it is all so terribly true.

QUOTED in Daniel Boorstin, *The Image* (1962).

Walter WINCHELL

American journalist (1897–1972)

1 [on Hollywood] A place where they shoot too many pictures and not enough actors.

ATTRIBUTED remark.

WING AND A PRAYER

US 1944; screenwriter: Jerome Cady; cast: Dana Andrews (Lieut. Cmdr. Edward Moulton).

2 *Moulton (quoting proposed citation)*: 'Congressional Medal of Honor, posthumously awarded.'

SOUNDTRACK. The film was about life aboard an aircraft carrier. President Reagan regularly liked to quote it, seemingly indifferent as to whether it was a film line or something that had actually once been said. He told a meeting (undated, but by 1986) of the Congressional Medal of Honor Society about an aircraft gunner who couldn't leave his post when his plane was crashing. The gunner was told by his commanding officer that he would win a 'Congressional Medal of Honor, posthumously awarded'. No such incident happened in real life.

Michael WINNER

English director (1935–)

3 Who says that actors are cattle? Show me a cow who can earn a million dollars a film.

QUOTED by David Lewin in *Cinema Today* (1 July 1970).
Compare Alfred **HITCHCOCK** 216:1.

4 [when asked what was the hardest part of directing] Keeping awake for ten weeks at a stretch.

REMARK in John Player Lecture at BFI (September 1970).

5 A team effort is a lot of people doing what I say.

ATTRIBUTED remark.

Kate WINSLET

English actress (1975–)

6 [on her performance in *Titanic*] She should get the Oscar for best bust. Anyone with those two floaters doesn't need a lifeboat.

COMMENT by Camille Paglia, quoted in *The Independent* (28 March 1998).

Shelley WINTERS

American actress (1922–)

1 I did a picture in England one winter and it was so cold I almost got married.

QUOTED in *Ritz* (March 1983). In *The Sunday Times* (2 May 1971) she had said she'd been so cold on a winter sports holiday she almost got married.

(Sir) Norman WISDOM

English comic and actor (1920–)

2 Anyone who doesn't have a child's sense of humour is not a very happy person.

QUOTED in *The Observer*, 'Sayings of the Week' (30 June 1991).

WITHNAIL AND I

UK 1987; screenwriter/director: Bruce Robinson; cast: Richard E. Grant (Withnail); Richard Griffiths (Uncle Monty), Paul McGann (and I/Marwood).

3 *Monty (to Marwood)*: Do you like vegetables? I've always been fond of root crops, but I only started to grow last summer.

SOUNDTRACK. An unusual line of seduction. Uncle Monty has designs upon Marwood (the 'I' of the title).

4 *Monty*: It is the most shattering experience of a young man's life, when one morning he awakes, and quite reasonably says to himself, I will *never* play the Dane.

SOUNDTRACK.

5 *Withnail (to waitress in tea shop)*: Cake and fine wine ... We want the finest wines available to humanity! We want them *here*. And we want them *now!*

SOUNDTRACK.

6 *Monty*: We live in a kingdom of rains where royalty comes in gangs. Come on, lads, let's get home. The sky's beginning to bruise, night must fall, and we shall be forced to camp.

SOUNDTRACK.

The WIZARD OF OZ

US 1939; screenwriters: Noel Langley, Florence Ryerson, Edgar Allan Woolf (based on Frank Baum novel); cast: Judy Garland (Dorothy), Billie Burke (Glinda, the Witch of the South), Margaret Hamilton (the Wicked Witch of the West), Jack Haley (the Tin Woodman), Bert Lahr (the Cowardly Lion), Ray Bolger (the Scarecrow), Frank Morgan (the Wizard).

1 For nearly forty years this story has given faithful service to the Young in Heart; and Time has been powerless to put its kindly philosophy out of fashion. To those of you who have been faithful to it in return … and to the Young in Heart … we dedicate this picture.

SCREEN TITLE at opening.

2 *Dorothy*: Some place where there isn't any trouble … behind the moon, beyond the rain … somewhere over the rainbow.

SOUNDTRACK. Leading into song.

3 *Dorothy (to her dog, arriving in the Land of Oz)*: Toto, I've a feeling we're not in Kansas any more.

SOUNDTRACK.

4 *Wicked Witch*: I'll get you, my pretty. And your little dog, too!

SOUNDTRACK.

5 *Dorothy (and the Munchkins)*: Follow the yellow brick road …
You're off to see the Wizard
The wonderful Wizard of Oz.
You'll find he is a whiz of a wiz
If ever a wiz there was.

SOUNDTRACK.

6 *The Cowardly Lion (in haunted forest)*: I do believe in spooks, I do believe in spooks, I do, I do, I do, I do, I do, I do.

SOUNDTRACK.

7 *The Wizard (on being exposed when Toto pulls aside the curtain)*: Pay no attention to that man behind the curtain! The, er, great Oz has spoken.

SOUNDTRACK.

8 *Dorothy (to Wizard)*: Oh, you're a very bad man!
The Wizard: Oh, no, my dear, I … I'm a very good man – I'm just a very bad wizard.

SOUNDTRACK.

9 *The Wizard (to the Tin Woodman)*: As for you, my galvanized friend, you want a heart. You don't know how lucky you are not to have one. Hearts will never be practical until they can be made unbreakable.

SOUNDTRACK.

1 *The Wizard (to the Tin Woodman)*: And remember, my sentimental friend, that a heart is not judged by how much you love, but by how much you are loved by others.

SOUNDTRACK.

2 *Dorothy (on what it is that she has learned)*: Well … I think that it … that it wasn't enough just to want to see Uncle Henry and Auntie Em … and it's that if I ever go looking for my heart's desire again, I won't look any further than my own backyard, because if it isn't there, I never really lost it to begin with.

SOUNDTRACK.

3 *Glinda (on how to get from the Land of Oz back to Kansas)*: Close your eyes and tap your heels together three times. And think to yourself, 'There's no place like home.'

SOUNDTRACK.

4 *Dorothy*: Oh, but anyway, Toto, we're home, and this is my room, and you're all here, and I'm not going to leave here ever, ever again. Because I love you all, and, oh Auntie Em, there's *no* place like home!

SOUNDTRACK. Her final lines, alluding to the song 'Home, Sweet Home' by J.H. Payne (1792–1852): 'Mid pleasures and palaces though we may roam, / Be it ever so humble, there's no place like home.'

5 That rainbow song's no good, it slows the picture right down. Take it out.

COMMENT by Marty Rackin, head of production at Paramount, passing on the suggestion of Louis B. Mayer, who recommended the whole Kansas sequence be cut on the grounds that it was 'boring', after a screening for studio heads. The song 'Over the Rainbow' by Harold Arlen and E.Y. Harburg won the Oscar for Best Song.

(Sir) P.G. WODEHOUSE

English novelist and lyricist (1881–1975)

6 Everybody liked Bill Shannon, even in Hollywood, where nobody likes anybody.

EXTRACTED from novel *The Old Reliable* (1951).

The WOMEN

US 1939; screenwriters: Anita Loos, Jane Murfin (based on Clare Boothe Luce play); cast: Joan Fontaine (Peggy Day), Florence Nash (Nancy Blake), Dennie Moore (Olga), Joan Crawford (Crystal Allen), Norma Shearer (Mary Haines), Mary Cecil (Maggie), Mary Boland (Countess DeLove).

1 *Peggy*: I wish I could make a little money writing the way you do. *Nancy*: If you wrote the way I do, that's just what you'd make.

SOUNDTRACK.

2 *Olga (about Crystal)*: She's got those eyes that run up and down men like a searchlight.

SOUNDTRACK.

3 *Nancy*: I'm what nature abhors – an old maid. A frozen asset.

SOUNDTRACK.

4 *Maggie*: You know, the first man that can think up a good explanation how he can be in love with his wife *and* another woman is going to win that prize they're always giving out in Sweden.

SOUNDTRACK.

5 *Countess DeLove*: '*L'amour, l'amour. Toujours l'amour.*'

SOUNDTRACK.

6 *Crystal*: There's a name for you ladies, but it isn't used in high society – outside of a kennel.

SOUNDTRACK.

7 *Mary (on her lack of pride on rejoining her unrepentant husband)*: No pride at all. That's a luxury a woman in love can't afford.

SOUNDTRACK.

Joanne WOODWARD

American actress (1930–)

8 Acting is like sex. You should do it, not talk about it.

QUOTED in *The Mail on Sunday/You* Magazine (1987).

See also Paul **NEWMAN** 302:7.

The WORLD IS NOT ENOUGH

UK/US 1999; screenwriters: Neal Purvis, Robert Wade, Bruce Feirstein; cast: Pierce Brosnan (James Bond) , Denise Richards (Dr Christmas Jones).

9 The World Is Not Enough.

TITLE OF FILM. *See* ***ON HER MAJESTY'S SECRET SERVICE*** 315:2.

10 *Bond (in bed with Dr Christmas Jones)*: I was wrong about you … I thought Christmas only comes once a year.

SOUNDTRACK. Last line of film.

Fay WRAY

American actress (1907–)

1 At the premiere of *King Kong* I wasn't too impressed. I thought there was too much screaming … I didn't realize then that King Kong and I were going to be together for the rest of our lives.

ATTRIBUTED remark.

WUTHERING HEIGHTS

US 1939; screenwriters: Ben Hecht, Charles MacArthur (from Emily Brontë novel); cast: Laurence Olivier (Heathcliff), Merle Oberon (Cathy).

2 *Heathcliff*: What do they know of heaven or hell, Cathy, who know nothing of life? Oh, they're praying for you, Cathy. I pray one prayer with them – I repeat till my tongue stiffens – Catherine Earnshaw, may you not rest so long as I live on! I killed you! Haunt me, then! Haunt your murderer! I know that ghosts have wandered on the Earth. Be with me always. Take any form, drive me mad, only do not leave me in this dark alone where I cannot find you. I cannot live without my life! I cannot die without my soul!

SOUNDTRACK. This is almost word for word what Emily Brontë wrote in *Wuthering Heights*, Chap. 26 (1847), but it is relocated at the end of the story with Cathy on her deathbed.

William WYLER

German-born American producer (1902–81)

3 [on the decision to film *Brigadoon* (US 1954) in the studio rather than on location] I went to Scotland but I could find nothing that looked like Scotland.

QUOTED in Forsyth Hardy, *Scotland in Film*, Chap. 1 (1990).

YESTERDAY'S ENEMY

UK 1959; screenwriter: Peter R. Newman (from his TV play).

1 When you go home
Tell them of us and say
For your tomorrow
We gave our today.

SCREEN TITLE – epigraph and apparently what inspired the title of this film set in Burma during 1942. Famously, these lines appeared on the 2nd British Division's memorial at Kohima War Cemetery, Assam (now Nagaland), in India (and on many other war graves round the world). They come from the poem 'For a British Graveyard in France', a suggested epitaph by J.M. Edmonds that appeared in *The Times Literary Supplement* (4 July 1918). The third line of Edmonds's original should *not* read 'For your *tomorrows*', as in the *Oxford Dictionary of Modern Quotations* (1991) and the *Oxford Dictionary of Quotations* (1992), and the fourth line should read 'These gave their today'.

YOU CAN'T CHEAT AN HONEST MAN

US 1939; screenwriters: George Marion Jnr, Richard Mack, Everett Freeman, from story by Charles Bogle (W.C. Fields); cast; W.C. Fields (Larson E. Whipsnade).

2 *Whipsnade (referring to his drink)*: Keep your hands off my lunch, will you?

SOUNDTRACK.

YOU ONLY LIVE TWICE

UK 1967; screenwriters: Roald Dahl, Harry Jack Bloom (after Ian Fleming novel); cast: Sean Connery (James Bond), Donald Pleasence (Ernst Blofeld), Akiko Wakabayashi (Aki), Karin Dor (Helga Brandt), Bernard Lee (M).

3 *Hong Kong policeman (after Bond has apparently been murdered in bed)*: Well, at least he died on the job.

SOUNDTRACK.

4 *M (referring to Bond's latest case)*: This is the big one, 007!

SOUNDTRACK.

1 *Aki (to Bond)*: I think I will enjoy very much serving under you.
SOUNDTRACK.

2 *Bond (to Helga Brandt)*: What's a nice girl like you doing in a place like this?
SOUNDTRACK. *See also* **CLICHÉS** 108:3.

3 *Bond (undressing Helga Brandt)*: Oh, the things I do for England!
SOUNDTRACK. *Compare The* ***PRIVATE LIFE OF HENRY VIII*** 336:8.

4 *Blofeld*: Allow me to introduce myself. I am Ernst Stavro Blofeld. They told me you were assassinated in Hong Kong.
Bond: Yes, this is my second life.
Blofeld: You only live twice, Mr Bond.
SOUNDTRACK.

YOUNG FRANKENSTEIN

US 1974; screenwriters: Gene Wilder, Mel Brooks (director); cast: Gene Wilder (Dr Frederick Frankenstein), Marty Feldman (Igor).

5 *Frankenstein*: Pardon me boy, is this the Transylvania Station?
SOUNDTRACK.

6 *Frankenstein*: I'm a brilliant surgeon. Perhaps I can help you with that hump.
Igor: What hump?
SOUNDTRACK.

YOUNG MAN OF MANHATTAN

US 1930; screenwriters: Daniel Reed, Robert Presnell (from Katherine Brush novel); cast: Ginger Rogers (Puff Randolph).

7 *Puff*: Cigarette me, big boy.
SOUNDTRACK.

YOU'RE TELLING ME

US 1934; screenwriters: Walter de Leon, Paul M. Jones (from a story by Julian Street); cast: W.C. Fields (Sam Bisbee).

8 *Sam*: It's a funny old world – a man's lucky if he gets out of it alive.
SOUNDTRACK.

Z

Darryl F. ZANUCK

American producer (1902–79)

1 [characteristic remark to minions] Don't say yes until I finish talking!

QUOTED in Mel Gussow, *Don't Say Yes Until I Finish Talking* (1971).

2 [Zanuck] is the only man who can eat an apple through a tennis racquet!

COMMENT by David Niven, quoted in Noël Coward, *Diaries of Noël Coward* (entry for 10 December 1954).

See also Jean **RENOIR** 351:5.

Sam ZIMBALIST

American producer (1904–58)

3 [asking Graham Greene to give a final polish to a rewrite of the last part of a remake of *Ben Hur*] You see, we find a kind of anti-climax after the Crucifixion.

QUOTED by Graham Greene in article in *International Film Annual* (1958). Reprinted in *Ways of Escape* (1980).

ZORBA THE GREEK

US/Greece 1963; screenwriter/director: Michael Cacoyanis (from Kazantzakis novel); cast: Anthony Quinn (Zorba), Alan Bates (Basil).

4 *Zorba (to Basil)*: Boss, why did God give us hands? To grab. Well, grab!

SOUNDTRACK.

5 *Zorba*: To dance, one must be a little mad.

SOUNDTRACK.

Adolph ZUKOR

Hungarian-born producer (1873–1976)

6 If I'd known how old I was going to be I'd have taken better care of myself.

REMARK on approaching his hundredth birthday, quoted by Benny Green in *Radio Times* (17 February 1979).

Index

This Index represents quotations in capsule form under keyword headings drawn from the one or two main or most significant words in the quotation. To keep the Index to a reasonable size, not every occurrence of words like 'film' or 'movie' has been recorded here. Note also that the Index is only to the *content* of quotations. It does not list characters from films. It does not include titles of films (for which see the alphabetical listings in the main text and also the TITLES OF FILMS special section). It only lists people who are the subject of quotations where these are not given under alphabetical headings in the main text. References are to page number and quotation number: thus, 305:4 refers to quotation 4 on page 305.

A

B

C

D

E

F

H

I

J

K

L

M

N

P

Q

R

S

T

take away fake t., 272:8

U

V

Y

Z